Journals
Of Australian
Explorations

by

Augustus Charles Gregory And
Francis Thomas Gregory

Double 9
BOOKS

Journals
Of Australian Explorations
by Augustus Charles Gregory And Francis Thomas Gregory

ISBN: 978-93-59327-03-7

Published by

DOUBLE 9 BOOKS

2/13-B, Ansari Road
Daryaganj, New Delhi – 110002
info@double9books.com
www.double9books.com
Tel. 011-40042856

ABOUT THE AUTHOR

Francis Thomas "Frank" Gregory was an Australian explorer and politician who lived from October 19, 1821 to October 23, 1888. He was born in England and moved to Australia with his family as a child. He was the younger brother of Augustus Gregory, an explorer and politician who also created a name for himself in the colony. Gregory was born in 1821 in Farnsfield, Nottinghamshire, England. In 1829, he and his family, including his older brother Augustus, immigrated to Western Australia. Gregory joined the Western Australian state service in 1841 as a cadet surveyor after receiving a rudimentary education. Gregory went to survey the land north of Perth with his older brother Augustus and explorer Henry Churchman in 1846. Sir Augustus Charles Gregory KCMG FRSGS was an English-born Australian explorer and surveyor who died on June 25, 1905. He led four important trips between 1846 and 1858. He was Queensland's first Surveyor-General. He was appointed to the Queensland Legislative Council for life.

CONTENTS

PREFACE.

Numerous inquiries having been made for copies of the Journals of the Explorations by the Messrs. Gregory in the Western, Northern, and Central portions of Australia, and as these journals have hitherto only been partially published in a fragmentary form, and are now out of print, it has been deemed desirable to collect the material into one volume, for convenience of reference, and to place on permanent record some of the earlier attempts to penetrate the terra incognita which then constituted so vast a portion of the Australian Continent.

Although, during the twenty-two years which have elapsed since the last of these expeditions was undertaken, the geographical knowledge of Australia has so far advanced as to fill in most of the details of its physical features and set at rest the speculative opinions and theories of early explorers, it has not been deemed desirable to alter or amend the impressions or views recorded at the time, but simply reproduce the journals as originally compiled.

MESSRS. GREGORY'S EXPEDITION TO THE EAST AND NORTH OF SWAN RIVER 1846

EARLY CONDITION OF WEST AUSTRALIA

The colony of Western Australia was established in 1829; but its isolation from the older settlement of New South Wales rendered it necessary to import all the horses, cattle, and sheep by sailing vessels from Tasmania, or other remote sources, while the heavy losses and difficulties attending long sea voyages prevented any large importations of stock--so that, though there was a fair rate of increase, the flocks and herds of the settlers had found sufficient pasturage for the first ten years on the banks of the Swan River and its upper valley, the Avon, together with the coast district southward to the Vasse Inlet; but after 1840 the stock-owners began to feel that all prospect of material increase must be relinquished unless additional pastures could be discovered.

Several public as well as private expeditions were undertaken for the purpose of ascertaining whether in the interior or along the coast on either side of the settlement there existed any available country, but they had only encountered dense scrubs of acacia and eucalyptus, with salt marshes and scarcity of fresh water in the interior. The coast to the east had been traversed from Adelaide to King George's Sound by Mr. Eyre, and found to be altogether unfit for settlement, while to the north the coast presented a series of sandy plains for more than 200 miles.

It may now appear extraordinary that the earlier explorers in Australia were so frequently unsuccessful in their endeavours to penetrate the interior; but the scarcity of suitable horses, the unsuitable character of the saddlery, cumbersome camp equipment, and deficiency of knowledge regarding the seasons in the interior, all combined to defeat the first explorers in districts which have since been traversed with comparative facility.

In 1846 the known country had become so nearly stocked to the full extent of its capability that the leading question of interest with the settlers was, where new runs could be discovered; and, among many others, the Messrs. Gregory proposed to attempt the further exploration of the interior.

Messrs. A.C. and F.T. Gregory, who were attached to the department of the Surveyor-General, applied for three months' leave of absence for the purpose; but it was eventually arranged that the expedition should be under the auspices of the Government, which provided four horses, and voted 5 pounds for the purchase of equipment, the remainder being supplied at private expense.

The party consisted of A.C. Gregory, F.T. Gregory, and H.C. Gregory, provided with four horses and seven weeks' provisions, the equipment being reduced to the least possible weight. The starting point was Mr. T.N. Yule's station, in the Toodyay district, sixty miles north-east from Perth.

The following is a transcript of the journal:--

DIARY

EXPLORATION TO EAST OF SWAN RIVER, 1846.

7th August, 1846.

Leaving Mr. Yule's farm at Boyeen Spring, passed Captain Scully's station at Bolgart Spring at 10.15 a.m.; thence steered north 70 degrees east over sandy downs, thinly timbered with eucalyptus; at 12.50 p.m. crossed a small watercourse trending in the direction of our course till 2 p.m., when it turned south; at 3.50 p.m. halted for the night on a small stream flowing to the south-west.

Latitude by observation 31 degrees 12 minutes 10 seconds; longitude 116 degrees 50 minutes.

8th August.

At 7.5 a.m. commenced a course 70 degrees; at 8.0 crossed a granite hill with some grass, after which the country was scrubby till 9.30, when we entered a grassy flat timbered with casuarina; at 10.25 the country was more open, but scrubby; at 12.45 p.m. observed a small lake bearing 10 degrees; steered on that course, and reached it at 2.10 p.m.; halted till 3.15, and then resumed our former course through a swampy country, and at 4.50 camped on the bank of another small shallow lake.

Latitude by observation 31 degrees 4 minutes 24 seconds; longitude 117 degrees 4 minutes.

9th August.

At 7.35 a.m. steered on a course of 95 degrees through a scrubby country with small wooded valleys; at noon observed several large shallow lakes five to ten miles to the north-east; at 3 p.m. altered the course to 45 degrees, and at 3.30 to north; at 4 p.m. reached a large open flat covered with salicornia and other salt plants, and with shallow lakes of salt water. At the edge of the flat found a native well with good water and a patch of grass around it, and bivouacked.

Latitude by observation 31 degrees 2 minutes 22 seconds; longitude 117 degrees 23 minutes 15 seconds.

10th August.

At 7.35 a.m. left the bivouac and steered 95 degrees, passed several small salt lagoons in a thick swampy country; at 9.15 entered a gum forest with close underwood, which rendered travelling slow and difficult, but it gradually became more open; at 1 p.m. observed several lakes to the north and east, six to seven miles distant; we then passed a succession of dense thickets and patches of gum forest till 4.25, when we turned north, and at 5.30 halted in an open patch of grass surrounded by swampy thickets.

Latitude by observation 31 degrees 1 minute 44 seconds; longitude 117 degrees 45 minutes 10 seconds.

11th August.

At 7.25 a.m. steered north-east through gum forest; at 8.30 passed a dry lagoon; at 9.10 changed the course to 95 degrees; the country became more open; at 11.35 ascended an elevated ridge, and saw several bare granite hills to the eastward; steered 75 degrees to the nearest; reached its summit at 1.40 p.m., and halted for the remainder of the day to refresh the horses, there being abundance of water in the hollows of the rock and some grass around the base of the hill.

Latitude by observation 30 degrees 58 minutes 47 seconds; longitude 117 degrees 59 minutes 47 seconds.

DRY COUNTRY. GRANITE HILLS.

12th August.

Leaving the bivouac at 7.30 a.m., steered 122 degrees through alternate patches of gum forest, underwood, and grass; at 11.50 reached the summit of a bare granite hill, from which we could see Lake Brown, bearing 93 degrees to 103 degrees, Eaglestone Hill, 100 degrees, also many other remarkable hills and peaks. Leaving this hill at 12.15 p.m., steered 58 degrees over undulating wooded country with several small watercourses trending to the south; at 4.30 bivouacked at a scrubby hill, near a small pool of rainwater, on a granite rock.

Latitude by observation 30 degrees 59 minutes 54 seconds; longitude 118 degrees 17 minutes.

13th August.

Resumed our course 58 degrees through level gum forest, then a spearwood thicket, then dense underwood and patches of gum forest till 1.25 p.m., when we came to a native well among granite rocks; having watered the horses, continued the course through the same description of country till 4.40, when we halted at the foot of a granite hill with plenty of rainwater in the hollows and grass on a narrow strip between the scrub and base of the bare rock.

Latitude by observation 30 degrees 48 minutes 34 seconds; longitude 118 degrees 40 minutes.

14th August.

Started at 10.35 a.m., and steered 41 degrees through a level country, with thickets of underwood, cypress, and gum, with some grassy patches; at 2.20 p.m. reached a bare granite hill, at the foot of which we bivouacked.

15th August.

Leaving the bivouac at 7.15 a.m., steered 50 degrees; at 8.50 crossed a steep ridge of white sandy rocks resting on granite; after this the country was grassy, with little timber, 10.30, when we entered a thick scrub; at 11.0 observed a high granite hill bearing 50 degrees, steered for it, and reached the summit at 12.55 p.m., descending into thick scrub on the other side. Having climbed a tree to get a view, observed a very remarkable peak and range of rugged hills distant about forty miles, the highest point bearing 57 degrees; at 2.30 came to scrubby country with only a few trees, and at 4.15 camped at a small waterhole in a granite rock.

Latitude by observation 30 degrees 31 minutes 43 seconds; longitude 118 degrees 52 minutes.

16th August.

At 7.15 a.m. resumed our march on a bearing 68 degrees, through well-wooded country till 9.35, when we ascended a fine grassy hill of trap-rock. From this hill several of a similar character were visible to the southward, while to the north numerous large dry salt lakes or marshes occupied the valley along the south-eastern declivity of which we had travelled for the last two days; the course was then 56 degrees, through scattered forest, with much underwood and a little grass. At noon struck the shore of one of the lakes, the bank being composed of gypsum and red sand, in some parts twenty feet high; following the shore of the lake to the east till 1.15 p.m., again resumed a course 56 degrees through dense thickets of wattle (acacia), with patches of gum forest and cypress, the soil a red sandy loam devoid of smaller vegetation; at 5.0 halted for the night.

Latitude by observation 30 degrees 21 minutes 40 seconds; longitude 119 degrees 11 minutes.

WHIRLWINDS. RED SAND.

17th August.

At 6.30 a.m. recommenced our journey 50 degrees; at 6.55 crossed a narrow swampy patch of salicornia trending east and west; altered the course to 63 degrees, and at 7.35 crossed a deep watercourse trending to the south; at 8.15 ascended a trap hill with a few granite rocks at the foot, among which we found a small pool of rainwater, at which we halted for three hours to refresh our horses, and then proceeded 40 degrees till 2.20 p.m., when we arrived at the foot of the highest hill in the range for which we had been steering. Leaving our horses, we ascended the hill, which was composed of trap-rock, and did not exceed 300 feet in height above the general level of the country. From the summit several similar ranges of trap hills were visible, extending from north to east-south-east; to the south-east the country appeared to be a level sandy desert without the least appearance of vegetation, while to the west and north the smokes of many native fires were visible in the distance. The extremely level character of the country between the ranges to the east and north, and the immense columns of red sand or dust which were raised by whirlwinds to a height of 200 to 500 feet, gave but little hope of finding water in that direction. Returning to our horses at 4.20, steered 350 degrees about three and a half miles to a small patch of grass which had been observed from the hill, which was named Mount Jackson. There was a small watercourse through the patch of grass, but no water, and the country was suffering from prolonged drought.

Latitude by observation 30 degrees 12 minutes 28 seconds; longitude 119 degrees 16 minutes.

18th August.

After six hours' ineffectual search for water, we were compelled to return to the water passed early on the previous day.

19th August.

Left the bivouac at 7.20 a.m. and steered 275 degrees through a scattered gum forest with much underwood; at 9.55 came on a dry salt lagoon of irregular form, which was crossed at 10.20; passing a native well among flat granite rocks, the country rose gradually till 11.50, when we arrived at a hill crowned by steep white sandstone cliffs twenty to thirty feet high.

The course was then changed to north, through dense thickets, till 12.20 p.m., when we again turned west through a well-wooded country, and at 3.0 camped on a high granite hill with some patches of grass and abundance of rainwater in the hollows of the rocks.

Latitude 30 degrees 19 minutes 33 seconds; longitude 118 degrees 55 minutes.

20th August.

At 7.30 a.m. resumed a westerly course through dense thickets of acacia and melaleuca, and at 5.15 p.m. bivouacked in a small patch of grass and a small pool of rainwater on a granite rock.

Latitude 30 degrees 17 minutes 40 seconds; longitude 118 degrees 35 minutes.

21st August.

At 7.45 a.m. started on a course 320 degrees over an undulating country with dense thickets and patches of cypress and gum forest; at 4.30 p.m. bivouacked near a small hole in a rock with about two gallons of rainwater remaining in it.

Latitude 30 degrees 5 minutes 43 seconds; longitude 118 degrees 22 seconds.

22nd August.

At 7.35 a.m. resumed a west course through a succession of thickets, gum forest, and scrub; at 12.30 p.m. observed a granite hill bearing 315 degrees; made for the hill, and finding some excellent grass around a native well, at 2.15 camped.

Latitude 30 degrees 3 minutes 36 seconds; longitude 118 degrees 8 minutes.

23rd August.

Started at 7.40 a.m. in a direction 320 degrees, over thinly-timbered scrubby country, which gradually improved and became grassy; at 10.5 altered the course to 336 degrees, and at 1.15 p.m. reached the summit of a granite hill from which a series of dry lakes, or salt marshes, were visible in a wide valley trending to the north-east. A very remarkable hill bore 316 degrees, about 35 miles distant. Steering in the direction of this hill, found the country covered with almost impenetrable scrub of acacia. At 4.20 halted at the foot of a high sandstone cliff, where some deep holes in the rock retained a small quantity of rainwater.

Latitude 29 degrees 51 minutes; longitude 119 degrees 55 minutes.

24th August.

Left the bivouac at 7.35 a.m. steering 312 degrees; passed over a nearly level country timbered with cypress and eucalyptus, with patches of acacia thicket; at 2.45 p.m. halted at a deep waterhole in a flat granite rock.

Latitude 29 degrees 42 minutes 31 seconds; longitude 117 degrees 41 minutes.

EXTENSIVE SALT MARSHES.

25th August.

At 7.30 a.m. resumed our journey on the same course as yesterday, and at 9.15 came on an extensive flat covered with salicornia, which formed the margin of an immense salt marsh or dry lake, extending to the north-east and south-west to the horizon, but narrowing to about three miles at the point we came to it. It was decided to attempt crossing at this place, and, after travelling for an hour across the salicornia flat, reached the bare salt marsh. This at first seemed firm; but, after half-a-mile, the hard crust of salt and gypsum, which formed the surface, gave way and three of the horses were bogged almost at the same time. After a long ineffectual struggle to extricate themselves they were quite exhausted, and we waded through the mud to the opposite shore, a distance of half-a-mile, and cut some small trees, and with them, combined with tether ropes and saddle-bags, formed two hurdles or platforms twelve feet long and two feet wide. These with much difficulty were taken to the horses, and by placing them alternately in front of each animal, worked them over the soft mud, and after six hours of severe exertion succeeded in reaching the firm ground. The hard salt crust, though apparently strong, having once been broken, its edges gave way like thin ice. After reaching the ground, which was dry enough to bear the weight of the horses, we had to travel about three miles through soft dust of white gypsum, in which we sank from one to two feet, but at length reached a large granite rock, at the foot of which there was a little grass and on the rock some small pools of rainwater.

Latitude 29 degrees 37 minutes 30 seconds; longitude 117 degrees 38 minutes.

26th August.

From the summit of the rock we had an extensive view, the lake extending twelve miles east, fifteen miles to the south and west, eight miles to the north and to the north-east, only bounded by the horizon. Shallow pools of brine, varying from one to three miles in diameter, with low-wooded and high bare granite islets, were scattered over this vast area of white mud gypsum and salt. At 8.35 a.m. started in a southerly direction along the shore of the lake in the hope of turning its west side; at 10.40 altered the course to 221 degrees; and at 12.30 p.m. camped on a grassy granite hill, about a mile from the lake.

Latitude 29 degrees 47 minutes 13 seconds; longitude 117 degrees 36 minutes.

27th August.

Steering a general course 200 degrees from 7.40 a.m. to 8.40, again reached the shore of the lake, followed it south-east till 9.45, then 80 degrees till 12.15 p.m., when we halted for one and a half hours under a very remarkable solitary gum-tree; we then steered 173 degrees till 2.20; then 204 degrees till 3.30, when we left the lake, which trended to the west, and, steering 250 degrees till 5.5, camped at a native well in a small grassy valley. Some good open grassy flats were passed during the day and a large number of wild turkeys were seen.

Latitude 29 degrees 59 minutes 4 seconds; longitude 117 degrees 39 minutes.

28th August.

Starting at 7.35 a.m. in a west-north-west course, at 8.45 passed several small dry salt lagoons; at 9.0 ascended a granite hill, from the summit of which it was discovered that further progress in this direction was impracticable, and that we were on a peninsula, as the lake still trended south to the horizon. We therefore turned east, and at 11.35 came on the southern extension of the eastern branch of the lake; followed it nearly east till noon, then north-east and north-north-east till 1.0 p.m.; then 17 degrees, leaving the lake and crossing extensive open downs till 2.5, when a small dry salt lake was passed, and we entered thickets of acacia, which changed to gum and cypress forest; at 3.0 came to a rich grassy hill, then thickets and grassy patches, and at 4.0 reached the summit of a lofty granite hill and had an extensive view over the country. On the north side of the hill found a native well and some good grass, where we camped.

Latitude 29 degrees 45 minutes 15 seconds; longitude 117 degrees 46 minutes.

GRANITE HILLS AND GRASSY COUNTRY.

29th August.

At 7.35 a.m. left the bivouac and steered 30 degrees through thickets; at 8.30 crossed our track of the 24th, and at 9.15 passed a salt marsh trending north-west and south-east; at 12.25 p.m. altered the course to north till 1.0; then, 37 degrees, ascended a granite hill, on which we found a few shallow pools of rainwater; then north till 4.0 p.m., and bivouacked in a grassy patch with a small hollow containing a little muddy water.

Latitude 29 degrees 30 minutes 46 seconds; longitude 117 degrees 51 minutes.

30th August.

Resumed our journey at 7.35 a.m., steering north over a level country with patches of brushwood and grass; at 10.35 ascended a steep grassy ridge, and found ourselves at the north-east extremity of the immense salt lake which for five days had baffled our attempts to proceed north. The lake, which was named Lake Moore, was at this part about five miles wide, and extended to the horizon to the south-west; to the north and west there were many bare granite hills; changing the course to 328 degrees, at 12.55 p.m. camped at a grassy granite hill.

Latitude 29 degrees 17 minutes 56 seconds; longitude 117 degrees 47 minutes.

31st August.

At 7.30 a.m. steered 328 degrees for two hours through thickets of acacia, cypress, and gum; then entered a grassy country with jam-wattle; at 10.35 passed a granite hill and altered the course to 357 degrees, and at 11.30 ascended a high granite hill, from which many similar hills were visible to the north and east, and a remarkable range of trap hills about thirty miles to the north-north-east; also some smaller trap ranges to the north-west, from ten to thirty miles distant. At noon steered 302 degrees towards the nearest of these ranges, traversing a level plain with brushwood and grass; at 4.45 crossed a small dry watercourse trending west, and at 5.5 bivouacked on a granite hill, with some grass and a fine pool of rainwater in a hollow of the rock.

Latitude 29 degrees 3 minutes 14 seconds; longitude 117 degrees 31 minutes.

1st September.

Resumed our route at 7.45 a.m.; at 8.45 reached the hills we had been steering for; from the summit there was an extensive view: to the north and west were many trap hills and several dry salt lakes; to the north the country was level for several miles, and then rose into a low range of granite hills, covered with brushwood and grass; at 9.20 steered 230 degrees over level country with dense thickets of acacia; at noon the country became more open; at 1.0 passed some small dry salt lagoons, the country more open and with some grass, and at 3.0 camped at the foot of a granite hill, with good grass and some water oozing out of a cleft in the rock.

Latitude 28 degrees 50 minutes 44 seconds; longitude 117 degrees 20 minutes.

2nd September.

Leaving the bivouac at 7.40 a.m., steered 330 degrees over a succession of grassy granite hills, with small watercourse trending to the west; at 12.40 p.m. came on a party of four aboriginals, who hastily decamped, leaving their spears and shields behind in the hurry of retreat; they appeared to be of rather small stature, and somewhat darker in colour than the blacks near the Swan River. Observing a remarkable hill bearing 312 degrees about twenty miles distant, steered for it; the country became more level, with grass and brushwood; at 3.5 turned north to a steep granite hill, crossing a dry watercourse thirty yards wide and sixteen feet deep trending north-west; at 4.40 halted in a gully in the granite range, and obtained water by digging among the rocks.

Latitude 28 degrees 34 minutes 9 seconds; longitude 117 degrees 2 minutes.

3rd September.

Started at 8.0 a.m., steering towards the hill seen yesterday, and which now bore 307 degrees. The country was nearly a dead level, with a few small dry watercourses trending south-west; the soil a red loam, producing some grass and small acacias; at 10.50 came on an extensive flat covered with salicornia, which extended to the base of the hill, the summit of which was reached at 12.25 p.m.; from this position the flat or marsh appeared to extend fifteen miles to the north-east, a branch also to the north-west, in which direction the water seemed to trend, though the dip of the country, if any, was so slight as to render it uncertain. To the north a range of trap hills, five to ten miles distant, intercepted the view. Having completed observations at 2.10, steered 300 degrees along the foot of a range of trap hills; at 3.50 passed a dry salt lake on our right, and at 5.15 bivouacked on the side of a trap hill, among some fine oat-grass growing on calcareous tufa. From the summit of the hill we could see salt marshes continuing in a north-west direction for many miles; all the hills within twenty miles were of a trap formation, and therefore gave no prospect of obtaining water, the soil being loose and the rock full of fissures; hitherto we seldom had found water except on or near granite rocks, which serve to collect the rainwater of even slight showers.

Latitude 28 degrees 24 minutes 20 seconds; longitude 116 degrees 42 minutes.

SCARCITY OF WATER. TURN TO THE WEST.

4th September.

As the horses had been twenty-four hours without water, and there was no prospect of obtaining any to the north or west, no rain having fallen for the past month, it was deemed advisable to return to the last bivouac, and then, by a westerly course, attempt to make the sources of the Hutt or Arrowsmith rivers, the mouths of which had been discovered by Captain Grey on the coast opposite our position. Accordingly, after six hours' ride, we got back to the well at the bivouac of the 2nd.

5th September.

At 7.50 a.m. left the bivouac, and, steering 240 degrees, at 8.15 crossed the dry watercourse trending west; at 11.0 ascended the ridge bounding the valley; at noon found a small pool of water in a gully descending to the westward; after this traversed a continuous thicket of acacia with narrow strips of cypress forest, and bivouacked at 5.50 without water.

Latitude 29 degrees 47 minutes 15 seconds; longitude 116 degrees 41 minutes.

6th September.

At 6.45 a.m., proceeding west, ascended a granite hill, near the top of which we found a native well, where we halted at 7.30. Having watered the horses and breakfasted, at 9.30 resumed our journey over granite hills, covered with brushwood and cypress with a few grassy patches; at 11.10 passed a native well; altered the course to west-south-west, crossing three small watercourses trending north-west; and at 1.15 p.m. halted at the foot of a bare granite hill, on the top of which there was a fine pool of rainwater in a shallow basin of the rock.

Latitude 28 degrees 50 minutes 51 seconds; longitude 116 degrees 29 minutes.

7th September.

Started at 7.15 a.m. on a course 255 degrees through acacia thickets; at 10.5 crossed a narrow strip of salt marsh, which spread out into dry salt lakes to the south; after this the country was grassy till 11.30, when we entered a dense thicket of acacia, melaleuca, cypress, and eucalypti, the ground gradually rising till 4.0 p.m., and then descending till 5.25, when we crossed a small dry watercourse trending south; at 6.10 bivouacked in a gum forest without water or grass, though a large flight of white cockatoos which roosted near seemed to indicate that water was not far distant.

Latitude 28 degrees 58 minutes 14 seconds; longitude 116 degrees 6 minutes.

8th September.

Leaving the bivouac at 7.0 am steered west; at 7.20 came to a grassy granite hill, then west-north-west to another hill, where we halted for half an hour to look for water, but being unsuccessful, again resumed a westerly course through acacia thickets, alternating with grassy gum forest, till noon, when the soil changed from a red loam to ironstone gravel; grass disappeared and was replaced by scrub; the country was much broken and continued to rise till 4.0 p.m., when it began to descend rapidly till 4.30, when we came to a small watercourse trending south; following it down for half a mile, found a small pool of water and some grass, and halted for the night, this being the only water seen for nearly fifty miles.

Latitude 28 degrees 58 minutes 50 seconds; longitude 115 degrees 45 minutes.

DISCOVER TWO SEAMS OF COAL.

9th September.

At 7.30 a.m. resumed a westerly course through grassy gum forest; at 8.0 a.m. crossed a large watercourse trending south, with many shallow pools of water; the country then became scrubby; at 9.10 crossed a granite ridge and entered a rich grassy valley timbered with eucalypti and raspberry-jam wattle, a small watercourse trending north. The ridge on the west side of the valley was destitute of timber, but covered with dense wattle brush; at 10.0 a.m. altered the course to 305 degrees, and at 10.35 came on the head of a small stream-bed with pools of water; following it west-north-west, at 11.30 it was joined by a running stream four yards wide, the water being brackish, and trended to the south-west; left it and steered west over an open scrubby country; at 12.30 p.m. entered a dense thicket of eucalypti and acacia, the soil being formed of fragments of granite and trap; at 1.0 p.m. entered a deep valley by an abrupt descent, and found ourselves once more on the banks of the brackish stream, which was much enlarged, and running through a narrow grassy flat backed by high sandstone cliffs from 80 to 100 feet high. Continuing our course along the river west till 1.55 p.m., when it turned north, and at 2.20 p.m. north-west; at 3.0 p.m. the banks of the stream became very high, and stratified in a remarkable manner, the lower rocks in thin beds dipping to the east, while the superincumbent rocks of red sandstone were horizontal. We therefore entered the bed of the river to examine it, and found two seams of coal--one five feet thick and the other about six feet thick--between beds of sandstone and shale. Having pitched the tent and tethered the horses, we commenced to collect specimens of the various strata, and succeeded in cutting out five or six hundredweight of coal with the tomahawk, and in a short time had the satisfaction of seeing the first fire of Western Australian coal burning cheerfully in front of the camp, this being the first discovery of coal in the western part of the Continent.

Latitude 28 degrees 57 minutes 10 seconds; longitude 115 degrees 30 minutes.

10th September.

At 7.20 a.m. left the camp and followed the river downwards on a general course 250 degrees; at 7.40 crossed to the left bank, the valley opening out and the soil improving, being formed by the decomposition of soft shales, which contain much gypsum in fine crystals. Oat and rye grasses were abundant, with plenty of saltbush; at 9.10 crossed to the right bank, and steered 220 degrees to an abrupt headland on the north side of the valley, which was here about two miles wide; the soil a stiff brown loam, with rounded fragments of granite, flinty trap, and quartz, resembling in appearance the French millstone burr; the grass improved, being chiefly of perennial species. After a halt of twenty minutes to take bearings from the hill, at 9.40 steered 200 degrees, and again crossed the river at 11.15, and altered the course to 235 degrees; the grassy country having a breadth of two miles. At noon ascended a sandy ridge with a few gum-trees on the top; there the valley closed in, the grassy flats below being only half a mile wide and backed by extensive elevated sandy downs, covered with heath and short scrub. The course of the river was about 230 degrees. At 1.35 p.m. ascended a remarkable red sandstone hill, with a table summit and steep rocks on all sides nearly blocking up the valley; at 2.15 p.m. resumed a general course of 242 degrees along the bank of the river, and at 4.5 bivouacked in a rich grassy flat thinly timbered with white-barked eucalyptus.

Latitude 29 degrees 10 minutes 42 seconds; longitude 115 degrees 15 minutes.

REACH THE SEA-COAST.

11th September.

Started at 7.40 a.m., and, steering 240 degrees, crossed the river, left the grassy flats, and entered the sandy downs; at 8.45 ascended a steep sandstone cliff, and from the top had a distant view of the sea; the river about one and a half miles to the south, where a large branch joined it from the east about two miles below the bivouac. At 9.35 steered 267 degrees over open sandy downs, and at 10.35 struck the river, running north through beautiful grassy flats timbered with York and white-gums and wattles; there were many fine pools of water, which appeared to be permanent.

After an unsuccessful attempt to cross the river, followed it northerly till 11.0; then west-north-west till 11.20, and then west-south-west till 11.45, when we found a practicable crossing to the left bank, and, steering west by south, ascended a sandy limestone ridge; then on a west-south-west course followed the valley of the river down to its mouth, which was reached at 3.40 p.m. The entrance of the river was choked up with sand and rocks, and not passable for even small boats. This river appears to be the Irwin River of Captain Grey, as this spot is only one and a half miles to the south of the position assigned to it on Arrowsmith's map of this part of the coast. At 4.30 left the beach and retraced our steps to where we crossed the river at 1.30, and bivouacked at 5.50.

Latitude 29 degrees 15 minutes 10 seconds; longitude 114 degrees 59 minutes.

12th September.

At 7.50 a.m. resumed our journey up the river, steering north-east till 8.25; then east along the north bank, through rich grassy flats timbered with York gum. At 10.20 left the river and entered the sandy downs; at 10.30 crossed a small stream with some fine springs; at 11.0 changed the course to east by south; at noon altered the course to 83 degrees, crossing the river at 12.50 p.m., where it is joined by the east branch, which is of equal size with the northern one; followed the east branch up through wide grassy flats till 2.0, and camped.

The country consists of elevated sandy downs covered with heathy bushes and a few small banksia trees, it being only on the alluvial flats of the river that there is any grass or good soil. Large flocks of cockatoos--white, black with white tails, and black with red tails--came to water near the camp; some were shot, also a turkey, the flesh of which was extremely bitter and scarcely eatable. Several kangaroos were seen on the sandy downs.

Latitude 29 degrees 11 minutes 20 seconds; longitude 115 degrees 18 minutes.

13th September.

At 7.55 a.m. left the Irwin River and steered a course 160 degrees, over open sandy downs of considerable elevation; at 11.45 halted for half an hour and shot a kangaroo, which proved a welcome addition to the commissariat; at 1.30 p.m. changed the course to 142 degrees, and at 2.30 came to a running stream three yards wide. This we assumed to be the Arrowsmith River of Captain Grey, and as there was little prospect of finding water farther on, we bivouacked, though there was only a little grass close to the bank of the stream and the rest of the country covered with short scrub.

Latitude 29 degrees 27 minutes 9 seconds.

14th September.

Left the bivouac at 8.35 a.m., and steered 160 degrees over sandy downs with ridges of red sandstone till 3.0 p.m., when the course was altered to 220 degrees, following down a shallow valley; at 4.0 turned west-south-west, and at 5.15 bivouacked in a swampy spot with some grass; obtaining water by digging in the sand.

Latitude 29 degrees 48 minutes 10 seconds; longitude 115 degrees 32 minutes.

15th September.

Leaving the bivouac at 8.0 a.m., steered 214 degrees over scrubby country with patches of gum forest; at 9.0 turned to 160 degrees, crossed a country of sand and ironstone of considerable elevation; at 3.30 p.m. altered the course to 170 degrees, and followed down a scrubby valley till 5.0; then 115 degrees for half an hour, and came to a native well in a patch of York gum-trees, where we camped. The last three hours our progress was scarcely six miles, as one of the horses knocked up.

Latitude 30 degrees 10 minutes; longitude 115 degrees 39 minutes.

STEER SOUTH OVER SANDY DOWNS.

16th September.

As there was no grass for the horses, we were compelled to push on our journey, and at 7.20 a.m. steered 160 degrees; the country was more broken up by valleys, the soil sand and ironstone, with heathy scrub, banksia, and grass trees (xanthorrhoea) with a few patches of white-gum forest; at 10.30 steered 138 degrees towards a high summit, distant twelve miles. The horse again knocked up, but by relieving him of his load, which was transferred to the other horses, succeeded in driving him a few miles further. At 2.20 p.m. changed the course to 180 degrees, and entered a level sandy piece of country, bounded on all sides by hills; at 3.40 altered the course to south-west; at 5.0 had to abandon the weak horse and continue our route in search of water; at 5.30 passed a small salt lake with a little grass on the margin; at 6.0, finding the country getting worse, returned to the salt lake and camped on the western side.

Latitude 30 degrees 27 minutes 19 seconds; longitude 115 degrees 47 minutes.

17th September.

After digging in about twenty different places around the lake, at length found fresh water, and then went back for the knocked-up horse, and with some difficulty got him to the well, where we decided to rest the horses this and the following day, before encountering the inhospitable sandy region to the southwards.

18th September.

One of the party made a short excursion to the west of the plain, and in about three miles reached the hills, which appeared very barren and scrubby; but after crossing the first ridge, the country was timbered with York and red gum and a large species of acacia, producing abundance of gum; the soil a red loam, producing some grass and abundance of the everlasting flowers and warran, or native yam. After penetrating this good country four miles returned to the camp, having shot a kangaroo and ten cockatoos.

19th September.

Leaving the camp at 8.5 a.m., steered 160 degrees, and soon ascended the sandy downs, which were destitute of trees, except a few banksia and floribunda; at 11.45 crossed a valley trending to the west; at 1.15 p.m. observed a range of wooded hills to the east and south; altered the course towards a remarkable gorge which bore 129 degrees; at 3.30 entered a gum forest, and at 3.50 came to a large stream-bed with many pools of water; followed it down south, and camped at 4.20.

Latitude 30 degrees 42 minutes 39 seconds; longitude 116 degrees.

REACH THE MOORE RIVER.

20th September.

Crossed the watercourse, which seemed to be a branch of the Moore River, and steered 163 degrees from 7.30 a.m. till 8.20, when the country improved, with grassy hills and brown loam, with fragments of granite and trap rock; the timber York-gum and jam-wattle. This description of country continued till 12.15 p.m., when scrub again prevailed on ironstone hills timbered with white-gum; at 2.20 entered a valley of better character, with quartz and granite rocks. After crossing several rocky ridges, at 3.20 reached the main branch of the Moore River, which we crossed, and camped. This was the first place where the poisonous gastrolobium was observed.

Latitude 31 degrees 39 seconds; longitude 116 degrees 13 minutes.

21st September.

At 7.30 a.m. followed the river upwards on a bearing of 130 degrees; at 8.0 passed a deserted sheep-station, the river coming from the north; continued our course over broken ironstone ridges, timbered with white-gum; at 10.0 the country became more level and sandy, and at 11.45 struck the road from Toodyay to Victoria Plains; followed the road southerly till 4.5 p.m., and camped at a small spring.

Latitude 31 degrees 14 minutes 19 seconds; longitude 116 degrees 34 minutes.

CAPTAIN GREY'S REPORT OF GOOD COUNTRY CONFIRMED.

22nd September.

This morning an hour's ride brought us to Bolgart Spring, after an absence of forty-seven days, during which we had travelled 953 miles, traversing three degrees of latitude and nearly four and a half of longitude.

The discovery of coal and country available for settlement on the coast to the north of Swan River was deemed to be of such importance that the Government dispatched Lieutenant Helpman in the colonial schooner Champion to procure a sufficient quantity of the coal to admit of its being practically tested as to quality, and also to ascertain what facilities existed for its conveyance to a port for shipment. A volunteer party, consisting of Lieutenant Irby, Dr. Meekleham, Messrs. Gregory and Hazlewood, accompanied Lieutenant Helpman to Champion Bay, now the site of Geraldton, and thence by land to the coal-seam on the Irwin River, a distance of ninety miles, and brought down about half a ton of coal to the vessel. This coal, though of fair quality and suitable for steam purposes, proved, however, to be so remote from any suitable port for shipment that it has hitherto not been available for commercial purposes.

The primary object of the voyage having been attained, it was considered desirable to avail of the opportunity to examine the country to the northward and ascertain its capabilities for settlement; for though Captain, now Sir George Grey, had seen some good country on his journey along the coast from Gantheaume Bay to Swan River, in 1839, Captain Stokes, who landed from the Beagle subsequently and ascended Wizard Peak about twelve miles inland, had distinctly negatived the existence of any country capable of occupation, though, as an illustration of the difficulty of ascertaining the real capabilities of country by partial and hurried inspection, it may be observed that this has since become one of the most prosperous districts of Western Australia in regard to its pastoral, agricultural, and mining industries.

For the purpose of making this examination of the country, Messrs. A.C. Gregory, H.C. Gregory, and Lieutenant Irby, taking three horses and three days' provisions, left Champion Bay on the 20th December, the following being a copy of the journal:--

20th December, 1846.

At 6.20 a.m. left the bivouac and followed the shore of Champion Bay about a mile northerly; then steered 87 degrees over a scrubby country; at 7.20 crossed the Chapman River; and at 8.0, being a quarter of a mile north from Mount Fairfax, altered the course to 66 degrees, the country being thinly covered with wattle scrub and some grass; at 8.45 crossed a large branch of the Chapman with several small pools of water in the bed; the country beyond was more scrubby and the soil gravelly; at 9.0 changed the course to 18 degrees, and at 9.20 again crossed the Chapman River just below a pool of apparently permanent water; at 9.50 crossed a granite ridge, beyond which the country improved, with many large patches of grass to the eastward; at 10.20 ascended a high flat-topped hill of red sandstone resting on granite, which proved to be the eastern point of Moresby's Flat-topped Range. From this hill Mount Fairfax and Wizard Hill were visible to the east; grassy hills rose gradually from the Chapman River for seven or eight miles; steering 10 degrees over grassy country, the soil was composed of detritus of granite and trap rocks; at 11.0 came on a large party of natives, some of whom accompanied us for about a mile, pointing out places where we should find water. At noon turned to the north-east and entered an extensive valley with some patches of grass, but not generally of a good character; at 12.30 p.m. crossed a small watercourse trending west; followed it about half a mile, and then steered north-west over scrubby flats till 1.0, when we struck a small stream-bed with small pools of water, and halted till 1.20, and then followed up the stream to the north till 3.0, when we bivouacked.

21st December.

At 6.35 a.m. steered north over a hilly country with scrub, grass, York-gum, and wattle--the prevailing rocks red sandstone, quartz, and granite; at 8.30 crossed a stream-bed with pools of brackish water trending east, and at 8.50 entered a good grassy country which appeared to extend ten to twelve miles to the east and north--clumps of York-gum, jam-wattle, and sandalwood were observed on some of the hills. After crossing several small watercourses, at 9.45 ascended an elevated sandy tableland covered with coarse scrub; and at 10.35, not seeing any prospect of better country, changed the course to west, and following down a deep gully, at 11.7 came to a small pool of salt water; following the watercourse south-south-west, at 11.25 came to a small hole dug by the natives, in which the water was fresh, though the pools above and below were salt. Halting till nearly 1.0 p.m., resumed a westerly course, crossing several deep grassy valleys trending south; at 1.35 steered 211 degrees over a hilly, quartz, and granite country with very good grass; at 2.30 again came on the stream-bed, the country improved and well-grassed, with scattered jam and black wattle trees as far as the country was visible; at 3.50 the stream was joined by a branch from the east, and following it to the west-north-west till 5.0, bivouacked in the bed of the stream, water being obtained by digging in the sand.

22nd December.

At 6.35 a.m. steered 220 degrees over a fine grassy country; at 7.0 ascended a small ironstone hill, from which we observed a deep valley trending to the south-west; to the north and west the country was open and grassy for twelve miles, presenting at one view fifty or sixty thousand acres of fine sheep pasture. Continuing a south-west course over granite country with some good grass, but not equal to that seen the previous day, at 8.0 crossed a small stream-bed, which we assumed to be the Bowes River of Captain Grey; we ascended steep limestone hills on the west bank, and from the summit observed the large white sand patch on Point Moore bearing 170 degrees; turning south three-quarters of a mile, crossed the Bowes River at its mouth, which was choked up with sand; we then steered south-east with the intention of following Captain Grey's route to Champion Bay; but, after traversing sandy downs with limestone rocks for four miles, one of the horses became so footsore that we descended a deep ravine to the sea-beach, which was followed southerly, and after crossing the dry mouth of the Buller and Chapman Rivers, reached the landing place in Champion Bay at 1.10 p.m.

On the 23rd the party and horses were shipped on board the Champion and reached Fremantle on the 28th.

THE SETTLERS' EXPEDITION TO THE NORTHWARD FROM PERTH, UNDER MR. ASSISTANT-SURVEYOR A.C. GREGORY 1848

As the stock belonging to the settlers on the Swan River had increased to the full extent of the pastoral capabilities of the known available country, it became of pressing importance to push forward the exploration of the Colony of West Australia, and accordingly, in 1848 the Surveyor-General, Captain Roe, conducted an expedition to the south-east of Swan River, while the settlers organised one to proceed to the north, and made application to the Government to grant the services of Mr. Assistant-Surveyor A.C. Gregory as the leader of the party.

THE SETTLERS' EXPEDITION TO THE NORTHWARD FROM PERTH, UNDER MR. ASSISTANT-SURVEYOR A.C. GREGORY.

We could not do justice to the enterprise and exertions of the gentlemen who discovered the new tract of good land to the northward in any other way than by giving Mr. Augustus Gregory's Journal entire:--

INSTRUCTIONS TO LEADER OF THE EXPEDITION AND ITS OBJECTS.

Colonial Secretary's Office,

Perth, August 28, 1848.

SIR,

I am directed by the Governor to inform you that you have been appointed to direct the exploring expedition about to proceed northwards on account of the zeal, energy, and enterprising spirit that have been exhibited by you on other occasions, and called into action with credit to yourself and advantage to the public interests. The party under your direction, it is intended, should proceed northward as high as the Gascoyne River. (The Gascoyne River flows into Shark Bay, in latitude 24 degrees 52 minutes South.) It is advisable to approach that river from the eastward, about 100 miles from the coast, after proceeding in a north-easterly and northerly direction from the country abreast of Champion Bay, it being desirable that part of your route which lies farthest in the interior country should be first accomplished, in order to avail yourself of the best chance of finding water.

You will examine that river as far as it may be practicable to do, with the view of tracing its course; of ascertaining, if possible, the nature of the bar at the mouth of it, and the question of its being practicable for boats, to what distance from the bar, and the nature of the soil in the vicinity of either bank.

After having examined thus the Gascoyne River you will proceed in a southerly direction and examine the river, as yet unnamed, about forty miles farther south, that flows into Shark's Bay, the mouth of which was seen by Captain Grey, and is placed by him at Point Long.

Should you proceed along the sea-shore for any distance you will pay as much attention as your limited means will allow you to do to the peculiarities of the coast, and of any estuaries, creeks, or roadsteads that may present themselves.

You will bear in mind that the primary object of this expedition is the examination of a new tract of unknown country for practical purposes, by practical men--that, in fact, the discovery of new land of an available kind for pasture has become a thing to be desired, of paramount importance, and an object in the attainment of which the interests and perhaps the fate of this colony depend.

You will thus conduct your expedition with the view of promoting this principal object to the best of your ability. But it is hardly needful to observe to you that this chief object may be promoted and attained without neglecting to observe the geographical, geological, and mineralogical features of the country you pass through; its productions--animal and vegetable; and the character, dialects, and customs, to some extent, of the aboriginal tribes you may fall in with. You have been so frequently employed in exploring expeditions, though of minor importance perhaps to the present, that you must be well aware it is no less impolitic than cruel to come into actual collision, wantonly, unadvisedly, and maliciously, with the natives; and, on the contrary, that it is no less humane than politic to leave no angry recollections of white people, where the footsteps of travellers, however few and far between, must be expected to follow yours.

Should your route, either in proceeding on the expedition or returning, be in the direction of that part of the Irwin River where for the discovery of coal the colony is indebted to yourself and brothers, it would be desirable that you should devote a short time to the examination of the locality where it was first found; to excavation, to some moderate extent, in the vicinity of the veins of coal of most promise; and, above all, to the ascertainment of the fact if coal crops out, or if there be in the soil any indications of it between the place where the mine was discovered by you in 1846 and the seashore, in that intervening space of about thirty-eight or forty miles, or to the northward of it in the direction of Shark's Bay, where Dr. von Sommer thought the coal-seam of the Irwin might again make its appearance.

In the event of accident, occasioning loss of provisions and beasts of burden, and a necessity arising for a prompt return to the settled districts, you will bear in mind the causes of impediment on the march which proved so disastrous to Captain Grey's party on its return from Gantheaume Bay; the want of vigilance at night manifested in another expedition in the murder of Lieutenant Eyre's European companion; and the want of caution, forgetfulness of the nature of barbarians, and the facilities for ambush afforded by a wilderness of trees and jungle, that have led to injuries fatal to life, as in the case of Mr. Cunningham in Sir Thomas Mitchell's expedition, and of two of his companions at another time; and in some instances, as in those of Captain Stokes and Captain Grey, that have led to results all but fatal to the explorers and their expeditions; injuries suddenly and unexpectedly inflicted on individuals straggling from the main body of their party, or venturing considerable distances in advance of it.

You are to bear in mind that it might be of some advantage throughout your expedition to keep a register of the depths at which water has been found by you, and of those depths to which you have penetrated in vain for it.

It will be requisite that you should ascertain the course of rivers of any magnitude, and direction of chains of high land, that you may meet with, and follow the same to some extent--at least wherever appearances may lead you to expect improvement of soil, a richer country, or one indicating mineral productions.

In the event of occurrences of unexpected disasters, impediments, and unavoidable accidents, arising from loss of provisions or of horses, or of any injury to the health or strength of the party, rendering it utterly impracticable for the expedition to proceed as high northward as Gascoyne River, your discretion then supplying whatever you may be unprovided for in your instructions, you will explore as far as it is possible for you to do, on your return, the country north of the settled districts of York and Toodyay; so that something of utility may be accomplished, and the great object for which this expedition was prepared may not be wholly frustrated.

I am further to add that His Excellency's best wishes accompany your party, and that the success of the expedition, and the return of all engaged in it in health and safety, will be hailed by him with very lively satisfaction.

I have the honour to be, Sir,

Your obedient servant,

R.R. MADDEN,

Colonial Secretary. To A.C. Gregory, Esquire, Perth.

GENERAL REPORT OF JOURNEY.

Perth, November 20, 1848.

SIR,

I have the honour to transmit, for the information of His Excellency the Governor, the following outline of the proceedings of the exploring party to the northward which His Excellency has been pleased to place under my direction. I regret that we have not succeeded in reaching the Gascoyne River, which your instructions for my guidance pointed out as the ultimate object of the expedition; but I trust that our attempts to render the expedition serviceable to the colony have not proved unsuccessful, especially as the result has been the discovery of several fine portions of good grassy land near Champion Bay, which, with the more minute examination of the country in the vicinity which had been previously discovered, will render available a tract of pasturage sufficiently extensive to relieve the present overstocked districts; the estimated quantity of land suitable for depasturing sheep being about 225,000 acres, exclusive of 100,000 acres on the Irwin, the greater portion of which, however, is better suited to agricultural purposes. The observations I have had the opportunity of making during this journey have confirmed my previous opinion, that, could the party have started in July instead of September, the chief obstacle to our progress--the want of water--might have been avoided; and although there would have been many minor difficulties to encounter, I feel assured that the same zeal and energy which enabled my party to contend so long with the obstacles which opposed their advance to the Gascoyne River, would have ensured their success in a more favourable season. The gentlemen who formed my party have my sincere thanks for their prompt and energetic co-operation on all occasions; nor can I omit to mention the cheerful and trustworthy conduct of private W. King of the 96th regiment. For minute details I beg to refer my journal and the plans of my route, which I am plotting.

I have the honour to be, Sir,

Your obedient servant,

A.C. Gregory,

Assistant-Surveyor.

The Honourable the Colonial Secretary, etc.

JOURNAL
LEAVE THE SETTLED DISTRICTS. STAMPEDE OF HORSES.

2nd September, 1848.

Started for Toodyay, with Mr. C.F. Gregory and five horses for the expedition to Shark's Bay; bivouacked at Worrilloo.

3rd September.

Proceeded to Toodyay, where Messrs. L. Burges, J. Walcott, and A. Bedart joined on the 4th, bringing six horses with them. Having had the horses shod at Ferguson's, we continued our journey to Mr. Lefroy's station, near Bebano, which we reached on the 7th. The following day the cart, with our provisions, etc., arrived, accompanied by private W. King. Having obtained another horse from Mr. Lefroy, on the 9th we left Welbing, with ten pack and two riding horses, carrying three months' provisions, etc. Steering north by west for the first twenty miles, generally grassy, we entered the extensive sandy plains which occupy almost the whole country between the Moore and Irwin rivers. The rainy season having scarcely ended, we found both water and grass for our horses every night; and, not meeting with any serious impediments, we reached the upper part of the Arrowsmith Brook on the 13th. Here the country improved, and the valleys, in which the stream takes its rise, were estimated to contain about 10,000 acres of tolerable sheep pasture. Early the ensuing day we entered the Irwin Plains; crossing the eastern branches of the river, we encamped, on the 15th, on the northern branch, three-quarters of a mile below the spot where the coal was first discovered. The Irwin Plains presented a beautiful aspect, being covered with rich grass and vegetation; the soil is generally good; but most of the grasses being of the annual species, would not afford good pasturage in the summer, and in consequence they are better suited for agriculture, while the open character of the country would render clearing for the plough a matter of little expense. While dinner was preparing, the horses, being herded, suddenly started off at full speed, in consequence of a large stone rolled down by one of the party in ascending the hill. Two of the remaining horses were immediately saddled, and Mr. Burges and myself started to catch them; in about a mile we came up with them at the foot of an almost perpendicular cliff; on seeing us they started off, and scrambling up the rocks like goats, left us far behind; we did not overtake them for several miles, when with some difficulty we captured one, but had the mortification of losing one of the saddled horses in exchange. Leaving the captured horse in charge of Mr. Burges, I followed the rest; caught another after a smart ride of three miles, but it was not till I reached the East Irwin that I could again overtake the rest, when, favoured by the steep bank of the stream, I succeeded in securing our truant steeds. It was now dark, and being unable to manage nine horses by myself, I tethered several of the wildest, and started with two of the best for the encampment ten miles distant, which, owing to the nature of the country, I did not reach till midnight. Mr. Burges had arrived about an hour previous with the horse first caught. Light showers in the morning.

16th September.

Messrs. Bedart, C. Gregory, and J. Walcott started to bring in the horses; the rest of the party was employed in repairing damages of the harness, and at 3.0 p.m. the party returned with the horses. Slight showers in the morning.

17th September (Sunday).

Light clouds from the south-west; thunder; rain in the evening. Read prayers.

18th September.

Left the bivouac at 8.15 a.m., and followed upwards the main branch of the Irwin to the north-north-east, through a steep and rocky valley, the sandstone hills in some parts approaching the river, so as to render it necessary to cross frequently with the pack-horses. The very level character of the summits of these hills gives the country the appearance of having been once a plain, through which the valley of the stream has since been worn by the action of water; the upper stratum is a hard red sandstone, resting on a softer rock of a sandy or clayey character, beneath which the shales and rocks belonging to the coal formation show themselves, lying in unconformable beds, and often at a very high angle. At 9.25 the stream divided into two branches, that to the east being the most considerable; at this spot the sandstone ceased, and we commenced ascending the granite range, the direction of which was about north-north-west. The soil was poor and stony, producing a little feed for stock; but it could scarcely be made available, as the country is completely covered with thickets of acacia of small growth. At 4 p.m. bivouacked on a small watercourse running through a level grassy flat, bounded on both sides by thickets of wattle.

SCRUBBY COUNTRY NORTH FROM THE IRWIN RIVER.

19th September.

At 8.15 a.m. steered a nearly north course, through a country of the same description as yesterday; crossed several small gullies trending west, in some of which a little water still remained; at 4.20 p.m. halted for the night at a brackish pool in a small gully trending west.

20th September.

Started at 8.0 a.m., continuing a northerly course, over a similar description of country as during the past two days, crossing three large gullies coming from the eastward, but apparently near their source. At 3.45 halted on a large stream-bed, with a few brackish or rather salt pools in its sandy channel, which was in some places nearly 100 yards wide; from our encampment we observed a very remarkable peaked hill, distant about twenty miles, and from its outline conjectured it to be composed of the same vein of trap-rock as that which forms similar ranges further to the eastward.

21st September.

The scarcity of water and the very level appearance of the country to the northward of our bivouac, added to the general denseness of the thicket of acacia and cypress, rendering a continuance of a north course unadvisable, we steered north-west from 8.30 a.m. till noon, when we ascended a scrubby sand ridge, from which we had an extensive view; neither hill nor valley could be discovered to the north, east, or west--nothing but one immense sea of dense thicket of acacia and cypress was visible in these directions; the course was therefore changed to west, and continuing it without much alteration over a succession of low ridges of drifted sand, the valleys being filled with dense thickets, until 6.20 p.m., when the approach of night compelled us to bivouac in a small patch of gum forest, which also afforded a few scattered tufts of grass for our horses. Although this was the lowest spot passed in a distance of more than ten miles, it was so completely dried up and parched that a search for water was fruitless, even by digging; the scanty allowance of very brackish water in our kegs was therefore much relished by the party.

22nd September.

The night having been cloudy, and a strong breeze preventing any dew, our horses were not much refreshed; we, however, started at 7.45 a.m., and steering nearly west till 3.15 p.m. through a succession of dense thickets, high scrubs, and thorny bushes, we entered open sandy downs, and changed the course to south-west, with the intention of making the Hutt River, should we not find any water nearer, when, almost hopeless of procuring this essential element before the next day, we unexpectedly came to a native well in the centre of the sandy plain; here we bivouacked at 5.40, but, from the loose sandy soil in which the well was dug, we could not obtain more than about two and a half gallons of water for each horse, the sides of the well continually falling in. Strong breeze from the north-west, and several light showers in the evening and night.

23rd September.

Having completed watering the horses, we left the well at 9.30 a.m., and steering about north-west over undulating sandy downs, covered with coarse scrub and patches of dense thickets, at 2.15 p.m. entered a small gully trending north-west. The country improved, but was so thickly clothed with wattles as to render travelling difficult; a few patches of grass were seen in some small watercourses, in which a little water remained. At 4.40 bivouacked on a large gully trending northwards, with several small pools of water in a rocky bed of gneiss, containing numerous small garnets. Strong breeze from the north-west and slight showers.

24th September (Sunday).

Although the feed for the horses was not very abundant, yet the long marches they had encountered the last few days made it expedient to give them a day's rest to recruit their weary limbs. Read prayers. Strong breeze from the north-west and slight showers during the day.

ENTER THE VALLEY OF THE MURCHISON RIVER.

25th September.

Started at 8.27 a.m.; passed over poor stony hills of granite formation and producing a little grass in tufts--the wattles growing so close together as to render travelling difficult and tedious. At 10.45 came on a large stream-bed, which had scarcely ceased to run; the channel was fifty yards wide, the bed steep and rocky, and, where crossed, ran over a dyke of trap-rock, the water slightly brackish and in long shallow pools, with samphire on the banks. This stream must be the Murchison River, as no other was passed for 30 miles to the northward; the effects of violent floods were visible, but it did not bear the character of a stream rising at any great distance inland, nor did the nature of the gravel and sand brought down by it indicate a rich soil on its upper portion, as I did not see anything besides fragments of siliceous rock and garnet sand. The valley through which it ran appeared to be five or six miles wide, extending twenty miles to the eastward, backed by sandy plains on both sides; a few patches of grass appeared in the lower parts of the valley; westward it seemed to contract and turn to the south-west, flanked by steep flat-topped hills of sandstone, resting on granite rock. Continuing north-north-east up a small valley, we passed through wattle thickets till 1.40 p.m., when we again ascended the level sandy tableland or plains, and changed the course to the north; the scrub increased in density as we proceeded. At 4.25 halted for the night in a patch of good grass, where the thicket had been burnt off by the native fires; the sandy nature of the soil rendered the search for water unsuccessful; we therefore contended ourselves with the allowance of one pint each.

26th September.

Left the bivouac at 7.15 a.m.; course north; the country more open; 9.25 came on a large native well of good water in a slight hollow trending westward; having watered the horses and filled the kegs, continued our journey over sandy plains, covered with short coarse scrub; many hummocks of loose sand, covered partially with scrub, lay on each side of our track. At noon passed the last sandy ridge; before us lay an immense plain, covered with thickets, and not a hill or valley could be observed--the country seemed to settle into one vast level of dense and almost impenetrable scrub or thicket. At 1 p.m. entered it, and continued our route through it; although the bush-fires, which had burnt some large patches, greatly assisted us; 4.15 not finding any grass, we steered west, but at 5.15 were compelled to halt for the night in a dense thicket, without a single blade of grass or even scrub of any kind which could afford food for the horses; water it was hopeless to look for; and after a supper of raw bacon, damper, and a pint of water each, we retired to rest.

WATERLESS COUNTRY AND DENSE SCRUB NORTH OF MURCHISON RIVER.

27th September.

At 7.0 a.m. set out on a north course; at 8.5, finding the thicket almost impassable, I ascended a cypress-tree, where a most cheerless view met my sight to the north, east, and west; not a break was visible--nothing but thicket in all directions, with scarcely an undulation of any kind; the view to the north-west was most extensive--nearly twenty miles of thicket could be seen, with a surface as level as the sea. Not considering it prudent to proceed onwards, the thicket being too dense to advance without the greatest difficulty, the saddle-bags being almost torn to pieces, and the horses quite worn out with continual exertions in dragging their packs through the thickets, we were compelled to return to the well passed yesterday morning. The country seen to the northwards was of too flat and sandy a character to give any hope of finding water or grass--and without these requisites, it would be incurring great risk of losing the horses, and of course defeating the object of the expedition; therefore, taking advantage of the partially cleared tracts of yesterday, we reached the watering place at 4.30 p.m.

28th September.

This day we employed ourselves in repairing our pack-saddles, which it was found necessary to restuff, as they had been padded with coarse rushes; the saddle-bags had been torn to pieces, and the repairs of these required more time than could be afforded in an evening's bivouac.

29th September.

Started at 8.35 a.m.; pursued a general course of 310 degrees, gradually ascending the sandy downs on the north side of the valley for three miles; it then turned to the north of west, and we again descended, and found the bottom occupied by a narrow samphire flat, 50 to 100 yards wide, over which the water runs during heavy rains, but it was now dry, and in some parts covered with a thin crust of salt; 11.26 passed a native well of slightly brackish water, amongst loose blocks of red sandstone; a small well was passed at 11.50; the samphire flat then changed to a small sandy channel, among large blocks of sandstone belonging to the coal-formation: in one place the slate also cropped out. Abundance of brackish water lay in small pools along the course of the stream-bed, which at 1.0 p.m. changed its direction nearly west; we followed it through a scrubby valley, with high hills on both sides, till 4.45, when we bivouacked just below the junction of a small gully from the northwards, with a very remarkable sandstone hill about three-quarters of a mile south; below this spot the valley trended to the south-west, and was bounded on the north-west by flat-tapped sandstone hills.

30th September.

Not being more than ten to fifteen miles from the sea, I steered north 330 degrees east magnetic. Starting at 8.5, and having ascended the high land, passed through a thick line of wattles and dwarf gum, growing on the eastern face of the limestone range, which forms the high barren range along this part of the coast. The country was covered with thick scrub, and some patches of gum and wattle thicket; about noon it was more open, and ascending an elevated sandy ridge, saw apparently a high range of hills extending north-north-west as far as Shark Bay, and terminated by a very abrupt and detached hill; but the excessive refraction caused by the heated and nearly level plain which intervened more than doubled their real height. We descended gradually over a succession of sandy hills or ridges till 2.0 p.m., when the lowest part of the plain was reached; we found it occupied by a small patch of spear-wood; the soil was hard dry clay, but on proceeding a little farther we found a patch of moist ground, encircled by a ridge of sand; at one foot deep we found water, but in such small quantity that we could only obtain sufficient for ourselves, and should have had to wait at least two hours to have given each horse only one gallon. Proceeding onwards, in hope of finding a more plentiful supply, we found the country became drier and full of circular hollows, filled with fine clumps of green wattle and a little grass; in one of these we bivouacked at 5.0, and dug six feet for water in red sand, but without any appearance of obtaining it even at double that depth.

REPULSED FOR WANT OF WATER.

1st October.

This morning started at 7.55 a.m., and steering north-west, in hope of finding water, at 8.40 came on dense thickets of wattle, which extended at least seven or eight miles farther north; we therefore turned west to avoid them; at 9.30 changed the course to 300 degrees magnetic, and with great difficulty forced our way for two miles to a narrow strip of open ground; 12.40 p.m. arrived at the foot of the range of hills seen yesterday; found them to consist of limestone and sand, covered with thick scrub; between the hills were many nearly circular hollows filled with thickets of wattles; although the bottoms of the hollows were at least fifty feet below the lowest part of the ridges around them, they were quite dry, and afforded no hope of water even by digging; the country northward appeared even less likely to afford a supply, so much required, as it seemed to consist wholly of limestone and loose sand, without swamps or watercourses; the nearest spot at which we could hope to find it in this direction was the south part of Freycinet Harbour, distant, according to the charts, about thirty miles, and great doubt existed of the accuracy of it in this position (error having been found in some other parts of the coast-line); nor was it certain that we could find water on the coast, in which case the loss of our horses would be almost a necessary consequence, several of them showing extreme fatigue. The circumstances of the case required a prompt decision; I therefore ordered an immediate return towards the last spot where we had seen water. The whole party felt convinced of the necessity of returning, though with the greatest reluctance to do so, as it seemed to put an end to almost every hope of reaching the Gascoyne River. We followed our route back, and halted at 5.30 in a wattle thicket.

A HORSE FINDS WATER.

2nd October.

Left our uncomfortable bivouac at 7.30 a.m.; steered south-east. Finding the horses scarcely able to travel from want of water, I took the strongest and rode over to the spot where we had obtained a little on the 30th September, to dig wells and have a supply ready, if it could be obtained in sufficient quantity; at 11.0 arrived, and found the wells we had dug nearly dry; by opening several trenches down to the rocks which lay about one and a half feet below the surface, the water oozed in, and when the party came up, at 12.0, there was about a gallon for each horse; taking off the packs, we commenced watering: four horses had received their small allowance, when it came to my horse Bob's turn; after drinking his share he marched off at a smart pace, which somewhat surprised us, as he started in the direction of what we had supposed to be nothing but a tea-tree scrub; on following him, we found the horse drinking at a small shallow pool of water in a hollow in the clay. This was a very fortunate discovery, as the trenches filled with water so slowly that a full supply could not have been obtained that night, and the horses had been sixty-five hours without water.

SAND PLAINS AND SCRUB. RETURN TO THE MURCHISON RIVER.

3rd October.

This morning Mr. Burges and myself started at 7.30 a.m. in a north-easterly course, to ascertain the practicability of proceeding in that direction, taking two of the strongest horses. After riding four hours over an open, scrubby sand-plain, with circular valleys, we again fell in with thickets of wattles so dense that, although burnt by the native fires about four years previous, they would have been impassable for the pack-horses; but, favoured by this circumstance, we penetrated the thicket in a north-north-west direction for about twelve miles. From one small sandy ridge we had an extensive view, but of a most discouraging nature; the whole country was one vast plain, covered with dense thickets and scrub as far as the eye could reach, except to the west-north-west, where rose a high and barren ridge, which would not have been visible but for excessive refraction, as it must have been more than twenty-five miles distant. The plain was still dotted over with the remarkable circular hollows or valleys which, by their extreme dryness, indicated a great depth of sandy soil, incapable of retaining water on the surface even for a short time, or any probability of our obtaining it by digging. We turned in disappointment towards the encampment, scarcely extricating ourselves from the thickets before it became dark. Having gained the sand-plain, we continued our return for several hours, steering by the stars, hoping by a night march to avoid the scorching effects of the sun, which at this season renders travelling over an extensive sandy plain very fatiguing. Having been more than eleven hours in the saddle, we halted for the night.

4th October.

Started with the dawn, and pushing our tired and hungry horses over the plain as fast as circumstances would admit, arrived at the encampment before the heat of the day became excessive. During our absence two more waterholes had been excavated, and sufficient water obtained for the horses; but, from the great evaporation, it did not seem likely to last longer than three or four days: the hardness of the sandstone precluded our sinking the wells more than one and a half feet. The extreme aridity of the country--the absence of water in consequence of the sandy nature of the soil, which renders it impossible that watercourses should exist--the dense and almost impassable nature of the thickets of acacia and melaleuca of small growth, and the heat of the climate--all tend to prove the fallacy of attempting to explore this part of the colony, excepting during the wettest of the winter months. Under the existing circumstances, I considered it my duty not to lead the party into a position from which it would most probably be impracticable to extricate ourselves without at least losing some of our horses; and even difficulties of a more serious nature might arise, which would prevent the more complete examination of the imperfectly known country to the southward of our present position, more especially as a successful advance to the northward seemed impossible.

5th October.

Left the encampment at 8.10 a.m.; steered north 135 degrees east magnetic over sandy country, covered with coarse scrub; at noon passed a narrow strip of wooded grassy land, the soil being limestone and red loam. The country again became scrubby, and, descending an open valley, came on a small watercourse at 1.5 p.m., trending south; followed it south-south-west. At 2.15 passed our bivouac of the 29th September, and turning south-west along the stream-bed, at 4.0 came on the right bank of the Murchison River, running through wide grassy flats, the stream forming large pools, some of them more than a mile in length; but, with the exception of the flats on each side of the bank, the country is poor and scrubby, destitute of trees, and the hills high and rocky, consisting of red sandstone, those to the west capped with limestone.

6th October.

The horses being much fatigued and nearly starved, having subsisted chiefly on scrub for the last two days, we determined to rest them for a few days, while we examined the river towards its mouth. I started with Mr. Bedart, and tracing the stream downwards to the south-west, reached the sea after a ride of six hours. Excepting the flats and a narrow strip of land on each side, the country was very indifferent, the hills being composed of sandstone and sand, covered with coarse scrub and a gigantic species of grass, the leaves of which, instead of affording food for stock, were a source of great annoyance to our horses, being armed with sharp thorny points, and was somewhat appropriately called bayonet grass by the party. The tide flows about five miles up the river, when it is obstructed by some slight rapids; although it seems shallow, and full of rocks and islands, I think it is navigable for small boats. Above the rapids the river is a succession of long reaches of water about 100 yards wide, and wide flats covered with reeds, the roots of which seem to form an important article of food with the natives. Many springs were seen on the left bank, but few on the right, the water of which was of excellent quality. After making observations of the bar, which appeared to be practicable for whaleboats in moderate weather if the wind be south of west, we returned along the south shore of the estuary, which is about one and a half mile long and half a mile wide; it does not appear to be of any great depth. My horse being quite knocked up, it was dark before we could reach a spot where we could obtain water and grass; having come to a convenient place, we bivouacked under a large overhanging rock, as it promised to be a wet night.

7th October.

At 6.0 a.m. we were in our saddles, but owing to the rocky nature of the country did not arrive at the encampment till 12.30 p.m. During our absence the party had been successful in fishing and shooting; a savoury mess of cockatoos, swans, and ducks, with fried fish, proved a welcome change to us, after living so many weeks on salt meat and damper.

8th October (Sunday).

9th October.

The valley of the river being rocky and impassable above the camp, we crossed to the left bank and ascended the sandy tableland; steered about south-east from 7.45 a.m. to 11.0, when we came on the stream in a deep valley formed by almost perpendicular red sandstone cliffs from 50 to 200 feet in height, broken at short intervals by enormous fissures (their general direction west-north-west and nearly at right angles with the river), which time, with the action of water, had worn into impassable ravines, frequently extending more than half a mile back from the river, and rendered travelling very tedious and unsafe, as it was requisite to avoid the thick scrubs covering the higher land. The course of the river now changed to nearly south, and preserved the same rocky and unapproachable character till 5.0 p.m., when a break in the cliffs enabled us to descend into the valley, although with some difficulty and danger to the horses, which had to slide down the steep rocks at the risk of breaking their necks, which would have been the almost certain result of a single false step; but the descent being accomplished, they were rewarded by an abundant supply of grass and water, the latter from a large spring at the foot of the cliffs.

10th October.

While breakfast was preparing, Mr. Burges and myself examined the right bank of the river, and after a short search, found a practicable ascent to the top of the cliffs, and having cleared a way through the thicket of melaleuca on the bank of the river, returned to breakfast. At 7.50 a.m. commenced ascending, and at 8.30 reached the summit of the rocky hills, and steering about south-east through a succession of thickets, rocks, yawning chasms, sand-hills, and scrub, we attained to a fine grassy flat at 12.30 p.m. The bed of the river here quite changed its character, the sandstones giving place to granite gneiss, with dark trap dykes intersecting it in a northerly and southerly direction, the dip of the strata being to the west at a very high angle, at times almost perpendicular.

A DEPOT CAMP. EXPLORE THE UPPER MURCHISON.

11th October.

As this appeared to be a good spot for the formation of a depot, while we examined the upper portion of the Murchison, I proceeded up the river in company with Mr. Burges, leaving the rest of the party to guard the camp and attend to the horses. After one hour's ride we came on our track where we crossed the river on the 25th September, the general course of the stream-bed being east-north-east, its channel averaging 100 yards in width, full of rocks, small trees, and sandbanks, with many shallow brackish pools of water, with the exception of one, which was both wide and deep, where we halted for two hours to rest the horses; few of the pools seemed likely to last through the heat of summer. At 1.0 p.m. we came on a party of natives, five of whom came up to us, following us for some distance. As they seemed to prefer mimicking our attempts to speak the York dialect to using their own, we could not obtain much information; they carried kylies and dowaks, but had left their spears and shields with the rest of their party, who did not make their appearance. At 3.0 passed several ridges of red sandstone rocks, the strata dipping to the east-north-east at an angle of from 20 to 60 degrees. The granite rock entirely disappearing, the country became quite level, and covered with one universal thicket of acacia and cypress, except the very slight depression which formed a shallow valley about three miles wide, through which the river runs in a deep channel from 80 to 100 yards wide in ordinary seasons, but when in flood must exceed 300 yards, and the rise of the water, judging from the rubbish drifted up in former years, must exceed thirty feet. The valleys did not seem to be more than 100 feet below the general surface of the country (which was quite level), filled with a dense thicket of wattles; a narrow strip of large gum-trees, growing in grassy flats close to the river, marked the course of the stream. At 5.0 we halted for the night by a small pool of fresh water in one of the back channels of the river, the pools in the main bed being all brackish.

12th October.

Started at 6.35 a.m., following the river, the general course being north-north-east; no change was observed in its character. At 11.20 halted to rest the horses, and again started at 1.40 p.m. At 3.40 came on a large party of natives at a fresh water pool; five followed us some miles, and were not to be satisfied until we had made an exchange of part of a handkerchief for a quantity of noolban, some dowaks, and dabbas, some of which we accepted as a token of our friendly intentions. The stream-bed turned east, and we followed it until 6.0, when we were halted for the night, having the good fortune to find a little fresh water by digging in the sand in the bed of the river, the pools being all brackish.

RETURN TO DEPOT CAMP.

13th October.

At 6.15 a.m., we were again in our saddles, and continued journey up the river--the general course north-north-east. In vain we looked for some rising ground or hill from which we might obtain a view of the country, but the same sandy level, covered with dense thickets of wattles, still met the eye till 11.0, when we observed a low sandstone cliff forming the eastern side of the valley. In this direction we steered, and after pushing through thickets of wattle growing on stony ground, with small patches of salsolaceous plants, we arrived at the foot of the cliff, which was about sixty feet in height, of white sandstone, full of rounded quartz pebbles. The top was nearly on a level with the general plane of the country, which was of a most cheerless aspect. The valley of the river trended to the north-north-east for eight or ten miles, then to the east; the width appeared about five miles, and one dense thicket of wattles seemed to fill the entire space. The rest of the country was, without the slightest exception, level in the extreme, covered with one universal thicket of acacia and cypress, the latter indicating the sandy nature of the soil. As no appearance of change in the character of the country within twenty or thirty miles was visible, and we had only two days' provisions left (not having expected the stream to extend so far), and the camp at sixty miles distant, we were obliged to leave the farther examination of the river to some future explorers; but we regretted it the less as, from the nature of the gravel and sand brought down by the stream, there seemed great probability that it takes its rise in large salt marshes similar to those known to exist 100 miles east of the Irwin, if it does not actually drain them, as the general trend of the most northerly marshes seen was in the direction of the upper part of the Murchison. Under these circumstances, we returned to our bivouac of last night, reaching it at 5.40 p.m.

14th October.

Started at 6.25 a.m., and retracing our route down the river, came to our bivouac of the 11th at 5.5 p.m. without any incident worthy of notice, but surprising three or four natives asleep in the bed of the stream; they were of the party seen on our route up the river.

15th October (Sunday).

Resumed our journey; passed two parties of natives; a few of them followed us some distance, and having overcome their first surprise, commenced talking in their own language, which, as far as we could understand it, had great affinity to that spoken by the natives in the York and Toodyay districts. After a smart ride of seven hours we arrived at the encampment, found the rest of the party all well, and the horses much improved by their few days' rest.

THE GERALDINE LEAD MINE DISCOVERED. THE HUTT RIVER.

16th October.

The two horses we had ridden up the river requiring a day's rest, which was also acceptable to Mr. Burges and myself, we remained at the camp and made preparations to move on to the Hutt River the next day. Mr. Walcott brought in some specimens of galena, which, on farther observation, proved to be abundant.

17th October.

Leaving our encampment at 9.10 a.m., we steered a southerly course, passing over a succession of low granite hills, thickly covered with acacia, to the exclusion of almost every other kind of vegetation, save a few scattered tufts of grass. At noon entered the sand-plains which occupy the high lands in this district; observed a patch of grassy land bearing south-west; proceeding in that direction, at 1.0 p.m. came on it, but found it to be a very small spot of grassy granite country, encircled by sand-plains and scrub. Continuing our course, at 2.5 struck a small stream-bed trending west-south-west; the valley in which it runs is bounded on both sides by sandy hills, covered with scrub; some patches of grass and wattles occupied the lower ground wherever the granite rock showed itself; tracing the stream-bed downwards, we found many brackish pools. At 3.45 crossed the left bank--found it running, but brackish; and at 4.20 we bivouacked at its junction with the Hutt River, which was here about ten yards wide, with narrow grassy flats on both banks. The hills are of sandstone and sand, producing little besides scrub.

18th October.

Started at 7.50 a.m., steering north 140 degrees east magnetic up the valley of the Hutt, which gradually widened and improved, the hills being grassy for an average distance of two miles back from the stream, of granite formation, and thinly sprinkled with wattles; behind the grassy land the country rose into sandy plains, covered with short scrub. At 9.20 crossed to the left bank; the river trended to the eastward. At 11.10 sighted King's Table Hill, bearing south magnetic. We then descended into the rich and grassy valley of the Bowes River; this we traversed till 4.0 p.m., when we bivouacked in a small stream tributary to the Bowes. As the country passed over this day had not been previously examined, we were much pleased to find it equal to the best land on the southern branch of the Bowes, visited by the Surveyor-General and myself on former occasions.

FINE PASTORAL COUNTRY.

19th October.

Messrs. Burges, Bedart, and myself rode down the Bowes to examine the country, and found it generally of good grassy character, suitable for sheep; the bed of the streams being filled with broad-leaved reeds, seems to indicate an abundant supply of water in the dry season; but the pools were very small, and the water all brackish, not even excepting the running streams. The hills are of gneiss, with garnets and trap-rock, the latter producing excellent grass of various kinds, the most conspicuous of which is a species of kangaroo-grass, but of a less woody character of seed-stalk than that found in other parts of the colony. The extent of land fit for sheep-feeding on this stream (it can scarcely be called a river) I should estimate at 100,000 acres, and Mr. Burges considered it capable of feeding about 17,000 sheep. The existence of garnets, iron pyrites, and a mineral resembling in many of its properties plumbago, specimens of which were found in the gneiss of this district, seems to indicate a metalliferous formation, and I have little doubt a further search might develop many of the present hidden sources of wealth. Near the coast we fell in with some natives (four men and five women), who were very friendly, but from their peculiar nature we were unable to accept of their civilities.

20th October.

Started with Messrs. Burges and Walcott to examine the upper part of the Buller river; after passing over the country examined by Lieutenant Irby and myself in December, 1846, we crossed the granite ridge which divides the valley of the Buller into two nearly equal portions. We found the land on the left bank of the eastern branch of very good and grassy description, consisting of a range of granite hills about ten miles north and south, and two miles in width; to the east of which the high sandy and level plains commence in an abrupt line of sandstone slopes and hills. Halted for the night in the east branch of the Buller, with water in small pools and abundance of grass for our horses.

21st October.

Continued the examination of the Buller Valley down to the spot where I bivouacked on the river in December, 1846; then followed up the stream for seven miles, where we dined, and then steering west-north-west, arrived at the camp at 6.30 p.m. We estimated the valley of the Buller to contain about 10,000 acres of good grassy land, and 30,000 acres of inferior feeding country; the good land is much broken into patches by that which is of indifferent quality. Timber is here, and also on the Bowes, very scarce, and the little that exists is very indifferent and small.

22nd October (Sunday).

Messrs. Bedart and C.F. Gregory walked to the hill which lies three-quarters of a mile west of King's Table Hill. The rock of which it is formed appeared to belong to the coal formation, as thin seams of black shale were seen in the rocks of which the lower strata of the hill are composed; but the natives making their appearance, it was not considered prudent to remain geologizing among the cliffs. Returning towards the camp, the natives followed for some distance, and on descending a cliff the women commenced pelting the party with stones, apparently in revenge for the refusal of certain courteous invitations, which perhaps are the greatest marks of politeness which they think it possible to offer to strangers.

CHAPMAN RIVER.

23rd October.

Left our encampment at 8.5 a.m., and steered 150 degrees magnetic over granite hills producing wattles and good grass. At 9.40 crossed the south branch of the Bowes, after which the country was not so well grassed, except in the valleys. The lower hills were of granite; the higher red sandstone of tabular form. At 11.0 the country became more sandy and covered with short scrub, gradually rising to the south. At noon we attained the high tableland; crossed two scrubby valleys bounded by sandstone hills, in the first of which the black shale peculiar to the coal formation showed itself, with a slight dip to the south. At 1.50 p.m. crossed the Buller in a rocky channel with reedy pools, apparently of permanent character. The land improved and became grassy, and ascending the hills on the left bank, passed Peak Hill at 2.50: this is the highest part of the range between the Buller and Chapman. From this we steered south down a small grassy valley; the hills with granite bases and sandstone table summits, with excellent grass, and thinly wooded with acacia and a few York gums. At 3.15 bivouacked in a patch of excellent grass with water in small quantities.

24th October.

A violent thunderstorm during the night was followed by a rainy and misty morning; the weather clearing up, we walked down to the Chapman River, which was running in a sandy channel with small shallow pools. The land on the bank of the stream was very indifferent and sandy for about a mile, when it rose into granite and sandstone hills, covered with excellent grass.

EFFECT OF REFRACTION. GREENOUGH RIVER.

25th October.

Accompanied by Messrs. Burges and Walcott, I proceeded to examine the country to the eastward of our camp. Starting at 7.20 a.m., steered east over grassy hills, with granite bases and table summits of red sandstone, the latter rock forming but a poor soil with scanty feed and scrub; crossed several small gullies running into the Chapman. At 10.0 passed a large sandy hill, covered with short scrub, and halted at 11.0 in a grassy gully in the bottom of a wide scrubby valley; at 12.45 p.m. again resumed our journey, and ascending the sandy downs, at 1.15 gained the highest ridge. Before us lay the valley of the Greenough River; the white and red sandstone cliffs, which bound the valley on the south-east, were distorted by excessive refractions, which, as we crossed each sandy ridge, changed their appearance, sometimes assuming the appearance of islands with high rocky shores, then like reefs with heavy breakers, followed by high cliffs and grassy hills; but as we approached they assumed their true character of low rocky hills and cliffs, scarce exceeding 200 feet in height, and generally covered with dense thickets of acacia growing on an otherwise barren stony soil. At 3.30 came on the right bank of the Greenough River; the bed was quite dry, and had no appearance of having run since the winter of 1847. Following up the stream-bed to the north-east, passed some shallow pools of salt water; and at 4.45 observed the black coal shales at the bottom of a deep cliff, which formed the left bank of the river. At 5.0 halted for the night, obtaining fresh water by scraping in the sand by the side of a pool of salt water; we also found sufficient grass for our horses on the bank of the river.

26th October.

At 7.10 a.m. left our bivouac, steering north 120 degrees east magnetic towards a high sandstone cliff, which, after a ride of three-quarters of an hour through thickets of acacia, we ascended; but the view was not satisfactory, as thickets and scrubs extended over the whole of the country. We therefore returned to the river, and followed it downwards to the south-west by south. At 11.30 found some fresh water in a small waterhole in the bed of the river; halted till 1.50 p.m. to refresh the horses. The river turned south, and at 2.27 was joined by a small gully from the west, and coming from a grassy valley. As it had run during the last winter, it quite altered the character of the river for quarter of a mile, filling the pools with water, and giving the grass and trees a freshness which formed a most striking contrast with the brown and parched appearance of the rest of the valley. At 3.55 altered the course to 210 degrees magnetic; the country improved, many patches of grassy land appearing in the valley, and the country became more rocky. At 5.30 crossed to the left bank, and found the river running with many large pools of water, some more than a half a mile long and 80 to 100 yards wide. The water was slightly brackish, being this year supplied principally by springs, taking their rise in the new red sandstone formation. We then followed the winding course of the river south-west amongst high hills of sandstone, many of which were covered with excellent grass, though the country was not generally good. At 6.20 halted for the night on the right bank of the stream, in a narrow but rich grassy flat; heavy rain in the night.

WIZARD PEAK. CHAMPION BAY. MOUNT FAIRFAX.

27th October.

Started at 7.0 a.m. and steering an average course of west by north, ascended the high land on the north bank of the Greenough. For the first hour the hills were of red sandstone, very steep and rocky, producing little but coarse scrub; some of the valleys and lower hills were well grassed; the country then improved, the hills being of the coal formation, and the limestones forming very rich and grassy hills. At 9.40 the granite and gneiss formed a basis of the high sandstone-topped hills, which rose about 500 feet on each side of the valley. At 10.15 crossed to the left bank of the river, and re-crossed to the right at 11.10. The lower parts of the valley were not so rich or well grassed as the hills, but would afford excellent summer feed for sheep. Having dined, and given our horses an hour's feed on the rich grass which grew in the bed of the river (which here turned to the south), we continued our route. After an hour's ride over rich grassy hills, reached the foot of Wizard's Peak. Here we left our horses and ascended the hill; arrived at the summit, to our great surprise, instead of the scrubby and sterile country described by Captain Stokes of the Beagle, beautiful grassy hills, stretching from north to south-east, met our view to the extent of about 20,000 acres; had it not been certain, from bearings to Mount Fairfax and other hills, that we were on Wizard Peak, I should have suspected its identity. Leaving Wizard Peak at 2.30 p.m., steered north along the western foot of the grassy range. The country to the east consists of grassy hills of limestone, rich in fossil remains of wood and shells, with an occasional granite hill producing coarse grass or short scrub; to the west the country was more level, but less grassy, and in many parts scrubby. We fell in with some of the natives, who appeared friendly disposed. Crossed the Chapman at 6.5, and arrived at the camp at 7.15.

28th October.

Left the camp at 7.40 a.m., steering north-west. Made the stream previously called the Buller at 9.0; followed it downwards to the south-south-west till 11.0, when it became evident that, instead of being the Buller, it was the north branch of the Chapman. The land on its banks was not generally good, although some fine patches of grass were seen. Leaving the stream, we ascended Moresby's Range; the valleys and sides of the hills were covered with fine grass, and the sandstone rocks were rich with fossil remains of shells and wood. With some difficulty we descended the western face of the hills; after which, an hour's ride over a scrubby plain brought us to the mouth of the Chapman River, running strongly over a ledge of limestone rock into the sea. We crossed the river, and over to the usual landing-place in Champion Bay; we then returned to the Chapman, and halted for the night.

29th October.

Two of the horses having broken from their tether during the night, we were obliged to put the three saddles on the remaining horse, and proceed to track the stray horses; after tracking them about two miles, we found them on their way back to the camp. We then rode along the western foot of Moresby's Range, and ascended Mount Fairfax; after taking sketches and bearings, we steered for the encampment, and reached it about 2.0 p.m.

30th October.

Messrs. Burges, Walcott, and Bedart rode out this morning to examine the grassy hills on the south side of the Chapman River, and on their return reported the country to be of a generally good grassy character.

NATIVES STEAL FRYING-PAN.

31st October.

Left the encampment at 8.0 a.m. and steering 200 degrees magnetic over alternately grassy and scrubby hills of granite sandstone, crossed the Chapman at 9.40. Our course then lay nearly parallel to the river till noon; the land on the river was indifferent and thinly grassed, but rose into good grassy hills about a mile from the river. We then entered a level scrubby plain, extending from the Victoria Range to the sea. At 12.30 p.m. altered the course to 175 degrees magnetic, and at 1.5 to 139 degrees magnetic. At 1.15 the plain became grassy, and the soil good (with the exception of a few patches of York gum, the only trees were wattles), and by a rough estimate contained about 8,000 acres of good grassy land; on the north bank of the Greenough River, which we reached at 3.15, the channel was about seventy yards wide, but dry and sandy; nor did we observe any sign of its having run during the past winter. A little below where we struck the river it turned to the south-east; following it in that direction till 3.45 we bivouacked, obtaining a scanty supply of water by digging in the sand. Shortly after halting, a party of about thirty natives came up, and appeared friendly; they told us that there was a fine spring at some distance to the westward, but we could not obtain any other useful information, as their dialect differs considerably from that spoken in the settled districts, although some few words are the same. They encamped a short distance from us, and in the night stole our frying-pan, to dig a well, but returned it next morning before the theft was discovered.

THE IRWIN RIVER.

1st November.

At 7.10 a.m. resumed our course south-east, along the eastern side of the grassy plain. The scrubby hills gradually approached on each side; at 9.30 the good land terminated, the estimate being 2,000 acres on the south bank of the Greenough River. The country then became sandy, producing little besides scrub and a few banksia trees. At 10.0 passed about one mile west of Mount Hill; passed a small pool of water in a watercourse trending south-west. At 12.50 p.m. altered the course to 170 degrees magnetic; at 3.0 entered a thick forest of York gum; at 3.25 changed the course to 130 degrees magnetic and entered a grassy flat extending to the Irwin River, which we reached at 3.55, and following it upwards till 4.15, bivouacked on the left bank in a large flat. Shortly before reaching the river a large party of natives came up with us, after tracking the horses for some distance. Seventy or eighty men came to the bivouac, and, with the exception of one man who shipped a spear, making a demonstration of throwing it at us, they evinced a desire for the more peaceable amusement of eating damper and fat bacon. A few of the natives spoke a little English, having been for a short time in the settled districts. At sunset they retired to the other side of the river, and all appeared quiet when my watch commenced at 10.30; but at midnight I detected a native crawling up amongst the thick grass about ten yards from the back of the tents. He lay quiet till I almost turned him out of his hiding-place with the muzzle of my gun, when he took to his heels, but I did not consider it prudent either to fire at or capture him.

2nd November.

The natives being too numerous to allow any of the party leaving the camp to examine the country around without incurring greater risk than seemed prudent, we left our bivouac at 7.45 a.m. and steered north 170 degrees east magnetic over sandy hills, covered with short scrub. After two hours the country became nearly level, with small patches of swampy ground, which would be very wet in the rainy season, but was at present quite dry; the rising grounds were sand, covered with short scrub with a few scattered banksia trees. At 5.40 p.m. struck the left bank of the stream which has been considered to be the Arrowsmith River of Captain Grey, though I have now some reason to doubt its identity. The banks of the stream are sandstone and sand, and the channel scarcely three yards wide, with a strip of grassy thicket twenty yards in width along the stream, which is the only feed near the river, as the plain through which it runs produces nothing but scrub and banksia with a few grass-trees. We bivouacked a short distance below the spot where we first struck the stream, which was still running.

3rd November.

Our horses having but a very scanty feed at this place, we moved down the stream to obtain better grass for them before crossing the sand-plains which lay to the south. After following the stream west for two hours, encamped in a small grassy flat, below which the stream ceased to run, the water being wholly absorbed by the sandy soil, which has a substratum of limestone of recent formation.

SEVENTY MILES OF SAND PLAIN.

4th November.

Accompanied by Mr. Bedart, rode to the westward; passing over sandy plains and ridges for four hours, came to the beach, which we followed northwards for three hours, hoping to meet with the mouth of the stream on which our camp was placed. Not perceiving any signs of it, we turned to the east, and after an hour's struggle through a thick jungle, we came on a wet grassy flat, on which the stream seemed to be lost. Steering a general course of south-south-east, we arrived at 9.10 p.m. at the camp, after a ride of thirteen and a quarter hours, and the country traversed almost wholly worthless sand and scrub.

5th November (Sunday).

Remained at our encampment to rest the horses. Read prayers.

6th November.

Leaving our encampment at 7.10 a.m., we steered north 170 degrees east magnetic, along the limits of the low scrubby limestone hills which extend along this part of the coast. To the east the level sandy plain extended from eight to ten miles, and then rose into high sandstone hills, covered with scrub and destitute of trees; but at the junction of the limestone and sandstone formation, along which lay our route, were several small lagoons and swamps of fresh water, with grassy margins. At 10.0 altered the course to southward; the line of swamps trending to south-south-west, we entered the level sandy plain. At noon passed a shallow pool of rainwater in a slight depression of the plain, and shortly after crossed two small watercourses trending west; a little brackish water remained in the deeper portions of their channels. The effect of refraction on this level country, when heated by the midday sun, was so great as to cause many of the low sandy ridges to appear like large lakes and inlets of the sea, as in some instances the more distant hills were obscured by its effects. At 2.45 p.m. we reached the sandstone range, and at 3.5 halted in a small patch of grass around a native well of good water, which had the appearance of retaining water throughout the summer. While here we obtained several additions to our small collection of birds.

MOUNTS PERON AND LESUEUR.

7th November.

At 7.20 a.m. resumed our journey southwards, over a high and somewhat rugged range of sandstone hills; passed a short distance to the east of Mounts Peron and Lesueur. The valleys were wooded with red and white-gum of large growth, but the hills produced little besides coarse scrub. At 2.20 p.m. passed a large mound spring; at 2.45 crossed the Hill River of Captain Grey; the land on its banks, with the exception of a few grassy hills on the northern side, was very scrubby and indifferent. Ascending the high sandstone country on the south side of the river, we halted at 5.35 in a sandy valley trending north-west, in which we found a small patch of grass around a native well; but we were not much in want of water, being completely drenched by a heavy shower of rain just after we halted.

8th November.

Resumed our journey at 8.0 a.m., steering north 105 degrees east magnetic over a range of high scrubby sandstone hills. At 1.15 p.m. crossed a small stream-bed trending westwards in a wide scrubby valley. At 3.5, having ascended the hills to the south of the valley, observed a remarkable sandstone hill which I passed on a previous excursion from Mr. Lefroy's station at Welbing. Altering the course to 170 degrees magnetic, we passed the hill; at 5.45 halted in a fine grassy flat on the banks of a small brook-course trending west, in which we found abundance of water in small pools. As we were only forty miles west of Mr. Lefroy's station at Welbing, and the country in that direction already examined, I instructed Mr. C.F. Gregory to proceed with the party and pack-horses to Welbing and thence by the road to Perth, while, accompanied by Mr. Bedart, I pursued a more direct but less eligible course for pack-horses.

THE MOORE RIVER.

9th November.

Leaving the rest of the party at the bivouac, at 9.50 a.m., in company with Mr. Bedart, we steered a general course of south by east magnetic over hills of sandy loam, producing a little grass and thickly timbered with red-gum. Passed several extensive grassy valleys, with many fine patches of rich limestone land on their slopes. At 2.0 p.m. the grass was replaced by scrub, and at 3.30 entered the wide scrubby valley of the Moore River, which we reached at 4.20. After some delay in crossing the river, in consequence of one of the horses falling down in the mud, from which we had some trouble to extricate him, we bivouacked about one mile below the spot where we first made the river.

10th November.

Leaving the Moore River we steered south by west, and after traversing a nearly level sandy plain, producing banksia and scrub, with many lagoons and swamps, in eight hours' riding reached the Norcott or Gingin Brook. The banks were low and swampy; after a short search found a suitable place for crossing, and having swam the horses across, we halted for the night on the left bank.

11th November.

Started at 7.0 a.m., steering east by south magnetic; ascended the western Wilbinga Hill at 9.0, and traversing a rough limestone country, with several reedy swamps, reached Lake Nowergup at 2.50 p.m., and at 4.0 halted on the western side of the Wanaginup Swamp.

12th November (Sunday).

Once more in the saddle, and following the road past Wonneroo, arrived in Perth at 2.30 p.m.

Mr. C.F. Gregory having accompanied the party to the Victoria Plains, proceeded with Private W. King by the Bindoon road to Perth, where he arrived on the 17th.

The total distance travelled in this expedition was, in round numbers, 1,500 miles, and the extreme point reached in latitude 27 degrees south, 350 miles from Perth in a direct line; and the period we were engaged in the expedition was ten weeks.

HIS EXCELLENCY GOVERNOR CHARLES FITZGERALD'S EXPEDITION TO THE GERALDINE LEAD MINE 1848

CHAMPION BAY TO MURCHISON RIVER. 1st December.

Sailed from Fremantle in the Champion for Champion Bay, where we arrived on the 3rd, swam the ponies on shore, and encamped at the mouth of the Chapman River.

4th December.

His Excellency the Governor came on shore, when the party, consisting of the Governor, Mr. Bland, and myself, with three soldiers of the 96th regiment, and the Governor's servant, started at 7.15 a.m., steering north-east, crossed Moresby's flat-topped range at 9.0, made the North Chapman at 10.0, followed the stream upward till 11.50, the general course north-east by north. One native man and two women came up, and then retired to the other side of the river, watching our proceedings. Having dined, we started again at 2.25 p.m., steering a general north course over an indifferent scrubby country till 4.40, when we halted for twenty minutes to examine the black shale-like soil which was seen on a former occasion, but on digging it proved to be only alluvial soil resting on sand; from this spot we steered north 330 degrees magnetic over high sandy hills covered with scrub; the country gradually improved, and at 7.0 we halted for the night in a small grassy gully trending north-west, obtaining water in a native well.

5th December.

Started at 6.40 a.m., continuing the same course as yesterday evening over a succession of grassy hills of granitic formation till 11.10, when we halted on the eastern branch of the Bowes River; several natives shortly came to the encampment, and having eaten some biscuit and pork which we offered to them, retired in the evening to the opposite side of the stream-bed, keeping a close watch on us from behind some large rocks; a strict watch was therefore maintained by us during the night.

6th December.

This morning the natives commenced by throwing stones at the men who went down for the water, but we did not see any method of resenting it, except by expressing our disapprobation in words, and at 5.35 a.m. we started on a north-north-west course, the natives followed for about a mile, and continued throwing stones at the party. The country passed over was generally grassy granite hills till 9.0, when we ascended the high tableland between the valley of the Bowes and Hutt rivers, which last we reached at 10.25, and halted during the heat of the day on a pool of brackish water; at 3.20 p.m., again started, and following the river downwards, in a general course 310 degrees magnetic, at 6.10 bivouacked at the spot where we had before halted on the 17th October; the water in the pools brackish, but by digging near a moist bank obtained abundance of fresh water.

THE GERALDINE LEAD MINE.

7th December.

Left our bivouac at 5.50 a.m., and steered north-east over high sandy downs, covered with coarse scrub; at 10.30 entered the valley of the Murchison River; at noon halted at our bivouac of the 24th September, obtained some brackish water by digging in the sand of the small stream-bed. Having dined, we resumed our journey at 2.30 p.m., and bivouacked about 5.0 on the left bank of the Murchison, 500 yards below the large lead vein, obtaining good water in the sandy bed of the river by digging a few inches, the pools being all salt. While the men were preparing the tents, etc., the Governor proceeded to examine the vein of lead, which we traced to a greater distance than on the former occasion of its discovery, the water having sunk two feet, exposing many portions of the vein which were before covered.

8th December.

Examined the lead vein, tracing it 320 yards in a direction north 30 degrees east magnetic, along the bed of the Murchison River, which was nearly dry; clearing the sand and loose stones from the surface, found it to vary from eight to twenty-four inches in width, the general average being twelve inches, the dip to the west-north-west at an angle of about 80 degrees from the horizon. Throughout the whole length the lead vein appeared to be one solid mass of galena; the northern end either terminates or alters its direction close to a vein of schistose rock, which intersects the adjacent rocks; to the south the lode was covered by several feet of sand, which prevented its being traced further, as we had not time to remove it; the whole of the vein which was traced was included within the banks of the river, and the greater portion was covered by shallow water. One specimen of galena showed traces of copper. The rock which prevails on each side of the vein is a hard compact gneiss, abounding with garnets, some of which are of good colour, but mostly full of flaws; the stratification of the gneiss is somewhat confused, but it generally dips at a high angle (sometimes nearly perpendicular) to the westward, the strike being north and south. The facilities which the position of the lode offers for mining are not very great, as it occupies the lowest part of the valley, and steam power would be requisite to free the mine from water, and at the same time, unless the small boat-harbour near the mouth of the Hutt River, or Gantheaume Bay (both within thirty miles), be found suitable for the purpose, Champion Bay, distant sixty-two miles in a direct line to the south, is the nearest port where the ore could be shipped. In the evening the Governor examined the spot where Mr. Walcott had discovered the small pieces of lead ore about two and a half miles below the lode, but as most of the pieces had been picked up on that occasion, we could only find a few fragments of it.

9th December.

Left the encampment at 4.40 a.m., and steering about south-west, made our former bivouac on the Hutt River about 1.0 p.m., and halted for the rest of the day.

10th December.

Started at 4.50 a.m., steering 160 degrees magnetic over sandy country; passed a small grassy valley at 8.0; halted on the north branch of the Bowes at 10.10 on a small pool of brackish water; dined and resumed our route at 2.40 p.m.; steered south over a grassy country till 6.10, when we halted for the night on a tributary stream to the Bowes; obtained fresh water by digging, the pools being very small and brackish.

CONFLICT WITH NATIVES. GOVERNOR SPEARED.

11th December.

Left the bivouac at 5.15 a.m., steering 175 degrees magnetic over an indifferent country till 6.40, when we crossed the south branch of the

Bowes, the country improving. Here we saw several natives, who at first hid themselves, but finding that we saw them, came after us. At first they did not exceed eight or ten in number, but, being joined by several other parties, gradually increased till they exceeded fifty, when they altogether changed their friendly manner, and began to bring up their spears. At 6.15 we passed to the west of King's Table Hill, and as the country was covered with dense wattle thickets, the natives took advantage of the ground, and having completely surrounded the party, commenced first to threaten to throw their spears, then to throw stones, and finally one man caught hold of Mr. Bland by the arm, threatening to strike him with a dowak; another native threw a spear at myself, though without effect; but before I could fire at him, the Governor, perceiving that unless some severe example was made the whole party would be cut off, fired at one of the most forward of our assailants, and killed him; two other shots were fired by the soldiers, but the thickness of the bushes prevented our seeing with what effect. A shower of spears, stones, kylies, and dowaks followed, and although we moved to a more open spot, the natives were only kept off by firing at any that exposed themselves. At this moment a spear struck the Governor in the leg just above the knee, with such force as to cause it to protrude two feet on the other side, which was so far fortunate, as it enabled me to break off the barb and withdraw the shaft. The Governor, notwithstanding his wound, continued to direct the party, and although the natives made many attempts to approach close enough to reach us with their spears, we were enabled, by keeping on the most open ground, and checking them by an occasional shot, to avoid their attacks in crossing the gullies. They followed us closely for seven miles, after which they were only seen occasionally, following in our track. Having reached the beach, we were enabled to travel more rapidly, and although one of the ponies knocked up, we reached Champion Bay at 3.30 p.m., and got the party and horses on board the Champion by 5.0, where we were gladly welcomed by Lieutenant Helpman. About sunset the natives came down to the beach, concealing themselves behind the bushes, whilst a single unarmed native stood on the beach, and called to us to come on shore, no doubt in the hope of making a sudden attack on the boat should we venture to do so.

A.C. Gregory,

Assistant Surveyor.

THE MURCHISON RIVER 1857

THE UPPER MURCHISON RIVER.

In the month of March, 1857, Mr. Surveyor F.T. Gregory, while engaged on the survey of the lower part of the Murchison, observed that the river came down in flood, though there had been no rain for several months near the coast, and taking advantage of such a favourable opportunity of extending the exploration of the country beyond the point at which previous explorers had been driven back for want of water and grass, he proceeded up the Murchison, accompanied by his assistant, Mr. S. Trigg, following the course of the river for 180 miles. For the last fifty miles the condition of the vegetation showed that there had been heavy rains which had caused the floods in the lower part of the river.

The following is an abstract of Mr. Gregory's report to the Surveyor-General, as published at the time in the Perth Gazette:--

We last week intimated that an exploratory trip had lately been made into the interior eastward of the Geraldine Mine. We have now the pleasure and satisfaction of laying before our readers some details of one of the most unassuming explorations, yet important in its results, which has ever been undertaken in this colony. In the latter end of March last, Mr. Assistant Surveyor F. Gregory and Mr. S. Trigg started from the Geraldine Mine with two horses and sixteen pounds of flour, to trace the Murchison to its source, and returned after thirteen days' absence. Mr. Gregory has made a short report of his journey to the Surveyor-General, from which we have been kindly furnished with the following extract:--

While at the Geraldine Mine I availed myself of the circumstance of the Murchison being in flood to ascend that river and complete the sketch of the unexamined portions, as also to gain any additional information that might facilitate the exploration of the country between this and the Gascoyne River. The fact that the natives describe a considerable tract of grassy country extending northward from the head of the Murchison, plentifully supplied with water, was an additional incentive to ascertain from whence the inundation came.

TROPICAL RAINY SEASON. GOOD PASTORAL COUNTRY.

Accompanied by Mr. S. Trigg, I proceeded up the river about 180 miles, at which point it ceased to run; we then ascended a hill in the vicinity of 600 or 700 feet elevation above the plain, which I have since found to be, beyond a doubt, Mount Murchison of Austin; unfortunately I was unable to procure a copy of his map or journal, and was thus prevented from laying out my route to the greatest advantage by pushing more to the northward and going over more new ground. As it is, the only information I have been able to gain, beyond completing the plan of the river, is that the principal fall of rain had been eastward of the 116th degree of longitude, and that the tract of country between the great South Bend and Mount Murchison, which proved barely capable of supporting Mr. Austin's small party of horses in November, 1854, is now yielding a pasture nearly equal to the average of the Champion Bay district, and in some parts most luxuriant, the grass having scarcely arrived at maturity was perfectly green; this remarkable change in the character of the country is, I am inclined to think, not entirely confined to this year in particular, but that from meteorological causes this district has not unfrequently the benefit of tropical rains falling during the months of January and February, although not always in sufficient quantity to cause the river to flow as low as the settled districts.

It has already been observed by many persons that during the summer months the prevailing sea breezes divide the northerly currents of vapour about 100 miles inland from the west coast, preventing the rain from falling throughout the same parallel of latitude.

As near the eastern limits of my route the Murchison throws off two branches nearly equal in magnitude to the main stream, I am induced to imagine that its extreme source does not lie more than sixty or seventy miles beyond that point, and had it not been that I did not feel justified in abstracting so large a portion of time from the regular surveys of this district, there is no doubt but that I could with every facility have completed the exploration of the country as far as the Gascoyne in two or three weeks.

On comparing the tracing of the Murchison, which I now enclose, with Mr. Austin's route, it will be observed that there is a difference of seventeen miles in latitude, and something more in longitude throughout the eastern portion, a discrepancy which I am at a loss to account for, as my dead-reckoning to both the outward and inward track agree well with my cross-bearings; my latitudes were, however, taken only with a pocket sextant with a treacle horizon, and might therefore not be implicitly relied on. I have, however, preferred plotting my route exactly as booked in the field, leaving the existing error to be cleared up at some future period.

From Mr. Trigg, who arrived on Wednesday by the Preston from Champion Bay, we have gathered the following additional particulars:--

The outward route was on the south bank of the river Murchison; the first sixty miles was but indifferent, but there were many spots of grass, sufficient to maintain travelling herds or flocks; afterwards the soil on the banks of the river improved and were continuously grassy, the general width being about half a mile. About latitude 26 degrees 50 minutes, longitude 116 degrees east, two large branches, almost if not quite equal to the main stream, join the Murchison from the eastward. About Mr. Austin's Mount Welcome the grass was found very luxuriant--from two to three feet high, and between there and Mount Murchison the country is described by Mr. Trigg to be very beautiful, and the soil superior to any he had previously seen in the colony, and equal to the best land in Victoria. Mount Murchison itself is an immense mass of quartz with granite round the base; this differs from Mr. Austin's description, but that gentleman does not appear to have ascended the hill. From the summit three high lands were observable, one an isolated peak fifty miles east, the others to the north and north-east apparently more distant; so far as could be seen, the country to the east and north-east appeared scrubby and indifferent. The return was on the north side of the Murchison; and here a large extent of good grassy land was found, not on the bank, but a mile and a half from the river, and reaching four or five miles in width to the base of some hills, and reaching westward to the large northerly bend of the river in longitude 115 degrees 30 minutes about forty miles from the Geraldine Mine; the good land in all cases was very flat, the soil a red loam, which when dry was very open; the whole country is singularly infested with white ants, of which every tree living or dead appeared to have its colony. Mr. Trigg regards the country around Mount Murchison as auriferous.

The striking difference there is between this account of the country on the Murchison and that given by Mr. Austin may be accounted for in several ways: first, Mr. Austin does not appear to have crossed, but skirted the country intervening between Mount Welcome and Mount Murchison, but he describes the land about the latter as improving, and found water; while it was the feed and water at Mount Welcome which, in all probability, saved his party from perishing. The land on the north side, spoken of so favourably by Mr. Trigg, was not seen by Mr. Austin, and also his party was so exhausted that it was out of his power to diverge from a direct line in order to examine the nature of the country on either side; whereas Messrs. Gregory and Trigg made such an examination whenever any favourable appearance presented itself, and thus determined the quantity of valuable land for a distance of six or seven miles on each side of the river, and have thus been the means of conferring on the Colony one of the greatest benefits it has received since the northern district was first opened by Mr. A. Gregory.

GASCOYNE RIVER 1858

PERTH TO CHAMPION BAY.

In consequence of the very satisfactory results of the exploration of the Upper Murchison River by Messrs. Gregory and Trigg in 1857, a number of settlers in the northern districts subscribed horses and equipment for an exploring party to examine the country still further to the east and north, and with the sanction of the Government, the Expedition was placed under the command of Mr. F.T. Gregory, the result being the discovery of a considerable area of available country on the Gascoyne and Lyons Rivers, as described in Mr. Gregory's journal, of which the following is a copy:--

MR. F. GREGORY'S REPORT.

Western Australia,

Perth, July 26, 1858.

SIR,

In accordance with the instructions conveyed in your letter of the 15th March, authorising me to take command of the Expedition to Shark's Bay, in course of organisation by the northern settlers, I have the honour to furnish the following report of our proceedings while in that service, for the information of His Excellency the Governor.

The preliminary arrangements having been completed, and the heavy portion of the stores forwarded by sea to Champion Bay, I left Perth on the 26th March, accompanied by Mr. James Roe as second in command, chainer Fairburn having started the previous day with the team and light equipment of the Expedition.

Proceeding by way of Toodyay to the Irwin River, the party were joined by Mr. W. Moore with three horses; passing on by way of Champion Bay, we arrived a Koobijawanna, the point of general rendezvous, by the 10th of April. On the 12th the remainder of the stores arrived from Champion Bay, the party being augmented to six persons by the addition of Mr. C. Nairn and Dugel, an aboriginal policeman. This day and the following were occupied in weighing and packing stores, shoeing horses, etc.

14th April.

The equipment of the Expedition being completed (with the exception of one horse to be procured at the Geraldine Mine), we moved on to Yanganooka, passing the Geraldine Mine on the 16th, and bivouacked on the Murchison River, six miles above the mine, having obtained the additional horse, making in all six saddle and six pack horses; our supplies consisting of sixty days' rations, on a scale of one and a half pounds of flour, eight ounces of pork, four ounces of sugar, and half an ounce of tea per diem, the party being all well armed and furnished with ammunition.

The mean of our observations with the Aneroid barometer gives 575 feet for the elevation of this part of the river above the sea.

ASCEND THE MURCHISON RIVER.

17th April to the 25th April.

Was occupied in ascending the Murchison River by easy stages to the junction of the Impey, the highest point attained by me last year. The only observations worthy of remark were that the inundation had not been so great as that which occurred the previous summer, the grass up to this point not being by any means so abundant as I had found it on my former visit; the volume of water now running in the bed of the river being, however, at this time about the same, although none of the tributaries, including the Roderick and Impey, had been in flood, little or no rain having fallen to the west of the 117th degree of longitude, except to the north of latitude 26 degrees.

I availed myself of the opportunity afforded to make several additions and corrections to the map of this part of the country, verifying the correction made by me last year in the latitude of Mount Murchison and adjacent hills. By an improved series of triangulation and a carefully observed set of lunar distances, I am inclined to place Mount Murchison in about longitude 116 degrees 30 minutes east, which makes it more nearly approximate to the longitude formerly given by Mr. Austin.

The variation of the compass I found by several amplitudes to be 2 degrees 30 minutes west. The bed of the Murchison River is here about 1,077 feet above the sea. In addition to the fish and game formerly observed on this part of the river, we met with large flocks of the gallinule, which have for so many years excited the curiosity of the colonists as to their habitat; from subsequent observations it is evident they come from much further to the north-eastward. But one party of natives had as yet been seen, consisting of eight or ten, who chased our native Dugel to the camp while out shooting, but it was difficult to ascertain whether with hostile intentions. From this time to our return we regularly mounted sentry during the night, and no one was allowed to quit the party any distance alone--a precautionary measure the necessity of which was fully borne out by the sequel.

26th April.

From our camp, which was situated about eight miles west of Mount Murchison, we fairly commenced the exploration of unknown country. Following the river nearly north-north-east for fourteen miles it turned abruptly to the east; we, however, held our course, which at four miles further brought us to the foot of Mount Narryer, which we ascended, and procured a valuable round of angles from its summit. This hill has an altitude of 1,688 feet above the sea, and is formed by the eruption of a coarse dark-coloured crystalline trap through a base of amorphous sandstone, the direction of the range of which it forms a part being nearly north and south. Skirting round the north end of this range, we struck east over a stony plain, thinly grassed amongst open wattles, and at five miles again came upon the Murchison some time after dark. The pools here were somewhat larger than for many miles below, being from sixty to eighty yards wide and half a mile in length, the water in them becoming decidedly brackish; samphire, atriplex, and other salsolaceous plants being abundant on the banks.

27th April.

We only advanced nine miles, owing to Mr. Moore and Dugel having to return for one of the water-beakers, which had been torn off the pack-saddle the previous night in a thicket. Towards our bivouac, which was in latitude 26 degrees 23 minutes 38 seconds, the country near the river improved much, the channel of the river becoming very shallow; the water had spread over the flats for more than half a mile on either side, large flooded-gum trees growing abundantly with a fine sward of grass beneath, the soil being a rich brown clay loam. Gallinule and cockatoos were in large flocks feeding on the grass seeds, which were now nearly ripe.

28th April.

To latitude 28 degrees 7 minutes the river continued to come from north by east through an extensive plain, bounded on the west by a low range of trap and granite hills, at an average distance of six or seven miles, while to the eastward only a few distant peaks were visible, flooded-gum growing plentifully for more than a mile back from the river, on flats of tolerably good pasture. Receding somewhat further from the river, the country opens out into extensive plains yielding but little grass; atriplex bush and thinly scattered stunted acacia and melaleuca trees forming almost the entire vegetation.

29th April.

A few miles nearly north brought us to where a considerable tributary joins the Murchison from the north, the river trending first north-east, then east, and finally towards the afternoon it came from the southward of east, our bivouac being only seven miles north of the previous night, while we had made nearly eighteen miles of easting. The bed of the river had gradually become more rocky as we ascended, gneiss with quartz dykes passing through it and yielding a large quantity of salt, rendered the running water of the river scarcely drinkable; the only fresh water was found in the back channels filled by the late inundations. The ranges which ran parallel to the river to the westward terminated some miles to the north of the bend. Another range, apparently granitic and broken up into detached peaks, commencing a little to the eastward of its termination, runs east for about twenty miles at the distance of six or seven miles from the north bank of the river.

To the eastward an elevated range with two conspicuous summits, which were respectively named Mount Matthew and Mount Hale, terminated the view in that direction, while to the south only a few detached peaks were visible.

To-day we first observed a very beautiful convolvulus, which we afterwards found to bear roots like a sweet potato, some of them more than a pound weight and well flavoured, forming a very important article of food to the natives. The flowers are numerous, and measure from two to three inches in diameter, their outer edges of a dark lilac, deepening to a rich purple at the centre, with a pale green convolute ribbing on the outside, the stem and leaf of the plant resembling the kennedya. Mr. Drummond, to whom I have described it, considers it an important discovery, as by cultivation it might become a valuable addition to our Australian esculents.

A small species of rock-melon was also found in great abundance about the size of a pigeon's egg, somewhat bitter to the taste, but they were not ripe; in other respects it much resembles the cultivated varieties.

The bed of the river at this night's bivouac had attained an elevation of 1,240 feet above the sea.

LEAVE THE MURCHISON FOR THE GASCOYNE RIVER.

30th April.

Finding that the Murchison was leading us too much to the eastward, the object of the expedition being to reach the Gascoyne with as little delay as possible, we quitted the river on a north-north-east course for about eight miles over a tolerably grassy plain, in some parts open, with atriplex and samphire, and in others rather thickly studded with acacia and melaleuca. Ascending a granite hill of 150 feet elevation, the plain was observed to the eastward to extend to the horizon, only broken by one remarkable bold trap hill at the distance of twenty miles, which was eventually named Mount Gould, the main Murchison flowing round its southern base, while a considerable tributary from the north-east passed close under it to the north-west. To the north of our position the country rose into a succession of stony ridges thinly grassed and nearly destitute of trees; in the valleys the kangaroo grass was tolerably plentiful and quite green--a sufficient evidence that we had now arrived within the influence of the rains that had produced the recent inundation, which gave us every hope of being able to push across the country intervening between this and the Gascoyne. We accordingly altered our course to north-west for the remainder of this and the following day, crossing several tributaries to the Murchison, in which we found plenty of water, and on their banks an abundant supply of grass for our horses, the streams being generally divided from each other by low stony ridges or plains of red sandy loam, yielding a rather scanty supply of grass.

3rd May.

Having rested the party the previous day, it being Sunday, in latitude 25 degrees 33 minutes 48 seconds, at a fine pool of fresh water in a stream running south, and apparently tributary to the Murchison, we resumed our course for three or four miles up a branch of the stream upon which we had been encamped, which terminated at a gentle stony ascent; another mile brought us to its summit, which proved to be the watershed between the Gascoyne and Murchison; its elevation was found to be 1,500 feet above the sea. From this ridge a short descent northward led us to the head of a watercourse, which we followed in the same direction for seventeen miles, augmented by several small tributaries; turning to the westward, it formed a junction with another river coming from the eastward, in latitude 25 degrees 14 minutes 23 seconds, at an elevation of 1,144 feet above the sea.

STONY PLAINS.

The country through which we had passed was a nearly level and barren plain, evenly and closely paved with small stones, amongst which a few stunted acacia found a precarious existence; to this portion of country we gave the characteristic name of Macadam Plains.

GASCOYNE RIVER.

4th May.

The river we had encamped upon the preceding night had a level sandy channel thirty-five yards wide, with several shallow pools in its bed; a narrow belt of flooded-gum lined either bank, which also produced abundance of excellent feed; several of the grasses were new to us, yielding a large quantity of seed; further back the pasture was more scanty, and of an inferior variety of grass, the trees consisting almost entirely of small hakea or acacia.

The features of the country are generally very tame, with the exception of a prominent hill of considerable altitude, nearly twenty miles to the northward, to which we gave the name of Mount Gascoyne. The summit of another range, of less elevation, a little to the northward of west, distant fifteen miles, was called Mount Puckford.

Having decided upon following the left bank of the river, with the view of ascertaining what tributaries might joint from the southward, we this morning took our course for Mount Puckford, touching frequently upon the bends of the river, which soon found a junction with a large channel coming from the eastward, which ultimately proved to be the main Gascoyne; it was still running in a small stream in the bottom of a sandy bed, eighty yards wide, traces of recent heavy floods being plentiful. At ten miles the river has broken through a ridge of opaline rocks, in irregular masses, resembling flints, lying north-east and south-west, and a few miles further coming in contact with the south-east foot of Mount Puckford, it doubles back round its north-east base, and there takes a general north-west course to latitude 24 degrees 36 minutes, and longitude 116 degrees east, which we reached by noon of the 7th, a considerable tributary joining at this point from the northward. A compact sandstone range, resting on a granite base (which was named the Lockier Range, after Mr. Lockier Burgess, one of the principal promoters of the expedition), here diverts the course of the river to the left, which, by sundown, we found was running nearly south. The country for the last fifty miles varies but little in character, extensive open plains alternating with low granite ridges; the banks of the river, which here has acquired a width of 100 yards, with a depth of forty-six feet, being in many places stony and cut down by deep muddy creeks, rendering travelling both slow and laborious. Several tributaries join from the north and south, all of which had very recently ceased to run.

To the north and east were several prominent peaks and ranges of trap hills clothed with short herbage; to the highest of the former, a single conical peak, with deeply serrated sides, was given the name of Mount James, after my friend and fellow-traveller, Mr. James Roe; while two lofty summits, far to the northward, were called Mount Samuel and Mount Phillips.

The principal feed was found near the banks of the rivers, the back country still yielding only a scanty supply of a red-coloured silky grass of little value except when quite fresh. A tree resembling the sycamore of the Murchison, but with the leaves arranged in triplets, and the seed pods in the form of a large bean, grows near the river and attains to two feet in diameter, with a height of forty feet; the wood is light and spongy, something resembling the Nuytsia floribunda, but not gummy. It is formed by the natives into shields, and near the coast into canoes. We also found on some of the rocky hills a tree with fruit and flowers resembling a small fig, the leaves like a lemon, but yielding an acrid milky juice.

Several new species of crested quail and dark-brown pigeons were first observed here; the beautiful small doves, common in the northern districts, were also seen by thousands; gallinule and the elegant Ochaphaps plumafera (crested pigeon of the marshes) were also very numerous.

SURPRISE A NATIVE CAMP.

8th May.

Pursuing our course down the left bank, we crossed several stream-beds which drain the large tract of country between this and the Murchison. The Gascoyne here divides into several broad sandy channels, sometimes as much as a mile apart. Towards evening we came upon a native encampment; few of the men appeared to have returned from their day's hunting, but we observed upwards of thirty women and children, who ran into the bed of the river to hide, some of the women immersing their children completely under water occasionally to prevent their cry of alarm attracting our attention. Although we had before met with and spoken to several natives, this was the first opportunity we had of examining into their domestic economy. Around their fires, of which there were many, were ranged a number of wooden scoops capable of holding from two to four quarts; these contained a variety of seed and roots; the most plentiful was a species of grain like small plump drake, gathered from a grass much resembling wheat, which is very abundant on the alluvial flats, and a root resembling an onion not larger than a pistol bullet, a few rats, which are very numerous in the grassy flats, and a small variety of samphire like a Hottentot fig, formed the principal portion of their evening's repast.

The few weapons left by the men consisted of heavy spears, with from three to eighteen barbs cut out of the solid wood, the shaft from ten to twelve feet in length, large shields resembling those in use by the natives at

Champion Bay, made from the sycamore, and few skins of the red kangaroo, formed their entire camp equipment.

A NIGHT ATTACK.

Leaving everything as we found it, we passed on about two miles and encamped for the night on a low sandy island in the bed of the river, which was here full of flooded-gums of large growth, there being just sufficient grass for our horses immediately around our fire. By 9 o'clock our supper had been disposed of, and I had just completed my observations for latitude, when we heard the shouts of a large party of natives approaching from the direction of their camp; leaving Mr. Roe with two others to guard the camp, I advanced with Mr. Moore and Dugel to ascertain the object of their visit, which we soon found to be evidently hostile, as they came on rapidly, all well armed to the number of sixty or seventy, the women and children retiring to some rocky ground, while the men advanced lighting the large stacks of drift which were abundant in this part of the river. When within about forty yards they halted a moment, as we had damped our fire and they could not exactly make out our position. Mr. Moore was in the act of removing his horse from the front when a fresh fire enabled them to see us, upon which ten or twelve of the leading men shipped their spears. Being still desirous, if possible, of avoiding a collision, I hesitated to fire upon them; but observing a large body of them advancing with the evident intention of attacking Mr. Roe and his little party in charge of the camp, I advanced a few steps and fired a charge of small shot at the leading men as they were in the act of throwing at us. The effect was instantaneous and most salutary, as they fled with some precipitation, some of them being evidently wounded. We mounted extra guard for the remainder of the night, but they did not again venture to attack us.

9th May.

Being Sunday, we only moved a few miles lower down the river for more grass, and again found ourselves in close proximity to the natives. In the course of the day several of them made their appearance at the top of the hill overlooking the camp, but appeared afraid to molest us; they had with them several large white dogs which were evidently of Australian breed.

10th May.

The river took a south-west course, receiving two large tributaries from the south-east, one of ninety and the other of fifty yards in width. The flats were wider and large trees more abundant; the recent floods had, however, been very destructive to the pasture, and removed much of the soil for a considerable distance back from the river. The trap hills here ceased to appear; the last remarkable one lay about ten miles south-east of our morning's camp, and had been named Mount Dalgetty. Our evening's bivouac was found to be in latitude 25 degrees 14 minutes, longitude 115 degrees 30 minutes east by account, and its elevation 700 feet above the sea.

11th May.

Until noon our course along the river was nearly north-west, sandstones beginning to crop out on the banks, and the country generally was poor and scrubby; from our noon halt to sunset our course was nearly west, our bivouac being in latitude 25 degrees 2 minutes. The bed of the river had here widened out to 300 yards with an average depth of thirty feet, a small stream running through the sand in the bottom. In addition to the flooded-gum which grows here abundantly, we observed in the bed of the river a melaleuca of large size, like a paper-bark tree, but having broad leaves resembling the eucalyptus. During the night the natives were very noisy in the vicinity, some of them approaching so close as to startle our horses, keeping us well on the alert; the horses on this as on several other occasions appear to have been our principal safeguard against sudden attack.

FRIENDLY INTERVIEW WITH NATIVES.

12th May.

By the time we had commenced loading our horses, a large body of natives had collected and approached to reconnoitre our camp; I advanced towards them to keep them in check until the loads were completed. On observing that I came alone three natives advanced to meet me, throwing three or four spears at me in a friendly way, which I picked up and stuck in the ground by my side; this token at once established a good understanding, and after an exchange of presents they followed us for many miles down the river before quitting us. Towards nightfall several of our friends of the morning again made their appearance with a number of strange natives, dodging us among the deep muddy ravines which abound at this part of the river; their manoeuvres being equivocal and unsatisfactory, we kept well on our guard; they, however, ran off at night, on my facing about on horseback to drive them away.

Our course during the day had been nearly west twenty-two miles, one large tributary having joined the river from the northward, which was afterwards named the Lyons, in honour of the gallant admiral of that name; this accession had increased the breadth of the channel to 400 yards. As we drew towards our evening's bivouac the river entered a gorge formed by the river cutting through the south end of a flat-topped sandstone range of about 1,200 feet elevation above the sea, presenting many bold and picturesque outlines and detached summits, terminating in abrupt and almost precipitous faces; to this we gave the name of the Kennedy Range, in honour of our present Governor.

To the south a detached mass of broken sandstone hills gradually falls away in the distance, apparently into a barren scrub similar to those on the banks of the lower Murchison, while to the west lay before us an extensive plain, unbroken by a single object save a few long ridges of red drift sand, clothed with a stunted scrub of melaleuca and acacia. The bottom of the gorge we found to be 480 feet above the sea.

13th May.

From this morning to noon of the 15th the country passed over was similar to that first described, the sand ridges running north-west and south-east at about a quarter of a mile apart; the river keeping a general course of west-north-west, its channel deepening to sixty feet, and maintaining an average width of 400 yards. Grass was only to be found in small patches along the margin of the river; the accumulated waters of the late inundations having been confined to one channel, had risen to the height of forty-eight feet, carrying away many of the largest timber trees, as also much of the soil from the banks, leaving a scene of devastation exceeding anything of the kind I had hitherto witnessed.

A small description of Spanish reed was here first observed to grow on the margin of the pools. Deep muddy creeks, having only short courses, were very numerous, rendering travelling both tedious and intricate.

From noon of the 15th the country gradually opened out to a thinly-grassed plain of light alluvial soil, atriplex bushes and acacia widely scattered forming almost the entire vegetation; the ground, with the exception of the bed of the river, being parched and dry, no rain having fallen during the summer to the west of the Lyons River, in longitude 115 degrees 30 minutes east.

16th May.

Being Sunday, we only moved four miles lower down the river for better feed, the channel widening out to 600 yards.

17th May.

Early to-day the river began to throw off numerous channels to the north and south, shedding, when in a flood, a considerable amount of water over the adjoining plains, clothing the country in the garb of spring, the grass growing luxuriantly along the numerous channels, atriplex and other low bushes generally covering the plain, the lowest levels of which were extensively covered with fields of mud from one to fourteen inches thick, the deposit of a single inundation, yet scarcely hardened by the summer sun.

REACH THE COAST AT SHARK'S BAY.

At twenty miles we ascended a sandy ridge of about sixty feet in height, from which we had our first view of Shark's Bay, Babbage Island, and the mouths of the Gascoyne, now only four miles distant.

Behind the ridge upon which we stood, and for many miles to the south-east, the country was still under water from the recent floods, while between us and the sea lay a low flat, on which were many patches of acacia thicket, alternating with open grassy glades, or fields of atriplex and samphire, terminating to the westward in a broad irregular belt of mangroves, resting on the shallow margin of the bay.

Descending to the flat, we encamped in a rank patch of grass on the bank of the river, about a mile above Babbage Island, the north end of which I found to be in latitude 24 degrees 52 minutes, which is four miles north of the position as given by Sir G. Grey.

KOLAINA PLAINS.

18th May.

We found no difficulty in crossing the southern mouth on to Babbage Island; the tide being low, it was quite dry at the junction. Having, with Mr. Roe, walked over the greater part of the island, making a rough sketch of its outlines, and completing the requisite observations, while the rest of the party were occupied in an unsuccessful attempt to catch fish, we retraced our steps and crossed the main channel opposite our last night's bivouac, where it is not more than 250 yards wide. Continuing our course north-east for nearly a mile, we crossed several back channels, some trending towards the Kolaina flat of Sir G. Grey, while others were lost in the deep sandy ravines that extend for some distance to the north of the river.

While on Babbage Island several natives had waded across the northern mouth of the river to meet us, and had returned after a friendly interview, in which they apparently described the recent landing of two boats with Europeans. We now again fell in with the same natives on the north bank, near a large encampment of women and children; the latter quickly hid themselves on our approach, but the men assumed a threatening attitude, following us for some distance with much clamour. As their numbers quickly augmented, and they appeared determined to commence a fight, we led them out on to an open plain, where, leaving the pack-horses in charge of two of the party, four of us suddenly faced about and charged them at a gallop. This harmless manoeuvre had the desired effect, several of them having narrowly escaped being trodden under foot by the horses. They were very quickly dispersed, and made no further attempt to molest us. We encamped this night about six miles above Babbage Island.

19th May.

As our object was to explore as far to the northward as circumstances would allow, we left the river on a north-east course; but two hours' ride across an open plain, through which several channels ran to the north-west, brought us to dry barren scrubs, in which it appeared hopeless we should find either feed or water; we accordingly altered our course to south-east, and made the river again about sundown.

RETURN UP THE RIVER.

20th to 23rd May.

Was occupied in tracing up the north bank of the river in the hope of finding a tributary coming in from the northward; but, with the exception of one small stream which drains the western face of the Kennedy Range, not a single tributary was met with until we arrived at the Lyons River, a distance of more than ninety miles from Babbage Island. The country on the north bank differs but little from that on the south, except that travelling was somewhat easier.

THE LYONS RIVER. ALMA RIVER.

24th May.

Our horses having had a rest, the previous day being Sunday, we made an early start, and by noon halted on the Lyons River, a short distance above its confluence with the Gascoyne; its channel here was equal in magnitude and similar in appearance to the main river; a small stream was still flowing through the wide sandy bed, and gradually increased in volume for nearly eighty miles up the river. Three miles to the north of our midday halt Mr. Roe and myself ascended a deep sandstone peak, from which we had a fine view of the Kennedy Range, the nearest part of which lay about six miles to the west, extending for nearly thirty miles to the northward; the eastern face presents an almost unbroken line of nearly perpendicular sandstone, of probably 500 or 600 feet elevation. To the north a few remarkable peaks served as valuable points to carry on our triangulation, which had been continued almost uninterruptedly from Mount Hope, on the Murchison.

To the east were several ranges of flat-topped hills, filling in the space between the Lyons and the great southern bend of the Gascoyne; while to the south, with the exception of a few very distant peaks, it appeared, as far as the eye could reach, to be an uniform plain of open but almost grassless scrub.

Having completed our round of angles, we struck south-east to a patch of forest on the banks of the river, which we did not reach until sometime after dark.

25th May.

From this point to latitude 23 degrees 56 minutes the Lyons maintains a general course of north-north-east. The country passed over during to-day had evidently been tolerably grassy, but the floods had been quite as destructive here as on the Gascoyne, the bed of the river and flats for half a mile on each side being mostly choked up or buried under fields of fine white sand, which had been brought down by the inundations. In several places we observed beds of gypsum and fossil shells with other strong indications of the existence of coal in the vicinity. Bivouac in latitude 24 degrees 41 minutes 18 seconds.

26th May.

A few miles along the river brought us to a gorge in the eastern edge of the sandstones, to the east of which it opened out into extensive plains in some parts well grassed, and in others much washed by the river. Several trap and granite hills were visible at some distance to the northward and eastward. Our bivouac was in latitude 24 degrees 31 minutes 0.5 seconds, about three miles south of a bold trap-range, the summit of which was named Mount Sandiman.

27th May.

The country still maintained its variable character, travelling near the river being exceedingly heavy on account of the sand. The morning had been calm and sultry, but towards noon a strong breeze set in from the north, bringing with it a dense cloud of fine red dust, against which it was no easy matter to make head with our horses. Towards evening the flats began to improve, and we halted for the night amongst fine grass; melons and tobacco growing very luxuriantly. To-night it rained for about two hours, clearing the atmosphere of its load of dust.

28th May.

Resuming our course up the river, at four miles we crossed a stream-bed forty yards wide, coming in from the north-north-west, and in the course of the day passed over several thin beds of opaque opalline rock resting upon the sandstone. At our camp, which was in latitude 24 degrees 0.3 minutes 0.8 seconds, granite began to make its appearance in the bed of the river.

29th May.

Our pack-horses having now been much lightened of their loads, we were to-day for the first time able to trot for several hours; and as the country still improved, several fine grassy valleys coming in from the eastward, we made considerable progress.

ALMA RIVER.

At our noon halt Mr. Moore and myself ascended a hill of red schist of 300 or 400 feet elevation, in latitude 23 degrees 57 minutes 15 seconds, which had been named Mount Thompson. From this hill we had an extensive view of the surrounding country; close to the northern foot the river divided into two nearly equal parts--one coming from the north-north-east we named the Alma. To the north, just resting on the edge of the tropic, lay a compact range through which there was apparently but one break, and that was on the line of the Alma; from the southern face of this range, which extends nearly forty miles to the eastward, numerous streams take their rise and flow southward into the Lyons, which had altered its course and was now coming from the east-south-east. Our intention had been to keep our course until we had touched upon the tropic; but as the Alma was not running, we decided upon following the main course of the stream, and accordingly adopted an easterly course for the remainder of the day, encamping about six miles to the east of Mount Thompson. The river here was much narrower, with a rocky bed containing many pools of permanent character, overshadowed by flooded-gums of large growth, much resembling the Eucalyptus piperita of the flats of the Swan, but not possessing the same pungent leaf.

30th May (Sunday).

Found our latitude to be 23 degrees 58 minutes 32 seconds, and longitude 111 degrees east by account.

31st May.

NATIVE TOBACCO.

We started off at a quick pace, clearing sixteen miles by noon, over some fine open grassy flats, timbered for nearly a mile back from the river; one tributary 100 yards wide having joined from the north, and a smaller one from the south. Leaving the party busily occupied catching fish, which were abundant in this part of the river and much resembling those found in the Murchison, but larger, some of them being upwards of a pound in weight, I walked with Mr. Nairn to the summit of a granite hill two miles to the northward, from which I had a number of cross-bearings to hills already observed from Mount Thompson. One of considerable elevation bearing north 121 degrees 30 minutes east, distance fifty miles, lay directly up the valley of the river, and was ultimately named Mount Augustus, after my brother, now conducting the expedition in quest of the remains of Dr. Leichhardt. Pushing on twelve miles further, we halted for the night in latitude 23 degrees 59 minutes 39 seconds. Tobacco here grew to sufficient size for manufacture, occupying many hundred acres of the best land; a plant much resembling stramonium was also abundant on the moist land, yielding a strongly offensive odour from its leaves.

1st June.

For the first twelve miles along the river the flats much improved, and were only occasionally broken up by stony ridges; good country was seen to extend up the tributaries, several of which came in from the north. To the south, at two or three miles distant, and running parallel to the river for many miles, was an even grassy range of moderate elevation nearly destitute of trees or bushes; the acacia and melaleuca, which had hitherto generally covered the plains, was evidently fast giving way to an open undulating and thinly-grassed country, the back lands being however still too stony to yield much pasture, the summer grass being already parched and dry, the flats alone continuing moist and verdant.

At our noon halt the main river had ceased to flow, but a tributary coming from the north-east had a small stream still running in the bottom of a muddy channel down which the recent floods had brought flags and portions of bulrush, the only instance throughout the district in which we had observed them.

The next ten miles passed over between this and sunset was chiefly an alluvial flat, much resembling the fertile lands near the mouth of the Greenough; the acacias and several varieties of melaleuca, amongst which was the Callistemon phoeniceus, with its beautiful scarlet flowers, were growing with tropical luxuriance, the soil in many places being still saturated with moisture. A water-melon was here first observed, the fruit not attaining to more than two inches in length, but not otherwise differing from the cultivated kinds; we also found a fruit in shape like a pear, three inches in length, growing on a small creeper, the interior of the fruit consisting of a number of small flat seeds, to which were attached a bundle of long silky fibres resembling cotton. Our bivouac was in latitude 24 degrees 7 minutes 52 seconds, near a fine pool of fresh water, with limestone cropping out in a thin bed on the banks; we had frequently met with it distributed in small nodules scattered over a large portion of the country on the Upper Murchison.

Since quitting the mouth of the Gascoyne we had seen natives almost daily; to-night we again found ourselves in close proximity to a large encampment of them.

2nd June.

Our neighbours paid us an early visit this morning, some of them evidently bent on mischief, but were restrained by others more prudent--not, however, before it had nearly cost one of them his life; having pointed a spear at Mr. Moore, Dugel, whose natural instincts are very destructive, hastily took aim at him, but fortunately pulled the wrong trigger, which just gave his adversary time to lower his weapon; on our mounting our horses they hastily fell back and joined their other companions at their camp, which was just in our line of march; about thirty of them awaited our approach with some tokens of defiance, but most of them decamped on our coming within spear's throw.

MOUNT AUGUSTUS 3,480 FEET ABOVE SEA LEVEL.

Directing our course for Mount Augustus, we pushed on at a rapid pace with the object of ascending it if possible before sundown; but after riding twenty miles, we found it to be farther off than we anticipated, and accordingly altered our course and encamped at a pool in the river about three miles north-east of the mount, in latitude 24 degrees 20 minutes, and at an elevation of 1500 feet above the sea.

We here met with strong evidences of the cannibalism of the natives; at a recently occupied encampment we found several of the bones of a full-grown native that had been cooked, the teeth marks on the edges of a bladebone bearing conclusive evidence as to the purpose to which it had been applied; some of the ribs were lying by the huts with a portion of the meat still on them.

Nearly the whole of the country passed over this day was an alluvial flat extending on the south-west to the grassy range already described, while to the north and east it extended for many miles, branching out into the numerous valleys that drain the different ranges in that direction; the grass and vegetation on these flats is not so rank as on that traversed the previous day, but more even, and the soil better adapted for agriculture; the amount of good land on this part of the Lyons River was estimated at 150 square miles, while on the tributaries between Mount Thompson and Mount Augustus I have no doubt that there is as much more. Water at this time was plentiful in the numerous channels that intersect the plain, their permanency being the only matter of doubt--our limited acquaintance with the nature of the seasons in these latitudes does not enable us to decide with any degree of certainty; the pools lower down the river are unquestionably of a permanent character, but many of them were already becoming brackish.

The quantity of game seen in this part of the country was also a favourable indication. Turkeys, and a new variety of pigeon, having a brown back and slate-coloured breast, on the wing resembling a tame pigeon, congregate in flights sometimes of a thousand together; emus, cockatoos, quail, and parakeets are also very numerous, particularly the latter.

3rd June.

A gentle ascent of two and a half miles brought us to the foot of Mount Augustus, where, leaving our horses in charge of Fairburn and Dugel, we commenced the ascent up the only accessible point on this side of the hill; it required two hours' heavy toil to bring us to the summit, the barometer gradually falling until it only registered 26.10, which, compared with the simultaneous observations kept at Champion Bay by Mr. H. Gray, gives an elevation of 3,480 feet above the level of the sea; the last 500 feet of the summit being clothed in thickets of melaleuca, amongst which grew a nondescript variety of red gum-tree, the only new thing observed in this locality. The air was fortunately very clear, enabling us to take bearings to almost every remarkable summit within eighty miles, and in two instances to hills more than a hundred miles distant.

From this commanding position I was enabled to sketch in the courses of the rivers for more than twenty miles, some of them probably taking their rise from 60 to 100 miles still further to the eastward. To the north-east the country continued to improve in appearance until the view was intercepted by bold ranges of trap and granite--one of which bearing north 32 degrees east magnetic, distant nearly 100 miles, having a sharp volcanic outline, reared its summit above all the rest. To the south-east the country was not quite so promising, the ridges presenting naked stony outlines, upon which was only a little scanty grass or a few bushes; to the south it was almost an uninterrupted plain, extending nearly as far as the Murchison River, over which lay our homeward course. Descending the mount, we encamped at a spring in some fine feed close at its foot.

RETURN TOWARDS SETTLEMENTS.

4th June.

As we had now been out fifty-one days, and our provisions were only calculated to last twenty-four days longer, although we had reduced our allowance shortly after quitting the Geraldine Mine, we were reluctantly compelled to turn our steps homewards, being still 360 miles from the settled districts; passing, therefore, over the eastern foot of Mount Augustus, we pursued a south-south-east course for twenty miles over alternating grassy plains and stony ridges, and encamped on the river with a sandy bed, in which were a few shallow pools, its trend bearing north-north-west, and probably joins the Gascoyne near the Lockier Range. The feed on this river, as well as on those between this and the Murchison, was principally kangaroo-grass of strong growth; the course of the streams being easily traceable from a distance by the flooded-gum trees that invariably lined their margins.

5th June.

A south course of ten miles over a poor stony country brought us to the head of a stream, which, following in the same direction to latitude 24 degrees 51 minutes 52 seconds, we found plenty of feed on its banks and pools of water in its bed, which was here thirty yards wide; the principal features of the adjacent country being low granite ridges, intersected by occasional quartz dykes, alternating with chlorite schist.

6th June (Sunday).

7th June.

Following a south-south-east course, at six miles the stream turned to the south-west. Passing over several miles of stony country, in latitude 24 degrees 59 minutes 32 seconds, we crossed another stream-bed forty yards wide, running to the westward, and forming a junction with the last at some miles distant. Towards sundown we came upon a recently inundated plain, and a mile further struck a grassy channel thirty yards wide, which had barely ceased running, the soil for some distance on either bank being a strong red loam, yielding a fair supply of pasture. This channel we afterward found to be only one of several which formed the main branch of the Gascoyne. The observed latitude was 25 degrees 6 minutes 30 seconds, and elevation 1,740 feet above the sea.

8th June.

A mile farther we came upon the main channel of the river, with a wide shallow bed, down which a small stream was still running; the flats were well grassed, and the flooded-gums growing for more than a mile back from the river. To the eastward the country continued level and grassy as far as the eye could reach; our time was, however, too limited to admit of our making any further examination of this promising tract. A party of twenty or thirty natives were encamped here, and were apparently living upon the roots of the convolvulus, which grows in the vicinity in great abundance.

For fifteen miles to the south-east it continued a level plain of red loam, tolerably well grassed and covered with an open wood of acacia; the next eight miles was over a poor stony ridge of moderate elevation, terminating at a large dry stream-bed, in latitude 25 degrees 24 minutes 16 seconds, with some fine kangaroo-grass on its banks.

9th June.

Ten miles south, over a granite country, we struck the head of a watercourse, which, after winding about for sixteen miles, ran close to the western foot of Mount Gould, where we encamped at its junction with another small stream coming from the northward. The country passed over to-day was generally very stony until we came within a few miles of Mount Gould.

10th June.

Taking our course direct for Mount Hale, the pasture rapidly improved; at ten miles the watercourse we had been following formed a junction with the main Murchison, coming in from the eastward. From the appearance of the river at this point, it is probable that it takes its rise nearly another 100 miles farther to the north-east. The next thirteen miles down the river was fair average cattle pasture, extending for several miles to the right and left; open flats of atriplex and samphire occurring at intervals.

11th June.

The river soon divided into several channels, shedding its waters over a fine alluvial flat, of considerable extent, yielding a rich sward of grass, under flooded-gums of large growth. A little after noon we came upon our outward track, and encamped at night near the north-west bend of the Murchison.

DOWN THE MURCHISON.

12th to 22nd June.

Was occupied in descending the river to the Geraldine Mine, cutting off several bends of the river, and making such additions to our sketch of the outward route as circumstances would admit.

RETURN TO PERTH.

23rd June.

We all arrived safe at the hospitable residence of Mr. W. Burges, on the Irwin; the following day being occupied in making up the accounts connected with the expedition, which, including the whole of the cash expenditure, did not exceed 40 pounds, which sum had already been subscribed by a few settlers interested in the undertaking.

Quitting the Irwin on the 1st of July, and proceeding by way of Dandaragan and Toodyay, I arrived, with Mr. Roe and chainer Fairburn, in Perth on the 10th instant, having accomplished a journey of nearly 2000 miles in 107 days.

On reviewing the foregoing report, I find it necessary to add a few observations on subjects that could not well be introduced into the body of the narrative.

GEOLOGY OF COUNTRY.

In the first place, viewing the geographical and geological features in combination, the tract of country contained within the 114th and 118th parallels of longitude, and the 24th and 27th degrees of south latitude, may be considered as an inclined plane, the eastern edge of which has an elevation of about 1700 feet above the level of the sea. Commencing from the coast, the first 100 miles is almost exclusively of tertiary sandstone formation, which the process of denudation has, in many instances, converted into either stony or sandy tracts, rarely fertile, except when subject to the influence of frequent inundation. This region seldom gives rise to rivers or watercourses; the flat-topped ranges, which are often found towards the eastern limits of this formation, do not generally exceed 500 or 600 feet in altitude, and are only those portions of country that have not as yet yielded to the waste of time, or the constant action of rivers, which, rising in the higher lands more to the eastward, rapidly abrade, and in their onward course remove the soft and porous sandstone from their bases.

In the deeper valleys, towards the eastern edge of these sandstones thin beds of oolitic limestone, containing numerous fossil shells, occasionally occur; also gypsum and clayey shales, with other indications of the probable existence of coal in the vicinity; following the series appears a compact, fine-grained amorphous sandstone, having an almost flinty fracture; this rock, in a few miles, gives place to granite and gneiss, frequently broken up by the upheaval of whinstone and porphyritic trap hills, having an elevation of from 100 to 500 feet above the plain.

As we proceeded eastward, the eruptive rocks became more numerous; chlorite slate, veins of quartz, chert, and variegated jasper, frequently forming the summits of the most elevated hills, while, on the general level of the plain, are occasionally found thin beds of ancient lava.

The rivers, unlike most others in Western Australia, have nearly an even fall throughout their entire length, amounting on an average to six feet per mile; this, in a country subject to the sudden fall of almost tropical rains, is what gives rise to the destructive inundations already described.

CLIMATE.

Of the climate and seasons so little is at present known that, allowing all other difficulties to have been overcome, it would be very hazardous to risk flocks and herds beyond the head of the Murchison until the country has again been visited at a different period of the year, as it is probably that it has as yet only been seen under the most favourable conditions.

The fluctuations of the temperature are occasionally considerable; in the middle of June it some days amounted to 46 degrees in six hours-- registering, at 7 a.m., 36 degrees, and at 1 p.m., 82 degrees; ice having been seen as far north as latitude 24 degrees 30 minutes.

The prevailing winds during the period of inundation appear to have been from the south-east, as most of the trees blown down while the soil was in a state of saturation lay with their tops to the north-west. In May and June the winds ranged between north-east and south-east.

Of the regularity of the return of the summer rains it is at present difficult to form a decided opinion; but, as far as observation would admit, I am inclined to think they cannot be relied on with any degree of certainty, to the southward of the 25th degree of latitude. The period at which they fall being about January and February, it is a significant fact that the grasses found buried beneath the mud during these months had generally attained only to nearly half their growth.

AREA OF AVAILABLE COUNTRY.

With regard to the quantity and distribution of the available lands, it will only be necessary to observe that, with the exception of 30,000 or 40,000 acres at the mouth of the Gascoyne, there is no land worth occupying for many years to come to the west of the Lyons River; the amount of land on this river has already been estimated at nearly 300 square miles, while on the Upper Gascoyne and its tributaries there is probably double that quantity; this, with the lands on the Murchison near Mount Hale, would make a total of about a million of acres.

A very important circumstance in connection with this district is the total absence, so far as we were able to observe, of any of the varieties of gastrolobium or euphorbia, which constitute the poisonous plants so fatal to cattle and sheep in other parts of the colony.

The means of access to the Upper Gascoyne and Lyons is another important matter for consideration. I am inclined to think that this district cannot be advantageously settled until the tract of country between it and the north coast has been explored, and a port established somewhere between Exmouth Gulf and Depuch Island, as, should the country in that direction fulfil its promise, the intervening space would very quickly be filled up, and the lands on the Gascoyne become available, its distance from the north coast being about 200 miles, while from Port Gregory or Champion Bay would not be less than from 340 to 360 miles--a difference of some moment in the transport of stores or produce.

From the lay of the country to the northward of the Lyons River there does not appear to be any reason to suppose that a river of any magnitude falls into Exmouth Gulf, as there would be hardly room for it between the sources of the Alma and the rivers flowing to the north coast.

I cannot bring my report to a conclusion without recording my acknowledgments to Mr. James Roe for the able and effective assistance he has rendered me throughout the expedition, the barometrical observations and management of the provision department having been especially under his charge.

My best thanks are also due to Mr. W.D. Moore and Mr. C. Nairn, who on every occasion endeavoured to relieve me as much as possible from some of the many arduous duties that usually devolve on the leader of an exploring party. Chainer Fairburn and the native Dugel also gave general satisfaction in the performance of their respective duties.

I may add that to the ready cooperation and unanimity that prevailed throughout the party may in no small degree be ascribed the successful issue of the undertaking.

I have the honour to be, Sir, etc.,

F.T. GREGORY,

Assistant Surveyor.

To the Honourable the Surveyor-General, etc.

NORTH-WEST COAST 1861

ORIGIN OF EXPEDITION TO NORTH-WEST AUSTRALIA.

The important additions to geographical discovery, and the large extent of valuable pastoral country that had been found on the Gascoyne River and its tributaries, attracted the attention of a number of English capitalists interested in cotton manufactures, which were then in a very depressed condition in consequence of the civil war in America, it was proposed to establish a new colony on the north-west coast of Australia, having for its special object the cultivation of cotton.

Advantage was taken of the presence of Mr. F. Gregory in London to urge on the Home Government and the Royal Geographical Society the desirability of fitting out an expedition to proceed direct to the north-west coast of Australia, accompanied by a large body of Asiatic labourers, and all the necessary appliances for the establishment of a colony.

Under the advice of Captain Roe, Surveyor-General of Western Australia, and other gentlemen well acquainted with the subject, the scheme was modified so as to have the country explored as a preliminary to actual settlement, and for this purpose a grant of 2000 pounds was obtained from the Imperial Government, to be supplemented by an equal subsidy by the Colonial Treasury.

Accordingly Mr. Gregory obtained a suitable outfit for the party in London, and early in 1861 proceeded to Western Australia to confer with the Governor as to the requisite details; but owing to the delays caused by a part of the funds having to be provided by a vote of the local Legislature, the expedition did not finally leave Fremantle until 23rd April, 1861--nearly two months later in the season than it should have done, as the rainy season in North-west Australia terminates about the beginning of March.

The following is an abstract of the journal and report of Mr. Gregory to the Governor of Western Australia:--

JOURNAL OF THE NORTH-WEST AUSTRALIAN EXPLORING EXPEDITION.

20th April, 1861.

All the preliminary arrangements in Perth having been completed, and the stores and equipment of the expedition already sent on board the barque Dolphin, I proceeded to Fremantle and shipped the ten horses that had been furnished by the settlers in this part of the colony; the remainder of the hay and water being also completed by 2 p.m., we were prepared to sail, when the agent for the vessel raised objections to our departure, on the plea that the arrangements for the payments on account of the charter were not satisfactory. Wrote accordingly by express to the Private Secretary for an acknowledgment that the requisite documents were complete.

21st April.

Received reply from the Private Secretary to the effect that everything necessary had been approved of already by the Governor; the agent would not, however, allow the vessel to leave until he had actually received the first instalment on account of the charter from the Colonial Treasurer.

22nd April.

Accompanied Mr. Manning and Captain Dixon to Perth, when they were informed by the Colonial Treasurer that the money would be forthcoming on the presentation of the accounts. Returned to Fremantle, where we were detained for the remainder of the day to enable the agent to close his accounts.

23rd April.

Went on board the Dolphin at 7 a.m., and by 11 a.m. got underweigh, with a fresh breeze from the east-north-east, and stood to the north-north-west. The portion of the exploring party embarked at Fremantle comprised the following persons: F.T. Gregory, commander; J. Turner, assistant and storekeeper; E. Brockman, W.S. Hall, and J. McCourt, assistants; and A. James, farrier. Supplies of flour, salt pork, dried beef, preserved meat, bacon, sugar, tea, etc., sufficient for eight months, were provided for a party of nine; three more volunteers and ten horses having yet to be taken on board at Champion Bay.

24th April.

Light winds from the north; at noon sighted land, in latitude 31 degrees 28 minutes 12 seconds south; all hands attending to horses.

25th April.

Experienced variable and contrary winds; made but little progress.

26th April.

Weather cloudy, winds unfavourable; had a distant view of Mount Lesueur.

CHAMPION BAY.

27th April.

Sighted Mount Hill soon after daylight, rain and squalls rendering it difficult to distinguish the coast; the weather clearing up, ran into Champion Bay, and came to anchor by noon, half a mile north of the jetty, in four fathoms; landed and procured a horse from the Government Resident, and rode out to Mr. K. Brown's station.

28th April.

Procured a horse for the expedition from Mr. W. Moore, on account of Hamersley and Company, and returned with it to the Bay.

29th April.

Sent round to the rest of the subscribers of horses to the expedition; party employed filling up ship's water-tanks.

30th April.

Mr. J. Harding arrived, as a volunteer, with two horses from Mr. W. Burges; also Mr. M. Brown, as a volunteer, with one horse. The following gentlemen also sent horses: Messrs. J.S. Davis, 2; F. DuBoulay, 1; C. von Bibra, 1; H. Gray, 1; M. Morrissey, 1; and J. Drummond, 12 sheep. Mr. P. Walcott joined as a volunteer for the collection of specimens of natural history and botany. Ship's crew employed discharging the remainder of the cargo from England, consigned to Champion Bay.

1st May.

With the assistance of a number of gentlemen who kindly volunteered their aid, the ten additional horses were safely swum off to the Dolphin; Captain Dixon and his crew being employed landing a steam-engine. Wrote to His excellency the Governor, reporting intention to sail to-morrow.

CHAMPION BAY TO NICKOL BAY.

2nd May.

Wrote to the Secretary of the Royal Geographical Society, reporting progress of the expedition. Transferred order for twenty sheep, subscribed by J. Williams, to Mr. T. Burges. Took on board twelve sheep sent by Mr. Drummond, and closed accounts at the bay. Party fitting up mangers, etc. At 5.30 p.m. got underweigh and stood to the north-west, the soundings for five miles varying from three and three-quarters to seven fathoms; the sea breaking heavily for about a mile in a northerly direction from the end of the sheltering reef, showing a much greater extent of shoalwater than is noted on the charts. Established a routine of watches of two hours each, for the members of the expedition to attend upon the horses.

3rd May.

By observations at noon, found the latitude to be 26 degrees 53 minutes south; longitude 112 degrees 33 minutes east. Party preparing equipment, drying horse-slings, etc. Wind light from south-east.

4th May.

Putting pack-saddles together, covering water-belts, etc.; light wind from south, ship making from one to four knots; course north by east. Increased allowance of water to horses from four or five gallons each, on account of the heat of the hold. Killed a sheep.

Latitude at noon, 25 degrees 40 minutes south; longitude 112 degrees 1 minute east.

5th May (Sunday).

Held Divine service; passed through several drifts of seaweed at noon, in latitude 25 degrees 43 minutes 34 seconds south, longitude 112 degrees 5 minutes east, showing a southerly current of nearly two miles per hour; cloudy, with light winds from south-east and south.

6th May.

At noon sighted Cape Cuvier, bearing east twenty miles; latitude 23 degrees 52 minutes; longitude 112 degrees 53 minutes east; current of nineteen miles south in twenty-four hours.

7th May.

North-west Cape was visible at noon, bearing east three-quarters north, distant twenty-five miles; our latitude being 22 degrees south; and longitude 113 degrees 18 minutes east. The Cape appears to have an elevation of 500 or 600 feet, and to be of a sandstone formation; the soil back of the hills appearing good, and clothed at this period of the year with an abundance of grass, wattles of large growth and flooded-gum trees growing on the slopes; the character of some of the lower hills and valleys is that of a mineral district.

8th May.

Passed through many patches of drifting seaweed coming from the eastward. Light south-east winds and cloudy weather.

Latitude 20 degrees 24 minutes south; longitude 114 degrees 37 minutes east, at noon.

9th May.

Richie's Reef cannot be in the position shown on the charts, as we sailed over it, and saw no broken water. At noon found our latitude to be 19 degrees 58 minutes south; longitude 115 degrees 23 minutes east; light winds from the south-east, and a current of half a mile per hour setting to the west or north-west.

10th May.

At daylight sighted Legendre Island to the south-east, distant ten miles. Ran east-north-east till 10 a.m., with fresh breeze; tacked to south-west with wind at east; by noon it fell calm, having fetched to within ten miles of the north end of Delambre Island. At 5 p.m. a light wind from the north-west enabled us to run in and drop anchor at 6.0 in thirteen fathoms, the south end of Delambre bearing east about three miles; at 11.0 a strong breeze sprung up from the south-east, freshening to a gale by 2 a.m. of the 11th. Tide setting to south-west at four miles per hour, with a rise of sixteen feet.

STRONG TIDES PREVENT LANDING.

11th May.

The gale continued to 11 a.m., when it moderated; the tide being full at about noon. Got underweigh at 1 p.m., and stood to the south-west, under topsails, stemming a strong ebb tide to 3.30, when we came to anchor in five fathoms (sand and shells), about three miles from the western shore of the bay, Sloping Head bearing north by east five miles. The water of the bay is much discoloured, being of a deep reddish-brown. In passing down the shore we observed that the whole of what is shown on the chart as a promontory, extending to the north of Sloping Head, is an island, with a channel nearly half a mile wide, separating it from the main; to the outer portion was given the name of Dolphin Island. At 4 p.m. left the ship in the life boat, accompanied by Captain Dixon, Mr. Hall, and four men, and took soundings for six miles to the south-west down the centre of the bay, finding five and six fathoms all the way; the water then shoaled to three fathoms, when, being within a mile of the head of the bay, it became dark. Pulling about two miles to the south-east, it gradually shoaled to one foot, when we grounded, and remained there till 11 p.m., when the tide being at full we pulled for the ship, but not seeing her lights by 1 a.m. on the 12th, and the men being much fatigued, we lay on our oars for an hour, and then took a stretch for two miles to the south-south-east, to get under the shelter of the south-east shore of the bay, when, having no anchor, we lay-to till daylight, by which time the boat had drifted into heavy rollers under the high rocky land at the south-west head of the bay; the wind having risen so much that the boat was only kept afloat by keeping her head to the sea. As we could not observe any spot at which we could land without the risk of swamping the boat and wetting our firearms, we continued pulling towards the ship, the ebb tide assisting us until 2 p.m., when just as all hands were becoming thoroughly tired out, a boat was sent from the Dolphin to our relief, with a timely supply of biscuit and brandy, which, with the assistance of a tow-line, enabled us to reach the ship by 3 p.m., very thankful that we had escaped what at one time appeared likely to have proved a serious disaster.

LANDING EFFECTED.

13th May.

In the morning it blew so fresh from the eastward that Captain Dixon did not like to move the vessel until 2 p.m., when we stood to the south for about four miles, and came to anchor in four fathoms. Taking the life-boat and cutter, both well-manned, we pulled south to the shore about three miles, the water gradually shoaling until at half a mile from the shore the boats grounded on a sandbank, from which we walked, through mud, shells, and coral, to a belt of mangroves about fifty yards through, behind which rose a sandbank about thirty feet high, covered with flowers and coarse grass; from this to the foot of a range of rugged metamorphic sandstone, a distance of half a mile, was an open, undulating, loamy plain, covered with grass just arriving at maturity, a few small wattles, hakea, and white-gum trees. As the sun had now set, we had only just time to ascend a few hundred feet up the rocky ridge, from which elevation could be discerned a sheet of water about a mile to the eastward, which we attempted to reach, but it became so dark that it was found better to return to the boats, which were now high and dry. By 8 p.m. the tide had risen sufficiently to admit of Captain Dixon's return to the Dolphin, while I remained with a portion of my own party to make further examination in the morning; the leaky state of the cutter keeping one of us bailing through the night.

14th May.

With Messrs. Turner, Brown, Harding, and Brockman, landed at 7 a.m., and walked to the sheet of water observed last night, but found it only a tidal inlet, terminating in a salt marsh. Continuing on our course for five miles to the south-east, across a grassy plain, the soil being a light brown loam, with occasional patches of quartz and gneiss pebbles, and beds of limestone in irregular nodules, in an hour and a half arrived at a deep stony watercourse, containing some small pools of brackish water. This stream was followed up to the southward about a mile, but found to be dry, and did not appear to come from a greater distance than twenty miles. This river was named the Nickol. The country to the south not being very promising, we turned to the westward, recrossing the plain more to the south, passing several hollows, in which the rainwater had very recently rested, leaving a rich alluvial deposit from which had sprung up a splendid sward of grass, which was still quite green. Not meeting with water in this direction, and the party not being yet in full training, we were glad to return to the boat, which was reached by 2 p.m.; the tide being now in, enabled her to come in close to the beach, the rise being found to be about sixteen feet. By 5.0 we had returned to the ship, all tolerably well fatigued with our first day's march on shore.

INTERVIEW WITH NATIVES.

15th May.

Not being satisfied to land the horses on a shore devoid of water, I determined to attempt a landing in a small sandy cove in the high rocky shore on the west of the bay, which we had been afraid to enter during the gale on the 12th. Leaving the ship with two boats and provisions for the day, we pulled for the little cove about four miles distant, bearing west by north. For the first three miles the soundings did not show less than three fathoms, with an even sandy bottom, the last mile shoaling gradually to the beach; the landing being easily effected, as there now was but little surf. The shore was found to be generally very sandy, a low flat valley extending from the head of the cove across the isthmus about two miles to Mermaid Strait, where it terminated in a muddy mangrove creek. In about half an hour several wells were found, some containing rather brackish water, but one, about eight feet deep, in a hollow under a steep range of bare volcanic and granite hills, not more than 200 yards from the beach, was found to contain an abundant supply of good water; grass being plentiful and of fine quality in the valleys under the hills. Our principal requirements being now satisfied, it only remained to bring the ship in near enough to land the horses. On our return to the Dolphin we found that she had been visited by two natives, who had paddled off on logs of wood, shaped like canoes, not hollow, but very bouyant, about seven feet long and one foot thick, which they propelled with their hands only, their legs resting on a little rail made of small sticks driven in on each side. At first they were afraid to come on board, but on friendly signs being made, they ascended the ladder that had been put down for them. They were both fine-looking men, of about forty years of age, above the middle stature, one measuring six feet four inches, and the other five feet eight inches; their hair straight and black, teeth regular, and general features characteristic of the tribes on the west coast; their bodies were rather more spare, and had not on them a vestige of clothing. The Champion Bay dialect was quite incomprehensible to them; they, however, knew the use of both biscuit and tobacco, some of which was given them.

After remaining several hours on board, they took their departure for the eastern shore of the bay, distant at least six miles, promising by signs to repeat their visit the next day. It is worthy of remark that neither of these natives were circumcised, or had lost the front teeth, as is common on this coast further to the eastward. Their fearlessness and confidence in the good faith of Europeans would lead to the impression that this was not their first acquaintance with vessels on the coast. It was not far from this place that Captain P.P. King had a visit from natives similarly equipped more than forty years ago. While on shore to-day several new and very beautiful plants and flowers were observed, amongst them one in particular, which, without exception, is the handsomest shrub I have ever seen in Australia; in form the plant resembles a large chandelier, with a series of branches springing from a centre stem in sets of five each; on these are short erect stems a few inches apart, carrying five beautiful deep crimson dragon flowers, nearly three inches in length, grouped like lustres, producing a very gorgeous effect; the leaves of the plant are elegantly formed, like those of the mountain ash, and are of a rich green. A purple flowering bean, the seeds of which are the size of the English horse-bean, is here found in abundance, and are eaten by the natives. Melons similar to those formerly seen by me on the Gascoyne, several varieties of brachychiton, a small variety of the adansonia, three or four different kinds of convolvulus (one of which runs along the sands near the beach with arms sometimes as much as forty yards in length), acacias, sterculia, and a variety of eucalyptus resembling a stunted red-gum, are also found growing among the hills in small quantities.

ACCIDENT FROM CARELESS USE OF FIREARMS.

16th May.

Early this morning the Dolphin was moved to within three miles of the cove visited yesterday, and anchored in two and a half fathoms at the lowest water, the landing place bearing west by north. By 11.0 a.m. the first pair of horses were hoisted out and placed in the water under the counter of the cutter, two other boats assisted in towing us to the shore, which occupied about an hour; the horses, on landing, being scarcely able to stand, from the length of time they were in the water. On reaching the beach, a serious accident occurred to Mr. Hearson, the second mate of the vessel, resulting from the negligence of James the farrier, who, notwithstanding my repeated cautions to all the members of the Expedition to keep snappers on the locks of the guns, had omitted to do so, in consequence of which, on its being handed out, the hammer caught on the gunwale of the boat and discharged a ball through both the hips of the mate, causing him to fall in the water, which circumstance fortunately tended materially to stop the haemorrhage; he was immediately carried to a sheltered spot, and a tent pitched over him.

On examining the wound, I found the ball had entered the right posterior, passing close below the joint, and taking an oblique direction through the lower edge of the pelvis, made its exit in front of the left thigh, between the femoral artery and the principal tendon, without injuring either. This mishap and the freshening of the breeze prevented our landing any more horses to-day, the remainder of it being spent in making a camp and attending to the comfort of our wounded companion, who occasioned me some anxiety, as the treatment must entirely devolve upon myself, who possessed but a very limited amount of experience in matters of this nature.

17th May.

Four more horses were safely landed this morning, and we were returning to the vessel for another pair when a party of fourteen natives made their appearance at the camp. At first they came boldly up, but on a gun being discharged as a signal for my recall, they appeared much alarmed, although they would not go away. Our numbers being small, I determined not to allow them to enter the camp, on account of their propensity to thieving, and the few that could now be spared to guard the stores was insufficient to keep a constant watch on their stealthy movements; I therefore tried at first to make them understand that we had taken possession for the present, and did not want their company; they were, however, very indignant at our endeavours to drive them away, and very plainly ordered us off to the ship. It was very evident that our forbearance was mistaken for weakness, and that mischief was preparing. I accordingly took hold of one of the most refractory, and compelled him to march off at double-quick time, when they all retired to some rocky hills overlooking our camp, from which it was necessary to dislodge them. Taking Mr. Brown with me, we climbed the first hill, which made them retreat to the next. Resting ourselves for a few minutes, and taking a view of the surrounding country, we were just on the point of returning to the camp, when we observed three armed natives stealing down a ravine to the horses, evidently with hostile intentions, as they shipped their spears on getting close enough to throw; we did not, however, give them time to accomplish their object, as we ran down the hill in time to confront them, on which they took to the rocks. Seeing that it was now time to convince them we were not to be trifled with, and to put a stop at once to what I saw would otherwise terminate in bloodshed, we both took deliberate aim and fired a couple of bullets so close to the principal offender, that he could hardly escape feeling the effects of the fragments of lead, as they split upon the rocks within a few feet of his body. After dark, it set in to rain heavily for an hour, when lights were observed moving in the direction of our horses, but the sentries being on the alert, no further attempt was made to molest us.

18th May.

Two more horses were landed this morning; but rain setting in from the north-west with a strong easterly wind below, a stop was put to landing any more to-day.

19th May (Sunday).

It had rained both heavily and continuously during the night; but as our tents were good, we did not experience much inconvenience from it, and it gave a fair prospect of finding a good supply of water on our contemplated trip into the interior. Mr. Hearson's wound was progressing favourably, and I was in consequence enabled to go off to the ship and procure a few additional comforts. On our return two more horses were brought ashore, reducing the number on board to one-half.

20th May.

We succeeded in landing six more horses during the day; the great distance they had to be swam ashore made the process very slow and fatiguing, some of the horses being scarcely able to stand for some time after landing. This morning I made a rough survey of the cove and surrounding hills, and while so employed observed seventeen natives pass across the shoals at low water, carrying nets but no weapons; they did not appear to fear us, or inclined to come up to the camp; nor did we offer them any encouragement, as in the present exposed state of our camp they would have been very troublesome.

In the evening Mr. Brown and myself rode across the isthmus to Mermaid Strait, and found it to form a very fine and romantic-looking little harbour, surrounded by a bold rocky coast, giving it much more the appearance of an inland lake than an open strait. I have no doubt but that it would afford an excellent harbour; there is, however, reason to think it is equally difficult of access from the main with the cove upon which our camp is, as a wide expanse of marsh land appears to extend all round behind the hills that bound it to the southward.

21st May.

The last four horses were landed this morning, as also the instruments and remainder of the stores required for our first journey. The farrier, with two assistants, was kept busily employed all day shoeing horses.

PREPARATIONS FOR JOURNEY INLAND.

22nd May.

The forge was in full employ during the day, and great progress made with the shoeing and preparations for our departure. Accompanied by Mr.

Brown, I rode out to-day to reconnoitre, and seek for a pass through the hills that encompassed our camp; the only practical outlet we found to be through some very rocky ravines to the south-west, where at about five miles we found--what I had for some time suspected to be the case--that the whole of the isthmus upon which we had landed was cut off from the mainland by an extensive salt-water marsh, commencing at the bottom of Nickol Bay and running parallel to the general line of coast, at least as far as Enderby Island. Skirting the northern edge of the marsh for several miles to the westward, we found it gradually getting wider and deeper; we accordingly returned to the narrowest part, and rode into it for about half a mile, the water being very shallow, and the bottom sufficiently firm to carry us, although with considerable labour to the horses. Finding it was getting late, we determined to try and return to the camp round by the head of Nickol Bay, and succeeded in climbing over the rocks and boulders that encumber this portion of the coast, until we were within a quarter of a mile of the camp, when the tide came in upon us so quickly that, after having been repeatedly thrown down by the surf, we were compelled to leave the horses jammed up in the rocks just above high-water mark, and proceeded on foot to the camp.

23rd May.

At 3.0 a.m., the tide having fallen sufficiently, Messrs. Brown and Harding were enabled to bring in the horses left imprisoned last night. During the day, all the arrangements for our departure were completed, and in the afternoon Mr. Hearson was removed to the Dolphin, having been kept on shore since the accident, to be constantly under my own attendance; he was now rapidly recovering, although much reduced. Wrote instructions for the guidance of Captain Dixon and Mr. Walcott during the absence of the expedition, the latter gentleman being left in charge of the stores, and to make such observations as the means at his disposal should admit of.

24th May.

Landed at daylight, intending to make a start, as it was the Queen's birthday; but owing to some of the horses having rambled, we did not succeed in getting them all in and saddled up before 2.0 p.m., when three or four of the horses that had not been accustomed to carrying packs commenced playing up and scattering their loads in all directions, straining and otherwise injuring several of the pack-saddles, which detained us until so late in the day that I deemed it best to return to camp, and as the forge had not been removed to the ship, to shorten some of the saddle-irons, to render them less liable to injury, which was otherwise a great improvement.

25th May.

The re-adjustments having been satisfactorily accomplished, we made a fair start this morning by 9.0 a.m., and arrived on the edge of the marsh by 11.30, where, having first taken a survey of the several channels from the summit of a high granite hill, we entered the waste of mud at a point where it did not appear to be more than two miles wide; an hour's struggle carried us fairly through on to terra firma, only one horse having to be assisted by the removal of his load. After resting an hour and a half for dinner, we resumed our route in a south direction, across an extensive low grassy plain of red clayey loam, passing over a few rocky ridges at sunset, and at 6 p.m. encamped on a dry creek twenty yards wide, water being found in some clay-pans in the adjoining plain. Camp 2.

MAITLAND RIVER.

26th May.

Being Sunday, the camp was only moved a mile further to a fine pool of water in a river eighty yards wide, with beautiful grassy banks, which I named the Maitland; it comes from the south-east, and may probably have a course of sixty miles, coming through a plain five or six miles wide, the greater part of which is occasionally inundated by floods from the interior. Cockatoos and other game were plentiful, sixteen of the former being killed by Mr. Brockman at one shot; they were white, with orange-tinted feathers in the crest, similar to those on the Murchison and Gascoyne Rivers. It may be as well here to observe that upon first starting a regular routine of duty had been established in the party, the care and loading of five horses being told off to each two of the party, as they could lift on opposite packs simultaneously, and their being all numbered, everyone could at once know the loads under his charge. The night was also divided into eight watches, commencing at 8 p.m. and ending at 6 a.m.; the duty of the first watch being to cook the bread for the following day, and the last to have breakfast ready in the morning by the time it was light enough to see. By this arrangement no time was lost, and everyone knew what was under his particular charge. Camp 3.

SUDDEN FLOOD.

27th May.

Having determined in the first instance to strike to the westward, with a view to cutting any large rivers coming from the interior that might serve to lead us through the rocky hills that hemmed us in in that quarter, we this morning took a south-south-west by south course to 11.40 a.m. when we crossed a dry stream-bed sixty yards wide, coming out of the granite ranges to the southward, the country becoming more barren as we edged upon the spurs of the rocky hills. At 2.0 p.m. we halted on the banks of another stream-bed of the same size as the last, when it came on to rain; resuming our march at 4.10, steering west to 6.0, when we encamped on a dry gully, with a little feed near it. Having pitched the tents, it continued to rain until 11.0 p.m., when a sudden rush of water swept down the valley, filling the watercourse and carrying away our fire, and before we had time to remove the baggage to higher ground, we had a foot of water in the camp. Fortunately nothing was lost or injured, and it only served as a useful lesson for the future. Camp 4.

28th May.

The early part of the day was employed drying the stores, so that we did not make a start until late. Four and a half hours' travelling over stony country, principally covered with triodia, but containing several patches of good grass, brought us to another river fifty yards wide, in which were a few pools. This stream was followed up to 5 p.m., when we left it, and halted on an open plain close to some shallow clay-pans containing rainwater; our course for the day having been about south-west eleven miles. Camp 5.

Latitude 21 degrees 7 minutes.

29th May.

By an azimuth of the sun's centre taken this morning, the magnetic variation was observed to be about 20 minutes west. Steering north 230 degrees east magnetic, soon brought us out of the hills into a plain extending as far as the eye could reach to the north-west, with a few patches of good grass upon it, but mostly covered with triodia, which was now just ripe, yielding fine heads of seed, which the horses are very fond of. At thirteen miles struck the channel of a considerable river coming from the south. As this offered us a fair prospect of working inland, and we had already attained nearly to longitude 116 degrees, or about the meridian of the mouth of the Alma, the stream was followed up for an hour, its average breadth being over 200 yards. At 4.40 encamped at a fine spring on the bank of a deep pool, under a cliff of metamorphic sandstone nearly 300 feet high; a cane, much resembling a Spanish red, growing in considerable quantities near the water. Camp 6.

Latitude 21 degrees 18 minutes; longitude 116 degrees 4 minutes.

SURPRISE A CAMP OF NATIVES.

30th May.

Soon after starting this morning, we came upon a camp of fifteen or twenty natives, on the bank of a deep reach of water, hemmed in by steep rocky hills, up which they hastily scrambled on our approach, and on reaching the summit, tried by various gestures to express their disapproval of our visit, but would not hold any parley with us. At five miles the river turned abruptly to the north-east, through a precipitous rocky defile, which induced us to make an attempt to cut across and strike the river some miles higher up; but after being for some time involved in impracticable ravines, we were again obliged to have recourse to the bed of the river, although encumbered with beds of large stones, over which the horses had great difficulty in travelling; so that by sunset we had not accomplished more than six miles in a direct east by south line from last night's camp. Camp 7.

Latitude 21 degrees 19 minutes 29 seconds.

31st May.

The general course of the river during the day was very little to the south of east, its banks still maintaining the same rocky and precipitous character, marks of inundation being frequently observed at the height of thirty feet above the present stream, which now was only running gently in a channel not more than thirty yards wide, but when in flood occupying the whole of the valley, which averages a quarter of a mile in width. The larger pools are lined with flags and reeds, and contain numbers of small fish resembling trout, similar to those found in the Lyons and Gascoyne Rivers. A very handsome tree, resembling an ash, grew on the margin, bearing a beautiful white flower, four to five inches across, having on the inside a delicate tinge of yellow, and yielding a sweet scent like violets. Several natives were met in the course of the day, but would not come near us; in one instance, however, we came upon one so suddenly that he had only time to jump into a pool to escape being surrounded by the party. After calling for some time most lustily for his friends, he gradually crept away amongst the canes and disappeared. Only one tributary of any size was observed to join the river in the course of the day's march, and that came in from the southward. At 5.20 p.m. halted on the banks of a deep pool, surrounded by fine cajeput-trees and flooded-gum, grass being plentiful for our horses. Camp 8.

ENCOUNTER DIFFICULT COUNTRY.

1st June.

There was a decided improvement in the appearance of the valley as we continued to ascend the river, the deep pools were more continuous, and grass more abundant; the high lands on either bank still, however, retained their rugged outlines, and were clothed with little else but triodia. Travelling along the bed of the river was nevertheless difficult and dangerous for the horses, on account of the immense quantity of rounded boulders of water-worn rocks that occupied a large portion of the channel, and frequently jammed the horses into narrow passes, where they could not be extricated without meeting with very severe falls, which very soon crippled more than one of them; their shoes also began to be wrenched off by being caught in the deep clefts of the rocks, very soon expending all the extra sets brought with us. Just before coming to our night's halt a large stream-bed, forty yards wide, was observed to come in from the southward. Camp 9.

Latitude 21 degrees 28 minutes 18 seconds; longitude 116 degrees 31 minutes by account.

2nd June (Sunday).

Having abundance of feed and water, we gladly availed ourselves of it to make it a day of rest; it also afforded me an opportunity to ascertain the rate of the chronometer, which, as I had reason to expect, had gone very irregularly since landing.

3rd June.

Made an early start, and as the valley of the river was not quite so rugged as that we had passed over during the last two or three days, by noon we had accomplished about eight miles, the course of the river still being very little from the southward of east; we had not, therefore, made much progress towards the Lyons River (our more immediate destination), and to quit the valley was out of the question, as there is no feed or water out of it within a reasonable distance. Both the valley and surrounding country are destitute of trees, and bold hills of metamorphic sandstone frequently jut out into the valley, and terminate in perpendicular cliffs 200 or 300 feet high. Towards the evening the river had been coming from the northward of east. Camp 10.

Latitude 21 degrees 27 minutes 48 seconds.

4th June.

During the forenoon the river became much hemmed in by steep rocky hills, the bed being a succession of rapids, over a bare, rocky channel; but after the noon halt the stream came more from the south-east, with wide grassy flats on either side, in many parts very boggy, and producing Melaleuca leucodendron, with tall, straight stems, and a variety of eucalyptus, resembling Eucalyptus piperita. White sandstone and shales began to make their appearance on the banks, and the water in the river had a saline taste. Several of the horses began to show signs of being much distressed, by falling and sticking fast in the mud, from which they had not strength to extricate themselves, even after being relieved of their loads. Ducks were plentiful, and tolerably tame. Camp 11.

Latitude 21 degrees 33 minutes 55 seconds; longitude 117 degrees 2 minutes by account.

SANDSTONE CLIFFS.

5th June.

Having marked a large double-stemmed gum-tree with NAE and the date, we made a start up the river, but at about a mile found the valley narrow in until the channel of the river, which was here full of water, was walled in on both banks by perpendicular cliffs, from which we were compelled to turn back nearly to our last night's camp. During the last two days we had caught an occasional glimpse of an elevated range of hills extending for many miles parallel to the river and about ten miles to the southward, which rendered it probable that some change would now be found in the character of the back country, enabling us to travel without being so frequently retarded by the rocks and bends of the river. A suitable spot was accordingly selected for ascending out of the valley, which was accomplished with some difficulty, when the country was observed to be intersected for many miles by deep ravines, terminating, however, to the south in a level plain, extending to the base of the range already referred to. After four hours' heavy toiling, we at length reached the summit of the plain, water having been found in one of the rocky gullies by the way. For the first half-mile, on entering the plain or tableland, the ground was stony and covered with stunted acacia, but it very quickly changed into a rich clayey loam, yielding a splendid crop of kangaroo and other grasses, melons, and small white convolvulus, yielding a round black seed the size of a pea, which we found scattered over nearly the whole surface of the plain for miles together. In the lower parts of the flat rainwater appeared to have remained in shallow clay-pans until very recently, killing much of the grass, which was replaced by atriplex bushes. As we approached the foot of the range the ground became stony and covered with triodia; good grass was still, however, to be found in the ravines leading out of the hills, and as our object was now to shape a course to the southward, we followed up one of the most promising valleys, in the hope that it might lead us through the range; we were, however, disappointed in finding that, after pushing some distance up very steep and rocky passes, they all terminated in cliffs of horizontal sandstone, running in parallel bands one above another to the height of 500 or 600 feet, and frequently extending without a break for ten or fifteen miles along the face of the range. The horses being much fatigued by the climb from the valley of the river, we encamped at 3.10 p.m., within the hills, and without water. Camp 12.

FINE GRASSY PLAIN. FORTESCUE RIVER.

6th June.

A light drizzling rain came on early in the morning, but not enough to supply the horses, who rambled so far during the night in search of it that it was noon before they were all collected. Quitting the range, which had been named after one of the most liberal promoters of the expedition, Hamersley Range, we took a north-east course, crossing over twelve or fourteen miles of beautiful open grassy plain, in many parts the kangaroo-grass reaching above the horses' backs; the soil being of the richest clay-loam, occasionally containing beds of singular fragments of opaline rocks, resembling ancient lava. By 5.30 p.m. we reached the river again, several miles above the deep glen that had checked our course on the 5th. The valley having again opened out, gave us easy access to its banks, which were here a rich black peat soil, containing numerous springs. Here was first observed a very handsome fan-palm, growing in topes, some of them attaining to the height of forty feet and twenty inches diameter, the leaves measuring eight to ten feet in length. The river had again opened into deep reaches of water, and contained abundance of fish resembling cobblers, weighing four and five pounds each. The whole character of the country was evidently changing for the better; and as I have no doubt that at no distant period it will become a rich and thriving settlement, I named the river the Fortescue, after the Under Secretary of State for the Colonies, under whose auspices the expedition took its origin, and the large expanse of fertile plain that lies between the river and the Hamersley Range, Chichester Downs.

7th June.

A quarter of a mile up the river brought us to a fine tributary from the south, running strong enough to supply a large mill. This had to be traced up for two miles before we could find a ford; it was found to take its rise in several deep pools, fed by springs issuing out of the plains crossed yesterday. Some powerful springs were also observed to flow into the river from the northward, through a dense forest of melaleuca, with a rank undergrowth of canes, flags, etc. At five miles the river again presented a wide reach of water several miles in length, after which it all at once broke up into numerous channels, wandering through a forest of white-gum, well grassed, the soil being highly fertile. Owing to my having been accidentally trodden upon by one of the horses, we were obliged to encamp early, having only made about twelve miles. Camp 14.

Latitude 21 degrees 40 minutes 42 seconds; longitude by account 117 degrees 17 minutes east.

8th June.

Following up the channel upon which we had encamped, in about an hour it was lost in open grassy plains, which we continued to traverse until noon, when we struck on a well-defined stream-bed, which had branched off a mile or two south of last night's camp. Grass and water being abundant, we halted till 2, when we resumed an easterly route to 5.30, over rather stony plains, yielding triodia. Encamped after dark without water or feed, tying the horses up short to prevent their rambling, having accomplished about twenty miles in an east-south-east direction during the day. Camp 12.

Latitude 21 degrees 49 minutes 40 seconds.

9th June (Sunday).

Less than a mile this morning brought us to a grassy channel containing water, which was followed up for a short distance, when we halted for the remainder of the day to refresh our tired and famished horses. Camp 16.

A NATIVE CHILD.

10th June.

The channel of the river was still followed for several miles to the eastward, when it again disappeared in open plains extending to the base of the Hamersley Range, which still continued to run parallel to the river at about seven miles distance to the southward. Pools of water were occasionally found in channels scooped out of the alluvial soil of which the plains were composed--the waters of the Fortescue, during the period of the summer rains, spreading over the country for miles and leaving a rich deposit of alluvial mud, adding greatly to its fertility. In the course of the afternoon we came suddenly on a party of natives, digging roots. One woman, with a child of about five years of age, hid close to our line of march, and did not move until she was afraid of being run over by the pack-horses, when she ran away, leaving the child gazing upon the monster intruders with a look of passive wonder. It was a poor, ill-conditioned-looking object, suffering from a cutaneous disorder. On giving it a piece of damper, it quickly began to devour it, tearing it to fragments with its sharp and attenuated fingers, with all the keenness of a hawk. We left it standing with a lump of bread in each hand, where its mother would no doubt find it when she came to see what had been left of it by the large dogs, as the aborigines of this part of Australia call our horses. Travelling on till late, we encamped in an open grassy plain, without water. Camp 17.

Latitude 21 degrees 55 minutes 57 seconds; longitude 118 degrees 3 minutes.

ROCKY RANGES.

11th June.

Four miles to the south-east we came upon a pool of brackish water, surrounded with bulrushes, in a channel coming from the south of the Hamersley Range, again apparently offering us a chance of getting to the southward. We accordingly struck for the gorge out of which this stream came, and succeeded in penetrating for three miles up a very rocky gully, filled with some of the harshest triodia we had yet encountered, and had to halt for the night in a narrow pass, where there was scarcely room to tie up our horses. Camp 18.

Latitude 22 degrees 12 minutes 52 seconds.

ASCEND THE RANGES.

12th June.

One of the horses having slipped his halter during the night, Messrs. Brown and Brockman returned down the gully to track it up, while we made an attempt to follow up the deep defile in which we were hemmed, but a quarter of a mile brought us to an impassable barrier of cliffs. Retracing our steps about a mile, we again made an attempt more to the eastward, and this time succeeded in reaching a considerable stream-bed, which ultimately proved to be the main channel of the Fortescue, and led us through the range. Resting till noon, Messrs. Brown and Brockman overtook us with the missing horse, when we resumed our route up the bed of the river to the southward, until again brought to a dead stand by the whole bed of the stream being occupied by deep pools of water, fed by numerous strong springs. As it was getting late in the day, I left the party to form a camp, while I climbed the hills to get a view of the country in advance. A laborious ascent of nearly an hour brought me to one of the highest summits of the range, at an elevation of about 2700 feet above the sea, and 700 above the bed of the river. From this hill I had a fine view to the southward, and observed that by following up a small dry ravine to the south-east there would be a fair prospect of reaching a large extent of open level plain that came within two or three miles of the camp in that direction. To the east and south-east the range was lofty and mountainous, while to the south and south-west stretched open grassy plains, occasionally interrupted by bold detached hills, apparently of the same formation as the Hamersley Range. On descending to the camp, I started a fragment of rock of a few tons weight, which rushed with fearful velocity towards the deep gorge in which the horses were feeding. After carrying all before it for a quarter of a mile, it made a clear spring over a cliff 200 feet in depth, and plunged into the waters below with a sound like thunder, inducing a belief at the camp that a large portion of cliff had fallen. Fortunately it did not produce an estampede, which I had known to have been caused on another occasion by a similar occurrence. Camp 19.

Latitude 22 degrees 15 minutes; longitude 118 degrees 4 minutes 30 seconds.

13th June.

Availing ourselves of the observations made yesterday, we succeeded, after a hard scramble of two hours, in getting through the remaining portion of the range, our horses having learned to climb like goats, or they never would have accomplished the passage. The plain appears to have a considerable elevation above those to the northward, and is drained by several deep breaks through the Hamersley Range. Resuming a south-south-west course to latitude 22 degrees 26 minutes 32 seconds, we passed at first over some very stony land, yielding little else besides triodia and stunted acacia; but for the last six or seven miles was a rich alluvial clay, covered with very fair pasture, and water was found in abundance in pools in the bed of a watercourse coming from the south-east. Camp 20.

Latitude 22 degrees 26 minutes 58 seconds.

14th June.

On our first landing at Nickol Bay the nights had been very mild, but we now began to feel them cold and bracing. This was partly owing to the increased elevation of the country we were now travelling over; the south-east wind coming off the mountainous country was very keen, and almost frosty early in the morning. Our course this day was at first over tolerably good country, which gradually became more and more rocky, the ridges increasing in elevation until the aneroid barometer fell to 27.33, giving an altitude of 2400 feet above the sea. Night overtook us in a deep rocky ravine, where we had much difficulty in keeping the pack-horses together, and were at last compelled to unload them amongst rocks in the bed of a dry watercourse trending to the westward; a little grass being procurable in the vicinity. Fortunately water had been met with at noon, so that we were not pressed for want of it. Camp 21.

Latitude 22 degrees 41 minutes 43 seconds.

15th June.

Following the gully upon which we had encamped, it led us to the westward, over a rocky line of country, until 1 p.m., when not meeting with any water, and the horses showing great weakness and symptoms of distress from the loss of their shoes, it was found desirable to quit the main gully and try and find feed and water up a promising tributary coming from the north with the view of ultimately falling back on the plains under the Hamersley Range, should we fail to meet with water sooner; fortunately, however, in an hour we came upon a small supply amongst rocks, surrounded by some tolerable feed. Had we failed to find this timely relief, it is probable that not more than half the horses would have been able to carry their loads to the nearest known waterhole. Camp 22.

16th June (Sunday).

This day of rest was alike acceptable to man and horse, and afforded me an opportunity, after reading prayers to the party, to clear a set of lunar distances, by which I found that the chronometer would have placed us forty miles to the west of our true position. I had long since observed that it could not be trusted under even ordinary variations of temperature, but could procure no other, the Acting Surveyor-General having declined to supply me with either of the two chronometers belonging to his department that could be relied on, and in consequence I now found I should be compelled to have recourse entirely to lunar observations and triangulation for the compilation of the maps, which would add very much to the amount of labour and liability to error. Several crested pigeons, white cockatoos, and crested quail or partridges, were shot as they came to drink at the waterhole.

METAMORPHIC ROCKS.

17th June.

The horses had so far recovered after the day's rest that we were enabled to resume a south-west course, following down the bed of the stream to latitude 22 degrees 51 minutes, the country slightly improving towards evening; but we again had to encamp without water, having, however, obtained a small quantity in some gravel at noon. The hills to the east of our track rose about 1000 feet above the bed of the watercourse, and consisted of metamorphic sandstones and shales, intersected by whinstone dykes, their summits being capped with red conglomerate. In one place the river had cut through a ridge of altered rocks, and exhibited a very singular contortion of the strata, the laminae being crippled up into an arch of 100 feet high, showing a dip on each flank of 45 degrees, forming a cave beneath running for some distance into the hill. Camp 23.

18th June.

Continuing to follow the stream-bed south-west for eight or nine miles, we came upon a patch of very green grass, on which we halted, to allow the horses the benefit, on account of their not having had any water since noon yesterday. In the meanwhile, accompanied by Mr. Brown, I started off and walked to a prominent hill six miles to the south, to get a view of the surrounding country. From the summit of this hill, which we found to have an elevation of 700 or 800 feet, we procured a valuable round of bearings, and had a distant view of the country to the southward. Level plains and detached ranges of moderate elevation appeared to be the general character of the country towards the Lyons River. We returned to the party by 3.0 p.m., and were glad to find that during our absence water had been found in shallow clay-pans a mile to the westward, to which we moved over and encamped. Camp 24.

Latitude 22 degrees 56 minutes 23 seconds; longitude by account 117 degrees 21 minutes.

19th June.

We were unable to proceed this day, owing to my having eaten some of the dwarf mesembryanthemum, which I had formerly observed to be used as food by the natives on the Gascoyne, but which had produced with me violent headache and vomiting. The horses were, however, enjoying excellent feed; and I contrived to work up my map and clear a lunar.

20th June.

Started at 7.25 a.m. with nineteen horses, having been obliged to leave behind a horse belonging to Mr. Lennard, so lame that he could not move. Following the stream-bed nearly west for ten miles, came upon a pool of permanent water containing flags--the first we had met with since quitting the Hamersley Range. This was of great value, as there was no water that could be depended upon on our return, in the last sixty miles. Pushing on quickly for twelve miles further, the river entered a wide plain, in which was some tolerable feed; we had again, however, to halt for the night without water.

DEPOT CAMP ON THE HARDEY RIVER.

21st June.

Although the size of the channel of the river we had been following down for the last sixty miles had considerably increased both in width and depth, yet very little water had been found in it, and as it took a decided turn in its course this morning to north-west, after two hours' ride, without observing any change, and there being every appearance of its keeping the same course for the next twenty miles, I was convinced that it could not be a tributary to either the Edmund or Lyons, which I had at first hoped it might prove. The barometer also ranged too high for it to be at a sufficient elevation to admit of it flowing into either of those rivers, as the elevation of the Lyons at the confluence of the Alma is at least of the same altitude above the sea. Having named the river the Hardey, we fell back upon the pools passed yesterday, where I had decided upon forming a depot camp at which to rest the weakest horses, while with a lightly equipped party I proposed to complete the expedition of the country intervening between this and the Lyons River. Camp 26.

Latitude 22 degrees 58 minutes 28 seconds; longitude 117 degrees 10 minutes.

22nd June.

In accordance with the plan decided upon yesterday, I started this day accompanied by Messrs. Brown, Harding, and Brockman, with three pack-horses, conveying eight days' provisions and fourteen gallons of water. Twelve miles on the south-south-west course, over a very stony country, brought us to a deep stream-bed trending in the same direction, which we pursued for thirteen miles, the country gradually improving until the channel was lost in an open plain of rich soil, covered with fine green grass. Several pools of rainwater of a deep red colour, but fresh and sweet, gave us a good camp for the night; a set of Stellar observations giving the latitude 23 degrees 19 minutes 16 seconds. To the south, at about six miles distance, lay a bold range of hills, running nearly east and west with many sharp summits, having an average elevation of from 600 to 1000 feet above the plain, and extending for twelve or fifteen miles to the eastward, while to the west it was lost in numerous broken hills of lesser elevation. Camp 27.

ASHBURTON RIVER. CAPRICORN RANGE.

23rd June.

As to pass the eastern end of the range appeared likely to take us too much off our course, we struck for what appeared to be a break in the hills about seven miles to the south-west. The first five miles was across an open grassy plain, at times subject to inundation, which brought us to the bank of a fine river, containing permanent reaches of fresh water, lined with canes, the channel generally being from 100 to 200 yards wide, with a depth of forty feet; it was now barely running, but it was quite evident that it was too large for either the Alma or Edmund, and its bed must be at least 200 feet below the level of those rivers. We, however, determined to follow it so long as it ran to the south of west, which it did until it came in contact with the range observed yesterday, when it altered its course to west-north-west, and appeared to continue that direction for many miles, probably until joined by the Hardey, when, in all likelihood, it continues its course direct to Exmouth Gulf. Anxious, as I naturally was, to continue the examination of this promising river, time and the condition of our horses' feet did not permit us to do so with advantage. Naming it the Ashburton, after the noble President of the Royal Geographical Society, we quitted its verdant banks, and took a south course up a stony ravine, which led us into the heart of the range, where we soon became involved amongst steep rocky ridges of sharp slaty schist, which very quickly deprived the horses of many of their remaining shoes, and retarded our progress so much that by nightfall we found ourselves to be in only latitude 23 degrees 28 minutes 15 seconds, hemmed in on all sides by rugged country yielding little else but small acacia-trees and triodia. A little water and grass was, however, obtained in the bed of a stream tributary to the Ashburton. The summits of the hills passed over during the day had been seen from the Lyons River in 1858, and were now named the Capricorn Range. Camp 28.

24th June.

A rather rough ride of four hours to the south-east brought us to a watercourse sixty yards wide, trending to the north-north-east, in which we found pools of water lined with reeds and flags. This was traced up to the southward till 3.0 p.m., when we entered a deep gorge in a sandstone range, the bed of the stream becoming very stony and full of melaleuca-trees; it, however, contained many fine pools and strong running springs, with a small supply of grass. There was now a fair prospect of our reaching the Lyons, as the range we were now entering must contain the sources of the Edmund, which river has a much more restricted course than was originally supposed. Camp 29.

Latitude 23 degrees 42 minutes 15 seconds.

25th June.

The country continued hilly for about ten miles, when we arrived at the summit of a granite and sandstone tableland, at the extreme sources of the watercourse we had been following up. From this point we had at last the satisfaction of observing the bold outlines of Mount Augustus, bearing south-south-east about thirty miles, while more to the westward could be discerned the summits of Mounts Phillips and Samuel, and yet more to the right the southern face of the Barlee Range. Descending to the south across an open plain, we struck for a remarkable gorge in a granite range (the only one now between us and the Lyons), at which we arrived by sundown. On examining this singular gorge, it was found to be an almost perpendicular cut through a narrow ridge nearly 300 feet in depth, the length of the pass not exceeding 200 yards, the plain on each side being nearly on the same level. From the summit of this pass the course of the stream could be traced across the fertile flats of the Lyons until it was lost in the numerous channels of that river, and I was able to obtain bearings to many well-remembered objects noticed on my former visit to this part of the country. Camp 30.

Latitude 23 degrees 56 minutes 45 seconds.

RETURN TO DEPOT.

26th June.

As we had only four days' rations left, and no further object could be attained by advancing further south, unless there had been time to examine the present condition of the pasture in the vicinity of Mount Augustus, we marked several trees on the north side of the gorge close to a pool, and retraced our steps to within a mile of our camp of the 24th, having improved upon our outward track by keeping rather more to the eastward. Camp 31.

27th June.

Instead of returning by the rough route by which we came through the Capricorn Range, we followed the stream to the north-north-east, through a good country all the way to the Ashburton, which river it joined in latitude 22 degrees 26 minutes, passing through the end of the range one mile south of the junction. In this pass we encamped on a fine deep pool, in which we caught a small quantity of fish, showing the water to be permanent. Camp 32.

28th June.

Making an early start, we soon crossed the Ashburton, and rode twelve miles across open plains, thinly timbered and yielding a large quantity of good pasture, principally of kangaroo-grass, which here grew to the height of six feet. Resting for several hours at the waterholes of the 22nd, at 4.30 p.m. we resumed our route, having filled our water-kegs, and pushed on to within sixteen or seventeen miles of the depot, encamping amongst some good grass on our outward route, but without any water except what we carried with us. Camp 33.

29th June.

Giving our horses rather more than a gallon of water each, we made an early start just as it came on to rain, which was the first shower we had experienced since the 27th May; it continued until noon, but not heavy enough to leave any surface-water on the parched and thirsty loam. Keeping more to the westward than our outward track, we escaped much of the stony ground then passed over, and arrived at the depot camp by 2 p.m.

30th June (Sunday).

Remained in camp and read prayers to the party.

1st July.

The horses left at the depot were much improved by their nine days' rest, and had we been provided with more shoes for them, I should have at once returned to the Ashburton, and traced that river up to the eastward, as it offered a fine opportunity of penetrating to the south-east probably at least another 100 miles; and our provisions on a reduced allowance would admit of our remaining out forty days longer; but the lameness of many of the horses and lacerated condition of their fetlocks convinced me that, should we meet with any more difficulties or rough country before obtaining a fresh supply of shoes, much valuable time would be lost, and we should probably fail to get many of the horses back. I therefore deemed it more prudent to return at once by a shorter route more to the eastward so soon as we had repassed the Hamersley Range, and, obtaining a refit at the bay, to throw all our remaining time into the second trip. We accordingly to-day returned to camp 24, where we found the horses left there on the 20th June sufficiently recovered to accompany the party, although incapable of carrying a load. The remainder of the day was devoted to obtaining bearings and adding to the triangulation of the many remarkable summits visible from this part of the country.

2nd July.

The country generally being very rough, except on the banks of the Hardey, on our outward track, we found it desirable to return along it, more particularly as there was a better prospect of procuring water by so doing. At about twenty miles we found a little water under a cliff in the bed of the stream, and halted for the night. Camp 34.

Latitude 22 degrees 32 minutes 13 seconds.

MOUNT BRUCE.

3rd July.

Still returning on our old track, at five miles I stopped to ascend a very remarkable hill which had formed an important point in the triangulation of this part of the country, to which had been given the name of Mount Samson. Sending the party onward to wait for me at camp 22, I commenced the ascent of the mount, which proved something more than I had calculated upon, as it occupied more than an hour's sharp toil to arrive at its summit; when gained, however, it amply repaid the trouble, as from it I could discern almost every prominent hill or peak within sixty or seventy miles, and amongst them the mountain which on a former occasion I had procured a bearing to from Mount Augustus, at a distance of 124 geographical miles, and which I now named Mount Bruce, after the gallant commander of the troops, who has always warmly supported me in carrying out explorations. This part of the country I believe to be the most elevated in north-west Australia--Mount Samson having an altitude of not less than 1000 feet above the valley of the Hardey, while Mount Bruce and the mountainous country to the eastward rose to a considerable height above its summit, which, by comparisons from the aneroid barometer, would give not less than 4000 feet for the elevation of those ranges. Having completed my observations, I descended the hill with somewhat greater speed than it took to climb it, and was met at the foot by Messrs. Brown and Harding, who had waited for me with a horse. In less than an hour we overtook the rest of the party at Camp 22, when the additional horses at once drank up all the remaining water left in the rocks; resting, therefore, less than an hour, we moved on, taking a north course, over a very rocky but highly fertile country of trap formation, the grass just now being much dried up. At sundown we halted in an open grassy flat, on which no water could be found, although it is probable there is plenty in the vicinity, as emus and cockatoos were numerous; one of the former walked boldly up to the horses, and was fired at, but without effect. Camp 35.

OPEN GRASSY PLAINS. PASS HAMERSLEY RANGE.

4th July.

Travelling at a rapid pace on an average north-east course for upwards of twenty miles, over plains mostly of rich loam, well grassed, and extending to the southern foot of the Hamersley Range, we came upon a low range of sandstone hills, covered with acacia bushes and triodia, extending for three or four miles, when we again emerged on open plains, in which was found a deep channel, thirty yards wide, containing pools of rainwater retained in the clay. The amount of fine pasture country passed over during the day could not be less than 200,000 acres; and although we had not time to go in search for it, I have no doubt that abundance of water will be found in the deep gorges of the range skirting the plain. This tract of country is, I imagine, well suited for the growth of either cotton or sugar, as it is apparently well-irrigated during the summer months, and the soil is remarkably rich and strong, while its limits to the westward are at present unknown, and most probably continues to skirt the hills for at least thirty or forty miles. Halted at the waterholes about four miles to the west of the pass through the Hamersley Range. Camp 36.

5th July.

Two hours brought us to the head of the pass, which we entered by a ravine a little more to the northward than on our outward route, and by so doing saved a preliminary ascent of nearly 200 feet, and a similar amount of descent, making a very successful passage through the range without experiencing the same difficulties we had formerly met with, and by 3 p.m. found ourselves once more in the open grassy country that forms the Chichester Downs. At 6 p.m. encamped in an open flat without water. Camp 37.

PROCEED TOWARDS THE COAST.

6th July.

Started at 7.30 a.m., and in an hour came upon a pool of water in one of the numerous channels into which the Fortescue is here divided, and at seven miles struck the bulrush spring passed on the 11th June. From this the river was followed down for thirteen miles, through grassy clay plains, thinly timbered with white-gum. Encamped on a pool, in latitude 21 degrees 53 minutes 4 seconds, about five miles north of a very remarkable bold projection of the Hamersley Range. Camp 38.

7th July (Sunday) was kept as a day of rest.

8th July.

The horses strayed so far back on our tracks during Sunday night that by the time they were brought in it was too late to make a start with advantage, as we were now about to enter a new tract of country, by striking for the coast somewhere between Breaker Inlet and Depuch Island. As a knowledge of this part of the country would greatly assist us in starting on the second division of our exploration, I availed myself of the delay here to fix by triangulation many of the summits and prominent spurs of the Hamersley Range, and take observations for the variation of the needle, which I found to be about 1 degree east by the prismatic compass I had in use.

9th July.

Our horses again gave us some trouble to find them, so that we did not start until 10.30 a.m. Two hours' sharp travelling across the plain brought us to the foot of low hills of trap and sandstone, covered with triodia; good feed being, however, plentiful in the valleys, although now rather dry. Tracing up a small tributary to the Fortescue, at sunset we halted on a small rocky pool near its source, in latitude 21 degrees 41 minutes 40 seconds. Several pools, supplied by springs coming from under the superstratum of sandstone, were passed during the day. Camp 39.

Longitude 117 degrees 47 minutes.

10th July.

For seven miles the country continued gently to ascend, the sandstone giving place to trap boulders, yielding a very rich soil, clothed with short green grass and melons, the soil being too stony for agricultural purposes, although I have seen country of a similar appearance in the island of Mauritius producing fine crops of sugar. Some of the melons weighed as much as five or six ounces, and were passably good eating, although rather bitter. At noon the country dropped suddenly to the northward, and we descended a deep rocky ravine, in which we soon found water and grass. Travelling now became difficult and sometimes dangerous to the horses; rugged and semi-columnar metamorphic sandstone cliffs hemmed in the ravines on either side, while large rounded boulders of trap-rock filled the bed of the stream, which in several places was running. We had a rather indifferent camp in latitude 21 degrees 29 minutes 10 seconds, the camp at Nickol Bay bearing west-north-west, distant seventy-five miles by account. Camp 40.

SHERLOCK RIVER.

11th July.

The stream we were upon continued to take a northerly course for eight or ten miles down a valley from 200 to 300 feet in depth, where it is diverted to the eastward for about the same distance by a cross range of black volcanic hills of loose ragged rocks, totally devoid of vegetation. The channel receiving several tributaries, here becomes a succession of fine open pools of water from eighty to 150 yards in width. We halted for the night on a wide bed of bare sand and rocks, the only feed being in the channel of the river, to which was now given the name of Sherlock. Camp 41.

12th July.

This morning the river resumed a north-north-west course, and very soon led us into an open plain, rather sandy in character, the channel dividing into several branches separating miles apart, the stream of water issuing from the hills soon being absorbed in the sandy bed; but a well-defined line of verdant trees served well to mark the course of the channels through the plain for many miles. Selecting the one that appeared the most promising, it was traced down to latitude 21 degrees 6 minutes 43 seconds, where we encamped on a shallow pool of brackish water--the only one seen during the day. Several natives were found here, employed capturing partridges by means of nets constructed out of the leaf of the triodia neatly twisted and netted in the same way as done by ourselves, the mesh varying from one to five inches, according to the purpose to which it is applied. It was very singular to observe the mode in which they induced the birds to enter the nets, or rather cages, prepared for them. In the first instance they place ragged bushes all round the small pools, with the exception of a few spaces five or six feet wide, from which openings they stick in a double row of twigs, arching so as to meet overhead in the centre one or two feet from the ground; these little avenues lead away for several yards, and then terminate with a net thrown over a few light sticks at the end. The birds first alight on the margin of the pool, but after drinking, do not take flight at once, but run up the only opening, which leads them first under the arch of twigs and finally into the net, which is then drawn to by the hunter lying in wait under a few bushes. In this way they must capture a large amount of game, judging by the quantity of feathers around some of the waterholes. Camp 42.

13th July.

Two miles north the river turned west, and kept that course for seven or eight miles, through a poor sandy and stony tract of country, and was then joined by a fine channel coming from the south. Near the junction are two reaches of water, half a mile long each and a rifle-shot across, containing a quantity of ducks and other water-fowl, amongst which our sportsmen were very successful, along with other game bagging the only two swans we had seen since landing; a number of fine fish, like cobblers, were also caught, weighing from 1 to 5 pounds a-piece. As it was Saturday, and our horses were showing unmistakable signs of knocking up, we halted for the rest of the day. Camp 43.

Latitude 21 degrees 6 minutes 5 seconds; longitude 117 degrees 32 minutes 30 seconds.

VOLCANIC HILLS.

14th July (Sunday).

After reading prayers, Messrs. Brown, Harding, and myself walked to the summit of the range of black volcanic hills that skirted the western bank of the river at about a mile distant. These hills consist of ragged scoria, elevated 300 to 400 feet above the plain, and are nearly destitute of vegetation. At their summits are deep fissures, the heat of the eruptive rocks from beneath having been sufficient to convert the trap and sandstone rocks into a deep bluish-grey scoria, having a specific gravity of nearly four; but we did not observe any instance of the actual overflow of lava, and consequently there was a want of the fertilising properties in the soil resulting from it that usually accompanies volcanic formations. A native dog had left a litter of pups under a heap of stones not eighteen inches beneath our feet, but such was the sharpness and ponderability of the fragments of rock that it fairly baffled our attempts to unhouse them. A valuable round of bearings was procured from this spot, Depuch Island being seen bearing north 14 degrees east, distant about twenty-eight miles.

EXTENSIVE GRASSY PLAINS.

15th July.

We resumed our course down the Sherlock, the stony nature of the country telling severely upon our horses' feet, who in other respects were in very tolerable condition. We had not proceeded more than three or four miles when Mr. Brockman's horse, Rocket, gave in, and could not move another step, the hoof being fairly worn through; leaving him close to a pool of water amongst plenty of feed, I hoped he might possibly recover by the time we returned from the bay. Below this the channel became sandy and dry, and we only procured a little water at night in a clay-hole. Plains extended from the river to the north and eastward as far as the eye could reach, only interrupted by occasional detached hills of granite or volcanic trap, the feed being generally coarse and the soil poor. Camp 44.

Latitude 20 degrees 54 minutes 45 seconds.

NATIVES FISHING WITH NETS.

16th July.

Leaving the valley of the river on a north-west course, in half an hour we came upon an open plain of rich clayey loam, covered with a fine even sward of good grass, on which were feeding large flocks of pigeons and white cockatoos; this change in the character of the soil being ascribable to the occasional overflow of the river, leaving a deposit of rich mud. This plain extends as far as we could see to the north and east, a few widely-scattered topes of trees being the only objects breaking the monotony of the sea of grass. To the north-west was a strong line of large timber, for which we steered. At three miles we entered the wood, and found it to contain the main channel of the Sherlock, in which were a few small pools of rainwater. Crossing the bed of the river on the same course, we soon came upon another branch coming from the south-west, which was named the George. Immediately below the junction of the two streams the river opened out into reaches of brackish water, evidently under the influence of the spring tides. From this point the left bank was followed down to within three or four miles of the sea, when, the country becoming low and flat, the grass coarse, and no fresh water procurable, we quitted the Sherlock and struck to the west for six or seven miles, crossing several salt-water creeks, until we were compelled to turn to the southward to avoid a channel much larger and deeper than the rest, at which a party of natives were engaged drawing their nets, but ran away on our approach. A little further on the plain became more fertile, and we found a small pool of rainwater in the clay, at which we encamped. There is no doubt but that the Sherlock and the creek we were upon discharged their waters, by the numerous creeks shown on Captain

King's charts, fifteen or sixteen miles to the west of Depuch Island. Camp 45.

Latitude 20 degrees 52 minutes 15 seconds; longitude 117 degrees 15 minutes.

RETURN TO NICKOL BAY.

17th July.

By observation of the sun at rising, the variation of the needle was found to be 1 degree 10 minutes east. We were now about forty miles from Nickol Bay; and as it was very doubtful whether water would be procurable in that distance, I became very anxious on account of the horses, as, should the country prove stony, I was quite certain they could not perform the journey in less than three days; I therefore determined upon following up a leading valley towards the Maitland River, with the intention, in the event of not finding water or a pass through the heavy mass of hills that back Cape Lambert, of pushing through the upper branches of that river, and by a round of sixty or seventy miles to approach the bay by our outward track; fortunately, however, in the course of the day we fell in with some small pools of rainwater, which enabled us to advance about eighteen miles over tolerably even plains, well grassed, our night halt being without water. Camp 46.

18th July.

From our position, and the observations I had made of the country on the eastern shores of Nickol Bay, I was satisfied that the breadth of stony ranges lying between us and our destination did not exceed eight or ten miles, which we therefore now determined to venture upon, although at great risk to the horses, some of which now walked upon stones as they would over red-hot coals. Entering the range by a small ravine, three hours' scramble over sharp rocks brought us out on the head of a small tributary to the Nickol River, the sufferings of the horses in crossing the range being quite painful to witness; they all, however, succeeded in getting through, and as a little water was found in the bed of the stream, we were enabled to push on late, and cross the marsh at the head of the bay before it was quite dark, the departing rays of the setting sun having first favoured us with a glimpse of the Dolphin, riding at anchor on the deep-blue waters of the bay--a sight which was welcomed with no small satisfaction by the little band of weary travellers. Camp 47.

19th July.

The camp was easily aroused by the morning watch, as there was now only six miles between us and the landing-place in Hearson cove, the horses appearing to partake of the general activity; so that it was only 10.0 a.m. when we arrived on our old camping ground, which we found occupied by ten or a dozen natives, engaged mending their nets. Coming upon them suddenly, they would not stop to carry off their gear, although not half an hour before they had been employed assisting a boat's crew from the Dolphin, in loading with wood and water. A rifle-shot soon recalled the boat, which was not a mile from the shore, when we were glad to learn that Mr. Hearson was fast recovering from his wound, and that all had been going on well since our departure. From Mr. Walcott I ascertained that he had been able to establish a friendly understanding with the natives who frequented the western side of the bay, and that they had been made useful in filling up the ship's water and wood, for which service they had been rewarded by a suitable distribution of biscuit. In one instance the natives on the eastern shore of the bay had shown a hostile tendency on the occasion of a boat landing on the reef to gather shells. One of the seaman, who had wandered from the rest, was chased into the sea, and menaced with spears and clubs until he was up to his neck in water, when the boat came to his rescue, the officer in charge of her firing a shot over their heads to drive them off. Mr. Walcott had also been successful in obtaining a very useful vocabulary of native words and other interesting particulars from the aborigines, as also many botanical specimens, shells, etc.--amongst the latter some very fine pearl-oysters, from which several pearls of good colour had been obtained, but appeared to be principally valuable on account of the size and beauty of the mother-of-pearl, which averaged six inches diameter, with more than half an inch in thickness of solid shell.

PARTY REFIT FOR JOURNEY TO EASTWARD.

20th July.

The forge, stores, and other additional supplies having been landed, and the party set to work shoeing horses, repairing saddle-bags, etc., I proceeded with Mr. Walcott and Mr. Angel in the boat to make a rough survey of the coves on the western side of the bay, with a view to selecting a suitable spot from which to re-embark the horses on our return from the next trip, as it would be too late in the season by that time to venture the trip overland to Champion Bay. I found that a good anchorage existed, with three fathoms at low water, one mile off the little cove from which the ship had been watered, and is approachable at all times, except in strong east or south-east gales, when a heavy swell sets in across the bay, rendering a landing unsafe. The fresh water runs down a rocky gully at the north-west corner of the cove, at the north end of a small patch of sandy beach, and the supply appears tolerably abundant; it is, however, rather difficult of access towards the end of the dry season, as the water has then to be carried over the rocks in small baracas fifty or sixty yards to the boats, but from the setting in of the rains to the end of August it runs down strongly at high-water mark. I walked back overland to the camp with Mr. Walcott, the distance being about four miles, heading by the way another deep cove, the margin of which was lined with a broad belt of mangroves.

21st to 28th July.

Was fully taken up in shoeing horses, making spare shoes, refitting and packing stores, etc., ready for our trip to the eastward, my own time being principally taken up in roughly plotting the country already explored, so as to secure all the information obtained, in the event of any accident occurring to my field-books.

29th July.

Everything being in readiness for our departure, I gave Captain Dixon instructions to wait for us in the bay to the 10th December, and in the event of our not then returning, Mr. Walcott would land one of the ship's iron tanks, and bury in it a quantity of stores, at a spot already agreed upon; the Dolphin would then proceed to Fremantle. It blew so fresh all the morning that I could not land until 3 p.m., when we quickly saddled up and proceeded three miles to a waterhole up in the volcanic hills, as it was probable we should have a very long day's march tomorrow without water. As we had now only nineteen horses, and one of these so low in condition as not to be able to carry a load, we could only take with us eighty-seven days' rations, at the rate of one pound of flour, seven ounces of meat, and four ounces of sugar per man per diem; we were, however, well provided with ammunition, and thirty spare sets of horse-shoes, with nails sufficient for at least two removes, the horses themselves being shod at starting with extra strong shoes tipped with steel. We had now only seven saddle-horses, so that one of the party was always on foot by turns of an hour each. It had been originally intended that the Dolphin should proceed to Roebuck Bay and meet us there; but it was now so late in the season that I did not deem it prudent to run the risk of removing her to an unknown anchorage, where it was possible we might not be able to reach, and thus lay ourselves open to the probability of a very embarrassing uncertainty. The result proved we had adopted the right course. Bivouac.

DIFFICULTY IN CROSSING MUD FLATS.

30th July.

This morning we crossed the marsh with some difficulty, as all the pack-horses but three fell and stuck in the mud, until we transferred their loads to our own backs and carried them through half a mile of the softest part. The operation detained us so long that we did not make more than eighteen miles, when we found a little water left in the pool seen on the 18th. Camp 48.

31st July.

Started at 8 a.m., following our old tracks to 3.30 p.m., when we turned to the south up a stream-bed crossed on the 17th. At the gorge where it issued from the granite ranges we found a fine pool of permanent water and abundance of beautiful green grass. This stream was now named the Harding, and, as the packs were heavy, we remained here the rest of the afternoon. Camp 49.

A FERTILE PLAIN.

1st August.

Passing under the northern foot of the granite ranges on an easterly course for sixteen miles, we came upon a fine reach of open water in a branch of the creek on which we had encamped on the 16th July. This pool was a valuable discovery, as it would not only form a useful halting place on our return, but, from being in the middle of a fertile plain containing at least from 15,000 to 20,000 acres of arable land equal in quality to the Greenough Flats, the whole could, if necessary, be easily irrigated from this large natural reservoir, the highest part of the plain not being thirty feet above the water-level at the driest period of the year. This fine tract of country, in connection with the lands already seen almost adjoining on the eastern bank of the Sherlock, would in itself support a larger population than is at present contained in the whole of the colony of Western Australia. We had seen more kangaroos on these plains than on any other portion of our route; one that was shot resembled the Osphranter, and was in very good order, the fur much thicker and softer than the common kangaroo of the western coast, and of a pale mouse colour. It weighed about forty-five pounds. Camp 50.

Latitude 21 degrees 54 minutes 18 seconds.

2nd August.

Proceeding eastward over grassy plains and stony ridges, at thirteen miles we struck the Sherlock only two miles below the pool at which we had left the horse Rocket, and hoped to find him improved by the rest; but, on approaching the spot, the presence of crows and a wild dog gave indications of a different fate; we found him partly devoured within a few yards of where we left him, inflammation of the feet having most probably produced mortification. Pushing on till sunset, we arrived at our old camping ground (Camp 43) at the bend of the Sherlock. Camp 51.

ASCEND THE SHERLOCK RIVER.

3rd August.

Followed up the left bank of the Sherlock to Camp 42, and found a little water still remaining in the bird-cage pools, where we halted for two hours. At 1.30 p.m. resumed an easterly route across a sandy plain, yielding little but hakea and triodia. Five miles brought us to a large branch of the Sherlock coming from the south-east, in which were several small permanent pools, surrounded by flags, at which we halted. Camp 52.

Latitude 21 degrees 7 minutes.

4th August (Sunday).

Although the feed here was very indifferent, yet, as we had again entered unexplored country, I was glad to make it a day of rest before entering upon the rather unpromising tract of country that lay in the outward route.

5th August.

Making a rather late start, on account of the horses having strayed very far in search of feed, we steered for a bold range bearing east-south-east, distant about twenty miles. At four miles crossed a dry channel coming from the south-south-east, and continued our course over a poor tract of country, covered with triodia and a few acacia, large bare red granite rocks cropping out here and there. At one of these was a small waterhole, near which a native was hunting mice. Although at first alarmed, he soon told us, in answer to our inquiries, that we should find no water to the east, but plenty to the south, which we found to be correct, as we had to halt, after a very long day's march, in a dry ravine in the ranges for which we had been making. Camp 53.

Latitude 21 degrees 10 minutes 35 seconds.

RECONNOITRE THE COUNTRY AHEAD.

6th August.

Having reconnoitred the country for some miles ahead overnight without finding water, it was no use leading our horses further into the rugged defiles, where we might get entangled for many hours; we accordingly struck to the south-west for four miles, when we came on a rocky pool of permanent water in the south-east branch of the Sherlock, just at the point where it emerges from the hills. Having watered the horses and given them an hour's rest, we followed up the stream to the south-east for seven miles, when it divided into numerous small dry ravines in the heart of an elevated range of granite, capped with metamorphic sandstone; water having only been met with within the first mile from where we struck it. Camp 54.

7th August.

The horses requiring water, we fell back upon the pool passed yesterday, where I decided upon leaving the bulk of the party for the day or two, while I explored the country for a pass to the eastward. Camp 55.

Latitude 21 degrees 14 minutes 28 seconds.

8th August.

Taking with me Mr. Brown and Mr. Harding mounted, and one pack-horse carrying water, we struck through the hills to the eastward, and at six miles came upon a stream-bed that led us to the north-east fifteen or sixteen miles, when, finding it contained no water, we resumed an easterly course over an open sandy and stony plain, covered with triodia, for twelve miles, and encamped in poor feed without water. Camp 56.

Latitude 21 degrees 4 minutes.

THE YULE RIVER.

9th August.

A heavy dew having fallen during the night, our horses were much refreshed, and we were enabled to proceed with the scanty supply of water carried with us. In an hour we struck upon the channel of a river with a sandy bed, 300 yards wide, in which were a few pools of water, under a bold sandstone bluff, rising abruptly 300 feet from the plain. From the summit of this hill the river was observed to trend to the north-north-west for eight or ten miles, and to come upon a gap in a granite range four miles to the south-south-east, towards which we now turned our steps, across extensive beds of soft drift-sand brought down by the river. Cajeput and acacia trees occupied a large portion of the channel, and it was not until reaching the gorge in the range that grass was met with in sufficient quantities to supply our wants. Several large pools, teeming with water-fowl, occupied the whole of the valley, which here was fully a quarter of a mile wide. The remainder of the day I devoted to sketching and triangulating the country, while the horses were enjoying the benefit of the fine feed. Camp 57.

Latitude 21 degrees 6 minutes 26 seconds.

10th August.

As this river, from its magnitude, afforded a fair chance of working to the south-east, I determined to bring forward the rest of the party. Having named this river the Yule, we returned to the depot party by a somewhat shorter cut, making it in about thirty miles, which we accomplished by sundown.

11th August (Sunday).

Party resting. Observed a set of lunars, which placed us in longitude 118 degrees 3 minutes east, the rate of the chronometer being still so irregular as to be almost useless.

12th August.

To-day the whole party proceeded twenty-four miles towards the Yule, finding a small pool of water in a rocky ravine by the way which we had missed on our former trip. Bivouacked in an open grassy plain six miles short of the river.

13th August.

Moved on to our camp of the 9th, and halted there for the remainder of the day. The latitude by meridian altitude of the sun I found to be 21 degrees 6 minutes 22 seconds.

14th August.

As travelling near the river was found to be very laborious, on account of the vast beds of loose drift-sand thrown up by the summer floods, we steered to the south-south-east for a pass in the ranges about twenty miles distant, through which the river was supposed to come, but on reaching the hills, the river was observed to the westward; we accordingly altered our course to south-west, and struck it at about six miles; the character of the river being still the same, the aggregate width of the several channels amounting to nearly half a mile; water being procured in them by digging a few inches in the sand. The country passed over during the day was an open plain of light sandy loam, interspersed with bare granite rocks, cropping out at intervals of a few miles. Giant ant-hills of from ten to sixteen feet in height, and thirty to forty feet in circumference (a few of which had already been met with on our first trip), were here remarkably conspicuous, on account of their size and bright brick-red colour. An emu was shot during the day, while running at full speed, at the range of over 200 yards. Camp 58.

Latitude 21 degrees 23 minutes 23 seconds.

15th August.

One of the horses was missing this morning, so we did not start until 10 a.m., when the river was followed up to the south-east through country the same as yesterday; halting for the night in latitude 21 degrees 32 minutes 13 seconds. Camp 59.

16th August.

Our average course to-day was nearly east, occasionally crossing channels coming from the south-east. Towards evening we found that the main channel, which it had been our intention to have followed, had escaped our observation to the southward, and we were only on a comparatively small tributary coming from a rugged range of hills to the eastward. Our object for the present not being to push too far into the interior, this tributary was followed until it broke up into numerous small valleys, in one of which water was obtained by digging three feet in the sand, amongst tolerable feed, the country having much improved in the course of the day. Camp 60.

Latitude 21 degrees 34 minutes.

ROCKY RANGES.

17th August.

Soon after starting this morning we came upon a camp of natives, but we could not prevail upon any of them to stop and hold parley with us. Four hours' travelling over rather rocky ground led us well into the range, which we found to consist of granite, capped with metamorphic sandstones and broken up by dykes of variegated jasper. In a deep ravine at the foot of a cliff we found a small pool of beautiful clear spring water, which was very acceptable, as the sun had now acquired considerable power, and the grasses were beginning to get very dry food for our horses. During the halt at this spring Mr. Harding and myself ascended the highest part of the range, which was found to be 500 or 600 feet above the plain. From this elevation I was enabled to select our onward route, and obtain bearings to several useful summits for triangulation--a few hills to the south-south-east being visible at the distance of sixty or seventy miles, which no doubt form part of the continuation of the Hamersley Range. Resuming an east course, the culminating point of the range was soon passed, when we descended to the eastward down some deep and remarkably picturesque rocky glens, in which were found several springs and pools of water, leading down to a fine grassy flat, in which were growing some fine large flooded-gum trees. Camp 61.

18th August (Sunday).

Found our latitude 21 degrees 36 minutes 8 seconds; longitude 119 degrees 13 minutes east by account.

THE STRELLEY RIVER.

19th August.

The country being very hilly, it was found best to follow down the stream upon which we had encamped, although it trended to the north of east. In a few miles the valley opened out with fine pools of permanent water, covered with numerous flights of ducks, and at eight miles it joined a wide valley from the south, down which flowed a river, divided into several channels, containing many fine pools from 50 to 200 yards wide, which were still running gently from one to another. The banks, although well grassed, were very rocky, rendering travelling excessively fatiguing to our heavily-loaded pack-horses, several of them being bruised and strained while jumping from rock to rock, the clefts being too deep and narrow for them to walk between, and the ranges bordering the valley were too steep to admit of our leaving the river, which we were compelled to follow down to latitude 21 degrees 26 minutes 52 seconds. Camp 62.

20th August.

The river, which had been named the Strelley, continued to hold a northerly course; we therefore availed ourselves of a smoother valley coming in from the east to resume our old course. At nine miles we met with a stream 100 yards wide coming from the south-east, evidently tributary to the Strelley, and taking its rise in elevated granite ranges with black volcanic ridges protruding through them, but not to any considerable height above the general level of the country. After a few hours' scramble over these ridges we came upon a small stream trending east, containing several springs, surrounded by high grass and flags, gradually leading us by sunset into a deep pass, walled in by cliffs and bluffs from 100 to 300 feet high; the stream, having joined several larger ones from the southward, now occupying nearly the whole width of the valley. We encamped in one of the wildest and most romantic-looking spots to be found in this part of Australia, to which we gave the name of Glen Herring, from a fish bearing a resemblance to a herring being found in the stream. Camp 63.

Latitude 21 degrees 20 minutes 35 seconds.

THE SHAW RIVER. NORTON PLAINS.

21st August.

With some difficulty we wended our way down the intricate windings of the glen for six miles in a north-east direction, when it opened out into grassy flats, turning to the northward. Leaving it at this point, a mile east brought us to the bank of a fine open river-bed 200 yards wide, down which a little water was still flowing, the country on its banks becoming much more promising and grass plentiful. This river I named the Shaw, and some beautiful grassy plains through which it came for twenty or thirty miles to the southward Norton Plains, after the talented Secretary of the Royal Geographical Society. In the afternoon a large tributary from the south-east was followed up for some miles, when, turning to the south, we quitted it to follow an open valley leading east towards a bold granite and schistose range, under which we encamped late without finding water. Camp 64.

Latitude 21 degrees 20 minutes.

22nd August.

As we did not find water for some distance to the eastward under the foot of the hills, we turned to the south-east, quickly emerging from the hills upon the Norton Plains, and at two miles came upon the stream quitted last evening, to which the name of Emu Creek had been given. It had altered its course, and was again coming from the east, and contained several fine springs. This creek was followed up for the rest of the day through a rather indifferent country, and, towards nightfall, led us into a deep rocky ravine, in which we encamped, a small supply of water being obtained from holes in the rocks. Camp 65.

Latitude 21 degrees 28 minutes.

23rd August.

As we advanced, the ravine divided into many branches coming from an elevated tableland to the southward; we therefore again resumed an easterly course for five or six miles, over rugged hills, and descended by a gully trending north-east, which led us in a few miles into open plains. Skirting the northern foot of the range until after dark, we encamped on a small watercourse, in which we obtained water by digging under some granite rocks. Camp 66.

Latitude 21 degrees 23 minutes 30 seconds.

24th August.

The horses having suffered much amongst the rocks during the last few days, I determined to follow the southern edge of the plain until a stream could be met with to lead us to the south-east. A few miles brought us to a small watercourse running gently from some springs in the plain, which, contrary to our expectations, ran into the ranges to the south-east instead of coming out of them. As here there was plenty of green grass and water, and the horses were not looking well, we encamped early in the entrance of the gorge. Camp 67.

Latitude 21 degrees 20 minutes 13 seconds.

25th August (Sunday).

Longitude by observation 120 degrees 17 minutes; variation 30 minutes east.

26th August.

The stream we were upon led us about five miles south-east through the hills, and then joined a river coming from the southward, 100 yards wide, which was followed down on an average course of east-north-east to latitude 21 degrees 18 minutes; reeds and rank grass lining its banks in many parts, while in others granite boulders and banks of drift-sand offered considerable impediments to travelling. Camp 68.

DEGREY RIVER.

27th August.

The river took us on a northerly course nine or ten miles, receiving many large tributaries, several of them still running slightly, forming altogether a stream of some importance, which, on account of the large extent of pastoral and agricultural lands afterwards found on its banks lower down, and its many fine tributaries, I named the DeGrey, in honour of the noble lord who took a lively interest in promoting the objects of the expedition. As the object at present in view was to push to the south-east, we left this promising river and resumed an east-south-east course for five or six miles into a hilly country, and encamped in a gully with rather scanty feed, a little water being obtained by digging. Camp 69.

28th August.

We soon became involved in deep ravines, which led up into high tableland, the summit of which was no sooner attained than we had again to descend equally precipitous gullies to the eastward, the horses sliding down amongst the loose rocks and stones with a velocity that threatened immediate destruction; they all, however, arrived safe at the bottom, although in so exhausted a state that two of them had very shortly after to be left behind, while we pushed on with the rest in search of water and feed, which was not met with until late in the day. After a short rest I sent Messrs. Brown and Brockman back for the two beaten horses, while I moved the party on a mile further to a fine spring in a grassy flat, where we encamped. Camp 70.

Latitude 21 degrees 9 minutes 3 seconds.

EXTENSIVE GRASSY PLAINS.

29th August.

The two horses left yesterday were brought into camp early in the day, and as they were too weak to carry their loads, they were placed on our saddle-horses, one of the party by turns having to walk. As the season was rapidly advancing, we could not venture to incur any delay, much as the horses required rest, and accordingly resumed an east course late in the day.

At five miles came upon a sandy stream-bed fifty yards wide, trending to the north-east, beyond which the country opened out into an extensive plain of white waving grass--to the north uninterrupted by a single elevation, while to the east and south, at eight or ten miles distant, rose ranges of granite hills, capped with horizontal sandstones. It was not until some time after dark that we arrived near the opposite edge of the plain, when we came upon a river 200 yards wide, running to the northward. The long drought had reduced it to a few shallow pools, running from one to the other through the deep sand in the bed; magnificent cajeput-trees lined the banks, and grass was in abundance. Camp 71.

OAKOVER RIVER.

30th August.

We did not start till late, as Mr. Brown had to go back some little distance for his horse, which had been again left behind overnight, knocked up. As it would have been useless, in the present condition of our horses, to attempt at once to enter the ranges to the east, we determined to follow up the river for a few days to the south-south-east and by so doing secure feed and water, and give the poor animals a chance of recovering their strength; we therefore followed the river up for seven or eight miles, through fine open forest country, and encamped near a deep pool, in which were caught ten or twelve dozen of small trout, which, with cockatoos and ducks, afforded an important addition to our ration of only seven ounces of meat. This river was named the Oakover. Camp 72.

31st August.

For nearly ten miles the river continued to lead us to the eastward of south; it then divided, the main channel coming from the south-west; we, however, followed the eastern branch until quite satisfied that it contained no water, and then fell back to the westward, striking the river near some cliffs, at the foot of which water was plentiful. Although only 1 p.m., I determined to halt for the remainder of the day, as it was too late to make an attempt to enter the hills without giving the horses the advantage of some hours' feed and rest. It also afforded me leisure to make astronomical observations and work up the plans of our route. A set of lunar distances, very carefully taken, placed the camp in longitude 121 degrees 3 minutes 30 seconds east, while that by account, carried on by triangulation and dead-reckoning from the Sherlock, placed us four and a half miles more to the westward; the latitude being 21 degrees 23 minutes 43 seconds. Camp 73.

1st September (Sunday).

Read prayers.

2nd September.

A march of three hours across the plains to the eastward brought us to the foot of the range, which we entered by a tolerably easy pass, and soon came upon a pool of water in a tributary to the Oakover, the mouth of which had been passed on our ascent of that river. Here we halted for two hours, and then resumed our route through steep and rocky hills, containing numerous fine springs. It was not until 7 p.m. that we finally got through the ranges, and emerged upon open sandy plains of vast extent, no object being observable from north-north-east round to south-south-east except low ridges of red drift-sand, in many parts nearly bare of vegetation. A large party of natives were encamped upon the watercourse down which we descended to the plain. Not wishing to alarm them, we passed the waterholes from which they were supplied, and proceeded a mile farther, but had in consequence to camp without water, although amongst abundance of grass. Camp 74.

Latitude 21 degrees 21 minutes 30 seconds.

NATIVE HEAD-DRESS. ENTER THE SANDY DESERT.

3rd September.

This morning we returned to the native encampment for water, and found that they had already deserted it, leaving many of their things behind--amongst others, a very singular head-dress, shaped like a helmet. It consisted of a circular band, made of twisted grass, the size of the head, into which were stuck ten or twelve upright twigs, brought together into a point two feet high, which was woven like an open basket, with yarn made of opossum fur; the whole no doubt being considered highly ornamental by the wearers, but of not the least service as an article of protection for the head, either from the sun or in war. Having watered the horses, we entered the sand-plain, travelling between the ridges, which ran in straight lines parallel to each other at the distance of several hundred yards apart, the sand being thrown by the south-east gales into acute ridges thirty to sixty feet high, their direction being almost invariably north 109 degrees east. Travelling to 2.15 p.m., we got over about eighteen miles, the valleys yielding little else but triodia, with occasional patches of stunted gum forest, in which was found a little good grass, on which were feeding flights of pigeons and a variety of parrot new to us, but which I believe to be the golden-backed parakeet (Psephotus chrysopterygius) of Gould. As no water could be found, and many of the horses gave signs of being greatly distressed, no change being observable in the country for many miles ahead, a few very distant ranges being the only objects visible, we were obliged to have recourse to the only safe expedient of falling back and forming a depot.

Resting to 5.10, we commenced a retreat until 7.20, having been obliged to abandon a horse of Mr. Brown's, quite exhausted. Camp 75.

4th September.

At 6.30 a.m. resumed our retreat, and by noon arrived at the waterhole of the 2nd, having left two more horses behind, which, however, Mr. Brown and myself carried out water to in the course of the evening and drove them in during the night.

5th September.

Leaving the party to rest, I walked ten or twelve miles round to the south-south-eastward, along the foot of the range, in search of water, and to ascertain if a better line of country could be found in that direction, but it continued to maintain the same arid appearance, and I only came on one pool in a gully four miles from the camp. Depot.

6th September.

Leaving Mr. Turner and four of the party in depot, with instructions to remain there three days, and then fall back upon the Oakover, where there was much better feed, I started with Messrs. Brown and Harding, taking six of the strongest horses, sixteen days' rations and six gallons of water, and steered south-south-east along the ranges for six or eight miles, looking for some stream-bed that might lead us through the plains, but was disappointed to find that they were all lost in the first mile after leaving the hills, and as crossing the numerous ridges of sand proved very fatiguing to the horses, we determined once more to attempt to strike to the eastward between the ridges, which we did for fifteen miles, when our horses again showed signs of failing us, which left us the only alternative of either pushing on at all hazards to a distant range that was now just visible to the eastward, where, from the numerous native fires and general depression of the country, there was every reason to think a large river would be found to exist, or to make for some deep rocky gorges in the granite hills ten miles to the south, in which there was every prospect of finding water. In the former case the travelling would be smoothest, but the distance so great that, in the event of our failing to obtain water, we probably should not succeed in bringing back one of our horses; while, in the latter, we should have to climb over the sand ridges, which we had already found so fatiguing; this course, however, involved the least amount of risk, and we accordingly struck south four miles, and halted for the night. Camp 76.

REPULSED FOR WANT OF WATER. INTENSE HEAT.

7th September.

The horses did not look much refreshed by the night's rest; we, however, divided three gallons of water amongst them, and started off early, in the hope of reaching the ranges by noon; but we had not gone three miles when one of the pack-horses, that was carrying less than forty pounds weight, began to fail, and the load was placed upon my saddle-horse; it did not, however, enable him to get on more than a couple of miles further, when we were compelled to abandon him, leaving him under the shade of the only tree we could find, in the hope that we might bring back water to his relief. Finding that it would be many hours before the horses could be got on to the hills, I started ahead on foot, leaving Messrs. Brown and Harding to come on gently, while I was to make a signal by fires if successful in finding water. Two hours' heavy toil through the sand, under a broiling sun, brought me to the ranges, where I continued to hunt up one ravine after another until 5.0 p.m. without success. Twelve hours' almost incessant walking, on a scanty breakfast, and without water, with the thermometer over 100 degrees of Fahrenheit, began to tell upon me rather severely; so much so that, by the time I had tracked up my companions (who had reached the hills by 1.0 p.m., and were anxiously waiting for me), it was as much as I could do to carry my rifle and accoutrements. The horses were looking truly wretched, and I was convinced that the only chance of saving them, if water was not found, would be by abandoning our pack-saddles, provisions, and everything we could possibly spare, and try and recover them afterwards if practicable; we therefore encamped for the night on the last plot of grass we could find, and proceeded to make arrangements for an early start in the morning. There was still remaining a few pints of water in the kegs, having been very sparing in the use of it; this enabled us to have a little tea and make a small quantity of damper, of which we all stood in much need. Camp 77.

8th September.

At 4.0 a.m. we were again up. Having disposed of our equipment and provisions, except our riding-saddles, instruments, and firearms, by suspending them in the branches of a large tree, we divided a pint of water for our breakfast, and by the first peep of dawn were driving our famished horses before us at their best speed toward the depot, which was now thirty-two miles distant. For the first eight miles they went on pretty well, but the moment the sun began to have power they flagged greatly, and it was not long before we were obliged to relinquish another horse quite unable to proceed. By 9.0 a.m. I found that my previous day's march, and the small allowance of food I had taken, was beginning to have its effects upon me, and that it was probable I could not reach the depot until next morning, by which time the party left there were to fall back to the Oakover; I therefore directed Mr. Brown, who was somewhat fresher than myself, to push on for the camp and to bring out fresh horses with water, while Mr. Harding and myself would do our best to bring on any straggling horses that could not keep up with him. By dark we had succeeded in reaching to within nine miles of the depot, finding unmistakable evidence towards evening of the condition to which the horses taken on by Mr. Brown were reduced, by the saddles, guns, hobbles, and even bridles, scattered along the line of march, which had been taken off to enable them to go on a few miles further.

EFFECTS OF WANT OF WATER.

9th September.

At dawn Mr. Harding and myself got up from our beds of sand stiff and giddy, but much refreshed by the cold night air. In four or five miles we met Mr. Brown with fresh horses and a supply of water, having succeeded in reaching the depot at 8 p.m. the night before, with only one horse. We were now enabled to proceed with the tracking up of the horses left overnight, which, after resting some hours, had commenced to ramble in search of water; Mr. Brown returning on our route and recovering the saddles and firearms left the previous evening, the stores abandoned the day before being too far off to attempt their recovery. By 8.30 p.m. we had all returned to the depot, having tracked up the three missing horses, the two left at the furthest point being too distant to carry relief to without incurring the risk of further loss. I cannot omit to remark the singular effects of excessive thirst upon the eyes of the horses; they absolutely sunk into their heads until there was a hollow of sufficient depth to entirely bury the thumb in, and there was an appearance as though the whole of the head had shrunk with them, producing a very unpleasant and ghastly expression. Depot camp.

10th September.

We were only able to move the camp a mile to another waterhole, for the sake of a little better feed. Bivouac.

COMMENCE RETURN JOURNEY.

11th September.

On taking into consideration the reduced number and strength of our horses, it was quite evident that we had but little prospect of being able to cross the tract of dry sandy country that had already occasioned us so much loss and trouble; yet there were many reasons to stimulate us to make the attempt. Not only had we now attained to within a very few miles of the longitude in which, from various geographical data, there are just grounds for believing that a large river may be found to exist, draining Central Australia, but the character of the country appeared strongly to indicate the vicinity of such a feature; added to which, the gradual decline in the elevation of the country, notwithstanding our increasing distance from the coast, tended towards the same conclusion. Nor should we omit the strong evidences that the remarkable ridges of drift-sand which encumbered the plains must in the first instance, have been brought from the interior by water, and then have been blown by the strong prevailing south-east winds across the country in a direction at least 50 degrees from that which they originally came from; this, with the clean water-worn appearance of the sand, the bold outlines of the hills seen to the far east, and the number of native fires observed in the same direction, must all tend to support the hypothesis that the western half of Australia is probably drained by a large river in about this meridian. I could not, therefore, help regretting more than ever that we should be driven back at such an interesting spot; but mature reflection convinced me that any further attempt with our present means, at this period of the year, was almost certain to be attended with the most disastrous results; I therefore decided upon adopting the only other useful course open to us--that of examining down to the sea the rivers already discovered. With this in view, we to-day fell back five or six miles across the ranges to a tributary to the Oakover, called the Davis, when one of the horses became so crippled by a strain in the loins that we were obliged to halt to give him a chance of recovery, affording me leisure to verify our position by observing another set of lunar distances, which I found to agree well with those formerly taken ten miles to the westward. Camp 78.

DOWN THE OAKOVER RIVER.

12th September.

We commenced the descent of the Davis, having much difficulty in getting along the sick horse, as it required the united strength of the party to lift him on his legs every time he fell, which he at last did so frequently that I ordered him to be shot, as it was hopeless to attempt to bring him on, and if left, he must have died of starvation. By 2.0 p.m. we reached the junction of the stream we were upon with the Oakover, and halted two miles south of Camp 72; most of the party being now dismounted, shoe-leather was beginning to get very scarce with us. Camp 79.

13th September.

This day we only travelled eight miles down the Oakover, and encamped near a deep creek, in which was caught a good haul of fish. Camp 80.

14th September.

The feed was so good on this river that we were able to proceed to-day to latitude 20 degrees 59 minutes 33 seconds; the country improving much, grassy flats extending for some miles to the northward, the channel of the river being augmented by the junction of the large tributary crossed on our eastward track on the afternoon of the 29th August. Camp 81.

15th September (Sunday).

Remained in camp to rest the horses. A few natives were seen near the camp during the day.

16th September.

After running four or five miles further north, the Oakover turned to the north-west for fourteen miles, having a clear sandy or stony bed from 150 to 200 yards wide, water and grass being plentiful, and the country generally being open forest, with a pleasing appearance. Camp 82.

Latitude 20 degrees 46 minutes.

17th September.

The course of the river was followed for about seventeen miles in a westerly direction, the bed widening out to 300 or 400 yards, the water being now confined to a sandy channel not above 150 yards in width, the depth of the valley through which it runs being about forty feet; timber of white-gum and cajeput is tolerably plentiful on the banks, the soil of which is a red loam of considerable depth. Many of the pools are lined with tall reeds. Camp 83.

Latitude 20 degrees 41 minutes 32 seconds.

REACH THE DEGREY RIVER. ABUNDANCE OF FISH.

18th September.

Started at 6.40 a.m. and in two and a half hours entered a deep and wild-looking gorge, at which point it formed a junction with the DeGrey, coming from the south-south-east, through a beautiful level tract of open grassy country, a broad belt of flooded-gum trees growing for some distance back on either side. Passing through the gorge, which was a quarter of a mile wide and about a mile long, we came upon a camp of natives, who, as usual, quickly dispersed without giving us an opportunity of showing them that we intended them no harm. The river here contains a fine reach of deep water, upon which was a large quantity of whistling ducks and other water-fowl. Two miles lower down we halted on the banks of a deep creek coming in from the northward; the rest of the day being employed re-stuffing pack-saddles, etc., while some of the party caught a quantity of fine fish--amongst them an eel, which, however, was allowed to escape, being taken for a water-snake by one of the party who had never seen one before. A large kind of bat, or vampire, was first observed here, measuring about two feet across the wings. Camp 84.

19th September.

We continued to follow down the DeGrey for about eighteen miles in a west-north-west direction, through open grassy plains extending for many miles on either bank, the channel of the river still maintaining the same sandy character, and with abundance of water in its bed. Camp 85.

Latitude 20 degrees 36 minutes 30 seconds.

20th September.

There was little or no change in the appearance of the country for the eighteen or twenty miles that the river was traced down during to-day. We encamped on the bank of a wide and deep reach of water more than a mile long, surrounded by tall reeds. Fish were caught here in great abundance. Camp 86.

Latitude 20 degrees 31 minutes 48 seconds.

NATIVE CAMP.

21st September.

Shortly after starting we crossed the bed of a tributary coming in from the southward, with a shallow sandy channel 200 yards wide, which must drain the high ranges between the DeGrey and Shaw Rivers, which we passed over on our outward track. In many places we began to observe patches of triodia in the midst of the alluvial plains through which the river continued to run, and distant ranges were observed both to the north and south. Towards sundown we surprised a large party of natives encamped in a dry channel of the river, and approached so near before we were discovered that we had separated a young child from the rest of the party, which was observed by the mother, who remained while the rest of the natives made a hasty retreat; it was not long, however, before an aged warrior returned to her aid, with his spear shipped, and came forward in a very menacing attitude to recover the child, who stood by us with a look of the most perfect unconcern. Finding we took no notice of his threats, he threw down his weapon, and, walking up to the boy, caught him up in his arms and bore him off, with a look of triumph, to his companions. No attempt was made to carry away their supper, which was ready prepared in a number of wooden scoops, and consisted of fish, rats, beans, grass-seed cakes, and a beverage made with some oily seed pounded. Leaving everything undisturbed, we pushed on for another mile, so as to prevent their being afraid of returning to their evening repast. Camp 87.

Latitude 20 degrees 25 minutes 15 seconds.

ATTEMPT TO SPEAR HORSES.

22nd September.

Being Sunday, we only moved a mile lower down the river to a fine reach of water, on the banks of which was a rich sward of green grass for our horses. Shortly after we had made ourselves comfortable for the day we were startled by six of the horses coming into camp at a gallop in their hobbles, followed by eighteen armed natives. Everyone sprang to their arms in a moment, which caused the intruders to fall back. I tried to make them comprehend that we did not approve of the horses being hunted; but as they would not go away, and they had a strong party concealed in the brushwood, I fired at a tree to show them the use of our arms. The moment they heard the report of the rifle and saw the splinters fly, they took to their heels and did not again trouble us. We afterwards found a spear sticking in the ground in the track of the horses, having evidently be thrown while in pursuit. Camp 88.

Latitude 20 degrees 25 minutes; longitude 119 degrees 21 minutes.

23rd September.

The river soon passed round the southern foot of a range of hills of 400 or 500 feet elevation, the country to the south again becoming very fertile, and clothed with a rich sward of kangaroo-grass; at ten miles we struck the Shaw River, coming from the south-east, with a broad, deep, and well-defined channel, in which were many fine pools of water. Below the confluence of the rivers the DeGrey widened out considerably, turning rather more to the northward, and seven miles further was joined by the Strelley, in latitude 20 degrees 16 minutes, and longitude 119 degrees 5 minutes east; the river being diverted to the northward by a rugged range of volcanic hills; its course being now direct for Breaker Inlet, which was distant about eighteen miles. Camp 89.

MAGNETIC ROCKS RENDER THE COMPASS USELESS.

24th September.

As it was very important that I should obtain a round of bearings before proceeding any further, the country having for some days past been too flat to afford many opportunities for triangulation. I to-day started with Messrs. Harding and Brown to ascend the ranges that lie to the west of the river. A scramble of three miles over very rugged rocks brought us to the highest point, which was found to be not more than 500 feet above the sea; our journey, however, turned out to be fruitless, the magnetic attraction of the volcanic rocks of which the hills are composed being so great as to reverse the needle, which varied so much that I could not even make use of the compass to take angles, and I had omitted to bring a sextant.

Kangaroos were numerous among these hills, but we did not succeed in shooting any; they appear to be similar to those seen on the plains near the Sherlock. The view we had of the country was very extensive. To the south is a vast gently-undulating plain, only occasionally interrupted by detached granite and sandstone peaks; while narrow green lines of trees intersecting the plain in various directions indicate the watercourses coming from the distant ranges, and wander in wide sandy channels towards the sea; the course of the Strelley being easily distinguished for many miles. To the north the eye could trace the broad sandy bed of the DeGrey, trending towards Breaker Inlet, the position of which was only distinguishable by the margin of deep-blue mangroves that line it, and the whole of the extremity of the delta formed by the alluvial deposits brought down by the river. To the east and west of this is a wide expanse of alluvial flats, covered in most parts with rich, waving grass, the sameness of the scenery being relieved by detached patches of open park-like forest of flooded-gum. Returning to the camp by noon, the remainder of the day was devoted by me to bringing up the arrears of mapping, etc., and by the party generally in providing a supply of fish and ducks, which here were found to be very plentiful.

25th September.

By 7 a.m. we were once more tracing down the DeGrey through the flats seen yesterday. At eight miles the river divided into two channels of nearly equal width, the eastern one being followed to latitude 20 degrees 5 minutes 16 seconds, travelling being very heavy, on account of the numerous rat-holes that completely undermine the banks of the river for more than a quarter of a mile back on either side. For the last few miles the water in the river was decidedly brackish, and at our camp was evidently influenced by the tides; we, however, procured some tolerably good water by sinking a well in a sandbank in the dry portion of the channel, which here was about 300 yards wide. Camp 90.

SUDDEN RISE OF TIDE.

26th September.

This morning we found the water in the well quite salt, in consequence of the tide having risen during the night; and as our horses required water, it was found desirable to fall back upon some of the fresh pools to form a camp, while a day or two could be devoted to the examination of this fertile and interesting tract of country. We accordingly crossed the channel and proceeded westward for nearly three miles, when we came upon the other branch, which proved eventually to join again several miles below, forming an island containing some 8000 or 9000 acres of alluvial flat soil, covered with a quantity of mixed grasses. To this was given the name of Ripon

Island. The western channel was found to be over 300 yards wide, and to contain several fine reaches of open water, some fresh and others slightly brackish; they were all teeming with ducks and a great variety of water-fowl. Having selected a suitable spot for a camp, I started with Messrs. Brown and Harding to examine the country towards the inlet. At a little more than two miles we crossed the river between two pools of salt water, subject to the influence of the tides, and proceeded northward over an open grassy flat for two miles further, when the grass gave place to samphire and small mangrove bushes, which gradually thickened to dense mangroves, cut up by deep muddy creeks, which put a stop to proceeding further in that direction. Here we observed several remarkable stacks of dead mangroves, evidently piled together by the natives, but for what purpose we could not ascertain, unless to escape upon from the tide when fishing. Having gained firm ground, we made a detour more to the eastward, and at last succeeded in reaching the bank of the river close to the head of the inlet. The tide being at the ebb, I was able to walk over the mud and sand to the mouth of the river, and obtain bearings to Points Larrey and Poissonier, and observe the character of the entrance, from which I formed the opinion that the breakers seen by Captain Stokes when surveying this portion of the coast, and which deterred him from entering the inlet, were nothing more than the sea-rollers meeting a strong ebb tide setting out of the DeGrey, possibly backed up by freshes from the interior which would, from a river of this size, occasion a considerable commotion where the tide amounts to twenty feet; at any rate, I could not observe any rocks, and there appeared to be a channel with at least five or six feet of water in it at low tide. For the first mile the river has a breadth of from 400 to 800 yards, and would admit with the tide vessels of twelve or fourteen feet draft of water with perfect safety up as far as Ripon Island, where they could lie completely sheltered in all weathers quite close to the shore, which here has steep banks twenty to thirty feet high; they would however, be left aground at low water, as we did not observe any pools in this part of the river. I had only just time to complete my observations when the roaring of the incoming tide warned me that no time was to be lost in returning to the horses, which were nearly a mile higher up the river. Although I ran part of the way, the mud creeks filled up so rapidly, there was some risk of my being cut off from the shore and having to take up a roost on the top of the mangroves until the tide fell; I had time, however, to observe that the head of the tide carried with it thousands of fish of great variety, amongst them a very remarkable one from three to six inches in length, in form resembling a mullet, but with fins like a flying-fish; it is amphibious, landing on the mud and running with the speed of a lizard, and when frightened can jump five or six feet at a bound; I did not, however, succeed in capturing one for a specimen. Swarms of beautiful bright-crimson crabs, about two inches diameter, were to be seen issuing from their holes to welcome the coming flood, on which was borne a great number of sea-fowl, who, it was evident, came in for an abundant feast in the general turmoil. Mounting our horses, that had stood for the last two hours without touching a mouthful of the rank grass around them for want of water, we returned to the camp by a different route, through open grass flats bordering the deep reaches of water that encompass the north-west side of Ripon Island.

SCARCITY OF WATER NEAR THE WEST.

27th September.

Accompanied by the same party, but with three fresh horses, we again started to explore the plains eastwards towards Mount Blaze. For several miles after leaving the island the country continued of the same fertile character as that passed over yesterday, and is at times subject to inundation from the river; but as we receded from the influence of the floods the soil became lighter and the grass thinner, with patches of triodia and samphire. At twelve miles we entered a patch of open grassy forest, extending for some miles; but as there was no promise of obtaining water, and the day was calm and sultry, we turned to the northward in the hope that water might be procurable under the low sand-hills that line this portion of the coast. In this we were, however, disappointed, as the fall of the country terminated in mangroves and salt-water creeks, between which and the sea is a narrow ridge of low sand-hills. Amongst them we observed many tracks of natives; but did not discover any water. The sea here is apparently very shallow for many miles off shore, more than half a mile of mud and sandbank being left dry at low water. Resting the horses for two hours, we returned to camp by a more direct route, passing for several miles over a plain of rich black mould, covered with a short sward of bright-green grass, the native fires having swept off the dry grass a few weeks previously; and although there had been no rain since, the heavy dews that fell during the night in these latitudes had been sufficient to produce a rapid growth.

28th September.

As I expected to meet with some difficulties for want of water between this and the Yule River, I thought it best to give the horses the benefit of a little rest before resuming our homeward route. Some of the party were also deriving much benefit from the abundance of fresh game, as they had been suffering from debility, brought on most probably by over-exertion while traversing the heavy country of the interior. While here we obtained several additions to our small collection of birds--amongst them a beautiful wader, the size of a large snipe, the head being covered by a remarkable membranous hood or sheath of a rich gamboge-yellow, resembling the leaf of a flower falling back from the beak, and lying close over the feathers, protecting them when the beak is plunged into the sand after food; they had also a remarkable sharp horn or claw projecting forward from the last joint of the wing, with which they can fight when attacked by birds of prey. A very handsome bird was also shot resembling a flamingo, the body being about the size, and in plumage like a pelican; the head and neck of a deep rich purple, and formed like the flamingo; the legs bright red, long and slender; it flies extended to its greatest length, measuring six feet two inches, and across the wings seven feet two inches; its weight being only 11 pounds. A white heron, with bird-of-paradise feathers on its back, was occasionally seen, but only one specimen procured.

29th September (Sunday).

DELTA OF THE DEGREY RIVER.

30th September.

We made an early start up the river, and at three miles struck out into the plains to the westward, where we found a large extent of open flat, yielding grass and atriplex, and timbered in many parts with flooded-gums. At ten miles we came upon a deep reach of water flowing to the north-west, which must empty itself into the sea four or five miles to the south-west of Spit Point, forming an island of a portion of the delta of the DeGrey, containing between 90,000 and 100,000 acres of alluvial land. This channel was followed up, and found to come from the river, close to the junction of the Strelley, and must be a very considerable outlet for the water during the summer rains. I regretted much not having time to trace this branch of the DeGrey to its mouth, as it might be found to be navigable, and afford a fine site for a seaport town. Fresh water is abundant, and building stone procurable in any quantity being found in the immediate vicinity on land superior to inundation. We remained at the junction the rest of the day. Camp 92.

THE STRELLEY RIVER.

1st October.

As the plains were now dry and parched, we determined to follow up the Strelley to the ranges before striking west to the Yule. At first the river spread out into so many wide grassy channels that it was difficult to trace it; but at four or five miles collected into one bed, about 100 yards wide, in which were a few small pools. Up to this point the country had been fertile, the soil being an alluvial clay, resulting from volcanic rocks; but after getting clear of the line of hills, the soil became poor and hungry, yielding little else but triodia and acacia bushes; water was procured in several places in the course of the day's march; our course having been nearly due south. Camp 93.

Latitude 20 degrees 32 minutes 30 seconds.

2nd October.

The river led us this morning a little to the eastward of south, through a country very similar to yesterday. Late in the day we crossed a considerable tributary coming from the south-east, which was now quite dry, and takes its rise in a bold range of granite hills now visible to the southward, at the distance of ten or twelve miles, and forms a part of the main tableland of this part of the coast; the plain we had been passing over being only a sea-flat, with a few detached ranges widely scattered over its surface. The river now began to trend to the westward, granite rocks showing themselves on the surface in large masses. Water was occasionally procurable, which was very important, as the horses could not travel many hours without it, although the heaviest packs were reduced below 100 pounds. We had now only six saddle-horses, so that two of the party had to walk by turns for an hour at a time. We halted late in latitude 20 degrees 45 minutes 17 seconds. Camp 94.

3rd October.

Started at 6.30 a.m., and in an hour came upon a fine pool in the granite, which was very acceptable, as we had encamped overnight without any water. The channel of the river here deepened considerably, was full of rocks, and contained plenty of water. Skirting the ranges for some distance, several tributaries joined from the southward. The country, although rocky, improved much in general appearance; grass was abundant, and game frequently met with. At night we encamped on a small pool in the bed of the river about five miles from the foot of the range. Cockatoos and pigeons came in great numbers to drink at the pool about sundown. Camp 95.

Latitude 20 degrees 56 minutes 33 seconds, longitude 119 degrees 10 minutes by account.

4th October.

Made an early start, and travelled four miles on a south-west course, when the river divided into two channels, the main one coming from a deep gorge to the south-south-east, exactly in the direction in which we had left the Strelley on our outward route, at a distance of about thirty miles; identifying the stream with some degree of certainty. Taking the western branch, which would lead us towards the Yule, we followed it up until long past noon into a hilly country, without meeting with water; we, however, saw a large extent of fine grazing land which would make an excellent summer station when the flats were inundated. Having rested during the heat of the day, which had lately become rather oppressive, we resumed a westerly course, having run out the head watercourses of the western branch of the Strelley. A few miles brought us to a considerable stream-bed trending to the north-west, which was followed down till some time after dark, having procured a few gallons of water from a native well in the bed of a creek. To-day we had travelled for nine hours, and accomplished a distance of twenty-two miles, the longest day's march we had made for many weeks past. Early in the day we had noticed what we took for a great number of native fires springing up in all directions, and quickly to die away again; we, however, found it to be a number of whirlwinds, carrying with them huge columns of charcoal and dust, which traversed the plains sometimes for miles before they broke. Camp 96.

Latitude 21 degrees 4 minutes.

REACH THE YULE RIVER.

5th October.

Our computed distance from the Yule was now only twenty-one miles, and the country promised well for travelling; but the long march yesterday, and the short allowance of water, rendered it very doubtful whether some of the horses would hold out long enough to reach it; we therefore had our breakfast before daylight, and as soon as we could see resumed our route to the westward. At five miles we crossed a sandy channel, 200 yards wide, full of cajeput and gum trees, but as we did not soon find any water in it, pushed on at a rapid pace, and in two miles more crossed a similar channel, 100 yards wide, trending north-west and running parallel to the first; beyond this the ground became rocky for a few miles, and by the time we had gone rather more than twelve miles, Mr. Burges' mare, Lucy, could go no further; giving her half a-gallon of water out of the little stock carried with us, I left Messrs. Brown and Harding to bring her on when rested, and with the rest of the party continued our route. A mile or two further, and another horse, Bob, was knocked up and left behind, having also had some water given him. With considerable difficulty we succeeded in getting the rest of the horses on to the Yule by 1.30 p.m., making it close to our camp of 13th August. Had the distance been ten miles further, probably not more than three or four of the horses would have ever reached it, so much were they reduced in strength. On reaching the pool, several of the horses, notwithstanding our efforts to prevent them, rushed headlong into the water with their packs on, and drank so much of it that it was with great difficulty we could drag them out again. In the course of the afternoon Messrs. Brown and Harding came in with the horse Bob, but had not been able to get the mare on more than two or three miles; being anxious, however, not to lose her, I sent McCourt and James with two of the strongest horses, carrying four gallons of water for her, after which they succeeded in getting her into camp by midnight. Camp 97.

6th October (Sunday).

Moved a short distance down the river to camp 57 for better feed.

CROSS DRY COUNTRY TO SHERLOCK RIVER.

7th October.

As the distance from the Yule to the last known permanent water on the eastern branch of the Sherlock is over twenty-five miles, and our means of carrying water very limited since abandoning our largest pair of kegs in the retreat on the 8th September, I to-day set to work and soldered up a number of preserved-meat tins that had been carefully opened and kept for this purpose, putting a small spout to each; eight of these (4-pound tins) we found to contain something over four gallons, which, added to our water belts and the two remaining kegs, would provide for the conveyance of twelve gallons of water, which I hoped would prove sufficient to enable us to pass the dry tract of country in safety, as it would allow half a gallon to each horse and an ample supply for the party for two days. I also succeeded in repairing the aneroid barometer, which had been crushed nearly flat by the fall of a horse; fortunately, however, without injury to the vacuum vase.

8th October.

Having rearranged the loads and lightened them by leaving hid amongst the rocks a pack-saddle and sixty pounds weight of horse-shoes and nails, at 3.45 p.m. we commenced a retreat on our outward tracks of the 13th August, travelling to 7.15 p.m., when we encamped on a patch of tolerably good grass in the plain at the foot of a volcanic range, without any signs of water near us. Camp 98.

9th October.

We were up before daylight, and by 6 a.m. had our breakfast, and were again on our march, visiting a waterhole seen on our outward route, but now found to be quite dry. We pushed on at the best speed of our horses, which was now not much over two miles an hour, to 10.0, when the heat of the day began to tell on the jaded animals; we therefore halted for an hour to give the horses half a gallon of water each, after which they travelled on much more briskly, so that by a little past noon we succeeded in reaching the large pool in the eastern Sherlock, near Camp 55; some of the horses were, however, so much exhausted that we had some difficulty in getting them to move for the last mile, although entirely relieved of their loads. Camp 55a.

10th October.

Although the horses were by no means in a fit state to continue the march, yet grass was so scarce, on account of the native fires having here swept it off, that we found it best to push on for the springs at Camp 52.

Following down the banks of the stream, we found several pools not yet dried up, which proved a great help to our horses; before noon, however, the mare Lucy again gave in, and was finally abandoned, as there was but little chance of her ever reaching the bay; it is possible she may live to be picked up by some future travellers, although too old to last many years. By 1.0 p.m. we reached the springs at Camp 52, and found an ample supply of water, but the grass was here also much parched up; we, however, remained for the rest of the day.

NATIVE DEPREDATIONS.

11th October.

This morning our route was resumed down the eastern Sherlock, tracing a portion that had not been before examined, and which was now found to be well supplied with water and grass; cockatoos and pigeons being seen in large numbers feeding on the banks. As we approached the junction of the two branches of the river we met a party of ten or twelve natives, who came boldly up to us, which was the only time we had known them to do so since quitting Nickol Bay. Hoping to gain some useful information from them, they were allowed to follow us to our old camp of 2nd August, where there are the large fish-pools, of which they gave us the native names. We were not quite so successful in procuring game here as on the former visit, although as much fish was caught as could be consumed while it was good. The natives kept rather aloof while we were shooting on the river, but after dusk eight or ten came to the camp, unarmed, evidently on a thieving excursion, and although narrowly watched, managed to carry off a portion of Mr. Hall's kit, which, however, he recovered next morning, on paying them an early visit, finding the articles buried under some rushes in their camp.

THEY SET THE GRASS ON FIRE.

12th October.

We were now getting so near our destination that, although provisions were getting low, we could afford to give the party a whole day's rest, while I was enabled roughly to plot out some more of my work and write up the journal, which, from having my time constantly taken up with more pressing duties, had fallen sadly into arrears. The natives again came to see what they could steal, but this time were made to sit outside a line drawn on the sand, some twenty paces from the camp--an arrangement they appeared highly to disapprove of, giving expression to their dissatisfaction in a manner anything but polite; finding, however, that we were inattentive to their impertinence so long as they confined it to harmless display, they watched their opportunity, and suddenly set fire to the grass in several places at once around the camp, and ran off as hard as they could. As this was an open act of hostility that it was necessary they should be chastised for, although I did not wish seriously to hurt them, they were allowed to run to a suitable distance, when a charge of small shot was fired after them, a few of which taking effect in the rear of the principal offender, induced him, on meeting some of the party out shooting, to make an apology, and try to lay the blame of the theft of the previous day on the dogs.

13th October (Sunday).

As the distances between the several watering places on the homeward route were too much to perform without intermediate halts, and the heat of the noon-day sun rather oppressive, it was found better to start from the pools late in the day, so as to make the halts without water during the cool of the night, travelling only very late in the evening and early in the morning. We accordingly did not start this afternoon until 4 p.m., and travelled on to 8.45, encamping in an open grassy plain under Black Hill--a volcanic eminence, the position of which is shown on the Admiralty charts. Camp 99.

14th October.

By 6 a.m. we were again on the move, and in an hour gained the banks of the George, which takes its rise in the volcanic hills to the southward. In its channel was an abundant supply of water, with many fine healthy trees overshadowing the pools. By 9.0 we arrived at our old camp (50), where we rested to 4.15 p.m., when we resumed and travelled on till nearly 8.0, encamping on the open grassy plains near the Harding River. Camp 100.

REACH THE HARDING RIVER. FLYING FOXES.

15th October.

An early start enabled us to accomplish the remaining six miles to the Harding by 8.30, where we halted for the remainder of the day, as it was not unlikely that we might have to travel the remaining thirty miles into the bay without finding any more water. As we had now only four days' rations left, and it was uncertain, in the present low condition of our horses, how long it might take us to reach the ship, the sportsmen of the party made the best use of the halt to procure game, while I proceeded to convert some more of the empty meat-tins into water-canisters, increasing our means for the transport of water to eighteen gallons, with which we had a fair prospect of getting in all the horses, even though no more should be found on the route. Our camp was enlivened this evening by the continued screeching of a number of large bats, which kept up a vigorous fight in the trees overhead the greater part of the night, notwithstanding our shooting ten or twelve of them. They were very fat, but emitted such an intolerable odour that it would require even an explorer to be hard pressed before he could make a supper of them, either roasted or boiled.

16th October.

This morning set in intensely hot, by noon the thermometer standing at 107 degrees in the shade, and at 3 p.m., when placed on a sandbank in the sun, rose to 178 of Fahrenheit; on the setting in of the westerly breeze it, however, fell at once to 96 degrees, and by 4.30 p.m. we were enabled to resume our route without feeling in any way inconvenienced by the temperature. We did not now attempt to pass through the rocky ranges so far to the eastward as on our outward route, but kept more to the westward along the open grassy valley, until opposite the narrowest part of the range, when, turning sharp to the north, we very quickly passed over the rocky portion of the hills, only encountering a few miles of extra rampant triodia, which was anything but pleasant to walk through, especially leading the party after dark. Following down a small watercourse for several miles, it at length joined the Nickol River, in which we shortly after found a small quantity of water in the bottom of what had been a pool, but which towards the close of the dry season sometimes goes dry; here we halted for a few hours to rest. Camp 101.

LAST DAY'S JOURNEY.

17th October.

Without waiting for daylight, by 2.10 a.m. we were again on the move, as there was now a fair chance of getting all the remaining horses into the bay, if we did but avoid travelling during the heat of the day. In an hour the hills were cleared, and it was now all open plain as far as the marsh at the head of Nickol Bay. By the time the morning broke we were in full view of the bay and several islands of the Archipelago, the long black hull of our ocean-home riding at anchor on the now placid waters forming by no means the least pleasing feature of the scene to those who had not seen a vestige of civilisation for many months. After halting for nearly two hours for breakfast, and to distribute the water amongst the horses, we again moved rapidly on, crossing the marsh with some difficulty, owing to the spring-tide having been recently over it, and at 1 p.m. arrived on our old ground at Hearson Cove, where we found a boat and party from the ship waiting for us, James having been despatched by a shorter route to signalize our return. Everything had gone on satisfactorily during our absence. The vessel's water-tanks had been kept filled up, ensuring a supply for our horses on the homeward voyage, as it would be utterly impossible at this season of the year, with the animals in such low condition, to attempt the overland route to Champion Bay. Amongst other discoveries during our absence was a bed of pearl-oysters at the head of the bay, from which the crew of the Dolphin had procured several tons of very fine mother-of-pearl, besides a small number of pearls varying in size from one to four carats.

18th October.

The party was fully occupied in clearing out the well and packing up saddles and outfit for shipment. It was also found that deepening the well had caused the water to become brackish, so much so that we had to bring water by boat from the spring at which the ship had been filled up; the horses however still managed to drink the well-water, although it produced great thirst. I have no doubt but that, had we had time to sink a fresh well closer to the foot of the hills, we should have obtained fresh water, as several ravines terminate there in a beautiful grassy flat, where a large proportion of the rainwater brought down from the hills sinks into the soil, from whence it gradually drains down and supplies the wells in the salt strata. I was disappointed to find that the cotton plants, that had thriven so well on first being sown, had been burnt in consequence of some of the sailors having thoughtlessly set fire to the adjoining grass; had they not been killed, by this time they would probably have been in flower, as their growth was very rapid.

EASTERN PART OF NICKOL BAY.

19th October.

As it was necessary to give the horses a few days' rest previous to swimming them off to the ship, I started this morning in the life-boat, accompanied by Captain Dixon and Messrs. Brown, Harding, and Walcott, to examine the eastern shores of the bay, for the purpose of ascertaining whether a more suitable spot for a landing place and site for a future town could be found in that quarter. Leaving the Dolphin at 5.30 a.m., we ran to the eastward with a light south wind, passing, at six miles, two small islands in the mouth of the small bay into which the Nickol River discharges itself. These islands had been visited already by Mr. Walcott, and I gave them the name of Pemberton and Walcott Islands. Continuing to run along the shore towards Cape Lambert, the soundings gave from two to three fathoms, with a good bottom of mud and sand, but the landing was generally indifferent and rocky until we came to within about nine miles of the cape, when a deep opening was passed, affording good shelter and landing for small craft. Two miles further we landed in a small rocky cove for breakfast, which gave me an opportunity of climbing a hill and examining the surrounding country, which proved very dry and rocky. A little further we passed a bold headland, against the extremity of which rested a singular flying buttress, forming half an arch of fifty or sixty feet span, and from thirty to forty feet in height. Turning this headland, another opening was observed, which we entered with the tide, and soon found that it communicated with the first one, forming an island of some extent and elevation, to which was given the name of Dixon Island. We continued to beat down the channel, which had an average width of over half a mile, until late in the evening, when we came to anchor in eleven feet of water.

20th October.

At daylight we found ourselves high and dry, only a narrow channel a few yards wide being left. Having walked over the mud to Dixon Island to breakfast, the vicinity was examined for water, but without success. At 6 a.m. the tide came in again so rapidly that it was not without some little difficulty that we gained our boat, when the wind set in so strongly from the south-west that, after several hours' almost ineffectual attempts to work to windward, we again landed not two miles from our last night's anchorage, the character of the country being equally unfavourable for landing, as it was cut up by deep mangrove creeks running far up the valleys into the steep rocky hills, forming a difficult and unpromising country. The breeze having moderated and shifted a point more to the westward, we again attempted to beat out into the bay, but by 9 p.m. had not made more than three miles, when we landed for the night, leaving two of the party in charge of the boat to keep her off the rocks when the tide fell.

21st October.

The wind and tide being now in our favour, by 3.30 a.m. we took to our boat, and arrived on board the Dolphin by 10, when she was very soon got underweigh for the purpose of taking her closer in to ship the horses; light and variable winds, however, prevented our working more than a mile nearer the landing cove by sundown, when we dropped anchor for the night.

22nd October.

With a light west wind the Dolphin was worked into eleven feet water, one and a quarter miles off the point near the cove; the vessel drawing over ten feet, brought the mud up to the surface in our wake. Eight horses were soon swam off without much difficulty, as we all had now some little experience in this sort of work.

EMBARK FOR FREMANTLE.

23rd October.

By 2 p.m. the remaining six horses and equipment of the Expedition were all safely shipped, and a conspicuous intimation of our sojourn on the coast having been painted in large white letters on a pile of granite rocks near the south corner of the cove, we took our final departure, getting the Dolphin underweigh by 4, with a light westerly wind, which carried us through the passage between Hauy and Delambre Islands by 7, when we hauled up and stood to north-north-west.

24th October.

The wind still holding to the west, we made but little progress, the Dolphin being only a good sailer in smooth water, or running before the wind.

Latitude 19 degrees 12 minutes south at noon.

25th October.

By noon observations we were only in latitude 18 degrees 42 minutes; longitude 113 degrees 32 minutes.

26th October.

The wind veering slightly to the south, we were able to make by noon to latitude 18 degrees 46 minutes 30 seconds; longitude 111 degrees 47 minutes 30 seconds.

27th October.

From this time to the 3rd November the winds continued to blow almost uninterruptedly from the south and eastward, which carried us as far west as longitude 101 degrees east, and latitude 31 degrees south, where we met with westerly winds, which enabled us to run up to within sight of Cape Naturaliste by the 8th.

9th November.

By 10 a.m. we were off Rottnest Island, when the pilot came on board and took us to the anchorage in Gage's Roads by noon. Having given instructions to Mr. Turner for the landing of the horses, etc., I landed with Messrs. Brown, Harding, and Hall, all of whom were, at their desire, at once released from the duties of the Expedition. Proceeded by steamer to Perth.

10th November.

Had an interview with His Excellency the Governor, and reported the safe return of the party and general results of the Expedition.

F.T. GREGORY,

Commander North-West Australian Expedition.

Perth, 6th February, 1862.

APPENDIX

Adopting the course which I have found most convenient on similar occasions, I now proceed to offer a few remarks on the general features, productions, and natural capabilities, etc., of the country traversed by the Expedition, which could not, without disadvantage, have been introduced into the foregoing narrative. These remarks have already appeared at the conclusion of my report published on the 18th November, 1861, but are equally applicable to the present publication.

Commencing with its geographical and geological peculiarities, that portion of the country that came under our observation consists of a succession of terraces, rising inland for nearly 200 miles, more or less broken up by volcanic hills towards the coast. The first belt averages from ten to forty miles in width from the sea, and is a nearly level plain, slightly ascending to the southward, with an elevation of from 40 to 100 feet, the soil being generally either light loam or strong clays, according as it is the result of the disintegration of the granite rocks that occasionally protrude above its surface, or of volcanic rocks of black scoria that frequently interrupt the general level; hills of this nature also constitute the greater portion of the more elevated islands off the coast, Cape Lambert, and the promontory that shelters the western side of Nickol Bay. The generality of these rocks do not, however, yield so rich a soil as might be expected from their origin. This is owing to the absence of actual lava, the eruptive heat having nearly been sufficient to convert the superincumbent primary and tertiary rocks into a vitreous scoria, having a specific gravity of 3.2, and is highly indestructible in its texture.

Proceeding inland for the next fifty or sixty miles is a granite country that has been originally capped with horizontal sandstones, and has an elevation of about 1000 feet. This range terminates to the southward in level plains of good soil, the produce of the next series of more elevated country, while towards the northern edges the granite and sandstones have undergone great changes through the action of numerous trap dykes, that have greatly disturbed its surface, producing metamorphic rocks, some resembling jasper, and others highly cellular and scoriaceous.

In about latitude 22 degrees, on the meridian of Nickol Bay, we came upon another and more elevated range trending away to the south-east, having an altitude of 2500 feet above the sea. This, unlike the last section, has a southern escarpment of 500 or 600 feet, and consists of horizontal sandstones and conglomerates, which have comparatively undergone little change, and has an average breadth of eight or ten miles, the southern flank being bordered by fertile valleys of strong loamy clays, merging gradually to the southward into stony ridges and hills, some having an elevation of nearly 4000 feet, the culminating point being attained at Mount Bruce, in latitude 22 degrees 30 minutes.

From this point the country gradually falls to the Ashburton, the bed of which river, in the same meridian as the bay, is about 1600 feet above the sea, and the adjoining ranges not above 2200 feet, or about the same as the country on the Gascoyne, Lyons, and Upper Murchison.

Of minerals I was unable to discover any traces, except iron. Quartz reefs occasionally traversed the country in a north-north-east and south-south-west direction, or nearly the same as the mineral lodes at Champion Bay; but I could not find any instance in which this rock offered much to indicate the probable existence of gold, it being far surpassed in this respect by the rocks on the Upper Murchison. Coal does not appear likely to be found within the limits of the country passed over, unless towards the easternmost point attained by the Expedition.

With respect to the harbours on the coast, I can only speak of Nickol Bay and the anchorage under Rosemary and the adjacent islands. The former I consider only second to King George's Sound, as it can be entered in all weathers, either from the north or north-east, and there is reason to believe that a safe passage exists between Legendre and Dolphin Islands, leading into Mermaid Straits, where there appears to be an excellent harbour at all seasons of the year.

The soundings towards the eastern and western shores of Nickol Bay, taken at low water, show sufficient depth for vessels of considerable tonnage to lie within a cable's length of the shore, the bottom being fine sand and soft mud. Towards the head of the bay the water is much shallower, not carrying more than two fathoms two miles from the shore. No reefs are known to exist in this bay, except quite close into land.

In making the running survey of the western promontory I found that all to the north of Sloping Head was an island, having a boat channel between from half a mile to a mile wide. To the outer portion I therefore gave the name of Dolphin Island.

The tides are tolerably regular, and average sixteen feet, but at the spring they rise twenty-one feet, on which occasions the whole of the western promontory, including the high lands for several miles to the westward, are entirely cut off by the sea, the other opening being under Enderby Island--a circumstance that greatly detracts from the value of these otherwise fine harbours, as it would require two miles of causeway to connect the best landing place, where water is to be found, with the mainland.

The average declination of the needle throughout this district I found to be 1 degree east, the result of many amplitudes and azimuths; there is, however, in the vicinity of many of the volcanic hills great local attraction.

Of the climate I can only say that during the five months we remained on the coast we never experienced the same inconvenience from it that we frequently have done within the limits of the settled districts of the colony; the weather was, however, principally fine, and the sky clear during our stay, only two showers having occurred--one at the latter end of May and the other in June. The meteorological register kept at Nickol Bay shows the following results, from observations taken at all hours of the day and night:--

Thermometer	Max.	Min
May	80	65
June	76	63
July	78	56
August	80	54
September	83	65
October	92	70

Under the peculiar circumstance of the thermometer being placed on a sandbank in the sun during the hot days in October, it rose to 178 degrees of Fahrenheit, whilst the lowest it ever fell to was up in the hills, in July, when it was 2 degrees below freezing just before sunrise.

The winds continued to blow almost uninterruptedly from the east and south-east during the first four months, veering to the south-south-east and south and occasionally to the north-east. Latterly the wind was alternately south-east in the morning, and north-west or westerly in the afternoon; the sky becoming frequently overcast, and every appearance of the near approach of the rainy season, which it has been observed by navigators and explorers to do about the beginning of November, and continue to March.

Amongst the natural productions I would first briefly refer to the beds of the pearl oysters, as they are likely to become of immediate commercial importance, considerable numbers having been gathered by the crew of the Dolphin at their leisure time, the aggregate value of which, I am told, is between 500 and 600 pounds; besides pearls, one of which has been valued by competent persons at 25 pounds. The limits of the bed are as yet undefined, but there is good reason to believe, from the position of it, that with proper apparatus ships could soon be loaded with them.

Sandalwood was found in small quantities, very highly scented, but too widely scattered to become of much importance as an article of export.

Of indigenous fruits, etc., we observed the adansonia, or gouty-stemmed tree of Sir G. Grey (nearly allied to the baobab or monkey bread-fruit of Southern Africa), sweet and water melons similar to those formerly seen by me on the Lyons River, but of much larger size; a small gourd; a wild fig, well-tasted; and a sweet plum, very palatable, were found in tolerable abundance.

I have already spoken of the palms which grow on the bank of the Fortescue; they are very handsome and grow to the height of forty feet, but not having brought in any specimens, they have not yet been identified as to their variety.

Tobacco does not grow so luxuriantly here as on the Lyons River, but the natives collect it, and after preparation, chew it; but we did not on any occasion observe them to smoke.

Many beautiful flowers were also collected, which will be forwarded to some of the most eminent botanists, to be described and classified.

It now only remains for me to give an opinion on the capabilities of the country for colonisation. It would be almost impossible to particularise the positions or define the limits of country adapted for grazing purposes beyond the reference already made to them. The total amount of land available for this purpose within the limit of our route I should estimate at not less than two or three millions of acres, and of this I may safely say 200,000 are suitable for agricultural purposes, the greater portion of which lies on the two flanks of the Hamersley Range, on the banks of the DeGrey and its tributaries, and on the Lower Sherlock.

Of the fitness of this district for the growth of wool, which, on account of its being an intertropical country, it is generally supposed it would be unsuitable, I would remark that its elevation above the sea appears likely to obviate the objection, and render it probable that sheep may not degenerate in the same way they are found to do in other tropical countries; at any rate, flocks are now being pushed over on to the same latitude in Queensland, and we do not hear of the wool-grower complaining that such is the case there.

As to its fitness for the growth of cereals, it is quite possible that wheat and barley may not come to the same degree of perfection they do in the more temperate latitudes of Australia, but there is no reason to doubt its capability of growing sufficient grain for the support of a numerous population.

What it appears more highly qualified for than anything else is the growth of cotton--a question which at the present juncture cannot be lost sight of. From my personal observation of the cultivation of this plant in Egypt, and the attention I have recently paid to this subject while in Europe, I feel confident that a very considerable portion of the arable lands on the DeGrey and Sherlock are precisely the soils adapted for the production of this valuable commodity. As, however, I purpose to make this the subject of a more lengthy paper at a future period, I will not now venture to enlarge upon it.

As the number and disposition of the aborigines is likely to have some effect on the first settlement of a district, I would give it as my opinion that these people will not prove particularly troublesome to the settlers, if properly and fairly treated. They are not numerous, and appear very willing to take employ under Europeans, and will no doubt soon be made as useful as in the other districts. In stature they rather exceed the usual standard, some of them measuring two or three inches over six feet.

In bringing my report to a close, I would wish to observe, that although the results of the Expedition have fallen short of my sanguine hopes with regard to Geographical discovery, and will, I am afraid, in some degree disappoint the anticipations of the eminent Geographers who have lent their valuable aid in promoting the undertaking, yet I cannot but hope that the large amount of additional fertile country it has brought to our knowledge will compensate in some degree for the deficiency. I am, however, unable to refrain from again expressing my opinion, that had not so many concurrent circumstances combined to retard the departure of the Expedition until so late in the season, and it had arrived on the coast at the time originally recommended by the Geographical Society, it would, in all probability, have resulted in the full accomplishment of the object they had in view.

It now devolves upon me to perform the pleasing duty of recording my entire satisfaction with the manner in which the whole of the members of the Expedition put forward their best energies in the performance of their respective functions. To Mr. Turner I am indebted for the care bestowed on the management of the store department, which came under his immediate charge. To Messrs. Brockman and Hall, J. McCourt, and James, are due my acknowledgments for the cheerful alacrity with which they performed the duties allotted to them.

Of Messrs. Maitland, Brown and J. Harding I cannot speak too highly. Accompanying me on all the extra services upon which I was engaged, they had to endure privations of no ordinary description, which they met with a spirit of steady fortitude deserving of the highest praise. Of the valuable services rendered to the Expedition and to science by Mr. P. Walcott I have already had occasion to refer, and I sincerely hope that his talents and zeal in the pursuits of Botany and Natural History may meet a more substantial reward than the thanks which are justly due to him and those gentlemen who have given their time and talents gratuitously in the service of their fellow-colonists.

To Captain Dixon and the officers and crew of the Dolphin every praise is due for the assistance which on all occasions they promptly afforded in aiding the Expedition, and for which I gladly avail myself of the present opportunity to return them my best thanks.

In conclusion, permit me to tender Your Excellency my acknowledgments for the readiness with which you have acceded to my various suggestions in carrying out the arrangements of the Expedition since the passing of the vote of money in aid by the local legislature.

F.T.G.

VOCABULARY OF THE ABORIGINAL LANGUAGE AT NICKOL BAY.

BY MR. PWALCOTT.

ENGLISH : ABORIGINAL.

Emu : Galiberie.

Kangaroo : Peckoora.

Kangaroo (Rock) : Noordee.

Barbed spear : Bilara.

Common spear : Wera Wera.

Foot : Jinna.

Sleep : Gnaree.

Water : Baba.

Sit down : Barnee Boongoo.

Come here : Gokie.

Eastern tribes : Kakardi.

Hair of head : Knuggnura.

Twine : Bingooro.

Nose : Moola.

Tongue : Talee.

Cockle (unio) : Yoondo.

Ears : Kulka.

Scars on the arms, etc. : Waarbungabo.

Red ochre or wilgee : Marder.

Sand : Narnoo.

Bean (scarlet runner) : Koordala.

Toe nail : Mindee.

Oyster (rock) : Jibboor.

Oyster (pearl) : Weerdee.

Grass : Warabo.

Fishing net : Takaroo.

Fetch or bring : Takora.

Acacia : Baragoon.

Breadfruit tree : Tangoola.

Gourd or calabash : Guabooraam.

Firewood : Tamara.

Granite rock : Caragnoo.

Come : Gokee.

Go : Wakkie.

Cowrie or Cypraea : Weelungooroo.

Sun : Yanda.

Biscuit : Mardomurrie.

Sea shag : Toorna.

Native dog : Wanga.

Vomit : Kalkalubata.

Knife : Chumberrie.

Horse : Gnoormiee.

Sponge : Banga.

Axe : Carama.

Black wattle : Eringgna.

Snake : Walee.

Tobacco : Gaanaree.

Scarlet trefoil : Beeban.

Hungry : Kamoongoo.

Knee : Manboor.

Shin : Kojaee.

Thigh : Woolagallu.

Eyelash : Gneearee.

Forehead : Wara.

Lip : Walee.

Knuckles : Munjee.

Elbow : Yarna Mangoola.

Big toe : Guangnaree.

Seaweed : Binda.

Iron : Tanga Tanga.

Boat : Kajuree.

Sneeze : Kanjeerneo.

Sugar : Kungknara.

NORTH AUSTRALIAN EXPEDITION 1855 TO 1856

The circumstances which led to the organisation of the Expedition for exploring Northern Australia, and the special objects of the Imperial Government in undertaking it, are best detailed in the following Despatch from His Grace the Duke of Newcastle, Secretary of State for the Colonies, to Captain Fitzgerald, Governor of Western Australia:--

The Honourable the Secretary of State for the Colonies, to the Governor of Western Australia.

Downing Street,

31st August, 1854.

SIR,

You will probably have been rendered aware by the reports of the Parliamentary Debates of last session, and from other sources, that Her Majesty's Government have been long considering the project of despatching an exploring expedition to lay open, if favoured with success, more of the interior of the great Australian Continent than the many energetic but partial attempts hitherto made have succeeded in developing.

This scheme originated with the Council of the Royal Geographical Society, who corresponded with the Colonial Department on the subject of it during last winter. But it was ultimately considered by Her Majesty's Government that the importance of the subject rendered it more advisable that the expedition should be undertaken under their own superintendence, and as a matter of public concern; and Parliament has now placed at their disposal a sum of 5000 pounds for the purpose, and will undoubtedly give further assistance should it be requisite.

Great difficulties have, however, presented themselves as to the necessary arrangements. The hostilities in which the country is involved have necessarily directed the time and thoughts, not of Her Majesty's Government only, but also of many of those whose professional knowledge and experience might have been of the greatest assistance, in another direction. Of the distinguished Australian explorers now in this country some are incapacitated by reason of health, and others by the circumstance of their services being required in other directions, from taking the command.

It would, however, be a matter of regret if, now that the money has been voted and the preparations partially made, the Expedition was not able to start at the best period for commencing operations next year, which on the northern coast of Australia seems generally thought to be from February to April.

I enclose copies of certain portions of the correspondence which took place early in the present year between the Colonial Department and Captain Stokes and Mr. Sturt, who were consulted in order to obtain the benefit of their advice, and the former of whom I had at one time the hope to secure for the command of the Expedition.

You will collect from these documents that the general view of those who have considered the subject appears to be that Moreton Bay would be a convenient rendezvous for the land portion of the Expedition; that they might be conveyed by sea to the mouth of the Victoria River, on the north-west coast; that it would be advantageous, if possible, that they should act in concert with a Government vessel, which might be employed in surveying operations in the Gulf of Carpentaria and neighbourhood, while the land explorers were engaged in the interior.

SELECTION OF COMMANDER.

Her Majesty's Government are, however, fully aware that such projects, especially where they involve so much combination, can only be submitted generally to the leader of such an expedition, to whom great latitude must be left as to the mode of carrying his instructions into execution.

They have now come to the determination of offering the command of the land expedition to Mr. A.C. Gregory, Assistant Surveyor, in Western Australia. They have been induced to take this course both by the very high testimonials which have been given to the abilities and fitness of this gentleman for the purpose by such authorities as they have been able to consult in England, and also by your own reports concerning him, particularly that contained in your despatch of the 6th January, 1852.

Should Mr. Gregory accept the charge, which I trust, notwithstanding its arduous and responsible nature, you will find him ready to do, it is the wish of Her Majesty's Government that without waiting for further instructions he should proceed immediately to Sydney, where he will find such instructions awaiting him, and where his party will be organised.

You are authorised to supply Mr. Gregory with the necessary funds for this purpose, which will be repaid to the Local Government, from the Commissariat chest.

If you are aware of any persons in your Government well qualified and willing to serve under Mr. Gregory in subordinate capacities, or if he has himself any assistants whom he would be anxious to engage, you are at liberty to place them at his disposal; but it must be understood that this permission does not apply to persons who are to take charge of scientific departments of the Expedition, as there are already gentlemen of this class with whom her Majesty's Government have been in correspondence; any such person who may wish to join the Expedition can do so only as a volunteer.

Copy of this despatch has been transmitted by the same mail to Sir Charles Fitzroy, and likewise to the other Australian Governors. Sir Charles Fitzroy will therefore be fully prepared to receive Mr. Gregory, and to render him all assistance in his power; and I have every reason to hope for the zealous co-operation of the several local Legislatures and Governments in a scheme intended for the development of the vast and unknown resources of their common Continent.

You will, on receiving this despatch, immediately communicate with Mr. Gregory, and if he should accept the command of the Expedition, inform both the Secretary of State for the Colonies and Sir Charles Fitzroy, and the other Australian Governments, immediately of his having done so, and of his intended movements.

I have, etc.,

(Signed) NEWCASTLE.

JOURNAL OF THE NORTH AUSTRALIAN EXPLORING EXPEDITION, BY A.C. GREGORY.

The preliminary arrangements for the North Australian Exploring Expedition being complete, the stores, equipment, and a portion of the party were embarked at Sydney in the barque Monarch and schooner Tom Tough, and sailed for Moreton Bay on the 18th July, 1855, and on the 22nd anchored at the bar of the Brisbane River. The next day the Monarch attempted to enter the river, but being taken by the Government Pilot half a mile to the east of the channel over the bar, grounded, and was not got off till the 26th, when she entered the river. The steamer Ballarat was engaged to tow the Monarch up to the town of Brisbane; but having struck on a rock near Ipswich, sank, and the steamer Hawk was engaged to tow up the river.

The Hawk, however, proved to be of insufficient power, and it was then decided to embark the horses and sheep, which had been collected by Mr. H.C. Gregory, at Eagle Farm.

HORSES EMBARKED AT MORETON BAY.

The horses having been got on board the Monarch on the 31st July, and the sheep the next day, the steamer Bremer was employed to tow her over the Bar. It was evident, however, that the Bremer did not intend to do this, for she slacked the tow-line, and then steamed ahead full speed and snapped the hawser, and went off without any explanation.

Having removed a quantity of stores from the Monarch to the Tom Tough, so as to reduce the draft of the former, on the 8th August warped over the bar and went over to Moreton Island, where about three tons of water were taken in from the fresh-water creeks near the Pilot Station.

On the 12 August weighed and left Moreton Bay; and this being the last point of communication with the civilised world, the Expedition might be considered to commence on this date.

The party consisted of eighteen persons, as follows: commander A.C. Gregory; assistant commander, H.C. Gregory; geologist, J.S. Wilson; artist and storekeeper, J. Baines; surgeon and naturalist, J.R. Elsey; botanist, F. Mueller; collector and preserver, J. Flood; overseer, G. Phibbs; stockmen, etc., C. Humphries, R. Bowman, C. Dean, J. Melville, W. Dawson, W. Shewell, W. Selby, S. Macdonald, H. Richards, J. Fahey. The livestock comprised fifty horses and 200 sheep.

The provisions consisted of flour, salt pork, preserved beef, rice, peas, preserved potatoes, sago, sugar, tea, coffee, vinegar, limejuice, etc., calculated to supply the party on full rations for eighteen months.

On 13th August passed Breaksea Spit, and Port Curtis next morning, the weather being fine with south-east winds; reached Port Albany on 26th. Landed on Albany Island, which is principally of sandstone formation rising into hills of moderate elevation, the soil generally poor and sandy covered with bush and small trees, with a few open grassy patches. Fresh water was found in a small cove 100 yards north from the landing-place on the sandy beach; the supply was so small as to be of little use, and the position inconvenient of access.

The mainland appeared to be covered with much dense bush, and the rocky sandstone hills did not indicate that the country was of any great value either for agricultural or pastoral purposes.

Port Albany is a narrow, but deep channel between Albany Island and the mainland of Cape York. It is easy of ingress and egress; but is neither safe or convenient, owing to the great rapidity of the current which sets through with the tide.

Some canoes with natives came to the vessels. They evidently have frequent communication with vessels passing through the Straits, and are well acquainted with the use and name of tobacco, which they smoke in large bamboo pipes. Their arms consisted of spears, bows, and arrows. The canoes, formed of a single tree, rudely hollowed out, and fitted with outriggers.

27th August.

Left Port Albany, and, passing through Endeavour Strait, were favoured with a light easterly wind as far as Port Essington, which was sighted on September 1st, and after passing through Dundas Strait anchored for the night.

The following morning passed Vernon Island with a light breeze. At 9.50 p.m. the Monarch grounded on a rocky reef off the entrance of Port Patterson, the master of the vessel not having made due allowance for the indraught of the tide. Unfortunately this occurred at the top of the spring tide, and the result was that, though every exertion was made to warp the vessel off, the tide did not rise sufficiently to float her until the 10th September, when, by cutting off the false keel and levelling the surface of the rock, we succeeded in hauling her off, with comparatively little damage, as the weather continued calm during the whole of this anxious period.

As the vessel lay on her side at low tide, the position of the horses was extremely inconvenient, and they suffered a greater amount of injury during these eight days than on the whole of the preceding voyage, and it is to this that the subsequent loss of so large a number of the horses is to be attributed; for though only two died on board the vessel, the others became so excessively weak that some had not the strength to go through the fatigue of landing and the journey from Point Pearce to the Victoria River, and at the same time the supply of forage was so reduced that it became necessary to land the horses immediately on reaching Point Pearce, and before the place could be examined for the best landing.

LAND AT THE ENTRANCE OF VICTORIA RIVER.

After getting off the reef, light winds and calms delayed the voyage to the Victoria River; but as the Tom Tough worked along the coast better than the Monarch, I went on with the schooner to examine the entrance of the river. Ascending the Victoria to Blunder Bay, found that the locality was not suited for landing horses, and therefore returned to Treachery Bay, near which Mr. H.C. Gregory had discovered abundance of grass and water under Providence Hill of Captain Stokes; commenced landing the horses on the 18th; but, in consequence of the strong tides and extensive mangrove flats, great difficulties were encountered, the horses having to swim more than two miles from the vessel to the shore, and were so exhausted that three were drowned, one lost in the mud and mangroves, and one went mad and rushed into the bush and was lost. Having transferred the stores to the Tom Tough, on the 24th the Monarch sailed for Singapore. Mr. Wilson was instructed to proceed in the schooner up the Victoria River, and to establish a camp at the highest convenient position on the bank of the river, while I proceeded overland with Mr. H. Gregory, Dr. Mueller, and seven of the men, hoping, by easy journeys of eight to ten miles per day, to give the horses time to partially recover the effects of the voyage.

MACADAM RANGE. RUNNING STREAM OF FRESH WATER.

1st October, 1855.

Accompanied by Mr. H. Gregory, I left the camp to search for a practicable route by which we could cross the MacAdam range; but, after proceeding about a mile, shot an emu, with which we returned to camp, and again started at 7.10 a.m., pursuing a south-east course, crossed a stony ridge, and at 8.0 a.m. came on a creek about twenty yards wide, with good pools of water and a grassy margin, but the country generally barren and stony. After several ineffectual attempts, we ascended the hills to the south-east of the creek, and traversed a very broken country of sandstone formation till 11.0 a.m., when we reached the head of a creek trending to the southward; this was followed down till 1.0 p.m. when we halted an hour, and again proceeded till 4.30 p.m., the country being very poor and rising into rocky hills on both banks of the creek; we then entered a wide grassy flat destitute of trees, extending six miles north to south, and fifteen miles east to west; on the south side there appeared to be a creek or river, which we supposed to be the Fitzmaurice River. This plain was bounded on all sides by steep rocky hills of sandstone of barren aspect. Returned up the creek till 6.0 p.m. and halted for the night. The day was hot and sultry, though a heavy thundershower somewhat cooled the air. The MacAdam Range is of sandstone, the strata of which dip about 30 degrees to the south, in which direction, as we advanced, the rock was more slaty, and broke into rhomboidal fragments. Water is abundant in the creeks, but the grass is scanty, and the rough surface of the sandstone and rocky ravines renders the country difficult to traverse. Timber is scarce, chiefly small-sized eucalypti; the cotton-tree was observed in a few of the valleys.

2nd October.

Returning to the camp we attempted to follow one of the creeks down to the plain on the north-west side of the range, but found the ravine too steep and rocky for the horses to pass, and were compelled to retrace our steps and cross several steep and rocky hills, reaching the camp at 2.0 p.m., at which time the thermometer stood at 94 degrees in the shade and 114 degrees in the sun.

3rd October.

Three of the horses had strayed, and this detained us till 11.0 a.m., when I started with the party, leaving Mr. H. Gregory and Bowman to look for the missing animals. Proceeding in a south-east direction to the crossing of the first creek, ascended the MacAdam Range, and steered east-south-east to the second creek; the course was then north-east and east to the head of the creek tributary to the Fitzmaurice River, and then encamped at 3.45 p.m. At the highest point on this day's route the aneroid stood at 29.40, and at the camp 29.55; thermometer, 88 degrees. The higher points of the range did not exceed 100 before the highest ridge crossed.

By a meridian altitude of a Cygni, the latitude 14 degrees 33 minutes 26 seconds.

4th October.

At 10.0 a.m. Messrs. H. Gregory and Bowen reached the camp with one of the missing horses, and, having obtained some provisions, returned to search for the other two horses. At noon started with the party, and followed down the creek in a south-south-east direction till 4 p.m., and encamped at the termination of the hilly country. One of the horses, Madman, showed symptoms of illness a short time before we started, and in crossing the creek half a mile above where we encamped he fell down and in less than three minutes died. This was a serious loss, as this animal was one of the most serviceable of our horses, having stood the voyage without losing his condition. The cause of death we were unable to ascertain; but the probability is that some poisonous plants existed at the place where we encamped last night.

By a meridian altitude of a Cygni, the latitude of the camp was 14 degrees 39 minutes 26 seconds. Thermometer: Sunrise, 80 degrees; at 11 a.m., 93 degrees; wet bulb, 80 degrees.

5th October.

This morning I started with C. Dean to examine the country to the east; after traversing the plain for two hours, came to a running stream ten yards wide, but the current very slow. The vegetation on its banks was very luxuriant, presenting a striking contrast to the surrounding country.

Followed the creek to the east and south for one and a half miles, when it changed to a salt creek, joining the Fitzmaurice River. We then steered south-east to a detached conical hill, which consisted of the same hard fine-grained sandstone as the ranges near the camp. Steering north-east and east for three miles along a salt creek, came to the termination of the salt water, where we saw four natives digging roots; on observing us they decamped. Our course was now south-east to a range of rocky hills, which we could not ascend with our horses from their steep and rocky character. We therefore steered north-west to a green patch of bushes in the plain, and at two miles came to a small lagoon 200 yards long and 30 yards wide, on which were numerous ducks and other water-fowl. Here we halted for one and a half hours, and then by a north-west and west course, passing through grassy plains and patches of forest, reached the camp at 8.30 p.m. Thermometer, 78 degrees to 104 degrees.

6th October.

Started at 8.10 a.m. with the whole party, and, steering east to the running creek, crossed it at the head of the salt water, and proceeding up the stream three-quarters of a mile, encamped. Near the creek we saw a native man and two women, who were much alarmed at the sudden appearance of the party, and retreated across the plain.

By a meridian altitude of a Cygni, the latitude was 14 degrees 40 minutes 4 seconds at this camp.

7th October.

At 8.0 a.m. steered an easterly course, crossing the grassy plain, beyond which we passed a low stony ridge thinly wooded with small trees; at 9.40 crossed a deep watercourse, with waterholes and grassy flats, and at 10.15 p.m. came to a second creek, which was followed up to the east-north-east till 11.20, when we halted at a small patch of grass; at 1 p.m. I rode to the north and east to seek a more suitable spot for an encampment, and having found a grassy flat and pool of good water one and a half miles higher up the creek, the party moved on to it at 4 p.m.

8th October.

Taking Dean with me, I proceeded to the south of the camp to ascertain the most convenient ascent of the rocky hills which bounded the plain. Following a small valley into the hills, after two hours' ride came to a creek trending to the south, the valley of which afforded a practicable line of route. We therefore returned to the camp at noon. At 3.0 p.m. started with the party, and moved the camp to the creek found in the morning. Thermometer, 114 degrees at 1 p.m.

9th October.

Started at 8.0 a.m., accompanied by Dean, and followed the creek through a rocky valley between sandstone ranges, the strata of which dip to the west at a high angle--30 degrees to 40 degrees; at 10.15 a.m. came to the tide waters of the creek, and after crossing several stony ridges which came close to the bank of the creek, at 11.30 a.m. reached a small running stream with a patch of good grass; here we halted for two hours, and then returned to camp; which we reached at 5.0 p.m., and found that Mr. H. Gregory and Bowman had arrived with the two stray horses, having found them about ten miles to the north-west of the camp, at the reedy swamp from which they strayed. Thermometer, 6 a.m., 77 degrees; noon, 114 degrees; 6 p.m., 92 degrees.

ENCOUNTER STEEP ROCKY RANGES.

10th October.

At 7.50 a.m. started with the whole party, and proceeded down the creek to the head of the salt water, and then by a detour among the rocky hills reached the running creek visited yesterday, and encamped at 11.0 a.m.; I then started with Mr. H. Gregory in a southerly direction, and after an hour's ride came to the Fitzmaurice River, which varied from 100 to 300 yards in width, the general course nearly east and west; the channel was full of rocks and banks which were dry at low water, the rise of the tide nearly twenty feet. The hills which bounded the valley of the creek we had descended terminated in an abrupt rocky ridge which left no passage between it and the river; we therefore returned about half a mile to the north, and, after a toilsome ascent of nearly an hour, crossed the ridge and halted at a small spring on its eastern side till 2.0 p.m., when we proceeded up the river, crossing two small dry creeks; after a fruitless search for a suitable spot to which the camp could be moved, there being no fresh water in the creeks, we turned towards the camp, but could not cross the range, as we everywhere encountered steep rocks and ravines, and were glad to extricate ourselves from the hills at 9.0 p.m., when we bivouacked in a grassy flat.

11th October.

At 4.30 a.m. resumed the attempt to cross the range, and at length found a practicable route for the pack-horses, passing a small spring of water at 7.0 a.m., and reached the camp at 8 a.m.; during our absence one of our best pack animals had died, apparently from poison. At 2.0 p.m. the party started to cross the range; but the horse Drummer was so weak that he fell several times, and we were at length compelled to abandon him. Having crossed the hills to the Fitzmaurice River, we proceeded up the valley and halted at a salt creek seven or eight yards wide, there being a little green grass on its banks.

Latitude by observation b Pegasi and a Andromedae 14 degrees 47 minutes 18 seconds.

HORSES BITTEN BY ALLIGATORS. CROSS THE FITZMAURICE RIVER.

12th October.

During the night the horses were several times disturbed, but it was not till morning that the cause was ascertained, when we found that they had been attacked by the alligators, and three were severely bitten and scratched. At 8.0 a.m. started to follow up the river; but the rocky hills approached so close to its banks as to leave no passage, and we had to ascend the range, which was not an easy task; after three hours of severe toil under a scorching sun we reached a more practicable country, and at 3.30 p.m. encamped on the bank of the river, above the influence of the tide, fifty yards wide. Two of the horses had been left about a mile from the camp quite exhausted, but at sunset they were brought in to the camp.

Latitude by observation a Cygni 14 degrees 51 minutes 37 seconds.

13th October.

At 7.0 a.m. crossed to the left bank of the river at a stony bar where the water formed a rapid twenty yards wide and two feet deep; we then followed the river up for half an hour and altered the course to south-south-east, along a running creek ten to twenty yards wide; at 8.5 a.m. crossed a running stream from the west; at 10.30 a.m. two of the horses were completely exhausted, but having rested them at a pool of water, one revived, but were compelled to leave the other. We then proceeded, but were obliged to return to the creek about a mile higher up, as several of the horses began to fail, and though we rested till 3.0 p.m., the second horse was unable to proceed, and was therefore abandoned. Since these horses were landed they have not had strength to rise without assistance, and it has been necessary to even watch them while feeding to lift them up when they fall down from exhaustion. Continuing our route, the valley was about two miles wide, with flat-topped hills bounding it on the east and west; there were a few pools of water in the creek, but the country was poor and stony with a few patches of grass; at 5.0 p.m. encamped.

Latitude by meridian altitude of a Cygni 15 degrees 1 minute 10 seconds.

14th October.

Started at 6.30 a.m. and pursued a south course till 8.0 a.m., when we crossed the ridge at the source of the creek and ascended some stony gullies to the south-west; at 10.40 a.m. halted at a small waterhole in a small creek. Re-commenced our journey at 3.0 p.m., and followed a valley to the south-east; but finding the country in that direction unsuited for our object, turned to the west and reached the creek again at 5.15 p.m.; followed it till 6.0 p.m. to the south-west, and encamped. There was abundance of water in the creek, and the rank growth of the grass on its immediate banks proved a great impediment to the horses. The back country, however, was very rough and stony, thinly timbered with white-gum eucalyptus of small size, and nearly destitute of leaves; and though the whole country was grassy, it was so much parched by the intense heat that it presented a very sterile aspect; at 4.30 p.m. there was a heavy thundershower.

15th October.

As the creek below the camp trended to the west and entered a deep rocky gorge in the sandstone range, we steered south at 7.0 a.m., crossing several stony ridges with small gullies and creeks trending west; at 10.20 a.m. crossed the highest ridge, and observed a succession of low stony ridges occupying the space between us and the Sea Range. Descending, we reached a creek, on the bank of which we halted at 11.30 a.m. Here we caught several small fish in a deep pool in the creek.

15th October.

Resuming our route down the creek at 2.30 pm, the average course was south-west till 5.30, when we were encamped at a large deep pool or reach of water three-quarters of a mile long and fifty yards wide, supplied by a small stream. Great numbers of large bats were seen hanging in the trees on the margin of the creek, some of which we shot; the flesh was white and was eaten, but it had an unpleasant flavour. The country during this day's journey has not been so hilly as yesterday, and near the camp the trees have retained a few leaves. The soil, however, shows no improvement, being universally stony, and though well-grassed, the country is useless for any purpose than feeding stock. The gouty-stemmed tree (adansonia) is more frequent on the banks of the creeks; pandanus and fig trees prevail near the water, and eucalypti on the hills.

Latitude 15 degrees 17 minutes 50 seconds.

THE VALLEY OF THE VICTORIA RIVER.

16th October.

Resumed our journey down the creek at 7.0 a.m., the general course south-south-west; the country became so steep and rocky that at 8.0 we left the valley and steered south, crossing several stony hills with rocky ravines, which were so rugged that they were scarcely passable. At 11.0 sighted the Victoria River, about six miles below Kangaroo Point; but, on attempting to descend the range, was intercepted by a deep valley bounded by sandstone cliffs 50 to 100 feet high; following the valley to the east and north-east in search of a break by which we could descend, but without success. At 3.0 p.m. one of the horses was so completely exhausted that he could proceed no farther; I therefore halted the party, and was examining the cliff to ascertain the best place for lowering one of the party by a rope into the valley for the purpose of procuring water from the pool which was visible 300 feet below us, when I found a small spring on the top of the cliff, at which we encamped. As soon as the horses were unsaddled, Mr. H. Gregory and myself proceeded to examine the valley to the east, but had not gone more than a mile when we observed a column of smoke rise from the camp, followed by a sheet of flame, which extended in a few seconds to the side of the adjacent hill. We therefore returned to the camp to subdue the fire, and, if possible, save some of the grass for the horses, which, with great difficulty, we succeeded in doing; but though checked, the fire had extended many miles over the country, and kept us busy all night. This fire originated for want of due precaution in clearing the grass around the fire at the camp, though the cook had been cautioned on the subject.

17th October.

At 5.0 a.m. left the camp with Mr. H. Gregory, and recommenced the search for a practicable descent into the valley, and about two miles from the camp found a break in the cliff. The hill was, however, so steep and rocky that it was necessary to form a path for the horses, and while Mr. H. Gregory returned, and was bringing up the party from the camp, I employed myself in filling up chasms with stones and removing rocks from the path, the steepness of the declivity greatly facilitating their removal, as it required but little force to hurl rocks of several tons weight into the valley below. Fortunately, we accomplished the descent without any accident, and reached the base of the hill at 11.30 a.m. Descending the creek, which occupied the lower part of the valley, for about two miles, encamped at a small pool of water. I then rode down the bank of the Victoria River, and ascertained that we were about six miles below Kangaroo Point. Returning to the camp, procured fresh horses, and, accompanied by Mr. H. Gregory, proceeded to Kangaroo Point, reaching the spot appointed for leaving a notice of the movements of the party in the schooner just as it fell dark, and though we found a small tree notched with an axe, there was nothing to guide us in any further search, and we therefore bivouacked.

18th October.

At daylight recommenced our search for some memorandum for our guidance to the camp or vessel, but only found five or six small trees cut with an iron axe, and the remains of a large fire; but if any memorandum had been left, there was no mark left for our guidance in the search for it, and I felt disappointed that my instructions had been so inefficiently carried into effect. As it was doubtful whether the vessel had proceeded up the river, I decided on continuing our route to some convenient spot for a camp near Steep Head, and accordingly returned to the party. The southern face of Sea Range is very abrupt and surmounted by a cliff of red sandstone 50 to 100 feet high, the whole height of the hills about 500 feet, the range being the edge of an elevated tableland, the upper strata being hard sandstone in horizontal beds which rest on soft shales which appear to be somewhat inclined; but its surface was so covered by fragments of the upper rocks that no satisfactory data was obtained. The soil of the level land between the Victoria and the Sea Range is very poor, and either sandy or covered with fragments of rock; there is no water, and the grass is very coarse and blady. Many flights of cockatoos came to drink at the pools near the camp, and about fifty were shot during the day.

ASCEND THE VICTORIA RIVER.

19th October.

Started at 7.0 a.m. and followed the river up to Kangaroo Point, and then by an easterly course ascended the salt-water creek which joins the Victoria at this point; at 4.0 p.m. we reached the termination of the salt water, beyond which it divided into several small dry channels, in one of which we found a small pool of fresh water, at which we encamped at 4.15. The result of our shooting this day was one turkey, one hawk, and thirty-nine cockatoos. The country near the creek is brown loam; but as the hills are approached the soil is very stony, but well covered with grass, and very thinly wooded with small eucalypti, which were nearly destitute of foliage. To the south of the creek the country appeared to be of somewhat better character.

THE TOM TOUGH WRECKED.

20th October.

At 7.0 a.m. steered north 160 degrees east till 10.0, over a level grassy plain wooded with small eucalypti and melaleuca, etc., the soil varying from a brown loam to a strong clay; altering the course to 190 degrees, we passed some low stony ridges, and at 11.30 halted in a dry gully to rest the horses during the heat of the day; at 3.0 p.m. again started and steered to the south-west for half an hour, when we camped at a sandy creek in which there was a shallow waterhole. At 4.0 I left the camp with Mr. H. Gregory and proceeded west-south-west to the river, which we reached at 5.45, and then followed it up for half an hour, when we observed a tent and boat on the opposite side of the river. Having hobbled the horses, we crossed over to the camp, which was established at a small spring, and found Mr. Elsey and two of the men in charge. Mr. Elsey informed me that the schooner had grounded on the bank below Mosquito Flat, and had received considerable damage. Fourteen of the sheep had been brought up to the camp, and the boat was expected up that evening with another lot of sheep. I now ascertained that a bottle had been buried near the marked trees at Kangaroo Point, and a pencil-mark made on one of the trees indicating its position, but this mark had escaped our observation. In the evening Messrs. Baines and Flood and one of the men arrived at the camp in the long-boat, bringing twelve sheep, having lost several on the passage up the river in consequence of detention on the shoals near the Dome. The whole stock of provisions at the camp consisting of ten pounds flour, ten pounds pork, six pounds sugar, and twelve pounds beef, I was unable to send the required supplies to the party in charge of the horses, and the sheep were too poor to be fit for food. The Tom Tough reached Entrance Island on the 25th September, and the next day anchored off Rugged Ridge; on the 27th was proceeding up the river, and grounded on a ledge of rocks on the south side of the river, about six miles below Mosquito Flats; and from that date was never sufficiently afloat to be under control, but gradually drifted up to about two and a half miles below Curiosity Peak. From the time of getting on the rocks she had leaked considerably, and a large quantity of stores had been destroyed or damaged, there being at one time four feet of water in the hold; but by nailing battens and tarred blankets over the open seams the leaks had been greatly reduced. The stock of water on board the schooner having been exhausted during her detention, Mr. Wilson had sent the boat up to Palm Island to bring down a supply; but having greatly miscalculated the time requisite for this expedition up the river, the distance being sixty miles, the sheep had been kept several days without a sufficient supply of water, and a great number had died.

21st October.

Proceeding down the river with Messrs. Baines and Flood in the long-boat, the tide being unfavourable, we only reached Kangaroo Point.

22nd October.

Started at 2.0 a.m., and reached the schooner at 11.0 a.m., having been delayed by the flood tide. The vessel had not moved during the last four tides, and the leaks had in some degree stopped. She was so deeply bedded in the sand that, though the bank was dry at three-quarter ebb, I could not examine her bottom. The deck beams, however, were strained and broken, and it was evident that the vessel had been much damaged by resting on her centre, when the current had worked deep holes at the head and stern. Only fifty-five sheep remained on board, and those in a miserable condition. At 5.0 p.m. despatched Mr. Flood in the gig with one month's provisions for the party at the camp; 8.0 p.m. the tide rose to five feet on the bank, but the vessel only just floated in the hollow in which she lay.

23rd October.

At 8.0 a.m. the tide rose to six feet on the bank, and the schooner was moved her own length towards the channel in shore; at 10.0 a.m. the tide ebbed, and she settled on an even keel. Mr. Baines having informed me that Overseer Humphries had refused to assist in pumping the schooner on the 9th, he had, therefore, put him off duty till Mr. Wilson returned, on the 14th, when he was put on duty again. I therefore fined him one week's pay. The night tide did not rise so high as in the morning. Landed to search for fresh water, and found a small spring on the bank of the river at the upper end of the stony beach, three and a half miles below Curiosity Peak; this spring is below high-water mark, but at half tide boats can approach close to it, there being deep water close to the bank.

24th October.

Landed at 2 a.m. to procure water, having opened a well at the spring; filled two casks and returned to the vessel at 7. At 9.30 the schooner floated, and we moved her to about a mile above Curiosity Peak, where she again grounded on a bank; while afloat the pumps had to be kept constantly at work. With the night tide we floated over the bank; but the breeze failing, she was swept against the shore two and a half miles above Curiosity Peak, and before the kedge could be laid out the tide fell.

25th October.

The morning tide did not rise sufficiently to allow us to cross the banks; but the schooner was warped into a better position in the channel, about one mile higher up the river. Landed the sheep and drove such as could walk to the waterhole at our camping place, one mile north of the Dome, and left a party in charge, consisting of Dr. Mueller, Mr. Wilson, Overseer Humphries, and W. Selby. Fifty sheep were landed, but only forty-four reached the waterhole, and of these one died during the night. The night tide rose eight feet, and we moved the schooner to the right bank of the river off Broken Hill and anchored in the channel. Before the full moon the tides have been higher during the day, but as the time of full moon approaches the higher tide is at night.

26th October.

At 10.0 a.m. weighed and ran up the river with the flood to the commencement of the reach below Kangaroo Point, when the schooner grounded on a bank. Proceeded with Mr. Baines in the gig to the sheep camp with the intention of moving the sheep across the river and then driving them to the upper camp, but found them so weak that this arrangement was not practicable. Returned to the vessel.

27th October.

At 3 a.m. the vessel floated, and she was moved about a mile above Kangaroo Point, when we anchored in three and a half fathoms. At noon weighed, and with a light breeze from the west and north till a thunder-squall from the south-east compelled us to come to anchor one mile below Sandy Island; a change of wind enabled us to move on to Sandy Island.

28th October.

At 2 a.m. weighed, and towed the schooner to the upper end of the spit off Sandy Island, when she grounded, but was warped off at 4; the wind and tide were now adverse, and we therefore anchored in two fathoms. There is two fathoms in the channel past Sandy Island, but a reef of rocks extend from the left bank of the river, which renders it necessary to keep close to the edge of the shoal off the island.

TOM TOUGH REACHES DEPOT CAMP.

29th October.

At 2 a.m. weighed with the flood, and towed the schooner up the river about four miles; at 6.30 a light northerly breeze enabled us to stem the ebb tide, and at 9.40 the schooner was moored at the camp, in two fathoms, close to the bank. Having obtained a supply of water, I despatched Mr. Baines, with Phibbs, Shewell, and Dawson, in the gig to bring up the sheep, the long-boat also going down the river with a crew from the vessel to bring up the kedge anchor and warp from Alligator Island, and also to assist in bringing up the sheep. In the evening there was a fine breeze from the east, and the thermometer fell to 65 degrees during the night. A few days before our arrival one of the kangaroo dogs had been seized by an alligator, and instantly drowned. The horses had been brought to the camp by the ford at Steep Head, and were looking well.

30th October.

Commenced the erection of a shed to protect the stores, as it is necessary to land the cargo of the schooner to effect repairs. The keelson is broken seven feet before the mainmast, three of the deck beams are broken in the centre, and the knees are strained, and the bolts drawn; there is also reason to think that the floor timbers are fractured, and some of the timbers broken in her bends.

31st October.

Messrs. Wilson, Baines, and Mueller, with the party in charge of the sheep, arrived at 7 a.m., bringing the remainder of the sheep, twenty-six in number, eleven having been drowned from want of proper care in bailing the boat, which consequently sunk during the night. Such of the party as are not otherwise engaged are employed in the erection of the store shed. Being desirous to examine the river above Steep Head, commenced fitting the portable boat, but found that the heat of the climate had destroyed the seams of three of the air cells, and the boat is therefore unserviceable. The general character of the materials of which inflated boats are constructed precludes any effectual repairs, as the intense heat of the sun decomposes the varnish with which the canvas is covered; it first becomes soft and adhesive, and then changes to a substance like tar, which does not consolidate with a lower temperature. Adjusted the aneroid barometer.

1st November.

S. Macdonald was reported for being asleep on his watch during last night; reprimanded him for this neglect of duty. Several of the sheep escaped from the fold last night; some have been found, but eight are missing. Commenced thatching the store; landed maize, bran, and other stores from the schooner. Though the thermometer stood at 100 degrees in the shade, yet a westerly breeze renders it cool enough to work. Mr. Baines employed repairing the portable boat; Richards clearing a plot of ground near the spring for a garden.

DAMAGE TO PROVISIONS.

2nd November.

Continued to discharge the cargo of the schooner; at the request of the master of the Tom Tough, examined sixteen small and four large casks of bread, which had been damaged by salt-water; the whole of this bread was found to be quite destroyed and unfit for use. Although the large casks had been carefully coopered in Sydney, yet the hot climate had opened the joints, and as there were three to five feet of water in the vessel when aground in the lower part of the river, the bread was completely saturated. The leakage of the schooner has been much reduced, and now only requires pumping every six hours. The dryness of the air has increased from 10 to 20 degrees of evaporation, and the heat is not so oppressive, though the mean temperature exceeds 85 degrees. Heavy thunder-clouds are visible on the horizon, and the lightning is frequent in the early part of the night, especially to the east. Since the spring tides the river has gradually fallen, and is now four feet lower than low water at the full and change, and it does not vary more than one and a half feet in the twenty-four hours. A small spring of water has been found below high-water mark close to the landing place.

3rd November.

Completed thatching the store; continued landing stores from the schooner; coopering the flour-barrels. Towards evening there was a strong breeze from the north, which suddenly veered to the west, with thunder and a little rain. The sheep are visibly gaining flesh, and the horses have improved, but they are still unfit for work, as the grass is very dry and not in a state to fatten animals.

4th November (Sunday).

The sky was overcast in the afternoon with a strong north-west breeze, and every indication of approaching rain.

5th November.

Landing stores from the schooner; general duties; light shower at 3 p.m.; evening cloudy. By observed altitudes on the meridian, the latitude of the camp 15 degrees 34 minutes 30 seconds.

6th November.

Messrs. H. Gregory, Elsey, and Mueller, with two men and the master of the schooner, proceeded up the river in the gig to ascertain the most convenient spot for procuring timber for the repair of the vessel; the men variously employed coopering casks, fencing garden, etc. Towards evening the sky was overcast, and a slight shower fell at 4 p.m., the thermometer varying from 85 degrees, 100 degrees, 90 degrees. Mosquitoes are very numerous in the evenings. Received from Mr. Wilson a copy of his diary while in charge of the party on board the schooner ascending the Victoria River. In going down to the well Richards fell down among the reeds, and a splinter entered his wrist, passing under the skin for one and a half inches; but no material injury has occurred, though the wound will disable him for a few days.

7th November.

Men employed coopering the flour-casks, fencing the garden, completing the store, and general camp duties. The party which went up the river yesterday in search of timber for the repair of the vessel returned in the evening, having found some suitable melaleuca-trees on the bank of the creek below Steep Head. The afternoon was again cloudy, with much lightning in the evening.

8th November.

Men employed clearing away the grass and bushes around the camp, landing cargo from the schooner, plotting map of route from Point Pearce to the Victoria River.

9th November.

Party employed as before.

10th November.

Party employed as before. On unpacking the rice and peas, found that 720 pounds of rice and half a bushel of peas were destroyed by salt-water, and much more damaged; much of the sugar is damaged; but as it is not prudent to open casks, the quantity lost cannot be ascertained. Wrote to the master of the Tom Tough, requesting information with reference to a complaint by Mr. Wilson, that on the 30th September his signals for a boat to bring him to the schooner had been disregarded.

11th November (Sunday).

TIMBER FOR REPAIRS OF VESSEL.

12th November.

Mr. H. Gregory, with Shewell and Dawson, accompanied Captain Gourlay to Steep Head to cut timber for the repair of the schooner. Erected a forge and continued the preparation of the garden, etc. Last night one of the sheep was strangled by getting entangled in the net which formed the sheep-pen. Received from the master of the Tom Tough a letter replying to my queries of the 10th instant. It appears that on the 30th September, while the schooner was aground in the lower part of the Victoria, Mr. Wilson landed to search for fresh water at Mosquito Flat; having made some indefinite arrangements with Mr. Elsey to signalize for a boat, should he require it, to return to the vessel; but he omitted to acquaint either the master of the schooner, or Mr. Baines, who was next in command to Mr. Wilson. The result was that when the signals were made there was some uncertainty whether they were fires lighted by Mr. Wilson as signals for a boat, and some delay ensued in preparing the boat, when it was found that the tide had fallen so much that there was not sufficient water to float the boat over the intervening sand-banks, and at low water Mr. Wilson waded across the deeper channels and walked over the dry banks to the vessel. As the affair appeared to be complicated with some private misunderstanding between the parties, and Mr. Wilson had neglected to make proper arrangements with the master of the vessel, I deemed it desirable that the investigation should not proceed any farther.

13th November.

Mr. Baines having succeeded in repairing the portable boat, I made preparation for an excursion up the river, as the horses were still unfit for the work of exploration, and I hoped to be able to cross the shallows which had obstructed Captain Stokes. Richards' arm does not progress in a favourable manner, and it is therefore necessary that Mr. Elsey should remain at the camp to attend to his case. The party proceeding with the boats will therefore consist of Mr. Wilson, Mr. Baines, Mr. Flood, and myself. Men employed as before, and the general duties of the camp.

14th November.

Party employed as before. At 3.30 p.m. I left the camp and proceeded to the creek, where the timber party were at work, reaching their bivouac at 7.30; six logs had been cut twenty to twenty-five feet long and twelve to fourteen inches square; the timber is a melaleuca with a broad leaf (Melaleuca leucodendron). The gum timber is generally unsound and worthless.

15th November.

Returned to the principal camp with Mr. H. Gregory at 11.0 a.m., and at 2 p.m. started in the indiarubber boat with Messrs. Wilson, Baines, and Flood; at 8.0 p.m. reached the creek near Steep Head, and remained at the camp of the timber party for the night.

16th November.

Started at 6.30 a.m. and crossed the shallows at Steep Head without much difficulty--as the tide was high, the water was six to eight inches deep. Three miles above Steep Head we observed three natives watching us, but they did not approach. At 10.0 a.m. reached Palm Island, which is only a bank of shingle with a few pandanus and melaleuca trees growing on it without a single palm-tree of any kind. One of the boats having been injured, hauled her up for repairs. Mr. Baines shot three whistling ducks on the island; they were very good eating. While at our dinner a native approached the bank of the river and came to us, and a parley commenced which was rather unintelligible, and when he found that he could not make himself understood by words, resorted to the language of signs, and expressed his contempt of us in an unmistakable manner. Having repaired the leak in the boat, we again moved up the river, but at one and a half miles came to a dry bar of rock, over which the boats were carried, and we passed a shallow pool of brackish water half a mile long to a second bar of greater breadth, and then entered a deep reach; but the day was so far advanced that we took advantage of a level rocky ledge and bivouacked.

INDIARUBBER BOATS FAIL.

17th November.

Proceeded up the river about a mile and came to a dry bank of shingle and rocks, which extended for at least a mile, and over which it was not practicable to carry the boats, which had been much injured in crossing the rocky bars yesterday, the heat having destroyed the texture of the waterproof canvas. I therefore decided not to expend any more time on this excursion, but return to the camp. We observed some blacks watching us from some thick scrub; but they did not approach near enough to hold any communication. At 2.0 p.m. commenced the return down the river and reached Palm Island after dark and bivouacked.

18th November.

At 3.0 a.m. there was a slight shower, and at 6.0 a.m. proceeded down the river, having dragged the boats over the shingle bank at Steep Head, where there was scarcely one inch of water; halted at the creek where the timber had been cut, to procure water for breakfast, and then sailed down the river and encountered a heavy squall, with thunder and lightning, just as we approached the camp; the rain continued nearly throughout the night. Captain Gourlay informed me that on the 16th three blacks had visited his party while cutting timber, and that in the evening some noise was heard, and being taken for the voices of the blacks, they had taken to the boat with great precipitation and returned to the schooner; the mosquitoes have nearly disappeared.

19th November.

Sent a party, consisting of Phibbs, Humphries, Shewell, Selby, and Dawson, to assist the master of the schooner in bringing the timber down the river; Richards' arm is somewhat better, but not progressing favourably; Fahey is on the sick list; the rain having moistened the grass, the horses did not come in for water to-day; the weather continues very hot, generally 90 degrees at sunrise and 105 degrees at noon in the shade.

20th November.

Commenced shoeing the horses and made preparations for a journey up the Victoria, to reconnoitre the country previous to starting for the interior.

21st November.

Fahey, being convalescent, was employed as cook; Mr. H. Gregory, Mr. Flood, Bowman, and Melville, shoeing horses; Dean making charcoal for the forge; in the afternoon there was a heavy thundershower; the flies are very troublesome and annoy the horses so much that they will not stand quiet to be shod, and some of the horses are nearly blind in consequence of the flies crawling into their eyes.

22nd November.

Shoeing horses, fitting saddles, etc.; the schooner leaks about seven inches per hour, and as the master is absent with the greater part of the crew, procuring timber, I have afforded assistance from the party at the camp, to assist in keeping the vessel dry.

EXPLORE THE UPPER VICTORIA.

23rd November.

Preparing equipment for the party proceeding to explore the Victoria River, towards the upper part of its course; the grass has become quite green and fresh water is also abundant, which has caused some of the horses to stray beyond the usual feeding ground on the Whirlwind Plains.

24th November.

Mr. H. Gregory and Mr. Flood brought in the stray horses, having found them beyond Sandy Island. The timber party returned to the camp with four logs of timber, which are intended to strengthen the keelson. While at work at the creek where the timber was procured the party had been twice visited by the blacks; these intrusions were neither decidedly friendly or hostile, but they stole some small articles which had been imprudently left lying near one of the logs of timber while the party was employed elsewhere; about 10.0 a.m. the blacks set fire to the grass about 200 yards from the camp, and then retired. At 2.0 p.m., left the camp, accompanied by Messrs. H. Gregory, Wilson, and Mueller, with seven horses and twenty days' provisions, the object being to examine the country through which the exploring party will have to travel on the route to the interior; at 6 a.m. bivouacked at Timber Creek; in the principal channel of the creek there were many small pools of water, and the grass was fresh and green on the flats. Except on the banks of the river and creeks, the country is very poor and stony; the geological structure of the country is the same as at Sea Range--the same bands of sandstone cliff resting on soft shales, the strata being horizontal; but beneath the shales chert and coarse siliceous limestone were exposed, and fragments of jasper are frequent. The principal timber is white-gum of small size, and the cotton-tree (cochlospermum), which sometimes attains the thickness of nine to twelve inches. Though grass is abundant on every description of soil, yet the greater part is of inferior descriptions and dries up completely at this season.

Latitude by altitude of Achernar, 15 degrees 39 minutes 43 seconds.

25th November.

Started at 5.45 a.m., and followed the creek to the south-south-east; it rapidly decreased in size, branching into small gullies, so that we had some difficulty in finding water for a midday halt. The flats on the bank of the creek are in some parts nearly a mile wide, well grassed and openly timbered; the hills are of sandstone, but chert and coarse limestone were frequently seen on the lower ridges. At noon halted at a small pool of rainwater. The day was cloudy and cool, the thermometer only 90 degrees at 2 p.m. At 3.0 resumed our route up the creek, which soon terminated in small gullies rising in stony ridges; as there was no appearance of water to the south, the course was changed to south-east and east, in which direction we followed down a gully, and at 7.20 halted at a small waterhole.

26th November.

Starting at 6.15 a.m., steered first north 70 degrees east and then 60 degrees till 3 p.m., traversing a level grassy box-flat extending along the northern side of a rocky sandstone range. At 3.0 p.m. reached the south-west end of the Fitzroy Range, which is a narrow ridge of sandstone hills ten miles long and one to two miles broad; at the north end of the range we found a small pool of rainwater, and, having watered the horses, pushed on towards the Victoria River, at the base of Bynoe Range; but although the country was level, we were so much retarded by the soft nature of the soil that the river was not reached till sunset, and the banks of the river were so steep that the water was not accessible for the horses, and we therefore encamped at a small hole of muddy rainwater. Our camp was about four miles above the furthest point attained by Captain Stokes, and consequently in Beagle Valley which we had traversed for more than thirty miles, the greater part of which was well grassed and openly wooded with box, bauhinia, and acacia. The Fitzroy Range is almost isolated, and there is a level plain five or six miles wide to the south-east, beyond which there is a high sandstone range surmounted by an almost unbroken cliff of sandstone near the summit, and which appeared to be quite impassable.

27th November.

Steering east-south-east through grassy flats for one hour and a half, found that the river had turned to the northward round a steep hill, but continuing our course, crossed a low stony ridge and again approached the river, the banks of which were so steep that the horses could not get to the water, and therefore followed it two miles and encamped on a stony bar where the water was easy of access. The valley of the river is much contracted by the steep sandstone hills, which come close on both banks. In the bed of the river several fragments of jasper and black shale were found, the latter appearing to belong to the coal formation. A slight shower in the afternoon cooled the air, and the temperature was only 92 degrees at sunset, and the wet bulb 79 degrees.

Latitude by Achernar 15 degrees 36 minutes 29 seconds.

DEEP GORGE IN TABLELAND.

28th November.

Started at 6.15 a.m. and followed the river, which first came from the east, then south-east and south-west till 10.40, when we crossed to the right bank and halted. The valley of the river is much narrower, and does not exceed half a mile, and is bounded by cliffs of sandstone varying from 50 to 300 feet high. The waters of the river occasionally rise 100 feet, as the marks of the floods extended to the base of the cliffs; the regular channel of the river is about 200 feet wide, the water forming deep reaches often more than a mile long and separated by dry stony bars of shingle and rock. The sandstone is thicker here than towards Steep Head, but there is no change in the geological character, except that the chert-beds are not exposed. The tracks of several natives were observed, but they were not seen by us; at 2.0 p.m. resumed the journey up the river in a generally south direction, and at 4.30 encamped, but had great difficulty in forcing our way through the reeds to procure water.

Latitude by meridian altitude of a Persei 15 degrees 41 minutes 54 seconds.

29th November.

Left the camp at 6 a.m. and continued the route up the river to the south till 10.10, when we halted till 2.15 p.m., and then proceeded on till 4.45, and encamped at a small pool of rainwater, the bank of the river being so steep and covered with high reeds that the water is scarcely accessible. The valley of the river is still bounded by sandstone cliffs; but as the strata are horizontal, and the bed of the river rises, the shales are not much exposed, and the alluvial banks reach to the base of the cliffs, which are so continuous that I have not yet seen a spot where we could have ascended the tableland in which the valley is excavated. Several tributary gullies having passed, but none worthy of special notice. Fragments of trap-rock are frequent in the bed of the river, and one specimen contained traces of carbonate of copper; at 6.0 thermometer 92 degrees, aneroid 29.80, at the camp--sixty feet above the river.

Latitude by meridian altitude of Achernar 15 degrees 50 minutes 30 seconds.

VALLEY SUDDENLY WIDENS.

30th November.

Resumed our route up the river at 5.40 a.m., the general course south; there being no change in the character of the country till 10.0, when the hills receded and the cliffs ceased; at 10.30 halted at a small pool in a back channel of the river. At noon the thermometer stood at 100 degrees in the shade, and the aneroid 29.75--forty feet above the river. Starting again at 2.0 p.m., soon entered an extensive plain extending to the east, south, and west; followed a large creek to the south-west till 6.15, and encamped.

Latitude by meridian altitude of Achernar 16 degrees 2 minutes 30 seconds.

1st December.

At 5.40 a.m. crossed the creek and steered east to the foot of a rocky hill, but not seeing the principal branch of the Victoria, returned to the creek and then steered south-south-west till 10.0 a.m., when we crossed two small creeks, in the second of which we found a pool of water surrounded by reeds (typha), and halted during the heat of the day. The country traversed was first a stony ridge, on which several small stone huts had been erected, but scarcely of sufficient size for a man to enter, and the roofs were only formed by a few pieces of wood and a little grass; they consist of a wall three feet high, in the form of a horseshoe, about three feet in diameter inside; the entrances of some had been closed with stones and afterwards partially opened, and I can only conjecture that, as the practice of carrying the bones of their deceased relatives prevails in this part of Australia, it is probable that these erections are used as temporary sepulchres. After crossing this stony ridge entered a level plain of clay, much fissured by the sun, and in some parts covered with fragments of jasper and sandstones; as the creek was approached limestone prevailed, but the exposed portion seemed to be formed by a rearrangement of the broken fragments of older rocks, which were visible in the gullies. The water at which we halted appeared to be supplied by a spring, and not to be the retention of rainwater. At 3.15 p.m. proceeded in a westerly direction in search of the principal branch of the creek, which we reached at 4.0 p.m., but found it much reduced in size, not exceeding fifteen yards in width; followed it up for an hour, and camped at a small but deep pool of water, which is evidently supplied by a spring in the limestone rocks, which form the banks of the creek.

Latitude by meridian altitude of Achernar 16 degrees 10 minutes.

JASPER RANGE.

2nd December.

Having filled our water-bags, we left the camp at 6.40 a.m., and steered a course of north 200 degrees east towards a range of hills composed of jasper rock, the highest point of which we reached at 10.0. The aneroid stood at 29.15; thermometer 94 degrees. Three miles to the south-west of this range the country rose into an elevated tableland higher than the Jasper Range; towards this we continued our route, following a small watercourse which gradually turned to the east. Finding the country very dry and rocky, and no prospect of finding a spot where the tableland could be ascended, we returned to the waterhole at which we camped last night.

3rd December.

At 6.0 a.m. were again in the saddle, and steering north till 7.20, ascended an isolated hill of trap-rock rising abruptly in the centre of the open plain about 200 feet. Having taken bearings of the surrounding ranges, steered north 30 degrees east till 10.30, across a level grassy plain to the creek, which, though much larger than at the camp, was destitute of water; but following its course downwards, at 10.50 halted at a small pool. Judging from the height that drift-wood was lodged in the branches of the trees, the floods rise about fifty feet; the regular channel is thirty yards wide; on the banks red, green, and white shales are exposed, but the bed of the creek is generally sandy. A large tributary appears to join this creek from the west, in which direction a large valley extends fifteen miles. At 3 p.m. steered east, and passed to the south of a remarkable sandstone hill, which we named Mount Sandiman, and at 5.30 reached the bank of the Victoria coming from the south-south-east; followed it up for one mile and encamped where a ledge of rock gave easy access to the water. In the evening there was a slight shower, and a heavy thunderstorm passed to the north.

4th December.

About 5.45 resumed our journey up the river, passing through wide grassy flats and over a sandstone ridge which was covered with triodia; from this ridge there was an extensive view of the country to the south and east, but no hills of greater elevation than the sandstone tableland were visible, and for twenty miles the valley of the river expanded into a wide plain thinly timbered with box-trees. Continuing a south-south-east course through a fine grassy country till 10.0, halted in a patch of green grass. The elevation of this part of the valley of the Victoria is not great, as the barometer stood at 29.77 forty feet above the river; thermometer, 101 degrees. The soil on the bank of the river is good and well-grassed, but the inundations during the rainy season extend on each side of the river several miles. The strata of the sandstone, where exposed, dip to the north, but there is no alteration in the character of the rocks. Abundance of portulaca grew near our halting place, and furnished us with an agreeable vegetable; this plant was afterwards found over the whole of Northern Australia, and proved a very valuable article of food. At 3.20 continued our route, and at 5.30 bivouacked at a small pool of rainwater in one of the back channels of the river, the banks of which were inconveniently covered with high reeds. During the night there was continuous light rain till 4.0 a.m.

ABUNDANCE OF FISH.

5th December.

Continued our route up the river to the south-south-west from 5.45 a.m. till 10.45, passing through open grassy box flats; a low grassy range approached the right bank and again receded; to the west a range of broken hills rose to 500 feet parallel to our course and five miles distant. Halted in the bed of the river, which formed fine reaches of water, with dry sand-bars between; caught several catfish and perch; mussels were abundant, the form of the shell much longer than I have before seen in the other parts of the river. At noon: Barometer, 29.80; thermometer, 104 degrees; at 3.0 p.m.: Barometer, 29.65; thermometer, 93 degrees. At 3.30 steered south from the right bank of the river, which turned to the westward; crossed some fine grassy country thinly timbered with box, and at 4.50 came to the southern branch of the river. This branch trended to the north-east, and consequently joins at a point lower down than where we crossed, the junction not having been observed. These two branches of the Victoria are so nearly equal in apparent size that it will remain for future examination to determine which is to be considered the tributary. Crossing to the right bank, we followed it upwards along the foot of the high land for half an hour, and encamped in the bed of the river.

Latitude by meridian altitude of Achernar 16 degrees 26 minutes.

RETURN DOWN THE VICTORIA.

6th December.

The day commenced with a heavy thundershower, which continued for several hours; but the rain not being quite so heavy at 6 a.m., we started and proceeded along the bank of the river to a hill about one and a half miles south-west of the bivouac. On ascending the hill, we found that though the elevation and position accommodated a fine view in fine weather, yet the rain at the present time obscured all distant objects, but the country to the south and west consisted of flat-topped sandstone hills with large open valleys between; to the east the view was obstructed by rising ground, while to the north lay the vast grassy plain which we had traversed during the last two days. The western branch of the river turned to the west-south-west along the foot of the sandstone ranges, its course being marked by a line of green trees, which contrasted strongly with the white grass on the open plains on its banks. The south branch of the river appeared to come from a valley trending south-south-east, but the thick mist obscured that part of the country. As we had now examined the country sufficiently to enable the main party to advance a whole degree of latitude without any great impediment, and ascertained the general character of the country and the nature of the obstacles to be encountered, and on which the equipment of the party would in some measure depend, we turned our steps towards the principal camp, crossing the western branch of the river at 9.50, and reached our camp of the 4th at 3.20 p.m. The rain this morning cooled the air to 74 degrees at 9 a.m. and 85 degrees at sunset.

7th December.

Resumed our journey down the river, following the outward track from 5.40 a.m. till 11.0, when we halted till 3.25 p.m. Thermometer at noon 102 degrees, with a cool southerly breeze; wet bulb, 78 degrees. Resuming our route, crossed to the right bank of the river, and bivouacked at the termination of the plains.

8th December.

At 5.45 a.m. proceeded down the right bank of the river, which was very rocky and steep; we therefore crossed to the left bank, and at 11.0 halted one mile above the bivouac of the 29 ultimo. Between 2.0 and 3.0 p.m. there was a heavy thunderstorm, when half an inch of rain fell; at 3.45 resumed our journey, and encamped about four miles lower down the river.

9th December.

Followed the left bank of the river from 6.0 to 11.0 a.m.; found the travelling less stony and intersected by gullies than the right bank; at 3.50 p.m. resumed our route, and at 6.30 encamped.

10th December.

Travelled down the river from 5.45 till 10.0 a.m.; when we halted a quarter of a mile above the camp of the 27th November. At 2.0 p.m. a heavy thundershower cooled the atmosphere from 100 degrees to 77 degrees. Resumed our journey at 3.0 and at 6.30 camped in the level plain at the foot of the Fitzroy Range, on the east side, water being abundant in every hollow, and since we passed up the river there has been heavy rain in this part of the country, and several of the gullies have been running eight feet deep. Shot a turkey and three black ibis. The Fitzroy Range extends about two miles north of a line from the gorge of the river to Bynoe Range, the Victoria winding round the north end of the range, and some tributary creeks appear to join from the north, as a valley extends several miles in that direction. The rain does not appear to have been general over the country, as it often occurs that after travelling over two or three miles of green grass where the gullies show signs of recent flood, that this beautiful verdure suddenly ceases, and we again encounter a dry and parched country which exhibits all the signs of an Australian summer.

11th December.

Left our camp at 5.45 a.m., and, steering west, crossed the low ridge of the Fitzroy Range, and having taken bearings of the features of the country, steered north 260 degrees east through the level plain which occupies the space between Wickham Heights and the Fitzroy Range, and which was named Beagle Valley by Captain Stokes. The soil of this plain is a brown clay, which in the dry weather crumbles into small pieces, so that the horses sink deeply into it; but in the wet season the whole is deep mud; it, however, appears to be very fertile, and produces an abundance of grass; the trees consist of bauhinia, acacia, and some eucalypti. Halting from 10.0 a.m. till 4.0 p.m. changed course to north 245 degrees east, and after traversing a grassy box flat for two hours, camped at a small watercourse with pools of rainwater in a rocky limestone channel.

BEAGLE VALLEY.

12th December.

Started at 5.30 a.m., and steered north 245 degrees east for one and a half hours, when we passed the high bluff of the range and changed the course north 330 degrees east, keeping three-quarters of a mile east of the remarkable hill called the Tower, by Captain Stokes, from a remarkable rock on the summit. The country was very rough and stony, though the ridge we passed over was not more than 200 or 300 feet above the river. Continuing a north-north-west course, at 9.45 reached the bank of the Victoria, which was followed on a course of 200 degrees till 10.10, when a large creek joined the river; this creek drains nearly the whole of Beagle Valley, and takes its rise in the north-west slope of Stokes' Range. The course was then westerly till 12.15 p.m., when we encamped in a grassy flat one-third of a mile from the river. Marked a large adansonia tree 12 on its south side.

13th December.

Leaving our bivouac at 5.30 a.m., followed the valley of the river, passing the ridge at back of Steep Head at 10.0., and halted at Timber Creek at 11.0. The heavy rains which occurred in Beagle Valley do not appear to have extended to this part of the country, and the grass is still dry and withered. At 2.30 p.m. resumed our route and reached the principal camp at

6.30, and found the party all well, except Richards, who was still suffering severely from the injury to his wrist. Mr. Baines was absent, having started on Wednesday in search of two horses which had strayed to the westward.

BAINES' RIVER.

14th December.

Messrs. Baines and Bowman returned with the stray horses, having found them on the bank of a small river fifteen miles to the west of the camp. This river, which I named the Baines River, has considerable pools of fresh water in its bed, which comes from the south-west, and flows into the large salt-water creek above Curiosity Peak. On one occasion Messrs. Baines and Bowman had halted to rest during the heat of the day, when they observed some blacks creeping towards them in the high grass; but, on finding they were observed, retired and soon returned openly with augmented numbers and approached with their spears shipped; but Mr. Baines and his companion having mounted their horses, galloped sharply towards them, and the blacks retreated with great precipitation. Mr. H. Gregory brought in the greater part of the horses; but as they had scattered very much in search of green grass, many of the horses were ten miles from the camp. Men employed cutting and carrying timber for the repair of the schooner, which work is progressing satisfactorily; computing astronomical observations.

15th December.

Party employed as before. One of the mares is reported to have foaled a fine filly. Thundershowers are frequent, and the country near the camp is clothed with verdure. Rode out with Mr. H. Gregory and Mr. Baines to bring in some horses which had strayed, and which, after several hours' tracking, we found and brought to the camp. The horses are now much improved, and, with the exception of three which are still very weak, are now in a serviceable condition, though few are capable of carrying heavy loads or performing long journeys; but as grass and water are now abundant for the first 100 miles of the route towards the interior, I hope that by travelling easy stages the horses will improve, and preparations are being made for commencing the journey early in January. The country being impracticable for drays, and as the sheep cannot be driven with advantage, owing to the high grass and reeds, it is necessary to constitute the party so that the whole equipment can be conveyed by pack-horses, to accomplish which the party proceeding to the interior must not exceed nine in number, for which the horses are capable of conveying five months' provisions and equipment. The remaining half of the party will have full employment in the repair of the schooner and care of the stores--points of vital importance to the

Expedition. It is therefore proposed to make the following division of the party, which, under existing circumstances, appears to me the most eligible.

PREPARATIONS FOR EXPEDITION.

16th December.

The exploring party to consist of the following: Commander, A. Gregory; assistant commander, H. Gregory; artist, T. Baines; botanist, F. Mueller; collector, J. Flood; overseer, G. Phibbs; farrier, R. Bowman; harness-maker, C. Dean; stockman, J. Fahey.

The party remaining in charge of the principal camp: Geologist, J.S. Wilson; surgeon, J.R. Elsey; overseer, C. Humphries; stockmen, Dawson, Shewell, Selby, Macdonald, Richards, Melville.

17th December.

Preparing a map of the late journey up the Victoria, shoeing horses, and other preparations for the expedition into the interior.

18th December.

Party employed as before.

19th December.

Removing the bones from the salt pork which is to form part of the provisions of the exploring party; the reduction in weight is 17 per cent. Packing flour in double canvas bags, containing forty or fifty pounds each. In the centre of each bag of flour one pound of gunpowder is placed as the most secure from accidents. Shoeing horses, etc., as before. At 10 o'clock last night it commenced raining, and continued till daybreak; the day has been cool and cloudy.

20th December.

Party employed as before; killed one of the sheep, which weighed thirty-eight pounds. During last night it rained for four hours, and there have been showers to-day.

21st December.

Preparing for explorations as before. The river commenced running, but is still brackish. The weather is cloudy, with frequent showers; the country is becoming very soft and boggy.

22nd December.

Frequent heavy showers, especially at night. Mr. Wilson, Dr. Mueller, and Selby went down the river to examine Sea Range and procure specimens of rocks and plants. The repairs of the schooner requiring some broad iron,

I had the ironwork of one of the drays appropriated to the purpose, as there was no iron of a suitable size on board the vessel. Party employed shoeing horses, fitting saddles, and general preparations of equipment for the exploring party.

23rd December.

Two of the horses have again strayed to the westward, and Mr. H. Gregory and Bowman were employed nearly the whole day in tracking them, and succeeded in bringing them in at night. The river is quite fresh, and running with a current from one to two miles per hour. Since the commencement of the rainy weather the general health of the party has improved; but this, perhaps, is due to the reduction of temperature, combined with greater regularity of habits and diet. Richards' arm is, however, in a very unsatisfactory state, though this is more the result of general ill-health than the original extent of actual injury.

24th December.

Preparing equipment, etc., as before. Dr. Mueller and Mr. Wilson returned in the boat from Sea Range. They report the river to be fresh at Sandy Island. Frequent heavy showers, which rendered the ground so soft that the horses cannot be hobbled without danger of their getting bogged, and it is scarcely possible to ride after them to herd them.

25th December.

Christmas day. Frequent heavy showers throughout the day and night. Killed a sheep; the weight, 38 1/2 pounds.

26th December.

Preparing equipment; fitting spare shoes for the horses, etc. Frequent showers.

27th December.

Packing stores, fitting saddles, etc. This has been the first fine day during the past week, having had only a single shower during the twenty-four hours.

FLOOD IN THE RIVER.

28th December.

Party employed as before. The schooner was moved into the stream, as the drift-wood collected in large quantities, and could not be easily cleared away from the bows when moored near the bank. The water of the river is very muddy, and has risen about six feet above the ordinary high-water mark. The current is about two miles per hour. In winding chronometer

2139, the chain, which was much corroded, broke, and the force of the recoil of the spring snapped it in so many places that I had to splice six of the links.

29th December.

As before--preparing equipment, etc.

30th December (Sunday).

31st December.

Preparing tracings of maps, etc., completed the preparations for the exploration of the interior.

A STAMPEDE.

1st January, 1856.

Wrote to Mr. Wilson, enclosing instructions for the guidance of the officer in charge of the camp on the Victoria. Wrote to the master of the Tom Tough instructions relative to the movements and repair of the Tom Tough, etc. Received from Mr. Wilson a letter requesting to be informed why he had been selected to take charge of the party at the principal camp. Wrote to Mr. Wilson in reply to his letter of this day's date. Having completed the preparations for the journey into the interior, the horses were saddled, and the party was on the point of starting, when a gun was fired on board the schooner, and the horses took fright and rushed wildly into the bush; and it was only after a hard gallop of two miles that they could be turned and driven back to the camp. Many of the saddles and loads were torn off by the horses having run against trees, and, as they had scattered very much, it took some time to collect the bags which had fallen from the horses, and four bags of provisions could not be found. A few of the straps of the colonial-made pack-saddles had given way, but there was no other damage done to them; but the English-made saddle was shaken to pieces. The party were occupied in the evening repairing damages.

2nd January.

Completed the repair of the saddlery, etc. broken yesterday; two of the missing bags were found, but a heavy shower having obliterated the tracks of the horses, two bags of sugar and sago were lost.

3rd January.

All arrangements being complete, the party commenced their journey at 11 a.m., and, proceeding up the river to Timber Creek, encamped there at 3.0 p.m.

The following is a memorandum of the arrangements and equipment of the party:

The Party: Commander, A.C. Gregory; assistant-commander, H.C. Gregory; artist, T. Baines; botanist, F. Mueller, collector, J. Flood; overseer, G. Phibbs; farrier, R. Bowman; harness-maker, C. Dean; stockman, J. Fahey.

Horses: 27 pack-horses with pack-saddles; 3 pack-horses with riding-saddles; 6 riding-horses.

Provisions for five months: Flour, 1,470 pounds; pork, 1200 pounds; rice, 200 pounds; sago, 44 pounds; sugar, 280 pounds; tea, 36 pounds; coffee, 28 pounds; tobacco, 21 pounds; soap, 51 pounds. Total, 3,330 pounds.

Equipment: Instruments, clothing, tents, ammunition, horseshoes, tools, etc., 800 pounds; saddle-bags and packages, 400 pounds; saddles, bridles, hobbles, etc., 900 pounds. Total, 5,430 pounds.

SENTRIES AT NIGHT.

The total weight was thus about two and a half tons, which, distributed on thirty horses, gave a load of 180 pounds each horse. Each person had a stated number of horses in his special charge, and was responsible for the proper care of the loads and equipment, the saddles and loads being all marked with numbers. A watch was constantly kept through the night, each person being on sentry for two hours in regular rotation, except myself, as I had to make astronomical observations at uncertain hours. The cook was on watch from 2.0 till 4.0 a.m., and having prepared breakfast, the party concluded this meal at daybreak, and thus the most valuable part of the day was not lost.

4th January.

Started at 7 a.m. and followed up the creek; but Dr. Mueller having wandered away into the rocky hills and lost himself, I halted at the first convenient spot, having despatched several of the party to search for him, but it was not till 4 p.m. that the Doctor reached the camp. At noon there was a shower of rain, which reduced the temperature to 92 degrees.

ASCEND TABLELAND.

5th January.

The day broke with a heavy shower, which continued till 7.30 a.m., when it was followed by a cool breeze from the west; at 8.30 steered north 150 degrees east magnetic up the valley of the creek till 11.0, when, crossing a low rocky ridge, we descended into Beagle Valley, and, steering 160 degrees till 2.10 p.m., halted at a small creek. The country is now covered with fine grass, and water is abundant, though the smaller watercourses have ceased to flow. In the evening walked to a hill about a mile from the camp; it was only 150 feet high, but gave a fine view of the distant ranges.

6th January.

It rained continuously during the night, with thunder and lightning. At 8.0 a.m. steered 160 degrees and soon came on a small creek with water-pandanus on its banks; followed it to the south-south-east; at 11.0 crossed it and changed the course to south-east, and at 11.30 encamped in a small gully; I then went with Mr. H. Gregory to look for a practicable ascent of Stokes' Range; having been successful in the search, we returned to the camp at 6 p.m. There are few spots where this range can be ascended, as a line of cliffs run along the brow of the hills varying from 10 to 100 feet in height. While on the hill we saw a few blacks, but they did not approach; the day was cloudy and cool, clearing after sunset.

Latitude by Canopus and Capella 15 degrees 59 minutes 57 seconds.

7th January.

The day again commenced with heavy showers, which lasted till 7 a.m. At 7.30 started on a course of 120 degrees; reached the foot of the sandstone range at 8.50, and the summit at 9.30, the tableland on the top of the range being intersected by deep ravines trending to the south-west; we steered east till 11.40, when we came to a deep valley trending east-south-east; having made the necessary observations for elevation, commenced the descent of the hills, which was practicable in few places, as the valley was walled-in by steep hills crowned by sandstone cliffs 20 to 100 feet in height, with only an occasional break. At 1.0 p.m. reached the base of the hill, and encamped at a small gully. The summit of the range is nearly a level tableland, the undulations not exceeding 100 feet, but is intersected by deep ravines with perpendicular sides, which vary from 100 to 600 feet in depth. The upper rock is sandstone, and the soil on it very poor and sandy, producing small eucalypti, hakea, grevillia, and a sharp spiny grass (triodia); this is the spinifex of Captain Sturt and other Australian explorers. The character of the country is similar to that of the interior of some parts of the western coast.

Latitude by Capella 15 degrees 59 minutes 32 seconds.

JASPER CREEK. GRASSY COUNTRY.

8th January.

Heavy rain till 7.0 a.m.; at 7.15 started and followed down the valley of the creek to south-south-east and south till 9.0, when it joined a larger valley trending east, in which a large creek in high flood obstructed our course. As the water was too deep to ford, we fixed a rope to a branch of a tree and passed the packs over the stream. This was accomplished at 3.0 p.m., and the water having also sunk a foot, the horses crossed over, and we encamped on the south side of the creek. The valleys are well grassed, and vary from a quarter to three-quarters of a mile in width, the hills rising steeply from the base to near the summit, where they are crowned by a sandstone cliff 20 to 150 feet high; the summits are level, or nearly so, as the valleys are only deep ravines excavated in the tableland. The valley of the larger creek appears to expand about five miles to the west of the camp, and the hills all rounded in their outline.

9th January.

A light shower at night was followed by a cool cloudy morning. At 6.50 a.m. followed down the creek to the east, and crossed to the left bank to avoid a rocky hill. On attempting to cross lower down, one of the pack-horses was carried down the stream some distance by the force of the current, and the saddle-bags were recovered a quarter of a mile below. The valley contracted as we proceeded, and at length the steep cliff left no passage on the left bank, and we had to return one and a half miles up the creek and cross to the right bank, when our course was again obstructed by a large tributary, which was crossed with some difficulty, and we passed through the rough rocky gorge of the creek, where the cliff approached the bank of the stream so closely that there was scarcely space for a horse to pass. At 12.10 p.m. camped on the bank of the creek at the termination of the hilly country, and, ascending a rocky elevation, obtained a view of the valley of the Victoria, and ascertained that we were on one of the branches of Jasper Creek. The afternoon and night were showery.

10th January.

Started at 6.30 a.m. and steered south-east, leaving the creek to the north; the country soon changed to a level plain well-grassed, but, owing to the late rain, very soft and muddy; at 10.20 passed to the north end of Jasper Range, and came to a creek fifteen yards wide trending north-east. Having forded the creek, camped on the right bank. The soil of the country traversed this day is a good brown loam on the plains, but rough and stony on the hills. The trees are of a small size, principally box and bauhinia. Sandstone is the prevailing rock, sometimes passing into jasper, and also into chert and coarse limestone. Small veins of quartz intersected the jasper, and contained small crystals of sulphuret of copper and iron.

Latitude by Aldebaran and Capella, 116 degrees 6 minutes 54 seconds; variation of compass, 3 degrees 6 minutes east.

11th January.

One of the mares having foaled in the night, she was not fit for a day's journey; we therefore remained at the camp, and employed the day in repairing and adjusting the saddles, and other works of indispensable nature; marked a large gum-tree NAE, 11 Jan., 1856.

12th January.

The night was fine, with a heavy dew and a light breeze from the south. At 6.15 a.m. steered north 150 degrees east over the level country which extends along the east side of Jasper Range; the soil is stony, but well grassed, and the fine weather had allowed the surface to become firm, so that the horses were not often bogged. At 12.25 p.m. camped on a small creek between the Fitzgerald and Jasper Ranges; marked a gum-tree at camp Number 9. The general character of this part of the country is good and well suited for stock, though not equal to the basaltic country to the eastward on the Victoria. Hard sandstone, jasper, and coarse limestone are the prevailing rocks.

Latitude by Aldebaran, Saturn, and a Orionis 16 degrees 16 minutes 22 seconds.

FINE PLAINS.

13th January.

The night cool and clear; thermometer 62 degrees at sunrise with heavy dew; steering an average south course from 6.40 a.m. till 11.25, reached the western branch of the Victoria River and encamped. The country traversed was nearly level and well grassed and thinly wooded with eucalypti and bauhinia; the soil is brown loam with small fragments of limestone; the river was running strong, but not in flood; the greatest rise this season had been only ten feet, and the usual flood-marks were twenty feet higher.

Latitude by Aldebaran and Capella 16 degrees 25 minutes 12 seconds.

14th January.

Followed the river to the west-south-west, crossing two large tributary creeks from the north-west, approaching the sandstone ranges on the western side of the plain; the soil did not improve, but became very sandy; the country is thinly wooded with box-trees and bauhinia of small size; grass is abundant and good. At noon one of the pack-horses, Sam, knocked up, and his load being transferred to one of the riding-horses, he was left to rest while we sought a suitable spot for a camp, and at 12.15 p.m. halted at a small gully, as the bank of the river was unsafe for the horses, being very boggy. Sent back for the horse Sam, and brought him to camp; ascended the hill to the north-west of the camp to take bearings, but no important features of the country were visible; in ascending the hill the aneroid (B) fell from 29.62 to 28.55 degrees, and on descending only rose to 28.80 degrees, the estimated height being 300 feet; as this indicated a change in form of the metal of the instrument, I re-adjusted it to the aneroid (A), 29.45 degrees. The continuance of fine weather and forward state of the grass led to the supposition that the wet season had already terminated, though only two months have elapsed since the first rains. It is probable that the wet season is much shorter in the interior than on the coast, and at no great distance inland the tropical wet season will cease altogether, as Captain Sturt, in latitude 26 degrees, only observed a fall of rain in the month of August; but this might be exceptional, as in the case of Dr. Leichhardt, who never encountered a rainy season during the journey to Port Essington.

Latitude by Aldebaran and Capella 16 degrees 27 minutes 20 seconds.

15th January.

Started at 6.45 a.m. and followed the river to the west-south-west; the hills coming close to the bank for some miles, caused the journey to be slow and difficult; crossed two large creeks coming from the west-north-west, the second seventy yards wide; at 10.35 encamped in a fine grassy flat. The course of the river was now more from the south, and the valley expanded into a plain several miles wide.

16th January.

As several of the horses required a day's rest, at 6.0 a.m. I started with Mr. H. Gregory to examine the country to the southward, and followed the river through a fine grassy plain till 10.0, when it entered the sandstone ranges, and the valley contracted to half a mile; the hills were steep, but the level ground in the valley, except where intersected by gullies, was good travelling and well grassed. The river is much reduced in size and the water is confined to the smaller channels of the principal bed; the water is clear, and had not that muddy appearance which characterises it lower down. The geological character of the rocks is unchanged; but the bed of the river being less deeply excavated, the lower beds of limestone and jasper are not so largely developed, the summit of the hills are not quite as level, and large blocks of sandstone, the remains of an upper stratum, gives the country a very rugged appearance. Returned to the camp at 6.30 p.m. In the evening there was a heavy thunder-squall from the north, but the weather cleared at midnight.

LOSE A HORSE.

17th January.

Started at 7.5 a.m. and steered a south-west course till 10.30 a.m., passing over a level grassy flat the whole distance; but the soil became more sandy as we proceeded up the river; there is very little wood of any description;

the few trees that exist are white-stem eucalypti and a few acacia with pinnate leaves; the horse Sam is very weak, and two other horses are lame and can scarcely travel; since the 3rd of January the distance travelled has not exceeded ten miles per diem; water and grass everywhere abundant, and the loads not heavy, yet the greater part of the horses appear to be unable to perform a greater amount of work.

Latitude by Aldebaran 16 degrees 36 minutes 43 seconds.

18th January.

Some of the horses having strayed towards our last camp, we were detained till 8.10 a.m. and then steered south for three miles; the sandstone hills here closed in on each side of the river, scarcely leaving a passage at the base of the steep rocks; here the horse Sam fell into a pool of water, and when extricated could not stand; this having caused considerable delay, we encamped in a grassy flat half a mile farther on; in the evening sent Bowman and Dean to bring the horse to the camp, but they found him dead; marked a tree near camp 14.

19th January.

The night was fine, with heavy dew, the temperature 73 degrees at sunrise; having collected the horses and saddled at 6.45 a.m., left the camp and followed the valley of the river on an average south-west course, crossing a large creek from the north-west; the valley of the river expanded to three miles and then narrowed to one mile, and the course of the river was nearly west till 10.50 a.m., when we encamped; the soil of the valley is a brown loam, producing abundance of grass; but the hills, though less rocky, are more barren than lower down the river; the character of the channel of the river has altered, and has the appearance of a stream which continues to run late into the dry season, as the channels are narrow and fringed with pandanus, melaleuca, and other trees which grow near permanent water; the banks are of less height and the timber on them grows to a greater size than lower down the valley; at 1.0 p.m. the thermometer 100 degrees, and the wet bulb 76 degrees, indicating 24 degrees of evaporation.

CROSS THE WICKHAM RIVER.

20th January.

Left the camp at 6.55 a.m. and followed the river in a west-north-west direction till 8.5, when we crossed at a ledge of rocks which caused a fall of about one foot, the water being twenty yards wide and one to two feet deep; but above and below the rapid the river formed fine reaches seventy yards wide; the course was now west-south-west till 9.0 a.m., when the river turned west, and at 10.50 came to a large stony creek from the south-west, at which we encamped; the country on the banks of the river rises gradually as it recedes, and, except within the influence of the floods, is poor and stony, producing little besides a sharp grass (triodia)--this is the spinifex of some Australian explorers--a few small gum-trees and bushes. As we progress towards the interior the wet season appears to have been of less duration and the fall of rain less, yet the great heat has forced the vegetation towards maturity, and many of the grasses have already ripened their seeds, while there are many other indications of the dry season having fairly set in; the wind is steadily from the south and south-east, and is very dry; the sky is clear and bright, and the creeks have ceased to run; the almost total absence of birds or animals shows that we are approaching the limits of the dry summer season of the southern interior; in the afternoon rode out with Mr. H. Gregory to examine the country, and found that the river came through a gorge in the sandstone range; this gorge is two miles long, a quarter of a mile wide, and 400 feet deep, with nearly perpendicular sides, the winter channel of the river occupying nearly the whole breadth, and intersecting the otherwise flat bottom of the valley with dry sandy channels and long pools of water; beyond the gorge the valley opened, but the view was intercepted by hills.

A HORSE KILLED.

21st January.

Resumed our journey at 7.10 a.m., and, following the right bank of the river nearly west through the gorge, at 9.0 entered an open valley, through which the river came from the south-west; but at 10.0 we entered a second defile, which, from the inclined strata of sandstone, was almost impassable for the horses. In crossing some soft ground between the rocks one of the horses fell on a sharp stump, and was deeply wounded in the belly. The wound was sewn up; but the injury was so severe that the horse died in the night. Having extricated ourselves from this ravine, we encamped at the foot of a sandstone hill, the strata of which dipped 60 degrees to the south-west. Ascending the hill, which was about 300 feet high, the country appeared more level to the south, rising into sandstone ranges at ten miles distance. The course of the river was from west-south-west, the channel being bounded by sandstone cliffs 100 to 200 feet high. The general aspect of the country was wretched in the extreme, as little besides a few small gum-trees and triodia clothed the rugged surface of the red sandstone. The weather continues fine, with only an occasional cloud or flash of lightning in the early part of the night. The temperature is increasing, being 104 degrees at 1.0 p.m. Some catfish and a small tortoise were caught in the river.

22nd January.

At 7.0 a.m. continued our route up the river; but, to avoid the deep ravines on its banks, made a sweep to the south, and at noon encamped in a grassy flat on the bank of the river. The country traversed was very barren and rocky, and the horses had great difficulty in crossing the deep ravines; many of their shoes were torn from their feet during the day's journey. The highest ridge crossed was 500 feet above the bed of the river, the height of which is approximately 500 feet above the sea-level, and thus the general level of the tableland may be considered to be 1000 feet above the sea. The general course of the river being from the west, it appears advisable to reconnoitre the country to the south.

Latitude by Capella 16 degrees 47 minutes 58 seconds.

RECONNOITRE TO THE SOUTH.

23rd January.

Leaving the camp in charge of Dr. Mueller, at 6.30 a.m. started in a southerly direction, accompanied by Messrs. H. Gregory and Baines, taking with us four horses and six days' rations, etc.; after clearing the deep rocky gullies near the river, we passed over a more level country with some fine open plains covered with fine grass, but the intervening ridges were very stony; at 9.45 a.m. reached the highest part of the range, and the country declined to the south-east, and intersected by deep rocky ravines trending towards a large valley, which is probably drained by the southern branch of the Victoria; the course was now south-east, descending to the valley of a creek, through a very barren and rugged sandstone country, producing little besides stunted eucalypti, acacia, and triodia. At 11.15 a.m. halted at the creek, and resumed our route at 3.0 p.m., and followed the valley to the south-east till 4.40 p.m., when it turned east through a rocky gorge between cliffs 150 feet high; but notwithstanding the dense bush of pandanus, fallen rocks and deep muddy channel of the creek, we succeeded in forcing our way through the gorge of the creek, and bivouacked in the open valley below at 5.30 p.m., there being a fine patch of grass in the flat, though the surrounding country is rocky and barren. The sandstone rocks show a great disturbance and dip at all angles and directions, so that no general angle or strike could be determined; the upper rocks, however, show a new feature in a coarse conglomerate of fragments of the lower sandstones and a few fragments of basalt; some of the enclosed pieces of rock are nearly a foot in diameter, and are mostly angular, though occasionally round; this rock forms a horizontal bed of 100 feet in thickness. Towards evening the sky was clouded, with lightning to the east, but no rain.

BASALTIC PLAINS.

24th January.

At 6.0 a.m. crossed the creek, and steered south-east over broken sandstone ridges till 8.0, when we entered a plain of basaltic formation covered with good grass, and where the ground was not entirely composed of fragments of rock the soil was a rich black loam; crossing the large creeks trending north, at 10.0 a.m. halted on the second. These creeks appear to rise in a steep range of sandstone hills which bound the basaltic plains to the west, about two miles from our track. At 3.0 p.m. resumed our route and traversed the trap plain for one and a half hours, and bivouacked in a small gully; the country on both sides of our track seems to be of trap formation for several miles, and then rises into sandstone hills with flat tops. The basaltic rock of this plain is not of great thickness, as the sandstone rose in a few spots above its surface and formed small islands covered with coarse vegetation, surrounded by the open grassy plain. The basalt seems to have been poured out into the valley after it had been excavated in the sandstone, and not to have been much disturbed subsequently. The surface of the plain is very stony, and the horses' feet were much injured by the roughness of the rock.

STONE SPEAR HEADS.

25th January.

The night was cloudy, and it was not till after daybreak that I could get observations for latitude by altitudes of Venus and b Centauri. At 6.5 a.m. were again in the saddle, and steered south-east to a rocky hill, which we reached at 7.0; the hill was sandstone, rising about 150 feet above the trap plain; from the summit the view was extensive, but from the broken nature of the country to the east nothing could be traced of either the courses of creeks or rivers; to the south the trap plain rose to a greater elevation than the summit of the hill we were on, and was surmounted by table hills of sandstone at ten miles distance to the east and north-east; the country appeared to consist of plains of basaltic formation, well grassed, and very thinly wooded. Leaving this hill at 8.0, followed a dry rocky creek to the east and north-east, through basaltic plains with sandstone hills and ridges, till 10.30, and halted during the heat of the day. At this place the bed of the creek had been cut through the basalt into the sandstone, exposing a fine section of the junction of the two rocks; the sandstone was much altered at the line of contact, and, having been deeply cracked, the basalt had filled the fissures of the older rock. This altered sandstone and also a white quartz-like rock are much used by the natives for the heads of their spears; and during this day's journey great quantities of broken stones and imperfect spear heads were noticed on the banks of the creek. At 3.45 p.m. recommenced our journey, and proceeded down the creek to the north-east till 6.30, and bivouacked.

Latitude by Capella, Saturn, and Canopus 17 degrees 24 seconds.

ROE'S DOWNS.

26th January.

Having ascertained that the party could be moved across the range to the basalt plains with advantage, commenced our return to the camp by a westerly route across the plain, which rose gently for ten miles, and was well grassed, but thinly wooded; the soil was stony, with fragments of altered sandstone and basalt. On the higher part of the plain there were several hills of trap-rock, forming flat-topped ridges trending north and south; the highest of these we named Mount Sanford, and the plains Roe's Downs. The country now generally sloped to the bank of the creek near the western limit of the plain, at which, after six hours' ride, we halted at 11.35. The banks of the creek are of trap-rock; but the sandstone is exposed in the bed; the pools of water are deep and apparently permanent. At 4.0 resumed our route and passed over about one mile of sandstone, and then two miles of basalt, and bivouacked at a small gully at the western limit of the valley.

27th January.

At 5.30 a.m. steered north-north-west, over several ridges of sandstone, till we struck our outward track, which we followed with some deviations to the camp, which was reached at 2.0 p.m. The evening was cloudy with a smart thunder-shower. Dr. Mueller informed me that he had traced the river about six miles to the west-south-west, but that beyond that point it appeared to come from the north-west, in which direction there was a low range of hills.

28th January.

Having collected the horses, at 7.15 a.m. steered south to the rocky creek, and followed it down to the rocky gorge and encamped. As the valley was completely walled in by steep rocks, it appeared to be a suitable spot for a depot camp, as it would prevent the horses from straying; and, from the rapidity with which the water in the creeks was drying up, it became desirable that no time should be lost in pushing to the head of the Victoria while it was practicable to cross the ranges in which it was supposed to rise; but as many of the horses were quite unfit for the journey, it became necessary to leave them in some convenient spot while a small party pushed on with a light equipment.

FORM A DEPOT CAMP.

29th January.

Preparing equipment for the party proceeding to the interior and making arrangements for the formation of the depot camp; the party to consist of myself, Mr. H. Gregory, Dr. Mueller, and C. Dean, Mr. Baines remaining at the depot in charge. Selected eleven of the strongest horses and had them re-shod; fitted four with riding and seven with pack saddles. The following provisions were packed for the journey: 150 pounds pork, 300 pounds flour, 50 pounds rice, 10 pounds sago, 8 pounds tea, 6 pounds coffee, 48 pounds sugar.

30th January.

Left the camp at 7.30 a.m. and steered an average course south-south-east till 10.20, over stony ground, at the junction of the sandstone and trap formation, and camped at a fine running creek which came from a rocky gorge in the sandstone range to the west of our course. Messrs. Baines and Bowman, who had accompanied us thus far, returned to the camp, which I had instructed him to move to this creek as better for the horses, as one of them had shown symptoms of poison, and I feared to leave them in that locality. A severe attack of the fever, from which I had been suffering since the beginning of the month, precluded our proceeding farther this day, as I had at first intended. At 5 p.m. it commenced raining, and continued till midnight with incessant thunder and lightning.

31st January.

Being able to mount my horse, at 8 a.m. left the camp and steered a course south-east by south, along the foot of the sandstone range--the basalt plain extending to the north-east. At 12.45 p.m. camped on a shallow watercourse trending to the south-south-west. The whole of the country to the east of our track, except some isolated hills, appear to be covered with excellent grass. The evening was raining, with continuous thunder.

1st February.

Steered north 160 degrees east from 6.25 a.m. till 7.0 across the basaltic plain, then crossed a large creek trending east, in which there were some large pools of water. We then entered the sandstone country, and crossed several rocky ridges; at 9.10 we had a good view from one of the ridges to the north and east. Fine grassy plains extended almost to the horizon, to the south the country consisted of sandstone ranges, and to the south-east large grassy plains and rocky ridges appeared to alternate with each other. Changing the course to south-east, traversed a fine plain covered with grass, beyond which was a rocky ridge, and then a second plain, in which we halted at 11.10, as I was unable to keep on my horse, owing to an attack of fever. At 2 p.m. again proceeded, and after crossing some rugged country with deep rocky ravines, at length reached a large creek, at which we encamped, though there was nothing but reeds and triodia for the horses to eat.

2nd February.

Left the camp at 6 a.m. and followed the creek up for three-quarters of an hour before we could find a crossing place; the course was then south-south-east over very broken sandstone country; at 9.50 halted in a grassy valley to feed the horses, and at 2.30 p.m. resumed our route south-east, crossed a sandstone ridge, and descended into a wide valley, the centre of which was occupied by a basaltic plain, at the edge of which we encamped at 3.55 p.m.

CRESTED PIGEON.

3rd February.

At 6.0 a.m. ascended the trap plain and steered north 190 degrees east; at 6.45 a.m. came to a large creek from the west, which joined the Victoria three-quarters of a mile to the east; but the deep and rocky character of the valley, or rather ravine, in which it ran precluded our approaching it, and we had to turn to the west, and descend from the basalt to the sandstone before the creek could be passed. Continuing an average south course, at 10.10 a.m. came to the Victoria River; the whole channel did not exceed 150 yards in breadth, of which only twenty to fifty were now occupied by water, and the rest by dry rocks and gravel, overgrown by bushes. With great difficulty we followed the river upwards, and were compelled to follow up a tributary creek for about a mile, and then encamped. Near this camp I saw the crested pigeon of Western Australia for the first time in this part of Australia.

Latitude by Leonis 17 degrees 41 minutes.

4th February.

Left the camp at 5.55 a.m. and steered nearly south for six hours, and then encamped on the bank of the Victoria River, at the end of a fine deep pool seventy yards wide, but at the lower end the water was contracted into a shallow rapid ten yards wide. The country traversed is of basaltic formation in the valley, but the hills are of sandstone, and rise on each side from 200 to 300 feet, and the whole appearance of the country shows that there has been little change in the form of the surface since the basalt was poured into the valley. On the banks of a small creek we saw a flock of tribonyx--a bird which has created some speculation as to its proper habitat, as it often makes its appearance in large numbers at the Swan River, on the western coast.

Latitude by Canopus 17 degrees 52 minutes 19 seconds.

THUNDERSTORM AND SQUALL.

5th February.

Started at 5.55 a.m., and steered south-west, keeping parallel to the river at about a mile from it, as the creeks cut so deeply into the rock near the river that they are impassable; at 9.20 a.m. crossed to the right bank of the river, and continued a south-west course, but found the country exceedingly rough and rocky, and therefore turned to the north-west to the river, and at 11.30 a.m. camped at a fine pool of water. In the afternoon we were visited by a sudden thunder-squall; fortunately the tents had not been set up, or they must have been blown to pieces. The valley of the river has contracted to about fifteen miles, and turns to the west, but a branch seems to come from the south, and a second from the north-west. The country is, however, nearly level, and it is difficult to ascertain the limits of the valley, as many portions of the original tableland exist as detached hills and ridges. Though the horses are well shod, they are becoming lame and footsore from continually travelling over rough and stony country, as more than half of the last 100 miles has been so completely covered with fragments of rock that the soil, if any exists, has been wholly concealed.

6th February.

Leaving the camp at 6.20 a.m., steered south up the valley of a large creek. At first the ground was very rough and rocky, but as we proceeded it became more level and sandy--the bed of the creek being worn in the basalt, and the hills of sandstone conglomerate rising 100 to 200 feet. Except on the bank of the creek, there was no grass, the hills being covered with triodia. Encamped in a grassy flat at 11.30 a.m.

Latitude by Pollux 18 degrees 48 seconds.

CROSS WATERSHED TO INTERIOR. HOOKER'S CREEK.

7th February.

At 6.30 resumed our journey to the south-south-west, and reached the head of the creek at 8.0 a.m. Ascending the tableland by an abrupt slope of 100 feet, our course was south one mile, when the southern slope was reached, and a large shallow valley extended across our course, beyond which a vast and slightly undulating plain extended to the horizon with scarcely a rising ground to relieve its extreme monotony. Descending by a very gentle slope into the valley, at 9.40 a.m. crossed a small watercourse trending south-east, and then passed through a plain densely covered with kangaroo-grass seven to nine feet high, and at 10.40 a.m. encountered the level sandy country beyond, which was covered with triodia and small acacia and gum trees, or rather bushes. Seeing little prospects of either water or grass to the southward, turned east to the creek, at which we encamped at 12.30 p.m. The bed of the creek was dry, except a few shallow pools of rainwater, and there had been so little rain this season that no water had flowed down the channel. A level grassy flat extended nearly a mile on each side of the creek, which indicated the extent of occasional inundations, beyond which the country was very sandy and covered with small gum-trees, acacia, and triodia.

Latitude by Pollux 18 degrees 3 seconds.

8th February.

The country to the south being so level and barren that we could not expect to find either water or grass in that direction, at 6.0 a.m. steered north 110 degrees east along the course of the creek, which turned somewhat to the north of our track for a few miles; but at 8.0 again came on its banks. The country was very barren and sandy, with small trees of silver-leafed ironbark and triodia, except on the inundated flats of the creek, which were well grassed and thinly wooded with box-trees. The course of the creek was now nearly south-east, but the channel decreased in size, and was quite dry till 10.0 a.m., when we reached a fine pool which had been filled by a tributary gully. Here we halted and shot several ducks. At 2.45 p.m. resumed our route, and at 3.20 came to a level grassy flat, on which the channel of the creek was completely lost. Crossing the flat to the east, the country was quite level and sandy; therefore turned to the north, where there seemed to be a slight depression, and at 4.50 came to a shallow pool of rainwater, at which we encamped. Frequent showers during the night.

THE DESERT INTERIOR.

9th February.

On winding the chronometers this morning, found the chain of 2139, by Arnold, was broken. Taking advantage of the cool cloudy morning, we steered south at 6.5 a.m. to ascertain if the water of the creek, after spreading on the grassy flat, collected again and found an outlet to the southward, but found the ground rise in that direction; observed a slight hollow to the west, for which we steered, but found it terminate on the sandy plain, and the country became a perfect desert of red sand, with scattered tufts of triodia and a few bushes of eucalypti and acacia. At noon, finding it hopeless to proceed further into the desert, we turned our steps to the north-north-east, and returned to our camp of last night. In returning to the camp we ascended a slight elevation, from which there was an uninterrupted view of the desert from east to south-west. The horizon was unbroken; all appeared one slightly undulating plain, with just sufficient triodia and bushes growing on it to hide the red sand when viewed at a distance. The day was remarkably cool and cloudy; the temperature at noon 86 degrees. Though the rain at the camp had been abundant during the previous night, it had not extended more than five miles into the desert, which is more remarkable, as the clouds were moving to the south.

TURN TO THE WEST.

10th February.

As the horses required a day's rest, we remained at our camp, which enabled us to repair our saddles and perform other necessary work. Repaired the chronometer and one of the aneroid barometers, which had been broken by the motion of one of the pack-horses. As there was no practicable route to the south, and the sandstone hills to the north seemed to diminish in elevation to the east, I decided on following the northern limit of the desert to the west till some line of practicable country was found by which to penetrate the country to the south. In selecting a westerly route I was also influenced by the greater elevation of the country on the western side of the Victoria, and the fact that all the larger tributaries join from that side of the valley. It is also probable that, should the waters of the interior not be lost in the sandy desert, they will follow the southern limit of the elevated tract of sandstone which occupies north-west Australia from Roebuck Bay to the Gulf of Carpentaria, both of which points are nearly in the same latitude as our present position, from which it may be assumed that the line of greatest elevation is between the 17th and 18th parallels. None of the rivers crossed by Leichhardt are of sufficient magnitude to drain the country beyond the coast range, and therefore any streams descending from the tableland to the south will either be absorbed in the sandy desert or follow the southern limit of the sandstone and flow into the sea to the south-west of Roebuck Bay. There is, however, reason to expect that, as the interior of north-west Australia is partly within the influence of the tropical and partly the extra-tropical climates, it does not enjoy a regular rainy season; and though heavy rain doubtless falls at times, it is neither sufficiently general or regular to form rivers of sufficient magnitude to force their way through the flat sandy country to the coast.

Latitude by Capella 18 degrees 20 minutes 49 seconds.

11th February.

At 6.30 a.m. proceeded up the creek, and at 12.30 p.m. camped at a shallow pool of rainwater on the flat, the channel of the creek being dry. On the northern bank of the creek we passed a small lagoon with a great number of duck and other water-fowl on it. The afternoon was cloudy, with a fresh breeze from south-east.

Latitude by Pollux 18 degrees 15 minutes 26 seconds.

12th February.

Three of the horses having strayed some distance, we did not start till 7.0 a.m., when we steered an average course of north 300 degrees east till 11.45 a.m., when we camped at a small pool of water in the bed of the creek, which was reduced to a small gully; for the first four miles we traversed the grassy flats of the creek, after which we passed over a level sandy country producing nothing but triodia, stunted eucalypti, and acacia till we again approached the creek, where the grassy flat was nearly half a mile wide, but of inferior character.

Latitude by b Tauri 18 degrees 9 minutes 44 seconds.

13th February.

At 6.50 a.m. followed the valley of the creek to the west, passing some fine flats with high grass, but the country generally very poor and thinly wooded with white-gum and silver-leafed ironbark; at 10.40 halted at a small waterhole at the foot of a low granite ridge; at 3.0 p.m. ascended the granite hills, which rose abruptly 100 to 150 feet above the plain, and extended about five miles to the south and east; to the west the sandstone covered the granite and formed a level tableland or plain; to the north a valley trended to the west, on the northern side of which the hills appeared to be granitic. Returning to the camp, examined a deep rocky ravine and found some small pools of water which might last for nearly another month.

Latitude by Castor and Pollux 18 degrees 11 minutes 20 seconds.

PIGEONS AND SEA-GULLS.

14th February.

Leaving the camp at 6.0 a.m., steered an average course of north 300 degrees east; crossing the granite ridge, we entered a level sandy country with much scrub, which was traversed till 8.40, when we entered a wide grassy plain extending to the north-west, in which direction we steered till 2.10 p.m., when we halted at a small muddy puddle two inches deep and three yards wide. Then rode on with Mr. H. Gregory to search for a larger supply of water, and found a shallow pool about a mile distant, to which the party moved and encamped. Although this pool was not 100 yards long and six inches deep, a large flock of ducks, snipe, and small gulls, were congregated at it, several thousand pigeons of species new to us came to drink. These pigeons keep in flocks of from ten to more than a thousand, feeding on the seeds of the grass on the open plains, as they never alight on trees. They are somewhat larger than the common bronze-wing; the head is black, with a little white at the base of the beak and behind the eye; back pale brown; breast, blue; throat marked with white; wings with white tips to the feathers and a small patch of bronze; tail short, tip white; feet, dull red. The evening and night were cloudy.

WILD RICE.

15th February.

At 6.5 a.m. followed a line of small trees and bushes which grew on the lower part of the grassy plain and indicated the course of the water in the wet season, and at 9.0 came to the head of a small creek trending north-west. Water was now abundant and formed large pools, and at 11.15 camped on the right bank of the creek at a pool a quarter of a mile long and fifty yards wide. This spot seemed to be much frequented by the natives, and large quantities of mussel-shells lay around their fires. The plain traversed this morning was well grassed; the soil a stiff clay loam; this plain extended three to six miles on each side of the track, and was bounded by a low-wooded country, which, in some parts, rose nearly 100 feet above the plain. In the lower part of the plain we observed the salt-bush (atriplex) and a species of rice; but as it was only just in ear, we could not judge of the quality of the grain. In the afternoon there was a fine breeze from the east which lasted till 8.0 p.m., the sky being cloudy.

Latitude by Canopus and Pollux 17 degrees 53 minutes 50 seconds.

16th February.

At 6.25 a.m. resumed our journey down the creek, which turned first west and then south-west, and at 12.20 p.m. encamped at a small pool; on the right bank of the creek wide grassy plains extended from three to five miles back towards a low-wooded ridge, but on the left bank the scrubby country came close to the creek.

Latitude by a Orionis, Canopus and Pollux 17 degrees 59 minutes 40 seconds.

17th February (Sunday).

As the water and grass were abundant on this camp, we were not compelled to move on in search of these requisites, and were enabled to observe it as a day of rest.

18th February.

Resumed our journey at 6.30 a.m., and steered an average south-west course till 11.10, and then south till 12.25 p.m., and again camped on the creek. The country consisted of wide grassy plains on the bank of the creek, without trees and well grassed; beyond the plains, at one to six miles distance, low-wooded ridges were visible; but the general aspect of the whole was extremely level. A great number of ducks and a few geese were seen on some of the pools in the creek.

Latitude by Canopus 18 degrees 4 minutes 40 seconds.

STURT'S CREEK.

19th February.

Commenced our day's journey at 6.0 a.m., followed the bank of the creek till 8.15, thence south-south-west till noon, when the course was altered to south-south-east to close in with the creek, but found that the channel was completely lost on the level grassy plain, and at 1.40 p.m. encamped at a small puddle of muddy water as thick as cream. Before the creek was lost in the level plain it spread into some large, though shallow pools, which swarmed with ducks of several species, but principally the whistling duck. The grassy plain gradually extended to a greater breadth, and the back country was so nearly level that it scarcely rose above the grassy horizon, while to the south the country was so level that the clumps of bushes appeared like islands, and the grassy plain extended to the horizon. Near one of the waterholes in the creek we surprised a native, who was sitting at his fire with a couple of women, who decamped with all possible despatch. Several smokes have been observed to the south and south-west, which shows that water must exist in that direction, though it may not be in sufficient quantity to supply our horses. The morning was cloudy, and at midnight there was a heavy shower of rain. Judging from the general appearance of the country, the waters of the creek, after spreading over the plain, must escape to the westward, as the grass has been bent in that direction by the current last year, but there has been so little rain this season that the channel of the creek has not been filled.

20th February.

As it appeared that the waters of the creek trended to the west in the wet season, at 6.5 a.m. we steered north 250 degrees east, through a level forest of box-trees, with abundance of good grass; the soil brown loam with fragments of limestone; the shower last night had left many shallow pools of water on the surface. At 8.40 a.m. passed a small swampy salt flat covered with salicornia; at 9.10 came on the grassy plain which we skirted on a west course, but as it turned to the north-west, again changed the course to 320 degrees; the plain was now reduced to about a mile in width, and we therefore crossed it in search of a definite channel, but without success, though there were some slight indications that during inundation the water flowed to the north-west. At 11.50 we camped at a shallow puddle of rainwater, on the north side of the plain. From the camp, till 8.0 a.m., the grass, though very backward, showed that there had been sufficient rain to cause it to spring; but as we proceeded it was perfectly dry and parched up, as at the end of the dry season, showing that little or no rain had fallen for many months in this part of the country. The day was cloudy, with thunder, and was followed by a heavy shower at night, which prevented my ascertaining the latitude by observation.

ENTER WESTERN AUSTRALIA.

21st February.

As we were now three days' journey from the last water which could be depended on for more than a few days, and the channel of the creek had been so completely lost on the plain that it was uncertain whether the marks of inundations near this camp had been caused by the creek flowing to the west, or by some tributary flowing to the east, I determined to attempt a south-west course, in the hope that, should the country prove rocky, the heavy showers might have collected a sufficient quantity of water to enable us to continue a southerly route, and accordingly selected the most prominent point of the rising ground to the south of our position, and at 6.5 a.m. started north 235 degrees east. After leaving the open plains we entered a grassy box forest, which continued to the foot of the hills, which we reached at 8.0. The slope of the hills proved very scrubby, with small eucalypti and acacia, the soil red sand and ironstone gravel; at 9.0 reached the highest part of the hills for many miles round. To the south the country was slightly depressed for ten or fifteen miles, and then rose into an even ridge or plain, the whole country appearing to be covered with acacia and eucalyptus scrub. To the west and north the view was more extended; the low ridge of sandstone hills extended to the west-north-west, on the northern side of the grassy flats for thirty miles, and only broken by a large valley from the north. Throughout its whole extent this range appeared to rise to 150 or 200 feet above the plain, and had the appearance of being the edge of a level tableland. South of the grassy plain, the western limit of which was not seen, the country rose gradually to eighty or 100 feet, and presented an extremely level and unvaried appearance. It was evident that our only chance of farther progress was to follow the grassy plain to the west till some change in the country rendered a southerly course practicable, it being probable that some creek from the north might join the grassy plain, and that the channel which had been lost might be reformed. At 9.30 steered north-west, and at 12.30 p.m. cleared the acacia scrub, and at 1.30 reached the bank of the creek, which had formed a channel twenty yards wide, with pools of water, which was brackish; but we were too glad to find any water which we could use without detriment to object to it because it was not agreeable in taste, and therefore encamped. We have thus been a second time compelled to make a retrograde movement to the north after reaching the same latitude as in the first attempt to penetrate the desert; but I did not feel justified in incurring the extreme risk which would have attended any other course, though following the creek is by no means free from danger, as very few of the waterholes which have supplied us on the outward track will retain any water till the time of our return. The weather was calm and hot in the early part of the day, and in the afternoon it clouded over, and there was a slight shower of rain. According to our longitude, by account, we have this day passed the boundary of Western Australia, which is in the 129th meridian.

Latitude by Canopus and Procyon 18 degrees 26 minutes.

STURT'S CREEK.

22nd February.

Leaving the camp at 5.40 a.m., followed the creek to the west-south-west and crossed a small gully from the south; at 11.30 a.m. camped at a fine pool of water in a small creek from the south, close to its junction with the principal creek, which we named after Captain Sturt, whose researches in Australia are too well known to need comment; the grassy plains extended from three to ten miles on each side of the creek, which has a more definite channel than higher up, there being some pools of sufficient size to retain water throughout the year; the plain is bounded on the north by sandstone hills 100 to 200 feet high, and there is also a mass of hilly country to the south, the highest point of which was named Mount Wittenoom; about noon a thunder-shower passed to the east and up the creek on which we were encamped, and though the channel was then dry between the pools, at 4.0 p.m. it was running two feet deep; the grass is much greener near this camp, and there has evidently been more rain here than in any part of the country south of Victoria yet visited; a fresh southerly breeze in the morning, thunderstorms at noon, night cloudy with heavy dew.

23rd February.

At 5.50 a.m. resumed our journey down the creek, the general course first south-west and changing to the south-south-west; the channel was gradually lost on the broad swampy flat, which was overgrown with polygonum and atriplex, etc., and had a breadth of half a mile to a mile, being depressed about ten feet below the grassy plain; the grassy plain also extended to about fifteen miles wide, the hills decrease in height, and the whole country is so level that little is to be seen but the distant horizon, scarcely in any part rising above the vast expanse of waving grass. At 10.50 a.m. camped at a shallow puddle of muddy water, just sufficient to supply the horses; I walked about a mile into the polygonum flat, but could not find any water, though the ground was soft and muddy in a few spots. Mr. H.C. Gregory, when rounding up the horses in the evening, saw eight blacks watching us; we therefore went out to communicate with them; but they hid themselves in the high bushes and grass. The night was clear, and I took a set of lunar distances, which the cloudy weather had prevented for more than a week, though I had been able to get altitudes for latitude.

Latitude by Canopus, Castor and Pollux 18 degrees 39 minutes 54 seconds.

EFFECT OF SEASONS ON APPEARANCE OF COUNTRY.

24th February.

At 6.0 a.m. resumed our journey down the creek, which spread into a broad swampy flat about a mile wide, and covered with atriplex, polygonum, and grass, the general trend south-west; at 7.30 crossed a large watercourse from the south-east, with a dry sandy channel, no water having flowed down it this season; at 9.0 a.m. crossed to the right bank of the creek; there were many shallow muddy channels and one with running water four yards wide and one foot deep; the largest channel was near the right bank, but, except a large shallow pool, it was dry. As we advanced the country showed effects of long-continued drought, and though the creek contained some large shallow pools, the channel was dry between, the dry soil absorbing the whole of the water which was running in the channel above; at 11.50 camped at what appeared to be the termination of the pools of water, as the channel was again lost in a perfectly level flat. Great numbers of ducks, cockatoos, cranes, and crows frequented the banks of the creek above the camp, and appeared to feed on the wild rice which was growing in considerable quantities in the moist hollows, as also a species of panicum; to the south-east of the creek there is a level box-flat which extends two to three miles back to the foot of some low sandy ridges covered with triodia and a few small eucalypti; to the north-west and west the grassy plain extended to the horizon, with scarcely even a bush to intercept the even surface of the waving grass.

Latitude by Canopus and Pollux 18 degrees 45 minutes 45 seconds.

25th February.

The small number of water-fowl which passed up or down the creek during the night indicated that water was not abundant below our present position, and we were therefore prepared for a dry country, in which we were not disappointed, for leaving the camp at 6.15 a.m. we traversed a level box-flat covered with long dry grass; at 9.10 a.m. again entered the usual channel of the creek, which was now a wide flat of deeply cracked mud with a great quantity of atriplex growing on it, but which had lost all the leaves from the long continuance of the dry weather. The flat was traversed by numerous small channels from one to two feet deep, but they were all perfectly dry and had not contained water for more than a year; there were, however, marks of inundations in previous years, when the country must have exhibited a very different appearance, and had it been then visited by an explorer, the account of a fine river nearly a mile wide flowing through splendid plains of high grass, could be scarcely reconciled with the facts I have to record of a mud flat deeply fissured by the scorching rays of a tropical sun, the absence of water, and even scarcity of grass. The creek now turned to the south, and we followed the shallow channels till 12.30 p.m., when we fortunately came to a small pool which had been filled by a passing thunder-shower, and here we encamped during the day; a fresh breeze at times blew from the south-east and south, and the air was exceedingly warm; thermometer 106 degrees at noon, but being very dry, was not very oppressive.

Latitude by Canopus, Castor and Pollux 18 degrees 55 minutes 45 seconds.

LEVEL COUNTRY.

26th February.

As the course of the creek was uncertain, we steered south at 5.45 a.m. across the atriplex plain, and at 6.35 reached the ordinary right bank of the creek, which was low and gravelly, covered with triodia and small bushes; we then passed a patch of white-gum forest, and at 8 entered a grassy plain which had been favoured by a passing shower; green grass was abundant, and even some small puddles of water still remained in the hollows of the clay soil. At 10.50 came on the creek, which had collected into a single channel and formed pools, some of which appeared to be permanent, as they contained small fish. At one of these pools we encamped at 11.10. The channel of the creek is about fifteen feet below the level of the plain, and is marked by a line of small flooded-gum trees, the atriplex flat has ceased, and the soil is a hard white clay, producing salsola and a little grass; the morning clear with a moderate easterly breeze, afternoon cloudy with a few drops of rain at night.

Latitude by Canopus and Pollux 19 degrees 7 minutes 30 seconds.

27th February.

Resumed our journey down the creek at 6.5 a.m., when it turned to the west and formed a fine lake-like reach 200 yards wide, with rocky banks and sandstone ridges on both sides of the creek; at 11.0 camped at the lower end of a fine reach trending south: the general character of these reaches of water is that they are very shallow and are separated by wide spans of dry channel, the water being ten feet below the running level. The country is very inferior, and the grassy flats are reduced to very narrow limits, and the hills are red sandstone, producing nothing but small trees and triodia.

Latitude by Canopus and Pollux 19 degrees 12 minutes 20 seconds.

28th February.

At 6.0 a.m. we were again in the saddle, following a creek which had an average west-south-west course, but the channel was soon lost in a wide grassy flat, with polygonum and atriplex, in this flat were some large detached pools of water, 50 to 100 yards wide and a quarter to half a mile long, although the dry season had reduced them to much narrower limits than usual, as they were now eight to ten feet below the level of the plain; at 11.45 camped at a large sheet of water, just above a remarkable ridge of sandstone rocks on the right bank of the creek. Ducks, pelicans, spoonbills, etc., were very numerous, but so wild that they could scarcely be approached within range of our guns; until the present time it has been doubtful whether the creek turned towards Cambridge Gulf, the interior, or to the coast westward of the Fitzroy, but the first point being now 220 nautic miles to the north, and the general course of Sturt's Creek south-west, such a course is not probable, and it therefore only remains to determine whether it is lost in the level plains of the interior, or finds an outlet on the north-west coast. The careful and minute surveys of the coast from the Victoria River to Roebuck Bay show that no rivers exist of such magnitude as the Sturt would attain in passing through the ranges to the coast, nor does the general abrupt character of the coast-line favour the supposition that any interior waters would find an outlet in this space. That the elevation of this part of the creek is sufficient to enable it to form a channel to the north-west coast is shown by the barometric measurement: the dividing ridge between the head of the Victoria and Hooker's Creek is about 1200 feet, at the head of Sturt's Creek 1,370 feet, and our present camp 1100 feet; thus the average fall of Sturt's Creek has been 270 feet in 180 miles, or one and a half feet per mile. Now the distance to Desault Bay (which appears the most probable outlet) is 370 miles, and allowing an increase of 500 for deviations, there would be more than two feet descent per mile, which would be sufficient for the maintenance of a channel. Should the creek turn to the south and enter the sandy desert country, the water would soon be absorbed, especially as the wet season at the upper part of the creek occurs when the dry season is prevailing in the lower part of its course. That it does lose itself in a barren sandy country is, I fear, the most probable termination of the creek, and that a level country exists for many miles on each side of our route is shown by the small number and size of the tributary watercourses.

Latitude by Canopus, Castor and Pollux 19 degrees 18 minutes 10 seconds.

29th February.

Leaving the camp at 5.40 a.m., traced the creek to the south-west for about three miles. It formed fine reaches of water fifty to 100 yards wide; but the channel terminated suddenly in a level flat, covered with polygonum, atriplex, and grass. In this flat we passed some large shallow pools of water; at 7.30 the creek turned to the west round the north end of a rocky sandstone hill, and was joined by a tributary gully from the north, below which point the channel was a well-defined sandy bed, with long parallel waterholes on each side, but very little water remained at this time; at 9.15 the course of the creek changed to south by west, and passed through a level flat timbered with flooded-gum trees; it was about one mile wide and well grassed, but completely dried up for want of rain. The back country was thinly wooded with white-gum, and gently rising as it receded, forming sandstone hills about 100 feet high of extremely barren appearance; at 11.45 camped at a small muddy pool which would last only for a few days. A strong breeze from the west commenced early in the day, and gradually changed to the south. Thermometer, 109 degrees in the coolest shade that could be found.

Latitude by Canopus and e Argus 19 degrees 28 minutes 5 seconds.

DESERT OF RED SAND.

1st March.

Our horses having strayed farther than usual in search of better grass, we were delayed till 6.20 a.m., when we steered a south by west course down the valley of the creek. Immediately below the camp the country beyond the effect of inundation changed to a nearly level plain of red sand, producing nothing but triodia and stunted bushes. The level of this desert country was only broken by low ridges of drifted sand. They were parallel and perfectly straight, with a direction nearly east and west. At 11.50 camped at a fine pool of water three to five feet deep and twenty yards wide. That we had actually entered the desert was apparent, and the increase of temperature during the past three days was easily explained; but whether this desert is part of that visited by Captain Sturt, or an isolated patch, has yet to be ascertained, and the only hope is that the creek will enable us to continue our course, as the nature of the country renders an advance quite impracticable unless by following watercourses.

Latitude by Canopus, Castor and Pollux 19 degrees 40 minutes 45 seconds.

2nd March.

Left our camp at 6.30 a.m., and steered south-west by west, which soon took us into the sandy desert on the left bank of the creek. Crossing one of the sand ridges, got a sight of a range of low sandstone hills to the south-east, the highest of which I named Mount Mueller, as the doctor had seen them the previous evening while collecting plants on one of the sandy ridges near the camp. At 10.15 again made the creek, which had scarcely any channel to mark its course; the wide clay flat bearing marks of former inundations was the only indication visible. At 12.35 p.m. camped at a small muddy pool, the grass very scanty and dry. Traces of natives are frequent. Large flights of pigeons feed on the plains on the seeds of grass. A flock of cockatoos was also seen.

Latitude by Canopus and Pollux 19 degrees 51 seconds 12 minutes.

3rd March.

At 5.30 a.m. started and followed the creek on a general course south-west. There was a very irregular channel sometimes ten yards wide and very shallow, and then expanding into pools fifty yards wide. The sandy plain encroached much on the grassy flats, and reduced the winter course of the creek to half a mile in breadth. At 8.0 the course was changed to south, and at 10.15 camped at a swamp, which was nearly dry, and covered with beautiful grass. The country differed in character from that seen yesterday, there being a few scattered white-gum trees and patches of tall acacia. Salsola and salicornia are also very abundant, and show the saline nature of the soil.

Latitude by Canopus and Pollux 20 degrees 2 minutes 10 seconds.

SALT LAKES.

4th March.

Left the camp at 5.50 a.m., and steered south-west over a very level country, with shallow hollows filled with a dense growth of acacia, and at 7.30 struck the creek with a sandy channel and narrow flats, covered with salsola and salicornia. The pools were very shallow, and gradually became salt, and at 10.15 it spread into the dry bed of a salt lake more than a mile in diameter. This was connected by a broad channel with a pool of salt-water in it, with a second dry salt lake eight miles in diameter. As there was little prospect of water ahead and the day far advanced, we returned to one of the brackish pools and encamped. The country passed was of a worthless character, and so much impregnated with salt that the surface of the ground is often covered with a thin crust of salt.

Latitude by e Argus 20 degrees 10 minutes 40 seconds.

5th March.

Started from the camp at 5.45 a.m., and steered south-south-east through the acacia wood to the lake, and then south by east across the dry bed of the lake towards a break in the trees on the southern side. Here we found a creek joining the lake from the south-west, in which there were some shallow pools. We then steered east, to intersect any channel by which the waters of the lake might flow to the south or south-east, and passing through a wood of acacia entered the sandy desert. As some low rocky hills were visible to the east we steered for them. At 2.10 halted half a mile from the hills, and then ascended them on foot. They were very barren and rocky, scarcely eighty feet above the plain, formed of sandstone, the strata horizontal. From the summit of the hill nothing was visible but one unbounded waste of sandy ridges and low rocky hillocks, which lay to the south-east of the hill. All was one impenetrable desert, as the flat and sandy surface, which could absorb the waters of the creek, was not likely to originate watercourses. Descending the hill, which I named Mount Wilson, after the geologist attached to the expedition, we returned towards the creek at the south end of the lake, reaching it at 9.30.

6th March.

As the day was extremely hot and the horses required rest and food, we remained at the camp. Ducks were numerous in some of the pools, but so wild that only two were shot. The early part of the day was clear, with a hot strong breeze varying from west to south-east. At 1 p.m. there was a heavy thunder-squall from the south-east, which swept a cloud of salt and sand from the dry surface of the lake. The squall was followed by a slight shower.

Latitude by Canopus 20 degrees 16 minutes 22 seconds.

DRY BEDS OF SALT LAKES.

7th March.

As I had frequently observed that in the dry channels of creeks traversing very level country a heavy shower in the lower part of its course often causes a strong current of water to rush up the stream-bed and leave flood marks, which would mislead a person examining them in the dry season, it seemed probable that this must be the case with the creek entering the salt lake at its south-west angle, as it might be the outlet of the lake when filled by Sturt's Creek flowing into it, though in ordinary seasons the flow of water would be into the lake; accordingly I decided on following the creek and ascertain its actual course. Leaving the camp at 5.50 a.m., steered nearly south-west along the general course of the creek till 7.30, when it turned to the north and entered the dry bed of a lake. As the beds of the two lakes were lower than the channel between them, the water during the last heavy rains had flooded both ways from the central part of the channel. Having skirted the lake on the west to intercept any watercourses which might enter or leave the lake on that side, we came to a large shallow channel with pools of water--some fresh and others salt--with broad margin of salicornia growing on the banks; at 11.0 camped at a small pool of fresh water. The soil of the country on the bank of the creek is loose white sand with concretions of lime, covered with a dense growth of tall acacia, with salsola and a little grass in the open spaces.

TERMINATION OF STURT'S CREEK.

8th March.

Started at 6.5 a.m. and traced the creek into a salt lake to the west, but this was also dry. After some search we found a creek joining on the northern side and communicating with a large mud plain, partly overgrown with salicornia, and with large shallow pools of muddy water two to three inches deep. On the northern side the plain narrowed into a sandy creek with shallow pools, the flow of the water being decidedly from the northward. At 12.15 p.m. camped at a shallow pool, near which there was a little grass, the country generally being sandy and only producing triodia and acacia. Thus, after having followed Sturt's Creek for nearly 300 miles, we have been disappointed in our hope that it would lead to some important outlet to the waters of the Australian interior; it has, however, enabled us to penetrate far into the level tract of country which may be termed the Great Australian Desert.

Latitude by Pollux and e Argus 20 degrees 4 minutes 5 seconds.

9th March.

Left our camp at 6.35 a.m., and followed the creek up for half an hour, and then steered east to Sturt's Creek, which we reached at 9.5, the country being level, sandy, and covered with triodia and acacia in small patches; we then steered a southerly course down the creek till 11.0, and camped at the large brackish pool.

COMMENCE RETURN TO DEPOT. HOT WINDS.

10th March.

We had observed that a creek appeared to join the salt lake to the north-east angle. There yet remained a possibility that the waters of the lake might find an outlet to the east and pass north of Mount Wilson; we therefore steered east from the camp at 6.45 a.m. and passed close to the south of a small salt lake (dry) three-quarters of a mile in diameter, and then traversed a level sandy country thickly wooded with acacia and a few white-gum trees. At 8.15 struck a small grassy watercourse with broad shallow pools; this we followed down to the south-south-west to the large salt lake, close to which it was joined by a small sandy creek coming from the east. Having reached the bank of the lake at 10.0, steered south along its shore till 11.15, when its shore trended to the west-south-west, and there was a small well-defined bank without any break to the point which had been the limit of our examination from the southern part of the lake, and thus determined that there was no outlet for the water to the eastward. As the whole country to the south was one vast sandy desert, destitute of any indications of the existence of water, it was clear that no useful results could arise from any attempt to penetrate this inhospitable region, especially as the loss of any of the horses might deprive the expedition of the means for carrying out the explorations towards the Gulf of Carpentaria. I therefore determined on commencing our retreat to the Victoria River while it was practicable, as the rapid evaporation and increasing saltness of the water in this arid and inhospitable region warned us that each day we delayed increased the difficulty of the return, and it was possible that we were cut off from any communication with the party at the depot by an impassable tract of dry country, and might be compelled to maintain ourselves on the lower part of the creek till the ensuing rainy season. Returned to the creek at the north-east angle of the lake and encamped. The morning was cloudy with a strong hot wind from the east and south-east; the night calm and misty.

11th March.

At 6.10 a.m. left the camp and followed the creek to the north-north-east, but it soon spread into a number of small gullies, which drained a patch of clay land. At 7.0 steered north through a wood of acacia growing on loose sandy soil. Entering the open sandy plain at 8.15, a few small white-gum trees were scattered over this part of the plain, which was quite level, the loose sand being covered with triodia, which partially concealed the glaring red colour of the ground. Observing a low abrupt hill a little to the east of our course, deviated towards it, and ascended it at 10.0. It was less than 100 feet above the plains, and composed of the same sandstone which prevails over the whole of the country south of the Victoria. The view was cheerless in the extreme. From north 26 degrees east to north 166 degrees east, the country was a level plain with small isolated or grouped hills of red sandstone, but not forming any definite ranges; the even height and peculiar table summits appear to indicate that they are only small remaining portions of a sandstone tableland or plain nearly the whole of which has been removed, the strata, however, had a dip to the east of one or two degrees. The vegetation on this part of the country was reduced to a few stunted gum-trees, hakea bushes, and triodia, the whole extremely barren in appearance. The remaining portion of the horizon was one even straight line; not a hill or break of any kind was visible, and, except the narrow line of the creek, was barren and worthless in the extreme, the red soil of the level portions of the surface being partially clothed with triodia and a few small trees, or rather bushes, rendered the long straight ridges of fiery-red drifting sand more conspicuous. The wind being strong, we observed the smoke of several fires along the course of Sturt's Creek, and also one near Mount Mueller, to the north-east, indicating the existence of natives in that direction, and doubtless of water in that locality, as it was a day's journey from the creek. Our course was now north 340 degrees east, and on approaching the creek passed through a patch of casuarina forest, which was remarkable, as they are the only trees of this genus we had seen on the coast since landing at the Victoria, though abundant in all other parts of Australia. At 1.35 p.m. reached Sturt's Creek and halted at our camp of the 2nd March; there was a strong hot wind from the east during the day.

12th March.

Resumed our route at 5.50 a.m. and steered north 20 degrees east till 8.0, then 40 degrees and 60 degrees till 1.0 p.m., when we encamped at a shallow pool of water near the creek, and about three miles above camp 48, as the route only traversed the level flats near the creek. Nothing worthy of further notice was seen, the channel being split into small hollows, some of which retained a little water. The grass was much dried up and limited to the flat near the creek, the more remote portions being covered with triodia. The day was hot and nearly calm, but at noon we were benefited by a few passing clouds, and at 6.0 p.m. a dry thunderstorm cooled the air from 100 degrees to 93 degrees, but the temperature rose at 8.0 to 96 degrees.

13th March.

At 5.50 steered north 10 degrees east, crossing the creek several times, and at 10.0 turned to the north-north-east and north-east, crossing the sandstone hills, round which the creek turns at a right angle, and at 12.10 p.m. camped on the creek near our track of the 29th February. Nearly all the pools of water had dried up, and the water at the camp had become brackish; some of the pools, however, must be permanent, as there were small fish in them. A great party of natives appeared to be travelling up the creek, as fresh fires are constantly seen to the north-east along its course. A cool breeze from the west to north-east moderated the heat, the temperature at 2 p.m. 103 degrees; passing clouds from the east in the afternoon.

FOLLOW UP STURT'S CREEK.

14th March.

Resumed our route and followed the creek upwards from 5.50 a.m. till 1.50 p.m., when we camped about three miles south-west of camp 45 at the first pool before the atriplex flat. A short distance above the camp we crossed a large sandy creek, which proved to be the cause of the change in the character of Sturt's Creek below that point. As our route was at a greater distance from the creek than in tracing it down, it gave a better opportunity of ascertaining the nature of the country beyond the influence of inundation; to the north-west a vast plain traversed by low ridges of gravel and drift sand, clothed with a scanty growth of triodia and a few hakea bushes, rose gradually from the creek, but on the south-east a more abrupt sandstone slope terminated in a similar plain of somewhat greater elevation, and showed that we were still within the bounds of the desert. Moderate breeze from the north-west changing to north-east; passing clouds; a slight shower at 11.0 p.m.

15th March.

Resumed our route at 5.50 a.m., steering north 40 degrees east, one hour into the triodia plain, then north 60 degrees east till 9.20 a.m., when we reached the first large pool in the creek, and rounding the bend camped at one of the narrow pools above the sandstone ridges. The water in the larger pools had sunk from six inches to a foot since we had passed downwards, and almost all the pools were now dry. The morning clear and cool, with clouds and light showers in the afternoon accompanied by thunder.

16th March.

As there was no water in the creek for the next thirty-three miles, we filled the water-bags and prepared for an early start; but unfortunately the horses had strayed farther than usual, which delayed us till 7.0 a.m., when following nearly the outward route, passed close to camp 43, the waterhole at which was dry, and at 1.0 p.m. halted under the shade of a few acacia-trees during the heat of the day, and resumed our journey at 3.0 p.m., following the south-east side of the plain through which the creek flows. The ground was stony and bad travelling, but as the moon was clear and bright we succeeded in reaching the first pool of water at 8.30 p.m.; this was one mile above Camp 42, the water at which had dried up, though four feet deep on the 24th February. The pool at which we now camped appears to be permanent; it is 100 yards wide and 300 long, the water three feet deep close to the bank. Ducks were numerous, and I shot four in the morning. An easterly breeze continued through the day, and as usual there were a few clouds towards sunset. Unfortunately, the dry weather had warped the scale of the thermometer to such an extent that it broke the tube.

DENISON PLAINS. WATER DRYING UP.

17th March.

We were again delayed by trifling circumstances, and did not leave the camp until 7.40 a.m., but having nearly cleared the desert the weather was comparatively cool. Steering an average course north-east, traversed the wide grassy plains on the right bank of Sturt's Creek, to which the name of Denison's Plains was given. At 2.0 p.m. camped at a small pool in the polygonum flat, which was all that remained of the water which had covered the flat to the extent of three-quarters of a mile in breadth, and was running when we passed down last month. Our course this day showed the great extent of the grassy plains to the north-west, as we did not see the limit at any point in that direction. Cool breeze from east with thin clouds all day.

18th March.

Left the camp at daylight and proceeded to Camp 40 on the outward route, and halted for the remainder of the day to rest the horses, as a heavy stage lay before us across the dry country. Large flocks of cockatoos came to the pool at this camp, and we shot thirty-three, which was a very welcome addition to our provisions. Strong easterly wind; passing clouds.

19th March.

Steered north 60 degrees east at 6.35 a.m., and followed up the course of the creek, crossing the right bank at 9.0, when there was nothing but the polygonum flat to mark its course; at 10.30 altered the course to nearly east, passing a large sheet of brackish water, which appeared deep and permanent at the lower end, but shallow at the upper part; at 11.20 encamped at a small pool of fresh water in a back channel, the creek being brackish, and we were anxious to procure a supply of good water before proceeding further, as the next three stages of the outward track were now destitute of water. Strong easterly breeze; light clouds.

20th March.

At 5.55 am steered 110 degrees; at 6.20 struck a small creek with steep banks; altered the course to 90 degrees, crossing two small watercourses from the north with a little water in the deeper portions of their beds, the general character of the country box flats and open grassy plains near the creek. At 7.25 entered a large grassy plain extending north and east for ten miles, and at 9.15 halted at a small watercourse which retained a little water in a grassy hollow, our object in halting thus early being to enable us to start fresh in the afternoon, and, should the country continue open, to push on through the night, by which the water could be reached before the heat of the sun was too great for travelling. At 3.5 resumed our march and traversed level grassy plains extending one to five miles on each side of our route; at 7.0 observed a native fire about two miles to the north, from which we concluded that water existed at no great distance, and at 7.15 were fortunate in finding a pool of rainwater in a slight depression of the plain, and encamped. We could not find sufficient wood near the camp to boil our tea, but were satisfied with the discovery of a sufficient supply of water.

21st March.

We were again in the saddle at 5.15 a.m., and continuing our course north 73 degrees east, reached the limit of the open plain, which turned to the south-east and extended to the horizon; at 6.40 entered the wooded country which bounded the plain, and the soil changed from a rich clay-loam to sandy and gravelly soil with fragments of sandstone, the vegetation consisting of small white-gum trees, shrubby acacia, and triodia, with a few patches of grass. The country gradually rose till 9.25, when we came to an abrupt descent into the valley of Sturt's Creek, but the country did not improve in character till 10.20, when we came to the grassy flats; at 10.50 camped at a large open pool of water in the bed of the creek. On the pools there were large flights of whistling ducks, but so wild that they could not be approached within range of our guns. Moderate breeze from east with light clouds from south-east during the day. The weather has for the past ten days been so misty that I have not been able to get a good set of lunar distances, and it is useless to observe unless under circumstances favourable for accuracy.

22nd March.

5.35 a.m. found us again travelling up the creek on a northerly course; at 7.20 changed the course north-east by north, and at 11.30 camped about a mile below Camp 35. The hill at the bend of the creek proved to be basaltic, with a stratum of ironstone conglomerate resting on it. The pools of water in the bed of the creek were much reduced and all the smaller ones dried up.

23rd March (Sunday).

The feed and water not being in sufficient quantity to permit of our resting at this camp, we followed up the creek nearly on the outward course. A few miles above the creek a party of blacks came out of the creek and commenced a distant parley, but on one of the party approaching them they picked up their spears they had secreted in the grass and ran away into the bed of the creek. After six and a half hours' journey camped at the lower end of the pool, where we had halted on the 15th February; near the northern bend of the creek we passed a fine deep pool, which appears to retain water through the dry season. All the smaller pools had dried up, and the larger ones had sunk two feet since we were here in February.

24th March.

As the horses had not had a day's rest for some time past, we remained at the camp to refresh them before attempting to cross the dry country which divides the southern waters from those flowing to the north-west coast. As the nearest water which we knew to exist was now fifty miles to the east, and the country in that direction very bad travelling, we were now, however, eighty miles in a direct line from the depot camp, and as that course would take us over new and unexplored country I determined to attempt a direct route.

1700 FEET ABOVE SEA LEVEL.

25th March.

At 6.20 a.m. steered north 40 degrees east, and, leaving Sturt's Creek, traversed open grassy plains till 9.5, when we entered a wooded country, with white-gum trees and underwood, acacia, triodia, and patches of grass; the soil a poor sandy red loam. At 11.0 passed to the south of an extensive grassy plain trending to the north-west; at 12.30 p.m. halted to ease the horses' backs from their loads, and resumed our route at 1.40, and at 2.0 crossed a ridge of stony country which the aneroid showed to be about 1700 feet above the sea level, and was the highest spot yet visited by the Expedition. At 2.20 altered the course to east, and followed a slight depression till 4.0, when we came to a dry watercourse trending north-west; this was traced down in search of water till 6.30, when we halted for the night, without finding any water. The day being very calm and hot, the horses were very much distressed for want of water; but as there was a little green grass on the bank of the creek, they were able to feed for a few hours during the night.

Latitude by Leonis 17 degrees 35 minutes 6 seconds.

26th March.

Proceeded down the creek, and at 7.20 a.m. came to a small pool of water, which the horses consumed in the space of a few minutes, but farther on came to a more abundant supply, and some of the pools appeared to be permanent, having a belt of water-pandanus and reeds round them; below this the channel was perfectly dry and sandy, but was much enlarged by numerous tributary gullies. At 12.50 p.m. came to a shallow pool, at which we camped. The country through which this creek passes is poor and stony, low hills of sandstone schist and limestone rising immediately behind the narrow strip of grassy land, which is fertilised by the overflow of the creek in the rainy season. The vegetable productions of the country seemed to be limited to a few small gum-trees, shrubby acacia, and triodia, with an occasional patch of grass. At the camp the bed of the creek was about forty yards wide, with banks fifteen feet high; the general course appeared to be north-west, a direction which renders it probable that it flows into Cambridge Gulf.

Latitude by Pollux 17 degrees 25 minutes 31 seconds.

SIXTY MILES WITHOUT WATER.

27th March.

At 6.0 a.m. left the camp and steered a course north 60 degrees east, gradually ascending among hills of schist and sandstone till 8.20, when we reached the level tableland. The principal trees were white-gum and silver-leafed ironbark, the soil a red loam of varying character, well grassed, but with patches of triodia, which affects a poor gravelly soil or deep sand. The country was now so nearly level that scarcely any rise or fall was discoverable, though the aneroid showed some slight undulations; at 1.15 p.m. halted for an hour, and at 6.0 camped in a patch of green grass, which enabled the horses to feed though they had no water. The weather was clear and hot during the day with a light easterly breeze, the night cloudy and very warm.

DEPOT CAMP.

28th March.

At 5.10 a.m. resumed our course north 60 degrees east through a grassy forest of ironbark and bloodwood, with patches of small acacia and triodia. At 7.45 entered a series of open plains covered with high grass. The plains continued till 10.0, when we passed through an open gum forest, and the country declined to the east, and at 11.15 came on a small watercourse, which was dry and sandy. This we followed down to the north-east till 11.40, when it passed through a rocky gorge in a sandstone ridge, which rose at an angle of 30 degrees to the south-west and 40 degrees to the north-east, the latter being the dip of the strata. In this rocky gorge we could see some pools of water, but they were quite inaccessible from that side of the ridge, and we had to make a considerable detour to the south before we could descend to the plain below, and found a fine pool of water at the termination of the gorge, at which we halted and watered our thirsty horses. As we were now only two hours' ride from the depot camp, we after a short rest started again at 3.10 p.m., and at 5.15 reached the depot camp, where we were welcomed by Mr. Baines and his party, and I was glad to find them all enjoying good health, and that the horses were in excellent condition. They had been, however, somewhat annoyed by the blacks, who had made frequent attempts to burn the camp, and also the horses, by setting fire to the grass, and on some occasions had come to actual hostilities, though by judicious management none of the party had been injured; nor was it certain that any of the blacks had been wounded, though it had been necessary to resort to the use of firearms in self-defence and for the protection of the horses.

29th March.

Returned our surplus provisions into store, when we found that the pieces of pork, originally four pounds weight each, were reduced to one-fifth of the original weight, as the long continuance of heat had melted the whole of the fat. Our ration had therefore been one pound flour, one-fifth pound salt pork, and two ounces sugar per diem. Mr. H. Gregory and Bowman rode out to round in the horses.

Latitude by Regulus and e Argus 17 degrees 2 minutes.

30th March (Sunday).

Read prayers to those of the party who were in camp, some of the men having been sent out to attend to the horses. Mr. Baines having handed me his journal, I regret to find that he has been compelled to make an entry regarding Mr. Flood, who had refused to attend to his order to carry arms while on watch at night on the 18th March. I therefore called on Mr. Flood for any statement he had to make in extenuation of his conduct. His replies were, however, extremely unsatisfactory, and only attempted to excuse the act on account of some private misunderstanding with Mr. Baines some months previous, and that the order to wear his pistol was given before he had time to put on his clothes. There had, however, been a distinct refusal to obey the orders of the officer in charge of the party, and those orders were neither vexatious or unreasonable, as they were simply in enforcement of well-established regulations. I therefore cautioned Mr. Flood that unless his future conduct was more satisfactory than it had hitherto been I should remove his name from the list of officers taking command in the Expedition, according to the general orders of the 27th August, 1855. The weather continues cloudy and calm, and, though the temperature is not extreme, it is very oppressive.

31st March.

Examining and packing stores in readiness for the exploration of the valley of the Victoria to the east of the depot. Found the stores in good condition, though the bags had been much injured by the rats and white ants. Although in some respects it would be more convenient to move the party at once to the bank of the Victoria before examining the country beyond, yet as the horses were now accustomed to the run near the depot, and the huts and stockyard rendered the station a more safe and convenient spot than any we could elsewhere select, I therefore decided on leaving the party here until I had explored the country to the east, and then move the whole party down the right bank of the river, by which the number and magnitude of the tributaries from the east would be ascertained, as this was an important point with reference to the contemplated journey to the Gulf of Carpentaria.

1st April.

Preparing equipment for a light party to explore the country to the east of the camp; shod six horses, and packed eighteen days' provisions for four persons. The weather continues cloudy, with light variable winds.

EXPLORE EAST OF THE DEPOT.

2nd April.

At 6.45 am started from the depot with Messrs. H. Gregory, Baines, and John Fahey, taking four riding and two pack horses, carrying eighteen days' rations, etc. Steered east over an undulating grassy country of basaltic formation with occasional sandstone ridges; the soil was generally good, but very stony. I had already traversed this country, and as the day was very misty with much rain, nothing worthy of further record was observed. At 1.30 p.m. altered the course to east-south-east, and at 3.15 camped on a large creek trending north-east, in the bed of which were large pools of a permanent character. The hills were basaltic, but the creeks having cut through the rocks and excavated the sandstone, the valleys were not of such a fertile character as the plains and ridges. Timber was wholly absent, and only a few small trees were seen at intervals on the hills. The morning was cloudy with light rain, but it cleared towards sunset.

Latitude by e Argus 17 degrees 4 minutes 6 seconds.

3rd April.

Resumed our route at 6.30, and steered east-south-east to a basaltic hill, which we reached at 7.40; from the summit a great extent of country was visible, but there were no marked features, as the broken ranges and isolated hills were nearly similar to each other. The whole country appeared to be a nearly level basaltic plain, with masses of sandstone rising 100 to 200 feet above its surface, while the valleys of the creek were excavated to the depth of 100 feet. The country was well grassed, but very stony; but this, though very inconvenient to the traveller, does not render it less valuable for pasture, as stony land always stands feeding better than any other. At 8.20 altered the course to nearly east towards a low ridge of hills. The plain was well grassed till 12.50 p.m., when the sandstone prevailed on the surface and triodia prevailed in the valleys. At 1.50 followed down a rocky ravine, and at 2.15 encamped.

THE VICTORIA RIVER.

4th April.

At 6.5 a.m. left the camp and followed the gully to the east-south-east; at 7.0 crossed a sandstone ridge, and beyond it a large creek from the south-west, in the bed of which there were some fine pools of water. We then ascended to a basaltic plain, and altered the course to south-east; at 8.0 the country gradually declined to the east, and sandstone was the prevailing rock, but grass was abundant. At 9.40 reached the Victoria, the course from south-south-west to north-north-east; the river had ceased to run and was now only in large pools; crossed to the right bank and steered south half an hour, and camped on the bank of a creek from south-south-east; at noon the sky was overcast, and at 2 p.m. it commenced raining and continued till 4.30, with thunder; heavy dew at night. After it commenced raining the aneroid fell 0.10, but rose again before it ceased. In this part of Australia neither wind nor rain appear to affect the atmospheric pressure to any great extent.

ECLIPSE OF THE SUN.

5th April.

The result of the rain yesterday was a thick fog this morning, and when we left the camp at 5.50 a.m. we could not see 100 yards, and we traversed the basaltic plain in an east course till 7.0, when the fog cleared away and we found ourselves at the foot of some low rocky hills of basalt, over which we travelled north 70 degrees east. These hills were very rough and stony, but covered with excellent grass. We then entered a basaltic plain, richly grassed and less stony than usual. At 9.30 crossed a basaltic ridge and entered a large valley trending to the north and east; at 10.10 ascended a rocky hill about 150 feet high, and got bearings of the ranges, etc. The country appeared to consist of grassy hills and plains, extending twenty to thirty miles to the north and east. To the south a range of basalt and sandstone hills intercepted the view. Steered east from the hill, and traversed an undulating country, the rocks being basalt, sandstone schist, and jasper; the basalt forming the higher ground, though on the banks of the creek the jasper rested on the basalt. At 2.10 p.m. encamped on a large creek with a gravelly channel twenty yards wide. Fahey obtained a large quantity of mussels from the pools in the creek; they proved an excellent addition to our supper, though rather deficient in flavour. The weather was cloudy, and, though there was an occasional sight of the sun, we could observe neither the commencement or end of the solar eclipse. I was therefore unable to avail myself of it for correcting the longitude.

Latitude by e Argus 17 degrees 9 minutes 6 seconds.

6th April.

Left the camp at 6.10 a.m. and steered east over a grassy plain; at 7.25 crossed some wide channels from the south-east, forming a large creek; at 8.15 turned south-east and followed the creek till noon. It then turned south, and at 12.15 p.m. we camped at a shallow pool of muddy water. The creek was here divided into several small channels, in which only a few pools of water remained. The whole of the country traversed this day was nearly level, well grassed, and very open. Basalt and jasper are the prevailing rocks.

Latitude by Regulus and Argus 17 degrees 15 minutes 45 seconds.

7th April.

As the creek appeared to come from the south and not to have a long course, but to rise in the low sandstone ranges which were visible in that direction, it was useless to follow it farther; we therefore steered northwards to intercept any streams which might join the Victoria River lower down its course, and, after travelling over open grassy ridges of basalt for six hours, at 12.25 p.m. camped at a small gully, in which there were some small pools, which appeared to be supplied by springs. The country for five to ten miles to the east of our track appeared open and grassy, basalt being the prevailing rock.

RUNNING WATER. FINE PASTORAL COUNTRY.

8th April.

At 6.0 a.m. left the camp, and steered an average west-north-west course over an undulating grassy country of basaltic formation; at 11.45 reached the bank of the creek, which formed fine pools fifty yards wide, with fine open grassy country on both sides, well suited for stock. Followed the creek west till 1.5 p.m., when we crossed to the left bank and encamped.

Latitude by Regulus and Argus 16 degrees 59 minutes.

9th April.

Continued our route down the creek in a northerly direction, leaving the camp at 6.15 a.m., and at 7.55 reached its junction with the Victoria. The river had high banks and formed deep reaches of water, with a dense growth of pandanus, melaleuca, flooded-gum, and other trees in the dry portions of the channel; the country on both banks was basaltic, and rose gradually into fine grassy downs; the soil very stony, but a good dark loam; sandstone showed where the river had cut through the basalt, which is not of any great thickness. At 2.35 p.m. camped on a back channel of the river, as the principal channel was difficult of access from the steep bank and dense growth of reeds. Although the upper part of the Victoria had long ceased to run, this part of the river was flowing with a strong stream ten yards wide and six feet deep.

Latitude by Regulus and Argus 16 degrees 45 minutes 30 seconds.

10th April.

Continued our route at 6.5 a.m., and followed the river northward till 8.10, when it turned to the north-west; the country consisted of nearly level grassy plains of various elevations, separated by low rocky ridges of sandstone and basalt, the whole well grassed, except some small patches where triodia prevailed; at 11.0 altered the course to average north-west by west, and at 1.30 p.m. camped at a small gully with a little water remaining from a recent shower. The horses suffered much from the heat, as the air was very moist; at 1.40 there was a shower of rain, and the temperature was reduced from 95 degrees to 84 degrees.

Latitude by Vega 16 degrees 35 minutes 8 seconds.

11th April.

Started from the camp at 6.30 a.m., steering west-south-west; at first sandstone prevailed, and triodia replaced the grass, but at two miles again entered the basaltic country, which was well grassed but very stony, and forming flat-topped hills of small elevation; the basalt appeared to be interstratified with sandstone, the latter much altered at the line of contact. At 9.15 came on the bank of the river, which was running in a deep channel with a dense line of pandanus, fig-trees, terminalia, flooded-gum, and melaleuca; followed the valley of the river to the north-west till noon, and camped at the foot of the hill which we had ascended, at the most southern point attained in December, 1855; ascended the hill and took the bearings, as on the former occasion the rain had obscured the features of the country.

Latitude by Leonis and Argus 16 degrees 27 minutes 30 seconds.

12th April.

Having connected this part of our route with that of December last, at 6.20 a.m. commenced our return up the river, crossing to the left bank at 7.15; the water was running strong twenty yards, and one to two feet deep; in examining the ford my horse trod on the back of a large alligator, which seemed to be equally astonished as the horse at this unexpected meeting; I then proceeded up the river a mile and a half and halted, as Mr. H. Gregory, who I had sent to examine the river in another part, had not come up with the party, but he shortly after overtook us, having found a good ford lower down the river; at 4.0 p.m. resumed our journey, and at dusk encamped in the bed of a large creek, which joined the Victoria from the south-south-west; at 7.0 it commenced raining, and there were frequent showers till midnight, with thunder and lightning.

HUTT PLAINS.

13th April.

As the creek in which we bivouacked seemed to come from the south-west, we followed the valley in that direction; at 6.40 a.m. the hills receding, the grassy flats appeared to extend to the Wickham River and form a continuation of Hutt Plains; the creek now came from the south-south-west and had some fine pools of water in the channel; at 2.10 p.m. camped at a shallow pool in the grassy flat, as the water in the creek was not very easy of access owing to the dense masses of reeds and grass. The hills which bound the valley of the creek are basalt, sandstone, and schist. In the level ground near the creek the grass was five to nine feet high, and greatly impeded our horses. The day was cool and cloudy with some light showers at night. The aneroid barometer was completely put out of adjustment by the principal lever having been moved from its position by a violent shake in crossing one of the deep gullies.

NATIVE PAINTINGS.

14th April.

At 6.10 a.m. resumed our journey up the creek in a southerly direction, the valley gradually narrowing, and in one part of the sandstone rocks came close to the banks of the creek, leaving scarcely space to pass between them and the deep pools of water; at 12.30 p.m. camped on the right bank. The basaltic hills appeared to turn to the south-east, and we now entered the sandstone country. The valley of this creek appears to offer the best line of access to the upper part of the valley of the Victoria, as it is nearly level from Hutt Plains to 10.40 in this day's journey, beyond which point drays would have to ascend the hills and turn to the south-east to reach Roe's Downs, which is the finest part of the country yet examined. A short distance below our camp we saw several native paintings on the sandstone rocks; they consisted of rude outlines of fish and snakes, some in red ochre and others in white clay. Mr. Baines sketched some of the most remarkable.

Latitude by Argus 16 degrees 55 minutes.

15th April.

At 6.25 a.m. recommenced our journey and followed the creek, which turned to the west, and the country became extremely rugged, and at length, as the valley became impassable, we ascended the hills and steered south-west across a very rocky sandstone country to the basaltic plains. Changing the course to west-north-west, crossed two tributary creeks, and at 3.40 p.m. camped on the bank of the creek, which was now much reduced in size. The country to the north of the creek consisted of very rough and rocky hills of red sandstone, extremely barren in appearance, while to the south it rose into the basaltic plain which forms Roe's Downs.

Latitude by Argus 17 degrees 6 seconds.

16th April.

Resumed our journey at 6.45 a.m. and travelled in a west by north course towards a remarkable basaltic hill, which I called Mount Sanford, traversing a fine open grassy country till 1.0 p.m., when we camped on a creek with permanent pools of water. The rough stony country has rendered the horses quite footsore, and their legs are much cut and bruised by constantly falling over the large rocks in crossing the deep ravines and rocky ridges.

Latitude by Vega 16 degrees 59 minutes 38 seconds.

RETURN TO DEPOT CAMP.

17th April.

Started at 6.25 a.m. and reached Mount Sanford at 7.30, the country passed being sandstone producing triodia and a little grass. The hill is of basalt with a flat top, but is based on sandstone; its form is nearly a truncated cone 150 feet high and 300 feet in diameter at the top. Having taken angles to the surrounding hills, we descended and steered south-west and west to the depot camp at 1.0 p.m. During our absence Dr. Mueller had found full employment in collecting the plants in the vicinity of the camp, and the rest of the party had been fully occupied in the care of the horses and duties of the camp. I was glad to find that they had not been again molested by the blacks.

18th April.

Preparing maps of the late excursion to the east of the depot; party preparing for the return to principal camp.

19th April.

Party employed as before.

20th April (Sunday).

A fine cool breeze from the south, with thin clouds.

21st April.

Several of the horses had strayed some distance from the camp, and we did not start till 12.30 p.m., when we steered north by west till 5.15 p.m. and camped at a small creek in a deep rocky valley; the country after leaving the basaltic plain was very rocky, the hills composed of schist with a superstratum of red sandstone; grass was abundant in the valley, but the hills produced little but triodia and small gum-trees.

START FOR MAIN CAMP.

22nd April.

At 6.45 a.m. steered east down the creek one mile to its junction with Depot Creek, which was followed north and north-north-east till 8.40. The back country rose into sandstone hills covered with triodia; but there were good grassy flats on the bank of the creek. The creek then entered a rocky gorge about 100 yards wide, with cliffs upward of 100 feet high on each side. With some difficulty we forced our way through the dense growth of reeds and brush, among huge masses of rock and deep pools of water, till 10.10, when we reached a more open part of the valley. The creek now turned to east-north-east, and the wide valley was bounded by low schist hills to the north and the sandstone range we had just passed to the south; except in the lower part of the valley and a few small patches on the hills the country was very poor and stony, triodia taking the place of the grass; water was abundant in the bed of the creek, where it formed large permanent pools, between which there was a small stream of running water in the upper part of the creek, but lower down the channel was dry between the pools; at 1.0 p.m. camped on the right bank of the creek; crossed to the left bank of the creek at 6.20 p.m. and followed it north-east one hour, when the creek turned east and our course was over stony ridges; it was now found that one of the horses was missing, having been lost in one of the dense thickets on the bed of the creek. Mr. H. Gregory therefore returned to search for the lost animal, and we halted till 9.20, and then went on with the party, leaving Mr. Baines to wait on the track till Mr. Gregory came up; at 10.20 p.m. reached the Wickham River and followed it down to the junction of Depot Creek, which we crossed at noon, and camped in a grassy flat about a mile lower down; at 2.0 am Mr. H. Gregory and Mr. Baines came into the camp, but had not been able to find the missing horse; at 3.0 a.m. Mr. H. Gregory and Bowman started to look for the horse.

24th April.

At 10.30 Mr. H. Gregory brought in the pack-horse lost yesterday. Fortunately, this horse was not carrying a load, and though the saddle got under the horse's belly nothing was injured.

25th April.

Followed the river down from 7.40 a.m. till 2.30 p.m. and encamped at 9.10 p.m.; crossed a large tributary creek from the south; the country was grassy near the river, but rose into rocky hills with flat tops at a short distance from it; light rain from 4.0 a.m. till 1.0 p.m., with light easterly breeze.

CROSS THE VICTORIA RANGE. STOKES' RANGE.

26th April.

Continued the route along the right bank of the Wickham from 7.45 a.m. till 3.15 p.m., the general course east-north-east, and camped; after passing the gorge in the sandstone range, which was very narrow and rocky, the country opened into level plains. The best line of route to the upper part of the Wickham is near Mount Warburton, as the sandstone hills which form the rocky gorge are detached; the day was cool and cloudy, with a strong easterly breeze in the morning, and it commenced raining at sunset.

27th April.

At 7.25 a.m. left the camp and steered east to the Victoria River, but as we could not find a fording place, turned north to the Wickham, and encamped on its banks at 12.25. The bank of the Victoria being so densely covered with reeds that the water was not accessible; at noon I rode out with Mr. H. Gregory to search for a ford, as I wished to keep on the right bank of the river to ascertain what tributary streams joined from the east; after three hours' search found a practicable ford and returned to the camp after dark. In the afternoon the blacks were heard calling on the left bank of the Wickham, near the camp, but were not seen, owing to the thick brush and reeds which filled the bed of the river.

28th April.

At 7.25 a.m. steered south to the Victoria and reached the ford at 8.35, and at 9.0 a.m., having accomplished the passage of the river with only a few slight accidents, followed the right bank of the Victoria downwards till 1.15 p.m., and encamped on the eastern side of the Victoria; the country was level and well grassed for several miles back, and then rose into the sandstone range to the south and basaltic hills to the east.

29th April.

At 7.10 a.m. steered north-east over a nearly level grassy basaltic country with low hills to the east of our route; at 8.0 a.m. altered the course to north and traversed a fine grassy country with table hills of basalt resting on chert and sandstone; crossed one creek from the south-east with a muddy channel fifteen yards wide; at 2.0 p.m. changed the course to north 300 degrees east, and at 4.15 p.m. reached the bank of the Victoria; but it was so steep that the horses could not approach the water, and therefore followed it to the rocky ford east-south-east from Mount Sandiman and encamped.

30th April.

Crossed the left bank of the river at 7.0 a.m., but one of the horses injured his leg among the rocks, and the wound had to be sewn up, which delayed us till 8.20 a.m., when we steered north-west to Jasper Creek, which, after much labour in forcing a passage through the reeds, we crossed at 11.25 a.m., and at 12.55 p.m. encamped on the bank of the Victoria, at the commencement of the rocky gorge through Stokes' Range.

1st May.

Proceeded down the river, leaving the camp at 6.50 a.m., and at 2.15 p.m. encamped a short distance above our camp of the 8th December, 1855.

2nd May.

Continued route from 6.45 a.m. till 1.0 p.m., and encamped one mile above our bivouac of the 28th December.

3rd May.

Resumed our journey at 6.45 a.m. and followed the left bank of the river till 10.10 a.m., when we encamped at the spot where we crossed the Victoria on the 28th November, 1855; at 2.0 p.m. crossed the river with Mr. H. Gregory, and rode to the east to examine a large creek which joined the Victoria two miles below the camp. The creek was thirty to forty yards wide, with high muddy banks covered with reeds, and the marks of floods were fifty feet above its present level; the general appearance was that of a stream having a course of forty to fifty miles. The wide flat on the left bank of the creek was well grassed; but the valley was bounded by steep sandstone hills covered with triodia and scrub; returned to the camp at 5.0 p.m.

6th May.

As we should have to pass this camp on our route to the Gulf of Carpentaria, I deposited 100 pounds of flour and a quantity of shot and lead, horse-shoes, etc., in a cleft in the rocks, and covered them with large stones, and then set the grass on fire to deface our tracks; at 8.15 a.m. left the camp and proceeded along our former track till noon, and camped on a small creek two miles east-south-east from Bynoe Range.

7th May.

Left the camp at 8.10 a.m. and steered north 240 degrees east over a level grassy country, wooded with bauhinia, acacia, and eucalypti--the latter being more abundant as we advanced; at 1.0 p.m. the country changed to low rocky ridges of chert and limestone, and at 2.0 p.m. encamped at a small creek trending north-west, and in which a few small muddy pools of water remained. At noon we passed a party of five or six blacks, who shouted to us from a distance, but would not approach within 200 yards. They were armed with spears, and seemed to be on their return from hunting, as the grass was on fire to the south.

8th May.

At 7.20 resumed our journey, and steering west crossed a fine creek with fine pools and water-pandanus growing on the banks. We then traversed a very rocky country, at the southern base of the sandstone range, till 11.0, when we came to a more level and grassy country, consisting of chert ridges. At noon steered north 300 degrees east down the valley of a small creek, and soon entered a deep valley bounded on both sides by steep sandstone hills. At 1.0 p.m. turned north 320 degrees east, and at 2.20 camped at a shallow pool in the bed of the creek, which was now in the limestone rock.

REACH THE MAIN CAMP.

9th May.

At 7.30 a.m. resumed our journey down the valley to the junction of the creek with the Victoria River, which we followed down, crossing the ridge at Steep Head at 10.20, and reached the principal camp at 5.30 p.m., where we were welcomed by Mr. Elsey, who was in charge, Mr. Wilson being absent down the river at the schooner, which had been laid on the shingle bank near the Dome to complete repairs. I was glad to learn that all the men belonging to the Expedition were in good health, except Richards, whose hand was still in a very unsatisfactory state, though better than when we left in January. The crew of the schooner had not been so fortunate, as the carpenter, John Finlay, had died, and three of the men were so ill that they had been left at the camp to be under the immediate care of the medical officer. This great amount of sickness is owing to the combined effects of previous disease and the inferior quality of the provisions with which the vessel is supplied. It appears that through damage by salt water and want of good management the provisions, which should have been sufficient for two years, are now reduced to salt beef of inferior quality and tea, the Expedition having had to furnish flour, rice, sugar, peas, and pork, as also medical stores, for the sick men. In consequence of the reduced number of the crew of the Tom Tough, Mr. Wilson had found it necessary to furnish men to assist in working the schooner, as well as to effect repairs.

10th May.

Much of the grass near the camp having been burnt, I sent the horses to the creek, three miles above the camp. Party employed in general duties of the camp. Twenty-nine sheep remained; they are now in fair condition; the average weight forty to forty-five pounds. They would probably have been much fatter had they been judiciously shepherded, but they had been kept close to the camp, where the feed had been eaten off closely. The natives have been frequently at the camp in small parties, and on these occasions were very quiet in their demeanour, but had made hostile demonstrations when met by small detached parties of the Expedition; and on one occasion Mr. Wilson had deemed it necessary to fire at them; but only one of the blacks appears to have been wounded, with small shot, in the arm, as he was afterwards seen at the camp.

11th May (Sunday).

12th May.

Preparing maps, arranging stores, etc.

13th May.

Drawing maps of the late journey and preparing for the Expedition to the Albert River.

THE TOM TOUGH REFITTED.

14th May.

Preparing maps, sifting flour, packing specimens, burning charcoal for the forge, preparing horse-shoes. At 6 p.m. Mr. Wilson returned in the boat from the Tom Tough. One of the boys belonging to the schooner was brought to the camp for medical treatment, as he was suffering from scurvy. The Tom Tough had been moored below the shoals, and was now moored in a secure position below Curiosity Peak. All the leaks had been secured, and she now only made about half an inch of water per hour. The crew of the vessel have been so much reduced by sickness that it will be necessary to send men on board to assist in refitting the vessel and procure a supply of wood and water. As it is necessary to replace the stores destroyed or damaged by salt-water, it appears desirable that the Tom Tough should proceed to the Gulf of Carpentaria via Coupang, in the island of Timor, where a supply of rice and sugar can be procured for the Expedition, and the vessel will be enabled to complete her stores. It appears desirable that the land party should refit with all possible despatch for the journey to the Gulf of Carpentaria, in order to take advantage of the cool season, and there is reason to expect that the horses will be sufficiently recruited in strength towards the end of June. I am, therefore, in hope that the party will be able to leave the Victoria before the expiration of the ensuing month. A small party of natives came to the camp in the morning and bartered a few trifles, and then retired.

15th May.

Continued preparation of maps; party employed in preparations for the journey to the Gulf of Carpentaria, camp duties, and preparing oakum for the schooner. Having found that the pork had been so much reduced in weight during the late journey, I made some experiments in the preparation of meat biscuits by mixing the preserved fresh beef with flour in equal proportions, with satisfactory results, as the reduction in weight by baking was 33 per cent.

16th May.

Party employed as before.

17th May.

Party employed as before.

18th May (Sunday).

19th May.

Messrs. Wilson, Elsey, and Mueller being desirous of proceeding up the Baines River to collect specimens, etc., made the necessary arrangements for the same, and they therefore proceeded in the boat with Phibbs, Humphries, and Shewell to the schooner; the men were then to return to the camp with a cargo of stores; and Messrs. Wilson, Elsey, and Mueller were to proceed up Baines' River in the small boat which they were to obtain from the schooner. Richards is in charge of the sheep; Macdonald cook during the week; Bowman and Melville in charge of horses; Dean preparing saddle-bags and harness; Fahey and Selby burning charcoal and general camp duties.

20th May.

Party employed as before. The weather continues fine, with southerly winds.

21st May.

Party employed as before.

22nd May.

Party employed as before. At noon the boat returned from the schooner with stores; Captain Gourlay also came up in the gig to the camp; he informed me that the schooner now only made ten inches of water per day, and that she would be ready for sea so soon as the upper seams were caulked, and that he considered her perfectly seaworthy for the purpose of the expedition.

23rd May.

Party employed as before.

24th May.

Despatched the boat to the schooner with three cases containing sationery, tobacco, clothing, etc. Captain Gourlay returned to the Tom Tough.

25th May (Sunday).

PREPARATIONS FOR JOURNEY EASTWARD.

26th May.

Party employed preparing equipment for the journey to the Gulf of Carpentaria.

27th May.

As before.

29th May.

Party employed as before. Messrs. Wilson, Elsey, and Mueller returned with the long-boat and gig from the schooner, having been about thirty miles up Baines' River to the south-west of Curiosity Hill. Mr. Wilson brought a native in the boat from Stony Spit.

30th May.

Party employed as before, and packing stores to be put on board the schooner.

31st May.

Party employed as before.

1st June (Sunday).

2nd June.

Party employed preparing saddlery and equipment for the journey to the Gulf of Carpentaria.

3rd June.

Mr. Baines proceeded in the boat to the schooner (which was now anchored below the shoals), conveying a quantity of stores. Boat's crew: Phibbs, Humphries, Dean, and Selby; remainder of party at the camp employed as before. Preparing map of route up the Victoria River, etc.

4th June.

Party employed as before, namely, shoeing horses, restuffing saddles, and other preparations for journey to the Gulf of Carpentaria. Received from Mr. Wilson a journal of his proceedings from 31st January to 3rd March, and 1st April to 14th May.

5th June.

Party at camp employed as before. Mr. Baines returned with the gig. Boat's crew: Phibbs, Humphries, Dean, Selby, and Dawson, also one of the seaman belonging to the schooner; received a note from the master of the Tom Tough, complaining that Dawson had used abusive language to Mr. Gourlay; but as it appeared that considerable provocation had been given, I only reprimanded Dawson for his conduct. Mr. Baines informed me that on the 4th instant he had landed early in the day from the schooner, in company with Captain Gourlay, Dawson, and one of the seamen (Adams), for the purpose of bartering with a party of natives, about twenty in number. The blacks having been allowed to come close to the boat, stole a tomahawk, and on Adams making a demonstration of detaining one of their number until the stolen article was returned, one of the blacks seized his gun and tried to wrest it from him; but, Captain Gourlay approaching, he ran into the bush, and the rest of the blacks retired; the party then returned to the schooner. The tomahawk was afterwards found in the water near where the boat had landed.

6th June.

Party employed as before; the shoeing of the horses progresses rapidly, Mr. H. Gregory and Bowman shoeing five horses each day, although some of them are very restive.

7th June.

Mr. Elsey proceeded in the gig with Phibbs, Humphries, Selby, and Adams, conveying the two sick men and boy belonging to the schooner crew to the Tom Tough. Mr. Wilson requested me to hold an investigation into the circumstances attending the landing of a party from the Tom Tough on the 4th instant, to traffic with the blacks, as he deemed it very imprudent, when so large a number of natives were assembled on the shore, to land with only four persons, though they were all armed; and adverted to the possible results of such a proceeding, which he said might have terminated the hitherto undisturbed harmony which had been maintained by the parties in his charge during my absence in their intercourse with the aborigines, and stated that he considered the evidence of men who were not present, but on board the schooner at the time of the party landing, was more to be relied on than Mr. Baines' statement, which had been made before the officers generally. As Mr. Baines had minutely detailed the whole transaction to me, and nothing farther was alleged by Mr. Wilson, who appeared to be actuated by no friendly feelings towards Mr. Baines, and my investigation would have only been an expression of a want of confidence in the veracity of Mr. Baines, which I could not entertain, I informed Mr. Wilson that I did not see any necessity for the investigation suggested. Party employed preparing equipment, shoeing horses, baking meat biscuits, etc. Rain at night.

8th June (Sunday).

MAKE MEAT BISCUITS.

9th June.

Completed shoeing the horses; party employed making small tents and saddle-bags, fitting pack-saddles, baking biscuits; Dr. Mueller collecting and arranging botanical specimens.

ARRANGEMENT OF PARTY.

10th June.

Party employed as before, and preparing extra shoes for the horses, etc. Mr. Elsey returned with the gig from the schooner; boat's crew: Phibbs, Humphries, and Selby; the sick men had reached the vessel without any serious difficulty, although the boat grounded on the banks, and was thereby detained till next tide, and thus kept them several hours exposed to the rain.

11th June.

Party employed as before.

12th June.

Completed baking 300 pounds of preserved beef and 300 pounds of flour into biscuits, which weighed 480 pounds when dry. A 6-pound tin of beef, with the soup and fat, was added to 6 pounds of flour, 1 ounce of salt (no water being used), and the whole made up into dough and baked in the ordinary form of sea biscuits; the result was 8 pounds, and thus 1 1/4 pounds contained 1 pound of flour and 1 pound of meat.

13th June.

Mr. Baines proceeded with Phibbs, Humphries, and Selby in the gig to the Tom Tough, with stores not required at the camp, and for the purpose of returning with soap and other stores required for the outfit of the land expedition. Party employed as before. Mr. Wilson completed and furnished to me a sketch of the Western branch of the Victoria River, which had been discovered by Mr. Baines in December, 1855, while searching for stray horses, and which I had then named after him. Preparing maps, etc., for transmission to the Governor-General of Australia.

14th June.

Wrote to Governor-General, reporting progress of the North Australian Expedition. Party employed as before; set of spare horse-shoes completed.

15th June (Sunday).

The weather has been remarkably cool and clear for several days, the temperature at sunrise 48 to 52 degrees.

16th June.

Mr. Baines returned from the schooner with the gig and long-boat (boat's crew as before) bringing the stores required for the land party. Party at the camp preparing equipment for expedition to the Gulf of Carpentaria. Mr. Wilson requested to be informed whether I had decided to attach him to the party which was to be organised at the Gulf of Carpentaria for the exploration of the country towards Moreton Bay, and in reply I informed him that so many unforeseen circumstances might occur before reaching the Albert River to require me to modify any arrangements made at the present time, that I should not select the individuals to form that party till we reached the Albert River. Received from Mr. Wilson a letter stating that unless I would now decide that he was to form one of the party proceeding from the Albert River overland to Moreton Bay, he was desirous of resigning his appointment of geologist to the North Australian Expedition. Wrote to Mr. Wilson in reply, stating that I could not comply with his request.

17th June.

Preparing copies of letters to Governor-General of Australia for transmission to the Secretary of State for the Colonies. Party preparing for journey to the Gulf of Carpentaria. Received from Mr. Wilson a letter stating that he declined to perform any further duties as an officer of the North Australian Expedition unless I complied with certain conditions therein named. Wrote to Mr. Wilson in reply, and informed him that he was henceforth suspended from any command in the Expedition. As I could not now include Mr. Wilson in the party proceeding to the Albert River by land, I requested Dr. Mueller to prepare to take Mr. Wilson's place in the party.

18th June. •

Issued a general order, Number 4, suspending Mr. Wilson from any further command in the exploring party till further orders. Party employed as before--preparing equipment. Received from Mr. Wilson a letter relative to his being suspended from any further command in the party.

19th June.

Wrote to Mr. Baines instructing him to take charge of the portion of the North Australian Expedition proceeding in the Tom Tough to the Albert River. Preparing equipment for explorations towards the Gulf of Carpentaria.

20th June.

Wrote to the Governor-General of Australia, forwarding copies of correspondence with Mr. Wilson. Wrote to Secretary of State for the Colonies forwarding copies of despatches to the Governor-General. Wrote to master of Tom Tough schooner, instructing him to proceed to Coepang for supplies, and thence to Albert River. Wrote to Mr. Baines two letters of instructions; inspected equipment, and fitted the saddles of the party proceeding overland to the Gulf of Carpentaria. Wrote to Mr. Wilson a letter in reply to his communication of the 18th.

START FOR GULF OF CARPENTARIA.

21st June.

At 10.0 a.m. left the principal camp on the Victoria with a party consisting of Messrs. H. Gregory, Elsey, and Dr. Mueller, Robert Bowman, Charles Dean, and J. Melville, seven saddle and twenty-seven pack horses, conveying five months' provisions of salt pork and meat biscuits, and six months' supply of flour, tea, sugar, coffee, etc., twenty-six pounds of gunpowder, sixty pounds bullets, 1 hundredweight shot, 5000 caps, etc. Proceeding up the left bank of the Victoria, crossed the ridge at back of Steep Head, and at 3.15 p.m. camped about three-quarters of a mile above it on the bank of the river.

22nd June (Sunday).

At 7.30 a.m. left the camp and followed the river up for ten miles, and then along a small creek four miles south-south-east; but the country proving very steep and rocky, returned one mile and camped at 3 p.m.

23rd June.

Left the camp at 7.0 a.m., and returned down the valley of the creek to the river, and kept along the bank of the Victoria to the junction of Beagle Creek. We ascended for five miles, and camped at 11.0, as there was no water between this point and the Victoria at Bynoe Range on the Beagle Valley route, and the distance was too great to be commenced at this late hour of the day.

24th June.

Started at 7.0 a.m., and steered east through an open box forest nearly level and well grassed. The grass had been burnt off by the blacks, but had shot up to a foot in height. Passed to the south of the Fitzroy Range; the valley between it and Stokes' Range similar to Beagle Valley, and about four miles wide. Keeping close to Stokes' Range, passed behind some of the detached hills at 4.20 p.m. Reached our old camp of the 5th May, and found the stores we had left secreted in the rocks undisturbed.

25th June.

Having distributed the stores which had been left here in May among the several pack-horses, at 7.15 a.m. resumed our route up the river, and crossed to the right bank two miles above the creek we intended to ascend, and camped at 11.0. Marked a large gum-tree Delta V.

Latitude by b and a2 Centauri 15 degrees 39 minutes 17 seconds.

LEAVE THE VICTORIA RIVER.

26th June.

Left the camp at 7.0 a.m., and followed the creek upwards to the east-south-east for five miles. The valley was about one mile wide, with fine grassy flats, bounded by sandstone cliffs 50 to 200 feet high, and forming tableland with deep ravines. The valley now turned to the east and east-north-east; some small tributaries joined the creek from the south-east, the sandstone cliffs disappeared, and the outline of the hills became rounded and rose about 300 feet above the creek. Shallow pools of water with dry shingle between, and an occasional deep waterhole, characterised the channel of the watercourse. At 1.30 p.m. camped on the left bank of the creek in an open grassy flat; the higher land very stony and indifferent.

Latitude by Canopus 15 degrees 40 minutes 49 seconds.

27th June.

The temperature was lower at sunrise this morning than on any other day since landing in North Australia, being only 41 degrees. A little dew on the grass, and a light air from the east. At 6.50 a.m. started and followed up the creek to the east-north-east till 1.0 p.m., when we camped at a deep pool of water 20 yards wide and 200 yards long. Our attempts to procure fish were unsuccessful. The country consisted of low stony hills, thinly wooded, and. the flats of the creek from a quarter to three quarters of a mile wide continued to be well grassed. On the north side of the creek a few miles back the hills rose to a greater elevation, and formed table-topped hills; some with cliffs of sandstone near the summits, and others smooth grassy slopes. The latter, from the colour of the grass, appeared to be of trap formation, and fragments of this rock were found in the bed of the creek. Soft shales were exposed in the gullies and on the sides of the hills, and were overlaid compact gray sandstones.

Latitude by b Centauri, a2 Centauri and Arcturus 15 degrees 37 minutes 15 seconds.

28th June.

Left the camp at 7.15 a.m., and followed up the creek to the east-north-east till noon, when we reached the last water in its channel near a steep range of sandstone hills, or rather tablelands; the country traversed was an undulating plain of trap formation resting on gray sandstone; it is thinly wooded, and well grassed; water was abundant in the creek below the camp; above the channel was dry, and soon divided into small gullies; in the afternoon ascended a hill three-quarters of a mile north-west of the camp; the lower portion was a dark compact trap or basalt, and the summit a horizontal bed of sandstone about 200 feet above the camp; the country to the north was very level, and only occasionally interrupted by flat-topped sandstone hills, the view extending at least thirty miles; to the south and south-west a country of trap formation extended for twenty miles, and to the east the tableland rose about 300 feet above the camp, and was composed of the same strata as the hill ascended, but surmounted by the ferruginous conglomerate, which is the highest rock of the new red sandstone series.

Latitude by b Centauri, a Centauri and Arcturus 15 degrees 33 minutes 13 seconds.

ARNHEIM LAND. DALY RIVER.

29th June.

At 6.45 a.m. left the camp with Mr. H. Gregory to reconnoitre the country to the east; ascending the tableland, steered east till 10.0 through a level forest of stringybark and other eucalypti; the soil a light gravelly loam, but well grassed; we then turned north-north-east for one hour, along a shallow watercourse, and then east through level forest country till 3.20 p.m., when we reached a small stream-bed trending north-north-east, tracing it through wide grassy flats, which were on fire; at 4.40 found a small pool of water, where we halted for the night.

30th June.

As this appeared to be a spot to which the party could be advanced with safety, we left our bivouac at 6.50 a.m.; returning across the tableland, reached the camp at 4.30 p.m.

1st July.

At 6.40 a.m. started an average course of 80 degrees magnetic, and reached the waterholes in the small creek at 3.30 p.m. with the whole party, and camped at our bivouac of the 29th June.

Latitude by b Centauri 15 degrees 30 minutes 19 seconds.

2nd July.

At 6.30 a.m. left the camp and followed the creek down to the east-north-east till 11.0 a.m.; it then turned more to the northward, and was nearly lost in wide level flats covered with high grass; the back country level stringybark forest, with good grass; at 2.25 p.m. the channel of the creek again collected, and we found a small waterhole twenty yards long and four feet deep, at which we camped; here we observed the fires of a party of blacks who had camped at the waterhole the previous day; small heaps of mussel-shells lay at intervals along the banks of the creek, though the channel was perfectly dry; but it appears that during the last wet season less rain has fallen than usual, and the soil has not been fully saturated, and consequently the waterholes have dried up sooner than in average years; although from the level character and geological features of the country, we are now on the tableland which divides the waters flowing to the north-west coast from those which fall into the Gulf of Carpentaria, the elevation of the country does not exceed 800 feet above the sea.

Latitude by Centauri and Arcturus 15 degrees 18 minutes 33 seconds.

3rd July.

Starting at 7.30 a.m., followed the creek to the north-east by east till 8.25, when it was joined by a small creek from the south; thus increased water was abundant in the bed of the creek, but the pools were shallow and not permanent. Grassy flats extended for a mile on each bank of the creek, beyond which the level forest of stringybark, bloodwood, and box was well grassed; the soil a good red loam. In a few spots fragments of limestone and agate were strewed over the surface, and an occasional ridge of ironstone conglomerate was crossed on which the grass was indifferent. At 12.45 p.m.

camped in a wide grassy flat, where the grass, having been burnt early in the season, had sprung up again quite fresh and green.

Latitude by a2 Centauri 15 degrees 11 minutes 24 seconds; variation of compass 2 degrees 10 minutes east.

4th July.

We were again in the saddle at 7.10 a.m., and, steering 70 degrees magnetic, diverged from the creek, traversing a level grassy forest of stringybark with abundance of green grass; at 8.0 turned north-east; the forest became more open, and the stringybark was replaced by bloodwood and box; limestone rock was frequent, and rendered the surface of the country very rough; and frequent depressions of the surface appeared to result from the falling-in of the roofs of caverns beneath which were farther indicated by deep clefts and holes in the rock, into which the surface waters flow during the rains. At 11.0 a.m. turned north, and at noon again struck the creek, which gradually turned to the north-north-east; limestone formed the banks, and only one small pool was seen till 4.50 p.m., when we found a little water in the sandy bed of a tributary creek from the south-south-east, at which we encamped. On the bank of the creek we this day first observed the casuarina, which is so frequent on the banks of the creeks trending towards the Gulf of Carpentaria.

Latitude by Arcturus and a Coronae Borealis 14 degrees 54 minutes 2 seconds.

5th July.

As the course of the creek was to the north-west, and we had already been driven further north than was desirable, we left the creek and followed up the tributary to the east-south-east, leaving the camp at 7.5 a.m. The channel was soon lost on the wide grassy flats, in one of which was a fine waterhole covered with nymphae, near which a party of blacks were encamped. On our approach most of the women decamped with their bags and nets containing their valuables, while the men stood spear in hand gazing on the strange sight, as we passed them. Continuing up the creek, the course of which was only marked for some distance by the nature of the vegetation, which indicated occasional inundations, it again formed a shallow irregular channel in the centre of an open box flat, and at 1.30 p.m. camped at a small waterhole in the channel.

Latitude by meridian altitude of the sun 14 degrees 55 minutes 15 seconds.

TABLELAND.

6th July.

The small size of the creek affording little prospect of water nearer to its source, and as Mr. H. Gregory was suffering from a severe attack of fever, which rendered travelling unadvisable, I proceeded with Charles Dean to examine the country to the east-south-east. Leaving the camp at 7.0 a.m., steered 120 degrees magnetic; at eight crossed a sandstone ridge covered with acacia scrub, and again descended into the valley of the creek, passing some fine grassy plains, and at 11.0 ascended the level tableland, the edge of which was covered with acacia scrub, beyond which we passed a level flat acacia scrub and small trees, and at noon entered a stringybark forest with occasional patches of bloodwood, leguminous ironbark, and sterculia. The soil varied from a brown loam to ironstone gravel, and in a few spots ferruginous conglomerate was visible. On the loamy soil the grass was good and abundant, but the gravel was covered with spiny treraphis. This tableland was so level that no declivity could be detected during the continuance of our day's journey, which lasted till 5.30, when we bivouacked without water; by taking the precaution of letting the horses feed on the outward track, and secreting ourselves after dark in the high grass, we passed the night without the necessity of keeping watch after midnight.

7th July.

Our horses having strayed back on the track, we carried our saddles and tracked them about two miles, and then mounting our horses steered north for some miles; but all was level forest without any sign of the existence of water, except a few cockatoos. I then turned to the south-west; crossing the outward track, and at length came on a shallow watercourse trending west, a ridge of rocks having confined the channel to a narrow space; three small waterholes were discovered in which a little water remained; below this the creek turned south-south-east, and I again turned towards the camp; but night overtaking us in the stringybark forest, we passed to the south of the camp without observing its position.

8th July.

Having ascertained that we had passed the position of the camp, turned to the north-east and reached the camp at 11.20. Mr. H. Gregory was somewhat recovered, but very weak from a violent attack of fever. During my absence a small party of blacks had visited the camp and had bivouacked a short distance up the creek.

9th July.

Moved the camp to the waterholes twelve miles south-east, and in the afternoon rode down the creek with Mr. Elsey; the creek turned to the south-south-east for a mile and a half, and was lost on a level flat, from which a channel trended to the west, which was again lost in a level flat extending to the west several miles. Heavy showers at night.

CIRCUMCISION PRACTISED.

10th July.

Accompanied by Mr. Elsey, I proceeded to reconnoitre the country to the south-east, and at 7.45 a.m. steered 130 degrees, gradually ascending the tableland, and which was openly wooded with bloodwood, box, and white-gum; acacia and sterculia occasionally appearing. The soil was brown sandy loam with a few ridges of sandstone rock of white colour; grass had been abundant, but was now burnt off. The small white-ant nests from two to five feet high were very numerous; at 12.40 p.m. a slight depression in the country was observed, and limestone appeared, and deep hollows were frequent. One of these hollows which I examined was thirty yards in diameter and fifteen feet deep; in the centre was a deep cleft of fifteen feet more, which extended to the east and west under the surface with a width of three feet; at 3.0 struck a small creek trending east-north-east with a few small pools of water in the channel; in following down the creek in search of a sufficient supply of water for the horses, we passed some blacks sitting at a fire near the creek; at 3.30 came to a pool sufficient for the supply of the whole party, below which the channel was dry; returning to the pool we met the blacks following our tracks, but, observing us, they ran away, and on being followed hid themselves; having unsaddled, we commenced our dinner and soon saw the blacks watching us from their hiding places, and after some time spent in making signs, they were induced to approach, the oldest of the party feigning to weep bitterly till they got close to us, when we commenced an attempt at conversation, and they appeared to recognise some few words of the language of the Victoria River. Their spears were formed of reeds with large heads of white sandstone, and also with three wooden points for fishing. They were circumcised and had their front teeth remaining; at 5.0 steered to the west-north-west for one hour, and bivouacked to secure ourselves from an attack during the night.

11th July.

At 6.30 a.m., resumed our route towards the camp, and reached it about 1.0 p.m., without observing anything of farther remark.

Latitude by a2 Centauri 15 degrees 2 minutes 49 seconds.

ABSENCE OF WATERCOURSES.

12th July.

The grass near the camp having been burnt off, the horses had scattered very much, and could not be collected and saddled before 10.0 a.m., when we followed our track of yesterday and reached the pool of water at sunset. The country was so level, although we were crossing the watershed between the north-west coast and the Gulf of Carpentaria, that the aneroid only varied from 29.55 to 29.62, and even of this change the greater part was caused by alteration of the temperature. The geological character of this portion of the country differs slightly from that of the Victoria River. The upper stratum is a bed of ironstone conglomerate about twenty feet thick, this rests on sandstone, the upper part of which is highly ferruginous, then passes away into a variegated sandstone imperfectly stratified, changing into a hard siliceous sandstone which is white and breaks with a conchoidal fracture; this rests on a hard cherty sandstone similar to that of the Victoria River. In this rock many depressions occur, which is apparently caused by the roofs of caverns falling in and there are usually deep fissures in the rock at the bottom of these hollows, in which all the water that drains into them is absorbed; in some places the sandstone resting on the limestone has sunk many feet below the general level, with areas varying from one to ten acres, sometimes sloping towards a centre ten to thirty feet below the plain, and in other spots with abrupt rocky banks five to eight feet high and a perfectly level bottom. The level character of the country is unfavourable for investigations of this nature, and the thickness of the several strata not easily determined; but I think that the collective thickness of the several strata above the limestone does not exceed 100 feet. The porous nature of the lower rocks preclude the existence of permanent surface water by draining the whole of the upper part of the tableland, while it forms strong springs in the lower ground towards the banks of the Roper River, where the limestone is exposed on the surface.

Latitude by a Coronae Borealis 15 degrees 14 minutes 31 seconds.

WHITE MAN'S CAMP.

13th July (Sunday).

Leaving the camp at 8.30 a.m., proceeding down the creek, mistook a tributary for the main creek; following it south for two hours, when it spread into small gullies, and we had to return to the creek, which had now a northerly course, and at 4.25 camped about three miles from our starting point in the morning. The country passed over was of a very poor character, stiff clay flats, with melaleuca scrub in the valley, while low but steep ridges of sandstone rose to the east, and were timbered with stringybark and bloodwood, etc.; to the south the country seemed to rise slightly, but was very poor and sandy. The smoke of bush fires were visible to the south, east, and north, and several trees cut with iron axes were noticed near the camp. There was also the remains of a hut and the ashes of a large fire, indicating that there had been a party encamped there for several weeks; several trees from six to eight inches diameter had been cut down with iron axes in fair condition, and the hut built by cutting notches in standing trees and resting a large pole therein for a ridge; this hut had been burnt apparently by the subsequent bush fires, and only some pieces of the thickest timber remained unconsumed. Search was made for marked trees, but none found, nor were there any fragments of iron, leather, or other material of the equipment of an exploring party, or of any bones of animals other than those common to Australia. Had an exploring party been destroyed here, there would most likely have been some indications, and it may therefore be inferred that the party had proceeded on its journey. It could not have been a camp of Leichhardt's in 1845, as it is 100 miles south-west of his route to Port Essington, and it was only six or seven years old, judging by the growth of the trees; having subsequently seen some of Leichhardt's camps on the Burdekin, Mackenzie, and Barcoo Rivers, a great similarity was observed in regard to the mode of building the hut, and its relative position in regard to the fire and water supply, and the position in regard to the great features of the country was exactly where a party going westward would first receive a check from the waterless tableland between the Roper and Victoria Rivers, and would probably camp and reconnoitre ahead before attempting to cross to the north-west coast. This creek is named Elsey Creek on the map.

ELSEY CREEK.

14th July.

Resuming our journey at 8.10 a.m., steered north-east down the valley of the creek, which I named Elsey Creek, after the surgeon of the expedition. Its course was generally to the north-east, but spreading into lagoons and swampy flats, became very tortuous and irregular. It then changed to a very winding reach of water fifty to sixty yards wide, with low banks covered with reeds and tall melaleuca-trees, beyond which was a belt of pandanus growing on the drier ground. Many small springs rose in the limestone rock and ran into the creek, on the banks of which large quantities of mussel-shells showed the frequent camps of the blacks. The banks of the creek and springs were so soft and boggy that our horses could not approach the water, and we followed its banks in search of a spot where they could drink in safety, till 4.0, without success, and having camped, had to water the horses with our leather buckets.

Latitude by a2 Centauri and a Coronae Borealis 15 degrees 5 minutes 35 seconds.

ROPER RIVER.

15th July.

Leaving our camp at 7.10 a.m., steered north-east till 9.0, over level country, which appeared to be very swampy in the rainy season; altered the course to 10 degrees magnetic, and crossed a small dry watercourse which proved to be a continuation of Elsey Creek. At 11.0 turned 60 degrees magnetic, and shortly came on the bank of a fine river with banks thirty to forty feet high, and fine reaches of water fifty to eighty yards wide; at 11.45 camped at the junction of Elsey Creek and the river, which appears to be the Roper of Dr. Leichhardt. The fan-palm was frequently seen on the banks of Elsey Creek, where it obtained a height of fifty to eighty feet, and had a thicker stem and produced a more palatable vegetable than the species growing on the banks of the Victoria River.

KILL AN EMU.

16th July.

At 7.5 a.m. recommenced our journey, following down the Roper River east and north-east; about a mile below the camp the limestone rocks formed a bar, over which the river ran with a rapid current ten yards wide and two feet deep; the banks became lower and the surface of the country extremely level. The overflows of the river had formed shallow lagoons, in which the nelumbium or gigantic water-lily was first seen. A ridge of low sandstone hills came close to the left bank, and on the right a vast level plain, covered with high grass and reeds, extending two or three miles back. This plain is evidently inundated during the wet season, though the soil was now dry and full of deep cracks. The river divided into several small shallow channels full of reeds, and each with a small stream of water, the deep green of the vegetation along the course of the running water contrasting strongly with the parched vegetation of the other portions of the plain. Clumps of melaleuca occurred at intervals, and at a distance appeared like low hills. At 2.0 p.m. camped at the end of a low basaltic ridge, which approached the bank of the river from the south. A range of flat-topped hills extended to the north-east from the river, about eight miles distant, to the north-west of the camp; they appeared wooded, and 200 to 300 feet high. Bowman rode down a young emu, which supplied us with a meal of fresh meat.

Latitude by a Coronae Borealis 14 degrees 50 minutes 56 seconds.

17th July.

At 7.0 a.m. steered east-south-east, following the bank of the river for a mile, when, to avoid the high grass and reeds, altered the course to south-east till 8.10; then steering 100 degrees magnetic till 9.25, when we camped on a small waterhole, there being abundance of water. The river appears to turn to the north and enter a range of hills, which trends north and south a few miles to the east of our camp. The country traversed this day is all well grassed and thinly timbered with terminalia, box, and silver-leafed ironbark; trap-rock visible in several places, and the soil was a good red loam. The metallic barometer has a second time suddenly deviated from the aneroid barometer, and the form of the vacuum vessel has visibly altered, the construction being too slight to bear the motion of the pack-horse, though one of the steadiest animals had been selected to carry the instruments, and they are always surrounded with blankets.

Latitude by meridian altitude of the sun 14 degrees 53 minutes 16 seconds.

18th July.

As this was a suitable camp for resting the party, and grass was abundant, I rode to the south-east with Mr. H. Gregory to look for a route towards the head of the Wickham River; our course was along a valley between the trap hills to the west and a sandstone range to the east. About eight miles reached a creek trending north-east; its channel was dry and sandy, but after some search found a small pool of water in a side channel; casuarina and flooded-gum trees grew on the banks of the creek, and there was some good grass on the flats, which were limited by sandstone hills densely wooded with acacia of the same species as that seen on the lower part of Sturt's Creek. After an hour's halt at the pool of water we returned to camp.

SILENT NATIVES.

19th July.

The horses having scattered much during the night, it was 8 a.m. before they were collected and saddled; we then followed our track of yesterday to the pool in the creek, eight miles south-east, reaching it at 11.45. The sandstones here showed a decided dip to the west, at angles varying from 5 degrees to 30 degrees, and the trap-rocks only extended five miles from the previous camp. In the afternoon five natives were observed watching the camp, and finding they were observed by us came up to the party, but could not be induced to speak a single word; they soon after retired. They had no spears, and were followed by a small dog. Their teeth were entire, but they were all circumcised. At 8.0 p.m. the blacks were detected stealing into the camp, and, though we called upon them to retire, only hid themselves in the grass; but as it was absolutely necessary for our own safety to dislodge them from their position, I caused a gun to be fired in the air, hoping that they would retire, but they commenced to ship their spears, and I therefore ordered a charge of shot to be fired at them, which had the desired effect of compelling them to retreat. What their object was in thus approaching the camp at night, unless for hostile purposes, we had no means of ascertaining; but the aboriginal Australian considers it an act of positive hostility to approach a camp in silence at night.

Latitude by a Coronae Borealis 14 degrees 59 minutes 6 seconds.

20th July.

Starting at 7.30 a.m., steered south-east over an undulating sandstone country, well grassed, but very stony and thinly wooded; a low range of rocky hills, nearly parallel to our route, lay to the south-west, and at 11.20 a.m. we camped at a fine running stream in a rocky ravine in this range; the grass was, however, very dry and inferior near the range.

Latitude by a Coronae Borealis 15 degrees 4 minutes 31 seconds.

21st July.

The horses had shown an unusual desire to stray during the night, and as we had reason to apprehend a visit from the blacks, they were kept close to the camp; at 6.20 a.m. steered south-east, crossing a tableland about 250 feet above the camp, and at 8.0 a.m. descended by a rocky gully, in which was a fine spring, into a grassy valley, which varied from a few yards to a mile in breadth, bounded by sandstone hills, the strata of which were not well defined, but appeared to have a considerable dip to the west-south-west; in the upper part of the valley the creek was well supplied with water, but as we advanced into the lower ground the channel was dry, though increased to twenty yards wide and ten to fifteen feet deep; at 11.15 a.m. one of the horses, Prince, was observed to be unwell, and at 1.20 p.m. a second horse, Bob, was noticed to be suffering from illness, having bled them, we proceeded down the creek in search of water at which the party could halt, and found a small waterhole at 2.20 p.m., but the two sick horses dropped dead about 150 yards before reaching it; their loads had been previously removed to the saddle-horses; as soon as the camp had been formed Mr. Elsey and Dr. Mueller examined the dead horses to ascertain the cause of death, and it appeared from the state of extreme inflammation of the stomachs that they had eaten some poisonous plant; but the food was too much comminuted to admit of the plants eaten being recognised.

Latitude by a Coronae Borealis 15 degrees 12 minutes 46 seconds.

22nd July.

At 7.10 a.m. resumed our journey down the valley of the creek to the east and east-north-east, passing a fine lagoon with nelumbium and a number of pelicans; at 8.30 a.m. crossed two large creeks and passed a second lagoon, 70 yards by 300 yards. The principal creek now turned to the north, and our course was along the foot of a sandstone range 200 feet high, till 12.40 p.m., when, altering the course to south-east, we ascended the range and crossed the level sandy tableland covered with scrub; descending to the south, found a small dry watercourse in an open valley, and followed it in search of water to the north-west till 4.0 p.m., when we found a small pool of rainwater, at which we camped.

Latitude by a Trianguli Australis 15 degrees 13 minutes 6 seconds.

23rd July.

The horses had strayed so far in search of green grass that we did not start till 10.30 a.m., when we steered south-east, crossing a spur of the tableland which lay to the south-west; then crossing several valleys and small watercourses trending to the north-east, camped at a shallow waterhole at 3.20 p.m. The country was of sandstone formation and the soil very poor, melaleuca scrubs prevailing on the lower ground, and eucalypti, acacia, and grevillia on the hills; to the south-west the hills were rocky, with a rounded outline, but to the north-east they were flat-topped and of less height. The sandstones are often at a considerable angle, but in no general direction, a thin bed of ferruginous conglomerate rests on hard gray sandstone, imperfectly stratified, beneath which shales of various colours exist; on the exposed surface of the shales observed an efflorescence of sulphate of magnesia.

Latitude by a Coronae Borealis and a Trianguli Australis 15 degrees 18 minutes 48 seconds.

SCARCITY OF GRASS.

24th July.

Resuming our route at 7.20 a.m., steered south-east and ascended a sandstone range with horizontal strata and very abrupt on the south-east side. Entering a wide valley, crossed two small watercourses, the second of which was running apparently from springs, as several clumps of the melaleuca grew on the slope of the sandstone hills from which they came. Crossing a second spur of the tableland, descended to a small creek with waterholes and narrow grassy flats, the general character of the country being very poor and scrubby.

Latitude by a Coronae Borealis and a Trianguli Australis 15 degrees 38 minutes 56 seconds.

25th July.

At 7.40 a.m. left the camp, and steered south-east through a succession of miserable scrubs of eucalypti, grevillia, acacia, and jacksonia, with patches of melaleuca. At 1.30 p.m. crossed a ridge of steep sandstone rocks, and gradually descended till 2.55, when we camped on a small gully coming from the south, and in which a little water remained, and on the bank some dry grass of very inferior kind. Since leaving the Roper River the general character of the country has been worthless; the small size of the watercourses indicating an arid country to the south-west of our route. Few traces of blacks have been seen, though vast columns of smoke rise to the east and south-east; animals or birds are rarely seen. The rocky nature of the country has caused the horses' shoes to wear out rapidly, and the day seldom passes without having to replace the shoes of several of the horses.

Latitude by a Coronae Borealis and a Trianguli Australis 15 degrees 40 minutes 19 seconds.

26th July.

At 8.0 a.m. steered south-east, soon entering a scrub of acacia, melaleuca, and grevillia, with a few eucalypti; the soil sandy, with a few blocks of gray sandstone; some small dry watercourses trended to the north. At noon crossed a large creek trending to the south-south-east through a very rocky valley, and the whole country was very barren and rocky. At 2.35 p.m. recrossed the creek, which here turned to the east and north-east. After following it down for an hour, found a small patch of grass, and encamped. The bed of the creek was very rocky and well supplied with water in shallow pools.

Latitude by a Coronae Borealis and a Trianguli Australis 15 degrees 50 minutes 2 seconds.

BARREN COUNTRY.

27th July (Sunday).

Resumed our route at 7.0 a.m., crossing a very rocky ridge of hills, in descending which one of the horses wedged his foot into a cleft of the rock, and falling down, was only released by beating the rock away with an axe. Fortunately, though much cut and bruised, there was no serious injury. With some difficulty we extricated ourselves from these rocky ridges, and, crossing a large creek, entered a level plain covered with melaleuca scrub. Crossing two sandy creeks fifteen and twenty yards wide with shallow pools, at noon reached a barren range of white sandstone hills, rising about 250 feet. Beyond this entered an open grassy plain, with clumps of melaleuca-trees, indicating the existence of springs of water, one of which we reached at 1.25 p.m., and encamped. The country passed is of a worthless description, there being very little grass, and the soil very poor and stony. The sandstones are of gray colour, and not regularly stratified; but where it could be ascertained the bedding was horizontal, and the lamina dipping 20 degrees to 30 degrees to the north, but often in the opposite direction. These sandstones are at least 200 feet thick, and rest on soft shales of white-brown and green colour.

Latitude by a Trianguli Australis 15 degrees 55 minutes 20 seconds.

28th July.

The indifferent character of the country having caused the horses to stray in search of better food, we were delayed till 8.30 a.m., when we steered south-east over several low ridges of sandstone, wooded with white and paper-bark gum, with triodia in the hollows. Small dry watercourses trended to the north-east and north. At 10.20 crossed a creek ten yards wide, with pools of water, and at 1.5 p.m. a second of the same size, which trended to the east, was followed till 1.50, when a small pool of water and a little grass enabled us to camp. The country continues to be of a bad description, and covered with scrub, though of a more open nature than before, the soil more gravelly, melaleuca less frequent, and eucalypti and triodia more abundant. The rock is a coarse gray sandstone, thick bedded with horizontal strata, the lamina dipping 30 degrees to north-east generally; but varying much, the peculiar marking on the surface of the rock resembling the rippling of water, is frequent, forming grooves two to four inches wide and half an inch deep.

Latitude by a Trianguli Australis 15 degrees 59 minutes 45 seconds.

29th July.

A dense fog was the unusual cause of delay in collecting our horses, as they could not be seen more than a few yards distant. At 8.45 a.m. steered south-east through scrubs of melaleuca, acacia, grevillia, and eucalypti; at 11.0 the country became more open, and entering a grassy plain extending five to eight miles to the east, where it was bounded by a low range of hills; to the south-west a level forest of white-gum ran parallel to our route. The soil was a brown clay-loam with pebbles of sandstone; a few box and bauhinia trees grew on the plain; the grass had been burnt off and sprung up again very green. At 1.20 p.m. came on a large dry creek trending north-east; it had several channels twenty yards wide with loose sandy beds, and was bordered by casuarina, melaleuca, and flooded-gum trees; following down the creek, at 1.15 camped at a shallow pool in one of the side channels. About three miles before we reached the camp Dr. Mueller had fallen some distance behind the party; but as this was a frequent occurrence in collecting botanical specimens, it was not observed till we reached the creek, when he was out of sight; after unsaddling the pack-horses I was preparing to send in search of him, when he came up to the camp, the cause of delay having been that his horse had knocked up. This was unfortunate, as the load of one of the pack-horses had to be distributed among the others, in order to remount the doctor, who requires stronger horses than any other person in the party, having knocked up four since January, while not one of the other riding-horses had failed, though carrying heavier weights.

Latitude by a Trianguli Australis 16 degrees 7 minutes 50 seconds.

30th July.

There being abundance of good grass at this camp, we remained this day to shoe some of the horses and repair harness, etc., and rest the horses; nor was I sorry to get a day of comparative rest, as I had been in the saddle every day since leaving the Victoria on the 21st June. Eleven of the horses were re-shod.

A SPRING OF GOOD WATER.

31st July.

Leaving the camp at 7.40 a.m., pursued a south-east course, soon leaving the grassy flats of the creek and entering a melaleuca scrub; at 8.20 ascended the tableland by a gentle slope; the country was now sandy with much bush of acacia, grevillia, and bossiaca, with triodia in the more open part of the forest, which consisted of paper-bark gums. The prevailing rock was ironstone conglomerate, and hard white sandstone sometimes appeared; after 10.0 the country declined to the south, and we passed through a belt of cypress scrub; at 1.15 p.m. altered the course to east-south-east; crossed a rough sandstone ridge and came on a deep valley with sandstone cliffs on each side; with some difficulty descended the rocks and reached a small watercourse which was quite dry; but observing some very green trees about a mile to the north-west at the foot of the rocks, turned towards them and found a fine spring of water flowing from the face of the cliff; selecting a suitable spot, encamped at 2.30. Near this spring were several huts constructed in the rudest manner by heaping branches together. From the summit of the hill the view extended thirty miles to the north-east, but no marked features were visible, the country only undulating slightly. The country too became more open and travelling easier, but no other improvement has been observed.

Latitude by a Trianguli Australis 16 degrees 17 minutes 5 seconds.

1st August.

At 7.30 a.m. left the camp and followed the valley to the south till 9.15, when a break in the sandstone cliffs which bounded the valley enabled us to ascend the hills and pursue our course to the south-east, crossing several ridges of sandstone, the strata dipping to the west, and becoming more shaly as we proceeded. Descending into a valley with a dry creek fifteen yards wide, the rocks on the south-east slope cherty limestone alternating with thin beds of shale, the strata dipping 20 degrees to 30 degrees west. The summit had a thin horizontal bed of ironstone conglomerate through which masses of white sandstone protruded. This limestone country was well grassed, and thinly timbered with eucalypti of small growth; at 1.20 p.m. altered the course to north-east and followed down a gully in search of water; but though it gradually enlarged to a considerable creek and we continued our search till 7.0, we were compelled to encamp without water. I then walked down the creek two miles, but only found one moist spot in which, by digging, a few pints of water were obtained.

2nd August.

At 6.5 a.m. resumed our search for water, and following the creek north-east for two hours reached a small muddy pool of rainwater, at which we encamped. The country near the creek was very level, and thinly-wooded low hills were visible in the distance to the south-east and north.

Latitude by a Trianguli Australis 16 degrees 16 minutes 25 seconds.

3rd August.

The water at this pool near our camp being nearly consumed, and nothing but thick mud remaining, we proceeded down the creek in search of a better supply; but it was not until we had followed its dry sandy bed for three hours that we attained our object, and encamped at a small pool in one of the back channels, the principal bed of the creek being perfectly dry. The country near the creek continues very level, and well grassed, but distant rocky hills are visible in almost every direction. In approaching the Gulf of Carpentaria heavy dews and fogs have become more frequent in the mornings, when it is usually calm. About 10.0 a.m. a breeze usually sets in from the eastward, varying from north to south-east; at sunset it falls calm, but commences again at 8.0 p.m. and blows moderately from the eastward for one or two hours; very thin misty clouds are frequent, and render the heat oppressive when they prevail. According to my reckoning, we are now only fifty miles from the sea-coast, and therefore much nearer Dr. Leichhardt's track than I could wish to traverse the country; but, however desirable a more inland route might be, it is evident, from the small size of the watercourses hitherto crossed, that we have been skirting a tableland which is doubtless a continuation of the desert into which we followed Sturt's Creek, and the small altitude of the country in which the watercourses trending towards the Gulf take their rise precludes the existence of any considerable drainage towards the interior.

Latitude by a Trianguli Australis 16 degrees 14 minutes 45 seconds.

THE MCARTHUR RIVER.

4th August.

The general course of the creek being northerly, and our distance from the McArthur about 20 miles on the chart, steered south-east from 6.35 a.m., crossing many rocky sandstone ridges and hills, the strata of which dipped 20 degrees to 40 degrees to the west. At noon from one of the higher ridges saw the valley of the McArthur River to the south-east; continuing our course, descended a small dry watercourse till 4.0 p.m., when we reached a large creek with a belt of casuarina, melaleuca and eucalypti along its banks. The channel was dry and sandy, about twenty yards wide, but showed the marks of high floods. Following the creek down for three-quarters of an hour found a small pool just sufficient for the supply of the party. Just below our camp a creek fifteen yards wide joined the principal one from the south, and, from the general lay of the country, it was evident that we were now on the McArthur River of Leichhardt; but though from the steepness of the banks the floods frequently rise thirty to forty feet, the creek did not bear the character of one which would take its rise at any great distance inland of our track. The country passed over was very thinly wooded with eucalypti of small growth, seldom more than one and a half feet in diameter and fifty feet high; a few leguminous ironbark, and sterculia were scattered on the hills, with much triodia and little grass. After crossing the highest ridge at 11.0 a.m. the sandstone strata were variously inclined, but generally to the west or north-east at high angles, except on the immediate bank of the McArthur, where the sandstones were horizontal. To the south-west of our route the country rose into stony hills of very barren aspect, but to the north the country appeared to be wooded.

Latitude by Vega 16 degrees 25 minutes 11 seconds.

5th August.

The country to the south-east being very rocky and broken, we followed down the river, leaving the camp at 7.20 a.m., the general course north-east; the sandstone hills rose abruptly from the bank of the river, the sandstone rock being frequently worn away in a partial manner, so as to leave isolated columns sometimes three feet in diameter and thirty feet high; a few miles below the camp a few pools of water were seen, but there was no grass near them, and we continued our route for four hours, and camped at a shallow pool with a small patch of grass on the bank of the river; the principal channel of the river was only twenty-three yards wide, but in times of flood the side channels carry off the greater portion of the water, which rises nearly forty feet; considerable quantities of mussel-shells lay at the old camps of the blacks along the bank of the river.

Latitude by meridian altitude of the sun 16 degrees 18 minutes 41 seconds; longitude by lunar distances 136 degrees 21 minutes.

6th August.

At 7.25 a.m. resumed our journey on a south-east course, over a miserable sandy country, with stunted eucalypti, grevillia, and triodia; at 11.0 reached a range of broken sandstone hills, which, with great difficulty and risk to the horses, we crossed in an east-south-east direction; but though the direct distance was only three miles, the deep ravines and rocks delayed us for three hours, and we were glad to emerge into an open valley, in which we camped at 2.30 p.m.; in the deep ravines of the sandstone hills water was abundant, but inaccessible for our horses, from the steep and rocky character of the country; a few small white-gum trees and triodia formed almost the entire vegetation; the rock is gray sandstone in horizontal beds with cleavage lamina, which varied so much in angle and direction that no general direction could be assigned, the cleavage of the upper beds often being the reverse of those immediately below them; the beds were from one to four feet thick, and the lamina half an inch to two inches, the grain very even and moderately fine.

Latitude by Vega 16 degrees 24 minutes 20 seconds.

7th August.

Resumed our journey at 7.10 a.m. on an average east-south-east course, along the foot of a rocky range of sandstone hills; at 8.30 came on a deep rocky creek, with long pools of water trending to the north; as our horses required rest, and the country ahead appeared very barren and rocky, we encamped.

8th August.

Steering a south-east course from 6.50 a.m., crossed a sandy tableland, with paper-bark and melaleuca with broad leaves; passed a small creek with pools trending north-east, and at 10.0 a low rocky ridge; then descended into a wide valley, with melaleuca and a few box-trees. At 1.25 camped on a large sandy creek with two channels ten yards wide, with low sandy banks; one channel was dry, but the other had a few small pools in it; a line of melaleuca and flooded-gum trees marked its course along the valley. When in flood the waters of the creek are 100 yards wide and ten to fifteen feet deep. The grass was inferior, but from having been burnt had grown up fresh and green.

Latitude by a Trianguli Australis 16 degrees 34 minutes 44 seconds.

IRON TOOLS USED BY NATIVES.

9th August.

Starting at 6.40 a.m., traversed an undulating sandstone country on a south-east course till 1.15 p.m., when we came on a large dry sandy creek, which we followed to the north-north-east till 1.50, when we found a shallow pool, at which we encamped. This creek had a sandy channel ten yards wide, with low banks, subject to flood to the breadth of fifty to eighty yards. Pandanus, melaleuca, and flooded-gum grow on its banks. The country generally is poor and stony, with paper-bark, gum, bloodwood, and narrow-leafed melaleuca. Shortly after reaching the creek the horse Monkey knocked up, though only carrying a pack-saddle since the 30th July; I therefore left the saddle, having removed all such portion of the fittings which might hereafter be useful. A few yards from our camp we found some spears and water vessels, which had been hidden under some sheets of bark by the blacks, who evidently were out hunting, as we heard them calling to each other in the afternoon, though they were not seen. These water vessels were formed by hollowing out a block of wood in the shape of a canoe, and had a capacity of three gallons, and it was evident that they possess tools of iron as also of stone.

Latitude by a Trianguli Australis 16 degrees 42 minutes 50 seconds; longitude by lunar distances 136 degrees 28 minutes.

10th August.

As there was a sufficient supply of grass and water, remained at the camp to rest the party. The morning was cloudy, but cleared up about 9 a.m., and I observed a set of lunar distances. Dean brought in some jasper from a hill one mile north-west of the camp. He also reported that the creek appeared to trend to the north for eight or ten miles.

11th August.

We continued a south-east route at 7.40 a.m., ascending hills of limestone and sandstone, with an upper bed of basalt, which on the higher land to the south-west was again covered by sandstone. The trap or basalt was much decomposed, and contained fragments of lower rocks. At 1.40 p.m. camped on a fine but small creek, with permanent pools of water in a rocky channel from five to thirty yards wide. The country was well grassed and openly wooded with box, sterculia, leguminous ironbark, and terminalia.

Latitude by a Trianguli Australis 16 degrees 51 minutes 55 seconds.

12th August.

At 6.50 a.m. resumed a south-east course, traversing a broken country with limestone, chert, sandstone, and trap hills, deeply cut by dry watercourses. The grass was abundant and good, though triodia appeared on the higher ridges; at 7.0 crossed a small river, with fine permanent pools of water in a rocky bed ten to thirty yards wide. The floods rise twenty feet, and extend over a breadth of 70 to 100 yards. It is the largest stream-bed crossed since leaving the river, and may possibly drain the country to a distance of sixty miles to the southward. At 1.25 camped on a small creek trending to the north-north-east, in which were pools twenty yards long and five feet deep.

Latitude by a Trianguli Australis 17 degrees 1 minute 31 seconds.

NATIVE FISHING NETS.

13th August.

Left the camp at 7.0 a.m. and continued a south-easterly course, crossing a succession of sandy valleys and broken sandstone hills; the strata horizontal, and lamina dipping to the north and east generally, but sometimes in the opposite direction; the soil poor and sandy, producing little besides white-gum and triodia. At noon ascended a high ridge, from which we saw a broad valley to the south-east, beyond which was a range of flat-topped hills terminating abruptly at the northern end, which bore east by north. Descending by a rocky ravine, at 1.30 p.m. reached a fine creek, on which we camped. This creek had deep pools of water fifty yards wide; but the steep rocky character of its banks caused the channel to appear larger than if it had been in a more level country. Under some large rocks Dean found a fishing-net made neatly of twisted bark, the mesh one and a half inch, the length perhaps thirty feet; some fishing spears showed the marks of iron tools. The rocks in this part of the country often contain angular fragments of the lower strata; thus the limestone includes fragments of chert and jasper, and the sandstone pieces of limestone, but I could not detect either granite, quartz, or slate.

Latitude by a Trianguli Australis 17 degrees 11 minutes 1 second.

14th August.

At 6.20 a.m. we were again in the saddle, and steered south-east across very rocky hills till 8.0, when we entered a fine valley with low hills of limestone and trap, well grassed and thinly wooded with box-trees and acacia; at 10.0 ascended a rough sandstone range with white-gum, acacia, and triodia; at 11.0 again descended into a valley bounded by sandstone cliffs on the northern side, and camped at a fine pool of water in a small creek at 12.5. Several trees near this pool of water had been marked by the blacks, the bark having been removed, the wood was painted yellow with brown spots at regular intervals, and vertical waved lines in black. It is evident from the outline of the hills that we are travelling on the edge of the tableland of Northern Australia, and this accounts for the small size of the watercourses, while the abrupt and broken nature of the hills has caused the rocks to form channels of sufficient size to retain water throughout the year, while the same disruption of the strata has exposed the limestone and trap-rock, has caused fertile patches of country, and thus enabled us to traverse a country which is otherwise barren and inhospitable in the extreme, our chief difficulty being the rocky character of the country, which can only be traversed with well-shod horses. It is possible that some small tracts of available country may exist between our track and the shores of the Gulf of Carpentaria, but to the south there is little to expect besides a barren sandy desert, as on every occasion that the tableland has been ascended, nothing but sandy worthless country has been encountered.

Latitude by Vega 17 degrees 17 minutes 56 seconds.

KANGAROO ABUNDANT.

15th August.

Resumed our journey at 6.35 a.m., and followed a large creek up to the south-east, and at 7.45 crossed it below a fine pool of water, above which the creek came from the south-west, in which direction the country consisted of low sandstone hills of barren aspect. We then crossed a few miles of sandy tableland and descended at 10.20 into a deep valley trending east. This brought us to a small creek with good water, on which we encamped at 11.30. The country is very poor and rocky, thinly wooded with box-trees in valleys and white-gum on the hills, where the grass is replaced by triodia. Kangaroos are more numerous than in any other part of Australia yet visited by the Expedition, and as many as twelve or fifteen have been seen each day. Early in the morning a light breeze from west; at 7.0 a fresh breeze from south-east which lasted till 4 p.m., and at sunset a light air from west.

Latitude by Vega 17 degrees 23 minutes 26 seconds.

16th August.

At 6.30 a.m. steered south-east and followed the valley of the creek till 8.0, when it turned to the north-east; continuing our course along the valley south-east, though there was now no watercourse in it, at 11.20 came on a creek in a trap valley trending north-east, across the larger valley, and crossing a ridge of sandstone and basalt, came on a large creek trending north, in which were long pools of water fifteen to twenty yards wide. Following this creek upwards to the south-south-east, as the valley widened the water ceased for some distance, but at 12.40 p.m. came on a pool supplied by a spring at the upper end. Here we encamped, as there was some good grass. The rock which formed the hills on this day's journey is a hard red-brown sandstone, the lower part thin-bedded, beneath which trap or basalt has been forced between the strata, and was exposed in the deep valleys excavated by the creeks. The view at times extended twenty miles to the north-east over a level depressed country, beyond which were low ridges of hills. The country generally was poor and stony, thinly wooded with eucalypti and acacia, except when the basalt was exposed, and by its decomposition formed a richer soil, well covered with grass and very open in character.

17th August (Sunday).

Grass and water being sufficient, remained at the camp to rest the horses, though, as several had to be shod, it was not altogether a day of rest to the party. A fresh breeze from south-east cooled the air at noon, but died away towards sunset.

Latitude by Vega 17 degrees 32 minutes 11 seconds; longitude by lunar distances 135 degrees 51 minutes 15 seconds.

18th August.

Collected the horses early, but two of them appeared to be much griped from eating the coarse grass, and I therefore delayed starting till 7.40 a.m., and then ascended the stony range to the south-east and reached the tableland. The soil was sandy with acacia scrub, paper-bark gum, stringybark, and bloodwood; at 10.0 the country became stony, with white-gum, tall acacia, and triodia, and we gradually ascended till the aneroid indicated an elevation of 1100 feet, and we appeared to be on a ridge parallel to the tableland of the interior and at a greater elevation; at 1.20 p.m. observed a clump of melaleuca in a deep rocky ravine, and steered south to it. Here we found a spring with a few acres of grass around it, and encamped.

Latitude by Vega 17 degrees 40 minutes 31 seconds.

BASALTIC RANGE. 1300 FEET ABOVE SEA.

19th August.

At 6.45 a.m. steered south-east and soon ascended a rocky range of altered sandstone and trap or basalt, thinly wooded with white-gum, tall acacia, and grevillia, triodia, and treraphis superseding the grass; at 7.30 the aneroid indicated the greatest altitude (1300 feet) which we had attained since leaving the Victoria River. From this point the view was extensive to the north and south. Towards the interior the surface of the tableland, not being so elevated as our position, appeared like a vast level plain without any marked feature whatsoever. To the north the country appeared to consist of low ridges of wooded hills gradually decreasing in height as they receded. Southward our view was intercepted by broken wooded hills of equal elevation with our position, while deep ravines trending to the south intercepted our route. I therefore altered the course to 200 degrees magnetic, and descended a rocky valley in which was a small watercourse which enlarged into a considerable creek with large rocky waterholes. The hills consisted of basalt and altered sandstone, which dipped 20 degrees to 60 degrees to the north-west, and by their outcrop formed parallel ridges which we passed with difficulty and great risk to our horses; at 12.30 p.m. we extricated ourselves from these ridges and entered a level valley extending thirty miles to the north-east and south-west. Here granite rock was exposed on the bank of the creek, which now trended across the valley to the south-east, with a broad sandy bed from a quarter to half a mile in width, but quite dry and overgrown with bushes; at 4.5 reached the hills which bounded the valley to the south-east, and the creek entering a deep gorge which, by concentrating its waters, had formed a fine pool, at which we encamped. The country after leaving the basalt hills, where the valleys were well grassed, was barren and useless sand, gravel, and rock.

Latitude by Vega 17 degrees 53 minutes 42 seconds.

20th August.

We left our camp at 7.0 a.m., and finding the valley of the creek impassable, crossed the hills in an east-south-east direction, the country consisting of steep sandstone ridges covered with triodia and a few stunted eucalypti; at 3.0 p.m. we again attained the bank of the creek and camped in a small patch of coarse rushes, as there was no grass for the horses.

Latitude by Vega 17 degrees 58 minutes 7 seconds.

21st August.

Leaving this miserable spot with our starving horses, followed the creek, which had now increased to a small river, to the east-south-east, and after two hours' travelling reached a small patch of grass and camped at 8.20 a.m.; the bed of the river is nearly dry, only a few shallow pools remaining in the sandy channel, which is ten to fifty yards wide, with smaller side channels, altogether occupying a breadth of nearly 200 yards, dense clumps of melaleuca-trees growing in the intervening banks of sand; large quantities of unio-shell, some five and six inches in length, are found on the banks of the river near the camps of the blacks; Bowman complains of an attack of scurvy, which causes pains in his legs and swelling of the gums.

22nd August.

Although our yesterday's journey was only of two hours' duration, the horses appeared very weak and fatigued when we started at 6.45 am, and it was with great difficulty that Boco and Monkey could keep up with the rest of the horses; we were frequently compelled to leave the bank of the river and cross steep rocky ridges of sandstone rock; the country was very rugged and barren, producing little besides triodia and a few stunted gum-trees. The bed of the river increased to 400 yards in width, consisting of sandy channels with narrow banks of sand covered with large melaleuca-trees between them. At 1.5 p.m. camped in a small patch of dry wiry grass; procuring water from a small pool in the bed of the river.

Latitude by Vega 17 degrees 59 minutes 2 seconds.

THE NICHOLSON RIVER.

23rd August.

Resumed our journey at 7.15 a.m., following the right bank of the river to the east-north-east; it soon passed between two steep rocky hills and turned to the north. Continuing our course a short distance, rocky hills compelled us to turn north-north-east to regain the banks of the river, following an ana-branch till 11.0 a.m., when it joined the main channel, which then trended north-east; at 11.30 came to a small grassy flat, along the banks of the river, and camped. The valley of the river is now more open, but the country of very barren character, with stunted eucalypti and triodia on the hills, and melaleuca and flooded-gum trees, with a little grass, on the bank of the river. The hills have decreased in height, the upper strata thick-bedded coarse sandstone with sandstone shale beneath; hard white sandstone exists in some of the lower ridges.

Latitude by Vega 17 degrees 56 minutes 37 seconds; longitude by lunar distances 138 degrees 22 minutes 7 seconds.

24th August (Sunday).

Although this was not a good spot for a day's halt, yet it was requisite the horses should have a day's rest, and, as it was Sunday, remained at the camp. While collecting the horses a native woman and child were seen at a distance, in the bed of the river; but on being approached hid themselves in the reeds, and though the grass was set on fire in several places by the blacks, they were not seen again.

25th August.

Resumed our journey down the river at 8.5 a.m., the general course being east; at 2.35 p.m. camped at a nymphae pool in one of the side channels of the river. The country was now more level and open, with grassy flats along the river, but the back country rose into low rocky sandstone hills, thinly clothed with white-gum and triodia. At noon we crossed a sandstone ridge, from which the view was extensive, but, except on a range of hills fifteen miles north of our position and terminating abruptly on a north-east bearing, there was nothing visible but low and flat wooded country. The bed of the river is a quarter of a mile wide, consisting of broad sandy channels with low sandy ridges between covered with melaleuca and acacia trees. Some of the party walked down the river and came to the camp of some blacks; but only one lame old man remained, who made a great noise to frighten away the invaders of his country.

Latitude by a Aquilae 17 degrees 54 minutes 18 seconds.

26th August.

Followed down the river from 6.45 a.m. till 1.40 p.m., the general course being east. The country is now more level, and ironstone conglomerate forms low steep banks to the river, the bed of which is unchanged, being broad dry sandy channels. The back country shows no improvement, and is covered with triodia. Some blacks were seen on the left bank of the river, but though within hearing of our horses' bells, did not appear to notice us.

Latitude by z and a Aquilae 17 degrees 54 minutes 10 seconds.

27th August.

The course of the river continued nearly east, and we followed its right bank from 7.30 a.m. till 1.5 p.m., when we camped at a fine pool of water in one of the side channels, the main channel continuing dry and sandy. The country on the immediate bank of the river was openly wooded with box, flooded-gum, leguminous ironbark, and melia, and was scantily grassed; the soil a brown sandy loam. Beyond the influence of the floods the ground was quite level; small terminalia, broad-leafed melaleuca, and silver-leafed ironbark, with dry triodia, formed the entire vegetation of this worthless plain. Ironstone conglomerate and sandstone boulders are the only rocks visible.

Latitude by Vega 17 degrees 56 minutes 32 seconds.

A FINE STREAM OF RUNNING WATER.

28th August.

Our day's journey commenced at 7.0 a.m., and following the right bank of the river to the east-south-east till 12.45 p.m., encamped in the bed of the river, which was nearly half a mile wide from bank to bank, the principal channel, eighty yards wide, was shallow and sandy, with a few small pools of water at intervals. The side channels of similar character, but smaller and without water. Beyond the bed the banks rose abruptly about thirty feet, and then appeared to decline as it receded, and no higher ground was visible. The soil was a sandy loam, thinly timbered with small box-trees and scanty grass.

Latitude by Vega and b Cygni 18 degrees 1 minute 3 seconds.

29th August.

At 7.20 a.m. steered east through level box flats, the country gradually becoming more open and better grassed, though very scantily; at noon crossed some open grassy plains, and altered the course to north-east, north-north-east, and north, and at 3.20 p.m. again came on the bank of the river and encamped at a small pool of water; the rest of the channel, which exceeded a quarter of a mile in width, being dry and overgrown with large melaleuca and flooded-gum trees. The general character of the country is a level plain about forty feet above the level of the river, thinly wooded with box and a few bloodwood, acacia, and bauhinia trees; the soil a brown loam, and the grass, though scanty, of good quality, but at this season very dry.

Latitude by Vega 17 degrees 55 minutes 40 seconds.

30th August.

At 6.50 a.m. steered east-north-east through box flats and open grassy flats, the course of the river nearly parallel to our route; at 10.10 came to a large tributary creek from the south. Its principal channel was 30 yards wide, with pools separated by dry banks, but two small side channels existed with small running stream. After half an hour's delay, we succeeded in crossing without further accident than resulted from some of the pack-horses falling down the bank into the water and wetting their packs, and getting a ducking myself, which wetted the chronometers. Water-pandanus, fan-palm, and casuarina formed a belt of trees along the bank of the stream, which bore quite a different character to that of the dry sandy bed of the river above the junction. Continuing our route, at 12.5 p.m. came to a second running creek, but of smaller size. This we crossed and followed down to the east till 1.5, when we encamped. Here we observed that, though the water was fresh, yet it was affected by the tide, which was now at the highest spring.

Latitude by Vega 17 degrees 52 minutes 35 seconds.

THE ALBERT RIVER. A MARKED TREE.

31st August (Sunday).

Rode down the creek with Mr. H. Gregory. At two miles from the camp came to the junction of a smaller creek from the south, the two forming a fine reach of water, which we recognised as the Albert River of Captain Stokes. This spot between the two creeks was the rendezvous appointed for the two sections of the Expedition, and though, from the short period which had elapsed since leaving the Victoria, the Tom Tough could scarcely be expected to have arrived before us, on approaching the spot we saw several marked trees:

CHUMLUT arrow pointing up ORE RCH TO 1856,

but were disappointed in our hope that the vessel had reached the Albert, as these marks consisted of several names of seamen, who appeared to have formed the crew of a boat sent up the river by H.M. steamer Torch. Search was made for directions for finding any memorandum which might have been concealed, as I first thought it probable that the object of the visit might have been to communicate with the Expedition; but the nature of the inscriptions and the absence of anything which led to even a surmise of what was the object of the visit caused us to come to the conclusion that it had no reference to the North Australian Expedition. From the state of the ashes of the fire and branches of the trees which had been cut and broken, it appeared that several weeks had elapsed, and consequently the Torch was not likely to still be in or near the river. In accordance with arrangements made with Mr. Baines, I marked a tree thus:

NAE AUG 30 DIG1YD TO E.

in order to apprise him of our having reached the Albert, and of our prospective movements. Returning to the camp, wrote a memorandum of the visit of the Expedition and a note to Mr. Baines, informing him that we intended leaving other marks and memoranda at the junction of the salt-water arm of the river, and then continue without delay our route towards Moreton Bay. These memoranda were enclosed in a powder-canister, and Messrs. Elsey and Bowman took them down to the marked tree and buried them. In the afternoon rode over with Mr. H. Gregory towards the Nicholson River, crossing Beame's Brook. Steered north-north-east four and a half miles over a level grassy plain with stripes of box-trees. As we could see four or five miles farther, and no indication of the river, returned to the camp, having ascertained that the Nicholson River does not join the Albert, unless many miles below the junction of Beame's Brook with the South Creek, which together form the Albert River.

1st September.

At 7.40 a.m. steered east to the South Creek, which we found at the distance of two miles, and followed it up for an hour in search of a crossing place, as the channel was very muddy. A suitable spot having been found, we filled up the channel, which was two yards wide, with pandanus stems, and crossed the horses over without accident. Steering east-north-east two miles across wide level plains, with patches of box-trees, turned north at noon and struck the Albert just below the junction of the South Creek and Beame's Brook. Finding the water brackish, we did not proceed farther down the river, and encamped. The existence of a narrow belt of mangrove along the bank of the river indicates that the water is often salt to the head of the Albert.

Latitude by Vega 17 degrees 51 minutes 55 seconds.

2nd September.

The water in the river being very brackish, it became evident that we should be unable to procure fresh water if we followed it towards the sea, and therefore I decided on leaving the letters I had written to Mr. Baines at this spot, and accordingly marked a tree thus:

NAEXPDN AUG 30 1856 DIG2YDN

and buried a tin canister with letters, stating that the exploring party was to start the following morning for Moreton Bay, and instructing Mr. Baines to remain at the Albert till the 29th September, 1856, in case any unforeseen circumstance should compel the party to return to the Albert within that period. Five months' flour, tea, sugar, etc., and three months' supply of meat at full ration still remained; and as our horses would supply the deficiency of meat, if required, we have sufficient quantity of provisions to enable the party to reach the settled part of New South Wales, unless extraordinary difficulties should be encountered; under the circumstances it did not appear prudent to delay at the Albert River, as the arrival of the Tom Tough might be deferred for an indefinite period.

3rd September.

Left our camp at 6.45 a.m., and steered east over level box-flats and open grassy plains; at 10.0 came on a small creek, which we followed half an hour to the north-east, when we came to salt-water, which had been left in pools at high tides. I therefore steered south-east till 5.0 p.m. and camped at a shallow pool in a large creek trending north. The country consists of vast open level plains, separated by narrow belts of box and terminalia trees; the soil a brown clay loam, producing rather short and dry grass. On approaching the waterhole at which we encamped, a black and three or four women were found camped on the opposite side of the creek; they climbed the trees and remained among the branches till dusk, when they descended to their fires and made a great noise till 9.0, when they decamped. This creek is probably the head of the salt-water arm of the Albert River or of the Disaster River.

Latitude by Vega 18 degrees 2 minutes 5 seconds; variation of compass 4 degrees east.

THE "PLAINS OF PROMISE," LEICHHARDT RIVER.

4th September.

Continued a south-east course through large open plains thinly grassed; passed a dry watercourse with a small waterhole in one of the back channels, but insufficient for our horses, and at noon camped at a shallow waterhole in a grassy flat. Mr. Elsey walked half a mile to the eastward; came to a river eighty yards wide, but observing some blacks, returned to the camp. In the evening nine blacks came towards us, and appeared inclined to hostilities; but, after a short interview, retired up the creek. These blacks were not circumcised, and their teeth were perfect; they had neither ornaments or any description of clothing, and were slightly scarred on the back and chest. Their spears were large and heavy, made of a single piece of wood, and thrown by hand; they had also smaller ones of reed, with wooden points, which were thrown with the throwing board, which were flattened vertically; clubs two and a half feet long and two and a half inches in diameter, and shields formed of a single piece of wood two and a half feet long and three inches wide. The river proved to be fresh, and in pools separated by rock flats, and is evidently the same that Dr. Leichhardt supposed to be the Albert--a mistake which has caused considerable error in the maps of his route; as it was not named, I called it the Leichhardt. The character of the country is inferior, as the grass which covers the plains is principally aristidia and andropogon; anthisteria or kangaroo grass only in small patches. The soil is a good brown loam.

Latitude by Vega 18 degrees 11 minutes 50 seconds.

ATTACK BY THE NATIVES.

5th September.

At daybreak we heard the blacks making a great noise up the river, and while the horses were being brought in nineteen blacks came to the camp, all armed with clubs and spears. They did not make any hostile demonstration, and the approach of the horses appeared to keep them in check; and a person unacquainted with the treacherous character of the Australian might have thought them friendly. When we started at 6.50 a.m. they followed the party to the bank of the river, and began to ship their spears, and when we were crossing a deep ravine made a rush on us with their spears poised ready to throw them at us, hoping to take advantage of our position; but just as their leader was in the act of throwing his spear he received a charge of small shot. This checked them, and we charged them on horseback, and with a few shots from our revolvers put them to flight, except one man, who climbed a tree, where we left him, as our object was only to procure our own safety, and that with as little injury to the blacks as possible. We did not pursue our advantage; by following the fugitives. Proceeding down the river a short distance, at 7.40 crossed to the right bank on a ledge of flat rocks. It was here about 100 yards wide, with shallow reaches of water, the banks rising steep--thirty to forty feet. Very little vegetation grew on the banks, which appeared to result from salt water occasionally reaching this part at very high tides. We now steered east over level grassy plains, with patches of box and terminalia. Passed a small but deep waterhole, near which were two black gins, who did not appear to notice us. At 10.0 the country was covered with an open scrub of terminalia, with silvery leaves, and triodia replaced the grass. At noon passed a small rocky gully with a waterhole, which our horses quite emptied of its contents. Altering the course to north-east, the country was covered with melaleuca scrub, with silver-leafed ironbark, triodia, and a little grass; but we soon re-entered the open plains which extended to the north, and, following a watercourse at 3.5 p.m. camped at a small muddy waterhole, on the banks of which the blacks had often encamped, as shown by the heaps of mussel-shells round their fireplaces. Our route has been along the southern limit of the open grassy plains, and to the south the country rises into low ridges and stony plains, covered with scrub and triodia.

Latitude by Vega 18 degrees 7 minutes 45 seconds.

6th September.

Starting at 6.25 a.m. our route was average east over a level country of very bad quality; the soil ironstone gravel, producing terminalia, triodia, and silk cotton-trees (Cochospermum gregoranum). Towards the latter part of the stage the country improved, becoming more open and grassy. At 12.15 camped on a large creek with a shallow pool of muddy water.

Latitude by Vega 18 degrees 9 minutes 45 seconds.

7th September (Sunday).

Remained at the camp to rest the party. A strong south-east wind blew during the night, and the day was cool and clear; the air very dry. Repaired our saddle-bags, which, from frequent contact with rocks and dead trees, were much dilapidated.

8th September.

Steered east-south-east from 6.40 am to 11.40, crossing low ironstone ridges and wide grassy plains, with belts of box, terminalia, white-gum, and silver-leafed ironbark of small size; the grass very inferior, with patches of triodia on the ridges; then traversed a level country covered with small trees and dry grass for two hours, after which we followed a dry watercourse, with large hollows in its bed, to the north-north-west for one hour; the shells of large unios abundant, but no water; altered the course to the east; passed two lines of box-trees crossing the plain from the south to the north, and at 5.50 p.m. camped in the plain without water; a strong breeze from the south-east during the day had rendered the heat less oppressive than usual.

Latitude by Vega 18 degrees 12 minutes 40 seconds; variation of compass 5 degrees east.

THE FLINDERS RIVER.

9th September.

Left our waterless camp at 6.10 a.m., steering north 50 degrees east magnetic over a level grassy plain; at 9.40 reached a fine river of fresh water 100 yards wide, but very shallow; pelicans, ducks, and other water-fowl were numerous, but very shy and wild; here we camped, although the grass was very inferior on the immediate banks of the river, the surface of the soil being very much furrowed by the rain; small fragments of limestone and a few quartz pebbles have been observed on the surface of the plain for the past twenty miles, and a dark limestone rock is exposed in the bed of the river, where it has horizontal stratification; fragments of flinty slate and trap exist in the gravel of the bed of the river, which, from its position, must be the Flinders River of the charts.

Latitude by a Aquilae 18 degrees 8 minutes 41 seconds; variation of compass 4 degrees 20 minutes east.

10th September.

6.10 a.m. again found us in the saddle, and crossing the right bank followed it to the south-south-east till 7.20, when it turned to the south-south-west, and changing our course to the east, passed through a fine grassy plain for two miles, and entered a level open box-flat, well grassed, the soil a brown loam; this continued till 2.30 p.m., when we entered a belt of terminalia, and at 1.0 reached a small watercourse, and camped at a fine waterhole fifty yards wide and 100 yards long, apparently deep and permanent water, with open grassy banks; this waterhole would render a great extent of the fine grassy country around available for pasturage; in passing through the box forest we observed several sleeping places which had been constructed by the blacks during the wet season; they consisted of four stakes two feet high, supporting a platform of small sticks five feet long and two and a half feet wide; three to twenty of these frames would be grouped together, and were frequent till we reached the Gilbert River.

Latitude by Vega 18 degrees 10 minutes 30 seconds.

11th September.

At 6.20 a.m. steered east for one hour through level box and terminalia flats, with good grass and brown loam; came to a fine lagoon eighty yards wide and nearly one mile long; beyond this was a creek with small pools of water; as it appeared to come from the south-east, we steered in that direction, but soon receded from it, as its course changed to south-south-east, and altering our course more to the southward, at noon came again on the creek, much reduced in size; melaleuca scrub and triodia growing close to its banks, and only a few shallow pools of water, nearly dried up, and very little grass; at 12.25 p.m. camped at a small pool. On the banks of the lagoon passed in the morning large heaps of mussel-shells showed the spots where, from the vast accumulation, the blacks had for many centuries camped successively on the same spots, and a well-beaten footpath along the bank showed that it was a favourite resort of the aboriginals. The common flies are very troublesome; very few birds, and no kangaroos have been seen during the last few days' journey.

Latitude by Vega 18 degrees 18 minutes 5 seconds.

12th September.

The course of the creek being from the south and water very scarce in its bed, it does not appear that we have yet reached the streams rising in the high land at the head of the Burdekin and Lynd rivers; it therefore appeared expedient to steer an east-north-east course till some stream-bed of sufficient size to retain water at this season can be found, and then to follow it up to the ranges where alone water can be expected to be found to enable us to steer to the south-east. At an earlier season of the year, when water is abundant, it would be more desirable to ascend the Flinders, and cross from its upper branches to the head of the Clark; but under present circumstances this course would be highly imprudent, and no experimental deviations from the most direct course would be justifiable. The grass being scanty, the horses had scattered much, and we did not leave the camp till 10.20 a.m., when we steered east-north-east. A short mile from our camp passed four blacks at a pool of water; they did not observe us till we had passed, though only 100 yards distant, and the country very open. Our route was through a level country, wooded with box, bloodwood, terminalia, grevillia, and broad-leafed melaleuca, triodia, and patches of grass. The soil is a hard ironstone gravel and clay. Passing several dry beds of shallow lagoons, came to a small dry watercourse coming from the east; at 12.20 p.m. camped at a shallow pool of water scarcely four inches deep. Near the camp were some fine grassy flats, but limited in extent, and the grass very dry. The cool southerly breezes have ceased, and the north-east and westerly winds are light and very warm.

Latitude by Vega 18 degrees 14 minutes 25 seconds.

13th September.

At 8.5 a.m. steered east-north-east through box-flats with broad-leafed melaleuca, with a little grass. The country gradually became more scrubby with grevillia, terminalia, bloodwood, and triodia; the soil very poor, and in some parts sand and gravel. At 2.0 p.m. altered the course to north, and at 5.50 came to a dry creek in a rocky channel trending west, which we followed down till 6.15, and camped without water.

14th September (Sunday).

At 5.50 proceeded down the creek on a nearly west course, searching the channel in its winding course for water, but without success, till 10.0, when we found a pool of good water fifty yards long and two feet deep, at which we encamped. Some blacks had been camped at this pool, and their fires were still burning. The country on the creek is very poor, with patches of open melaleuca scrub, box, bloodwood, leguminous ironbark, terminalia, white-gum, and a few pandanus, triodia, and a little very dry grass. The soil sandstone, with ironstone gravel. The native bee appears to be very numerous, and great numbers of trees have been cut by the blacks to obtain the honey.

Latitude by a Aquilae 17 degrees 59 minutes 26 seconds.

LEVEL COUNTRY. SCARCITY OF WATER.

15th September.

At 8.15 a.m. resumed our journey north 10 degrees magnetic, over a very level country thinly wooded with box, bloodwood, melaleuca, terminalia, grevillia, and cotton-trees, also a small tree which we recognised as Leichhardt's little bread-tree, the fruit of which, when ripe, is mealy and acid, but made some of the party, who ate it, sick. Several dry watercourses trending west were crossed, and at 2.5 p.m. camped at a small waterhole in a sandy creek, fifteen yards wide. By enlarging the hole we obtained, though with difficulty, a sufficient supply of water for our horses. On the flats near the creek the grass was good, but very dry.

Latitude by a Aquilae 17 degrees 46 minutes 11 seconds.

16th September.

Although our horses required a day's rest, none of our camps for some days had afforded a sufficient supply of water and grass for a second night; we therefore continued a north 20 degrees east course at 6.25 a.m.; at 7.30 a.m. came to a creek which we followed east an hour and a half, when it was reduced to a small gully, and again steered north-north-east, passing over much poor country with patches of melaleuca scrub, the country perfectly level; at 2.0 p.m. came to a sandy creek which we followed to the west till 6.5 p.m. without any water; camped in an open grassy box flat; I then walked down the creek, and was fortunate in finding a pool of water half a mile distant, and as soon as the moon rose we drove the horses to the water and filled our saddle-bags. Few parts of our journey have been through country so destitute of animal life as the level plain we have traversed since leaving the Flinders River--no kangaroo or even their track; emu tracks very rare, and very few birds were at the waterholes. Many of the sleeping-frames of the blacks have been observed, and thousands of deep impressions of their feet in the now dry and sun-baked clay show that during the rainy season the extremely level nature of the country causes it to be extensively inundated.

17th September.

The supply of water and grass being sufficient, we remained at this camp to refresh the horses, which had suffered much from the long stages.

Latitude by Capella 17 degrees 34 minutes 5 seconds; variation of compass 4 degrees 50 minutes east.

DRIED HORSE-FLESH.

18th September.

Starting at 7.0 a.m., steered north 10 degrees east magnetic till 12.30 p.m., crossing a level country with frequent hollows which form lagoons in the wet season, reaching a sandy creek with several channels, which we searched in vain for water; but found a fine lagoon about a quarter of a mile from it, in a grassy flat, in which we encamped. The country generally was more open, with grassy box-flats; melaleuca scrubs less frequent. As this camp appeared suitable for a halt of a few days, I decided on availing ourselves of the opportunity, and to kill one of the unserviceable horses and replenish our stock of meat and supply the party with fresh provisions. Old Boco, who had not carried a pack since leaving the Albert, and whose wandering and kicking propensities had rendered him a troublesome animal, was therefore shot, skinned and quartered.

Latitude by a Aquilae 17 degrees 21 minutes 20 seconds; variation of compass 5 degrees 15 minutes east.

19th September.

The horse was cut into thin slices and hung on ropes to dry by 10.0 a.m., the liver and heart furnishing the party with an excellent dinner.

20th September.

The night had been cloudy, but the meat dried well, and promised to be fit to pack the following day, the weather being very hot with little wind. Reduced the ration of flour to three-quarters of a pound per diem while fresh meat is abundant.

21st September.

Resumed our journey at 8.15 a.m. and traversed on a course north 40 degrees east a level plain grassy country thinly wooded with box, bloodwood, and terminalia, etc. The soil a dark loam of good quality, but very wet in the rainy season. At 11.30 a.m. came on a large creek or river with many sandy channels in which only a few small pools of water remained; followed it up to the east-south-east through fine open grassy flats till 2.35 p.m. and camped in the bed of the river. The banks of the river (which is probably the Gilbert of Leichhardt) are well grassed, and a dense line of melaleuca, leucodendron, flooded-gum, and morinda, mark its course through the plain; but being divided into many channels its size is difficult to ascertain. Considerable quantities of mica are mixed with the soil on its banks, which indicates that it rises in country of primary formation. Two kangaroos, some wallabies, and pink and sulphur-crested white cockatoos were seen near the river.

Latitude by a Aquilae 17 degrees 18 minutes 5 seconds.

THE GILBERT RIVER.

22nd September.

Leaving our camp at 7.25 a.m., steered north 120 degrees east across the plains on the left bank of the river, and at 1.30 p.m. camped at a small pool in the sandy bed of the Gilbert, which is broad, sandy, and retains very little water. Fragments of porphyry, quartz, and black slate are abundant in the drift, and mica, iserine, and minute garnets exist.

Latitude by a Aquilae 17 degrees 25 minutes 50 seconds.

23rd September.

At 7.5 a.m. continued our journey up the river's left bank, the average course south-east by east; at 2.50 p.m., camped at a small pool in the bed of the river; the principal channel is 200 yards wide, and the smaller ones occupy a breadth of half a mile; the banks are low, and the country quite level, thinly wooded with box-trees; the grass good, but not thick; water very scarce, except by digging in the sand of the river.

Latitude by a Cygni 17 degrees 36 minutes; variation of compass 5 degrees east.

24th September.

At 7.0 a.m. steered south-east, and at 8.0 crossed to the right bank of the river, the channel 300 yards wide, with banks fifteen feet high, beyond which the ground gradually declined, so that when the river overflows a great extent of country must be inundated. Continuing our course, the river turned more to the south, and we passed through some poor stunted forest of eucalypti, alternating with grassy box-flats. At noon altered the course south-south-east, and at 12.30 p.m. camped at a chain of small lagoons in the shade of some fine nonda-trees.

Latitude by a Aquilae 17 degrees 45 minutes 10 seconds.

25th September.

At 6.35 a.m. steered south-east through an open melaleuca scrub, the soil sandy loam, thinly grassed; acacia, bloodwood, silver-leafed ironbark, and grevillia forming open patches of wood at intervals. At noon turned south, and at 1.35 p.m. camped at a small lagoon nearly dry and half a mile from the bank of the river; a few hills rose close to the south-west of the river opposite our camp, the lower ridges grassy, the higher hills wooded, but not exceeding 500 feet above the plain. The bed of the river is broad, dry, and sandy, and the box-flats much reduced in width, seldom exceeding a mile. At 5.0 p.m. there was a heavy squall with rain and lightning, followed by a cloudy night and moderate breeze from the south.

26th September.

At 6.45 a.m. resumed our route, and, following up the right bank of the river in a south-east direction till 2.0 p.m., when we camped in the sandy bed of the river, procuring water from a small hole in the sand. The country on the banks of the river consisted of box flats, some parts well grassed, but usually very poor; this extended about half a mile, and then changed gradually to a poor country with little grass and small eucalypti and melaleuca, the soil gravel and sand. The bed of the river continues to be about 300 yards wide, dry, and sandy; a line of melaleuca, morinda, flooded-gum and fig trees, grow along it and mark its course.

Latitude by a Aquilae 18 degrees 10 minutes 10 seconds; variation of compass 5 degrees 20 minutes east.

27th September.

Steered an average south-east course up the river from 6.40 a.m. till 1.0 p.m., when we camped at some pools of water in a side channel of the river, where it was divided by a hillock of slate-rock. The country is inferior in quality, the flats narrowing to an average of half a mile with very dry and thinly scattered tufts of grass. The bed of the river is better defined, and formed at times a single channel 250 yards wide, dry and sandy, as water was only once seen during the day. Low rocky ridges of sandstone gradually approached its banks, and near the camp porphyry, slate, and coarse granite formed detached hills 50 to 100 feet high, seeming to indicate an approach to the ranges in which the stream takes its rise.

Latitude by a Cygni 18 degrees 15 minutes 21 seconds.

GRANITE, PORPHYRY, AND SLATE.

28th September (Sunday).

Walked out from the camp to a low hill about one mile south-south-east. It was composed of granite at the base and capped with horizontal strata of sandstone, some of the beds containing large water-worn pebbles, and the superstratum highly ferruginous. To the south-west of this hill the rock was slate, the strata nearly vertical; the strike north and south, but much contorted, and large pebbles of porphyry, quartz, slate, granite, sandstone, and agate formed banks in the bed of the river. The country, as seen from the hill, was generally level in appearance, but consisted of numerous low ridges and detached hills of granite, with sandstone on the summits. The valley of the river extended to the east and south, and a large branch appeared to join from the south about ten miles lower down, as a valley and some ranges of hills trended in that direction. The whole face of the country had an arid and desolate aspect, as there were no large trees except along the principal watercourses, and many of the hills appeared destitute of any other vegetation besides small acacias and scrub trees, the bare rock showing through its scanty covering.

29th September.

At 7.15 a.m. again steered east up the river, the country level and timbered with stringybark, box, bloodwood, leguminous ironbark, and rusty gum; the soil a red sandy loam, thinly grassed; at 10.30 a.m. came to low hills and ridges of granite and porphyry, timbered with box, leguminous ironbark, terminalia, and the grass somewhat improved. Altered the course at 11.0 a.m. to the south to close in with the river; but after crossing a great number of dry watercourses, and even steering west, only reached the bank of the river at sunset. The channel was dry, and all the vegetation had disappeared, only a barren waste of coarse sand and gravel 180 yards wide, with bare rocky banks, showed that it had once been a running stream. A few small hollows in the rocks retained water from the late rain, but not sufficient for our horses, and though we found a small pool in the sand, it was insufficient for the supply of the party. Encamped at 6.0 p.m. The geological structure of this portion of the country is wholly dissimilar to any other part of North Australia we have yet traversed. Granite, porphyry, and slate are the prevailing rocks. The whole appear to have been subjected to considerable disturbance, as the slate is much broken and contorted, and in several parts altered by contact with the porphyry, and no definite strike or dip appeared to exist. The porphyry is of a red-brown colour, consisting of grey paste with crystal of felspar and angular fragments of slate and granite sometimes one foot in length. The granite contains little mica, and the quartz frequently is arranged in rhomboidal crystals nearly parallel to each other; it readily decomposes, and from the predominance of quartz forms a coarse gritty soil. Quartz-rock forms large beds and veins in the granite, and has a general trend north and south. It often contains crystals of mica, and therefore not likely to contain metals. In washing the sand of the river near Camp 83, only a small quantity of titaniferous iron remained after the removal of the quartz and mica. It was in this locality that the Gilbert Gold Field was afterwards discovered.

Latitude by e Pegasi 18 degrees 25 minutes 33 seconds.

30th September.

Moved the camp about one mile higher up the river to some small pools of water, and then with Mr. H. Gregory ascended the hills to the south of the camp. From the highest ridge the course of the river was visible for nearly twenty miles, trending first seven miles south-south-west and then south-south-east; at the bend a branch appeared to join from west-south-west, in which direction the country appeared very flat for fifteen or twenty miles, as only a few distant hills were visible; from north round to south-east the country was very broken and hilly, rising highest to the north-east, but the view was limited to eight or ten miles; south-east a valley opened through hills, and more distant ranges were indistinctly seen beyond. The whole aspect of the country was barren, rock forming the principal feature. Returning to the camp, collected a quantity of the clustered figs on the bank of the creek; this fruit is rather insipid.

1st October.

Steering an average south-south-east course from 7.40 a.m. till 2.40 p.m., camped on the right bank of the river, which first came from south-west and then from south-east, throwing off two branches to the south-west, and was thereby diminished to 100 yards wide at our camp; only one creek and some gullies joined from the east, although the country in that direction was hilly; the bed of the river was still dry and sandy; water very scarce. Slate, quartz, schist, granite, and trap are the principal rocks, and by their decomposition do not produce a soil favourable to vegetation, the country becoming more desolate as we advanced. The only trees which retain their verdure are those which grow on the banks of the river.

Latitude by a Cygni 18 degrees 40 minutes 29 seconds.

RECONNOITRE TO THE EASTWARD.

2nd October.

The river above the camp coming from the south-south-west, it appeared desirable to pursue a more eastern course, and I therefore started from the camp at 6.30 a.m., accompanied by Mr. H. Gregory, to reconnoitre the country, steering east three miles over low slate hills (the strata dipping 60 degrees to 80 degrees to south by west); ascended a hill from which a range of hills were seen eight to ten miles to the east of a creek rising in them and joining the river near the camp to the east-south-east; at the head of the creek a gap in the hills showed a more distant range of hills; steering in this direction, came to the creek with a sandy and rocky bed ten yards wide and perfectly dry; ascending the range of hills, found them to consist of gneiss, schist, and slate, trap existing on the lower ridges. A large valley extended across our course to the east, beyond which a range of flat-topped hills or tableland bounded the horizon. Descending to the east the country improved and granite constituted the principal rock, ironbark and a few box-trees forming an open forest which on some of the ridges was well grassed; the soil a red loam. At 2.0 p.m. came on a small river with a dry sandy bed eighty yards wide; following it down to the south found a small pool of water in a hollow in the sand; here we halted till 3.30, and then followed the river south-west, south-east, south-west, west, and south; at 6.10 ascended a hill on the left hand, from which we saw that the river turned west and north-west, breaking through the hills and joining the Gilbert River. Having ascertained that we were still on a western watercourse, we bivouacked near the river without water.

3rd October.

At daybreak steered north-west, crossing several rocky ridges of hills, and at 2.0 p.m. reached the camp. Nothing of importance had occurred during our absence; the horses had improved by the two days' rest.

4th October.

At 7.15 a.m. left the camp, and, following an average east-south-east course for seven hours, reached the pools found on the 2nd, in the upper branch of the Gilbert River, and encamped. As this route nearly coincided with that on the 2nd, nothing was seen worthy of farther notice.

Latitude by a Cygni 18 degrees 47 minutes 54 seconds.

5th October.

At 6.45 a.m. left the camp and followed up the river in an east-north-east direction for three miles; water was abundant in the gullies owing to a heavy shower some days previous. Beyond three miles the water ceased and the country was dry and parched. Low hills of schist trap and granite formed a country near the river, and farther back high ranges bounded the valley; they appeared to be flat-topped and with horizontal strata of sandstone on the summits. At noon the river had divided into several small branches, and the character of the country did not promise the existence of water within the space of a day's journey; we returned down the river to the last water we had seen, and camped about three miles north-east of our last camp. As there was little prospect of finding water again till the range to the east of our present position was crossed, I decided on reconnoitring the country before moving the party farther, and as the weather promised to continue fine, the horse Monkey was shot and skinned preparatory to drying the meat during my absence.

6th October.

At 6.5 a.m. left the camp with Mr. H. Gregory, steering nearly east, crossed the south branch of the river, and reached the base of the higher range at 9.30; here we found a small spring a quarter of a mile south of a remarkable hill formed of a single mass of bare rock completely honeycombed by the action of the atmosphere; ascended the range, which consisted of porphyry with horizontal sandstone on the summit; we continued our east course over rocky hills with dry watercourses trending north; the grass was very thin and dry; and the country was openly wooded with acacia, eucalypti, cypress, etc., none of which attained a large size; at 1.30 p.m. halted to rest the horses, and searching among the rocks in the gullies obtained about three quarts of water by digging; at 2.45 resumed our route, traversing a hilly country, and at 4.15 ascended a granite hill with sandstone summit, from which the view was very extensive. Large valleys seemed to join and trend from south to north, and were bounded by ranges, except to the east, where a level plain or wide valley extended to the horizon. In the valley a line of green trees five miles distant marked the course of a creek. Descending the range we encountered a very rocky country with deep gullies, in one of which we found a few gallons of water, which our horses consumed. As there was no grass here, we pushed on till dusk, and bivouacked in a small patch of grass by the side of a dry gully. The country east of the range is entirely granitic; grass very scanty, and very thinly wooded with ironbark.

CROSS A GRANITE RANGE.

7th October.

Continued an east course at 5.50 a.m., and at 7.50 reached the large creek, which was 100 yards wide with shallow sandy bed; the banks low and thinly timbered with ironbark and a few box trees; the soil poor and sandy, producing little grass. Large casuarina and flooded-gum trees grew in the channel of the creek, which we followed three miles to the north-east without finding any water, and only two spots where it could be procured by digging; we therefore returned up the creek, and dug a well at the most eligible spot, procuring an abundance of good water; at 2.20 p.m. commenced our return route towards the camp, and following up the spurs of the range found a practicable route for the pack-horses; passed the highest point of the range at 6.0, and bivouacked at a small dry watercourse at 7.15 p.m.

8th October.

Resumed our route at 6.0 a.m., and deviating to the north of the outward route, found a small pool of water in a rocky gully, and following it down a mile came to a pool of sufficient size to supply the whole party. At 10.30 reached Bowman's Spring at the foot of the range, and by digging in the moist soil obtained a little water. As we approached the spring a small party of blacks shouted to us from the summit of one of the hills, but did not descend to us, though we halted till 12.30 p.m., and then resumed our route, reaching the camp at 4.0, and found the party all well; the horse-meat quite dry and fit for carriage. Bowman had also replaced the shoes on all the horses. The geological character gradually changes, in consequence of the larger development of the older rocks, as we proceed to the eastward. At the camp gneiss, porphyry, and trap have superseded the slates, and proceeding east, granite is visible at the western base of the range. This is covered by a thick mass of porphyry, containing large fragments of slate, gneiss and granite in its lower part, and in its upper portion it has a fine grain and light colour. Being deeply cracked by vertical fissures, it forms vertical columns of rhomboidal form, resembling basalt. The summits of the higher hills are formed by horizontal beds of white sandstone, containing water-worn pebbles of quartz. Granite supersedes the other rocks as the east slope of the range is approached, and is there occasionally intercepted by veins of dark trap.

9th October.

Proposed to start from the camp at the usual time, but four of the horses could not be found, and owing to the rocky nature of the country the tracks were not found till late in the evening, when tracing them some miles I found them at sunset in a secluded valley.

10th October.

This morning we were more successful in collecting the horses, and started from the camp at 6.35 a.m., and steering an easterly course reached the fate of the range at 10.20 and the summit at noon. Following our previous track, reached the pool of water at 1.0 p.m. and camped. Near the camp the xanthorrhoea first made its appearance.

CROSS THE MAIN DIVIDING RANGE.

11th October.

Leaving the camp at 7.0 a.m., steered an easterly course over somewhat barren granite country, timbered with cypress and ironbark; passed close to a hill on the highest point of the range, the summit of which, by approximate measurement, rose to 2500 feet above the sea. Then following a spur of the range we reached the well in the sandy creek at 1.5 p.m. Having cleared out the sand and banked it up with stakes and brushwood, a plentiful supply of water was obtained at about five feet below the surface of the dry channel.

Latitude by e Pegasi 18 degrees 45 minutes 53 seconds.

12th October.

At 7.0 a.m. steered north 60 degrees east over undulating granite country, timbered with ironbark and box, the grass scanty and very dry; at 8.45 crossed a large creek coming from the south. Its channel was 100 yards wide, dry, sandy, and a few pools of shallow water; the banks ten to twenty feet high. Crossing several gullies trending northward, at noon came on a dry sandy creek, also trending to the north. On its right bank was a level flat of cellular lava or basalt. Following the course of the creek, at 1.50 p.m. camped at a fine lagoon a quarter of a mile long and seventy yards wide, the water appearing to be about ten feet deep, although unusually low at the present time. A high range of hills exist to the north of this creek, and the watercourses all trend to the north-west; and, as our latitude is the same as the Reedy Brook of Leichhardt on the south-west side of the Valley of Lagoons, it is evident that these streams do not join the Burdekin, but are tributary to the Lynd, joining it probably at the southern bend.

Latitude by b Aurigae 18 degrees 38 minutes 12 seconds.

13th October.

At 6.25 a.m. steered east and traversed a slightly undulating granite country, with small watercourses trending west-south-west. Ironbark and box formed an open forest, the soil poor and gritty, with a few patches of black soil, with blocks of lava on the surface. At 11.15 ascended a small hill of lava, from which the country appeared very level to the east. To the north-east large hills rose about twelve miles distant; ranges also bounded the plain to the south, and some distant summits were visible to the south-east. Continuing an east course, lava became more frequent, and at length covered the whole surface. At 2.30 p.m. came on several streams of lava, forming ridges of rugged rocks, which were crossed with difficulty. These streams of lava appeared to have run from north to south, the thickness twenty to thirty feet, and breadth very variable. The level ground was lightly timbered with ironbark and box. At 5.25 turned to the south-east, following a small gully. Passed a small native well; but very little water in it, and the rock prevented it being enlarged. At 6.15 camped near some large rocks, in which five or six gallons of rainwater had collected. Walking down the creek one and a half miles in search of water, found two small pools of rainwater; but the darkness of the night and broken nature of the ground prevented the party moving to them.

14th October.

Moved the camp to the waterholes found last night, one and a half miles down the gully. The country is here granite formation, undulating and moderately grassed, and wooded with box and ironbark. The day was cloudy, but cleared at night, and I took sights for time, latitude, and lunar distance. Chronometer 2287 would not wind up in the morning, and stopped during the day, but, having run down, wound again without difficulty.

Longitude by lunar distances 144 degrees 33 minutes 15 seconds; latitude by e Pegasi 18 degrees 41 minutes 38 seconds; variation of compass 5 degrees 50 minutes east.

15th October.

Resumed our journey at 7.0 a.m., and followed the course of the creek to the south-east. The north-east side was a plain of lava, and the south-west consisted of granite ridges with sandstone on the summits. Several small creeks joined from the south-west, and increased the principal channel considerably. At 10.0 the country was more level and openly timbered with box and bloodwood; grass was abundant and green, owing to heavy rains, which appear to have been accompanied with hail, as the west-north-west sides of the trees were much bruised and the soil indented, and a great portion of the leaves torn from the trees. At 1.15 p.m. camped on a small tributary creek. The country appears to be chiefly granite and mica schist, with thin beds or streams of lava, which have come from the ranges to the north and advanced to various distances into the more level land. The surface of the lava is more thinly wooded and better grassed than the granite; but the roughness of the surface and scarcity of water rendered it less convenient travelling. From one of the higher ridges we had a wide but imperfect view of the country. The air being hazy, only a few of the marked features of the ranges to the north were visible; to the east a high hill twenty-five miles distant rose beyond an undulating wooded country. At 6.0 a heavy thunderstorm caused the creek to run for several hours.

Latitude by Capella 18 degrees 49 minutes 13 seconds.

THE BURDEKIN RIVER. A CAMP OF LEICHHARDT'S.

16th October.

The rain having passed away, the morning was clear and cool, and at 6.35 a.m. resumed our journey, steering average south-east, crossing the creek several times, and at 11.0 reached the bank of the Burdekin River, which had a strong stream of water flowing in its channel, which is here about 100 yards wide, but full of casuarina and melaleuca trees; the banks steep and cut with deep gullies. Following the river to the south-east, at 2.0 p.m. camped in a large open grassy flat a mile from the river, obtaining water from a small pool filled by the rain last night.

Latitude by e Pegasi 18 degrees 57 minutes 48 seconds; variation of compass 5 degrees east.

17th October.

At 6.30 a.m. resumed our journey, steering east and south for two hours over level flats; then turning east crossed a steep range of sandstone hills, the strata nearly vertical; the strike north and south; thin veins of quartz intersected the rock in every direction, forming a complete network. The steepness of the country compelled us to turn north-east to the bank of the river, which we followed to the south-east; the banks were high and cut by deep gullies. At 12.30 p.m. the hills receded, and we entered some fine flats. Here I picked up a fragment of the shoulder-bone of a bullock, and observed several trees that had been cut with iron axes; and as the latitude corresponds with that of Dr. Leichhardt's camp of the 26th April, 1845, the bone doubtless belonged to the bullock he killed at this place. At 1.5 camped on the bank of the river. The Moreton-Bay ash, poplar gum, and a rough-barked gum-tree with very green leaves, were added to the ironbark, bloodwood, and other eucalypti which constituted the forest, while casuarina and Melaleuca leucodendron grow in the beds of the larger watercourses. The channel of the river is about 150 yards, with a small stream winding along the sandy bed; much of the running water is due to the late rain, but it is evident from the character of the vegetation that it continues to run throughout the dry season.

Latitude by a Cygni 19 degrees 37 seconds.

18th October.

Continued our route at 6.25 a.m., steering nearly east till 8.30, when the river turned to the north round a range of sandstone hills, crossing which, reached the river again at 10.5 flowing south, with fine openly-timbered flats on the banks; steering south till 1.0 p.m., camped on the bank of the river just below a ridge of slate rock which crossed the channel. From the hills, at 9.0, we saw a fine valley joining that of the Burdekin from the east; it was bounded by a steep range to the south, which terminated two miles from the river. South-west of our position were several flat-topped hills, which appeared to be a continuation of the range crossed yesterday. To the south only a few distant hills were visible, the view being obstructed by trees. The flats on the banks of the river are well grassed and openly timbered with ironbark, Moreton-Bay ash, bloodwood, and poplar gum; the soil varying from a soft brown loam into which our horses sank deeply, to a firm black or brown clay loam; the ranges were stony and thinly grassed; the timber box and ironbark. The geological features consist of a fine-grained sandstone interstratified with slate and coarse conglomerates. The sandstone is intersected in every direction with veins of quartz, which do not appear to enter the slate. The dip of the strata is nearly vertical, the strike north and south. The whole appear to have been much disturbed and altered; neither granite nor trap has been observed since yesterday morning. Consumed the last of the dried horse-meat, and increased the ration of flour to one pound per diem.

19th October (Sunday).

Remained at the camp to rest the party; the day was cloudy, with variable breeze from the south-east to north-east and north; no observations for latitude could be taken till early on Monday morning, and even then the altitudes were imperfect; the stream of running water in the bed of the river has increased, but is still quite clear.

Latitude by Saturn 19 degrees 7 minutes 19 seconds.

CROSS THE CLARK RIVER.

20th October.

Resumed our journey at 6.40 a.m., steering south-east through fine grassy flats till 10.0, when we crossed the Clark River, and altered the course to east over well-grassed flats, to the foot of a rocky range of sandstone hills, which we reached at noon, and ascending by a steep spur, at 2.30 p.m. attained the highest ridge; here sandstone was the prevailing rock; xanthorrhoea, silver-leafed ironbark, and triodia constituted the principal vegetation; descending gradually, at 3.30 reached a small creek with a patch of good green grass on its banks, and at 3.45 halted at some small waterholes, which appeared to be permanent; except near the creek, the country was poor and stony, with a forest of ironbark and box trees; the country between the Clark and the Burdekin appears to be of excellent quality, consisting of well-grassed flats, timbered with ironbark, Moreton-Bay ash, poplar, gum, and box trees. The Clark is about 100 yards wide, with a sandy bed crossed by ridges of slate rock; the banks are sixty to eighty feet high, and the marks of last year's flood thirty to thirty-five feet, the trees being bent and broken by the force of the current; more water appears to come down the Clark during floods, but the Burdekin has a more constant stream, the Clark containing only shallow pools of water, separated by dry sand and rock; after leaving the immediate flats of the river the country was very poor and stony; the late rains had not extended so far, and the grass had the dry and parched appearance which characterised the country on the banks of the Gilbert.

Latitude by a Pegasi 19 degrees 14 minutes 2 seconds.

FRIENDLY NATIVES.

21st October.

6.15 a.m., resumed our journey and traversed an inferior country of sandstone and porphyry; box, silver-leafed ironbark, and triodia characterized the vegetation; in crossing one of these gullies, in which were some pools of water, Bowman's horse fell over the bank into the pool, and he got some severe bruises; at 10.15 came on the river, where it ran over a ledge of rocks forming a succession of rapids, below which it spread out into a broad sheet of sand a quarter of a mile wide, and turned to the south. As Bowman had fallen some distance in the rear, I selected the first suitable spot, and at 11.0 encamped, and shortly after Mr. H. Gregory came in with Bowman to camp. On the bank of the river we saw two black gins, who climbed a tree on our approach, and in the afternoon came to the camp with an old man, and after some unintelligible conversation departed; they had neither clothes or weapons, except a throwing-stick of the same form as those used by the blacks of the southern shore of the Gulf of Carpentaria. The geological character of the country has been sandstone, much altered by contact with porphyry which has been forced through it; both dip and strike are confused, and could not be ascertained to have any general angle or direction, except in the bed of the river, where the strata dipped 10 degrees to the north, but in the hills, on the left bank below the camp, the strata was horizontal; the river is now 150 yards wide at the narrowest parts, a small stream of water, one foot deep and ten to twenty yards wide, running in a winding course through the sand, and sometimes expanding into sheets of water occupying the whole breadth of the channel.

Latitude by a Pegasi 19 degrees 16 minutes 22 seconds.

22nd October.

At 6.15 a.m. steered south and followed the right bank of the river; for the first hour the country was hilly on both banks, with deep gullies; it then became more level, and opened into flats, well grassed; the timber box, ironbark, and Moreton-Bay ash; the soil a light brown loam in some parts, sandy and very soft from the numerous excavations of the funnel ant. These flats extended one to two miles back and then rose into low ridges of poor land, timbered with box and ironbark; crossed a sandy creek coming from the west, and at 1.30 p.m. camped on the right bank of the river. A short distance from the camp surprised a black and his gin and a child; the man climbed a tree and the woman ran off with the child, leaving a small water vessel, hollowed out of a piece of wood, and a calabash full of water. The rocks near the last camp were sandstone or porphyry; in the only exposed section the sandstone dipped to the north 5 degrees to 15 degrees. We also crossed a hill of porphyry which was remarkable for the regularity of cleavage into thick lamina, which were vertical, with a north and south strike; but though it had the appearance of a stratified rock, its structure was perfectly crystalline. About noon, granite, containing large plates of mica, was observed in some of the gullies.

Latitude by e Pegasi 19 degrees 29 minutes 43 seconds.

23rd October.

At 7.0 a.m. steered south-south-east and south-east over ridges of sandstone, timbered with ironbark and thinly grassed, for an hour and a half; again struck the river and passed at the foot of some limestone hills and ridges; this limestone contained fragments of shells and coral. Altering the course to south, traversed fine open flats half a mile to a mile wide, beyond which the country rose into low ridges of limestone. At noon basalt appeared covering the limestone and sandstone. The steep slope which formed the boundary of this rock was very rugged; but the level surface was covered with black soil and well grassed. At 12.55 p.m. camped in a fine grassy flat, walled in by steep rocks of basalt. We experienced some difficulty in watering the horses, as the bank of the river was so steep that they frequently fell back into the river in ascending it. The limestone rocks seen on this day's journey appear to rise from beneath the sandstones, some of which are very hard and close-grained; it dips about 10 degrees to the west and some of the adjacent sandstones 20 degrees west, in well-defined strata. The basalt covers all the other rocks, filling up the former inequalities of the surface and forming a perfectly level plain; where the softer sandstones were in contact, they were only baked into a coarse brick-like mass, which had had much the appearance of having been formed from the alluvial banks of the river.

Latitude by e Pegasi and a Gruis 19 degrees 42 minutes 10 seconds; variation of compass 6 degrees 15 minutes east.

DUCKS, GEESE, AND PELICANS.

24th October.

Leaving our camp at 6.0 a.m., steered south-south-east over well-grassed basaltic flats, timbered thinly with ironbark, etc.; the soil a red loam. At 9.0 a.m. came on a large reedy lagoon or swamp with considerable patches of shallow open water, on which were great numbers of ducks, geese, pelicans, etc. A broad and deep stream flowed from it to the south-east, varying from thirty to eighty yards in width, with a thick belt of reeds along the margin, beyond which the ground rose about fifty feet to the level surface of the basaltic plain. Following the winding of the stream till 10.35 a.m., crossed it at a ledge of basaltic rocks, when it formed a fine rapid with vertical fall of eight to ten feet. Beyond the running channel a dry sandy creek ran parallel at a distance of 80 to 100 yards from it. Our course was now between the creek and the steep rocky edge of the basaltic plain, which was too rugged for the horses to ascend till 11.20 a.m., when, crossing the basalt, we passed to the south of a shallow lake about half a mile in diameter. The country now became scrubby, with patches of grass. Altering the course more to the east, we again entered an open ironbark forest; at 2.0 p.m. crossed a large dry sandy creek, beyond which the country was poor and sandy, with pandanus growing on the ridges. On the bank of the creek we observed the marks of a recent camp of a large party of blacks, and a patch of ground twenty yards by thirty yards cleared of grass, and the surface scraped up into ridges, the whole covered with footprints, which showed that some dance or ceremony had been performed by a large number of men. At 3.30 p.m. entered a dense scrub of small crooked eucalypti and acacia, with a few sterculia. After losing an hour in attempting to penetrate the scrub, we turned north to the dry creek and followed it down till 7.0 p.m., when we camped near a pool of water; but the night was so dark that the horses could not be watered with safety, the banks being very steep and rendered slippery by a slight shower.

25th October.

The grass having been burnt near the camp, the horses had strayed considerably, and we did not start till 7.30 a.m., when, turning east, we soon came on the Burdekin, which now trended to the south-south-west and south-east; the basalt coming close to the river, we were compelled to cross a very rough ridge and came on a deep pool of water eighty yards wide and half a mile long; it terminated in a dry stony channel which joined a sandy creek, and entered the river. Crossing a granite ridge, we camped in a fine grassy flat on the bank of the Burdekin, the banks being high and steep, but the water easy of access.

Latitude by a Pegasi 19 degrees 58 minutes 48 seconds.

26th October (Sunday).

Remained at the camp. During the day there was a succession of showers without thunder, the clouds and wind from the east. At 10.0 p.m. the rain ceased, but the night continued cloudy.

GOOD GRASSY COUNTRY.

27th October.

The morning was cloudy, with light rain till 7.0 a.m.; at 7.30 steered east-south-east and east over fine grassy ridges of granite and trap formation, timbered with ironbark, box, Moreton-Bay ash, and bloodwood; the river taking a sweep to the north of the track, but at 10.40 came again on its banks. The course was now south till 2.15 p.m., when we crossed a large stream-bed from the south-west, with a sandy and rocky bed forty yards wide, which contained a few shallow pools of water. Below the junction of this tributary the river turned to the east and east-north-east, and we crossed low ridges of granite porphyry and trap, which came down from the high land to the bank of the river; at 3.30 encamped. The whole of the country traversed this day was well grassed, except about a mile of bauhinia scrub, which did not appear of any considerable extent. Ironbark, box, bloodwood, and Moreton-Bay ash formed the principal trees with which the country was openly timbered. The prevailing rock granite, traversed by numerous veins of dark trap, and in the latter part of the day porphyry and schist appeared; concretions of limestone were frequent near the trap veins. The soil was somewhat light and gritty loam, except on the trap-rocks, where it was rich black soil. The available country here appears more extensive than higher up the river; more rain has fallen in the early part of the season, and the grass is rich and green, especially where it had been previously burnt off.

Latitude by a Pegasi 20 degrees 7 minutes 23 seconds; variation of compass 6 degrees 20 minutes east.

28th October.

We resumed our journey at 6.25 a.m., steering an east-south-east course, but after crossing some fine grassy ironbark ridges, entered a dense scrub of acacia, sterculia, bauhinia, and thorny shrubs. Turning north, with some difficulty extricated the party from the scrub, which we then skirted to the east along the bank of the river till 9.10, when the scrub receded, and fine openly-timbered ironbark ridges replaced the scrub. These ridges were well-grassed, the rocks granite, trap, and porphyry. The country generally appeared well suited for stock; on both sides of the river no high ranges were visible. At 2.45 p.m. camped on a fine grassy flat, part of which having been burnt, was now covered with excellent green grass. The day was cool, with light showers from the east. The character of the granite was fine-grained, and intersected by veins and masses of trap, and in the latter part of the day's journey porphyry was superincumbent. In the scrubs sandstone existed; it was coarse-grained, and contained worn boulders of trap, quartz, granite, slate, and hard sandstone.

29th October.

As the river below turned to the east of its general course, at 6.20 a.m. steered east-south-east and south-east till 9.30, when we again came on the river trending south. The country consisted of openly-timbered and grassy ironbark ridges, but not equally good with that passed during the last two days. The river at 10.0 turned to the south-east, along the foot of some steep rocky hills of porphyry resting on granite, and at 11.45 was joined by a dry creek twenty yards wide, coming from the south-west; our course was now east-south-east, passing with difficulty between the river and a steep granite hill, beyond which the country became more sandy, and rose to the south in long gentle slopes scantily grassed, and timbered with bloodwood, ironbark, Moreton-Bay ash, and poplar gum, with a few pandanus; an immense number of deep gullies intersected the ground, cutting deeply into the granite rock beneath the soil, and rendering it difficult to traverse. A fine range of openly-wooded and grassy hills rose about two to three miles from the left bank of the river, attaining an elevation of 500 to 800 feet above the valley; these hills are probably porphyritic; they are the Porter Range of Leichhardt. At 2.45 p.m. camped on the bank of the Burdekin River.

THE SUTTOR RIVER. MOUNT MCCONNELL.

30th October.

At 6.30 a.m. steered north 120 degrees east, but at 7.0 a.m. came on the river trending south, the country gradually became more rugged, and rocky hills closed in on both banks forming a deep gorge through which the river forced its way. By keeping at the back of some hills we avoided much of the rocky ground, crossing at noon a high ridge, from which the view extended to the junction of the Burdekin and Suttor Rivers, Mount MccOnnell bearing 159 degrees magnetic, and the west end of Porter Range 334 degrees magnetic. A long range seemed to extend south from Robey Range, and bound the valley of the Upper Burdekin, while a high range appeared to trend north-east from the eastern side of the Suttor Valley, and to turn the Burdekin to the north of east. Continuing our route nearly south-east over steep rocky ridges, we encamped in a fine grassy flat, a quarter of a mile from the Suttor River, at 1.50 p.m., Mount MccOnnell bearing north 172 degrees east magnetic. About 10.0 a.m. we heard some blacks calling in our rear, and soon after came in sight, but would not allow any of the party to approach them, till one of the horsemen cantering up quickly, some of the blacks climbed into trees, where, after making signs to them that it was desirable that they should pursue an opposite route to ours, we left them to descend at leisure. The country passed this day was of a broken character, with deep gullies and rocky hills near the river, but was generally well grassed and openly timbered with ironbark and Moreton-Bay ash. Granite rock forms the base of the hills, and was covered by masses of porphyry, forming hills with rocky summits of columnar structure, as at the head of the Gilbert River a dark-coloured trap changing into porphyry formed some of the lower ridges, and was largely developed on the bank of the Suttor. Thin veins of calcareous spar and quartz intersected the granite. The bed of the Burdekin where we last saw it, one mile above the junction of the Suttor, was about half a mile wide with a stream of water varying from twenty yards wide to the whole breadth of the channel, which was very level and sandy. The Suttor is but a small river compared with the Burdekin. Near the camp it formed some fine reaches of water 180 yards wide, but of no great depth. The trees on its banks were much broken and bent by a violent flood which had occurred within the year. Considering the number of miles we have travelled along the banks of the Burdekin, few impediments have been encountered, while the extent of country suited for squatting purposes is very considerable--water forming a never-failing stream throughout the whole distance.

Latitude by a Gruis and a Pegasi 20 degrees 36 minutes 20 seconds; variation of compass 70 degrees east.

THE FIRST BRIGALOW SCRUB.

31st October.

A rainy night was followed by a thick fog in the morning, so that when we started at 6.30 a.m. it was with difficulty the deep gullies on the banks of the Suttor were avoided; steering south-west for one hour, crossed to the right bank of the Suttor, and then by an average south course passed to the west of Mount McConnell, which, by its isolated character and height (about 600 feet above the river) forms a very conspicuous landmark. It is wooded to the summit, and has fine patches of grass on the slopes, with cliffs of porphyry near the upper part, this being the prevailing rock; on the right bank white shaly rocks and dark trap, with veins of calcareous spar and limestone, prevailed on the left bank of the Suttor; the country on both sides well grassed and openly timbered with ironbark. The bed of the river was very irregular and sandy, with small shallow pools of water at intervals; at 11.0 the river came from the south-west, but continuing a south course we crossed some fine basaltic plains, covered with fine grass and separated by open box forest; at noon crossed a sandstone hill, the base of which was porphyry; traversing ironbark ridges for an hour, we crossed a sandy creek coming from the east, and at 1.0 p.m. encountered the first brigalow scrub; through this scrub we steered south-west till 3.40, and camped on a small dry creek with a narrow grassy flat; water was obtained from a small gully where it had lodged during a shower on the previous night. The country till we reached the brigalow scrub was well adapted for pastoral purposes; the rock trap, slate, and porphyry, with veins of limestone. The brigalow scrub grows on the detritus of a coarse conglomerate, the larger boulders of which lay scattered over the surface of the ground; these boulders consist of trap, porphyry, sandstone, and quartz, and show marks of being water-worn. A range of hills, apparently sandstone, bounds the valley to the east from three to seven miles from the river. They have no great elevation, and we did not obtain a good view of them from any point.

Latitude by Capella 20 degrees 52 minutes 25 seconds.

1st November.

The horses had strayed so far into the scrub in search of grass that it was 9.40 a.m. before they were collected and saddled; we then steered south-west through the scrub, which gradually became more open, and at 11.15 we again reached the river coming from the south-south-east; it gradually turned to south and south-south-west; two creeks joined the river from the east, but neither of any importance; the brigalow scrub came close to the bank of the river, only leaving a narrow flat open; the west side of the river we could see but little, except that it consisted of wooded ridges and scrub to the east at a distance of one to three miles; rocky hills of moderate height existed, and from their flat tops and red cliffs near the summit, evidently consisted of sandstone in horizontal strata; sandstone was also exposed near the river with a dip of 30 degrees to the south; at 3.30 camped on the right bank of the Suttor, where a fine grassy plain extended about a mile back, and was covered with beautiful green grass; water was abundant, as the river had been running during the past week and had filled the hollows in the channel, though it had now ceased to flow; the bed is very irregular, and consists of three to six channels, which separate and rejoin so as to form a complete network, with occasional isolated hollows. Being free from scrub, the bed of the river was good travelling ground, large flooded-gum trees and melaleuca-trees affording an agreeable shade.

Latitude by a Pegasi 21 degrees 4 minutes 43 seconds.

2nd November (Sunday).

Grass and water being abundant, we enjoyed a day's rest. Several cockatoos were shot; they are similar in colour and form to the sulphur-crested cockatoos of the Victoria and Gulf of Carpentaria, but much larger in size.

IRON TOMAHAWKS USED BY THE NATIVES.

3rd November.

Leaving the camp at 6.35 a.m., followed the river in a southerly direction till 11.0, when it turned to the east, and we ascended a sandstone hill; from the summit there was a fine view of the surrounding country. To the east several distant peaks and hills were visible, the most remarkable north 86 degrees east magnetic; to the south a low range about thirty miles distant, with one large peaked hill, bounded the horizon, the intervening country being very level and apparently covered with scrub. To the west the valley was bounded by low hills of sandstone. Although ironbark ridges are frequent, the general character of the country is very scrubby, and this combined with the scarcity of water will render it unsuitable for pastoral purposes. Descending the hill, steered south-east, crossed a fine basaltic plain, and entered open brigalow scrub, and at 2.0 p.m. again came on the Suttor River, which had completely altered its character, now consisting of level grassy flats with uncertain limits and intersected by long waterholes, which were mostly dry; the general course from south-south-west; at 3.30 camped at a fine waterhole. Two miles below the camp we surprised some blacks, who decamped into the scrub. The country along the river consists of open flats, thinly grassed and interspersed with patches of saltbush (atriplex), and openly timbered with box and flooded-gum, while ironbark, box and brigalow prevail over the rest of the country. The marks of iron tomahawks are frequent where the blacks have been cutting honey or opposums out of the hollow branches of the trees.

Latitude by a Pegasi 21 degrees 22 minutes 43 seconds; variation of compass 6 degrees 50 minutes east.

4th November.

Steering south-west from 7.40 a.m. till 8.5, the river turned suddenly to the south-east, and, changing our course to 170 degrees, traversed an open brigalow scrub with several shallow channels winding through it in an irregular manner. At 10.30 again came on the principal channel of the river, which was running, and very muddy from the effect of recent rains in the upper part of its course. The banks are very low, and the country so level that the floods must frequently extend more than a mile back into the scrub, which comes close to the bank on both sides. Box and flooded-gum trees grow along the larger channels, and sometimes box flats extend into the scrub. We now followed the river south-south-west, through a level country covered with dense brigalow scrub, passing only one low rocky hill, on the left bank, at 11.20. At 2.15 p.m. the river diverged to the eastward, and the course was altered to south. The country was more open, and at 3.0 encamped on one of the side channels of the river in a fine grassy box flat.

Latitude by a Pegasi 21 degrees 38 minutes 49 seconds.

5th November.

Steering south-east for one mile, reached the main channel of the river, which was followed south. Crossing to the right bank at 7.20 a.m., at 9.15 a dense brigalow scrub forced us south-west, and again came to the river at 10.30. A south course was then followed till 1.0 p.m.; then south-east till 4.0; then followed the river south-south-east till 4.50, and camped on a large grassy flat. The whole of the country is very level and covered with dense brigalow scrubs, except one sandy plain, on which triodia was more abundant than grass. Having now passed the latitude of Sir T. Mitchell's last camp on the Belyando, and thus connected his route with that of Dr. Leichhardt, I considered it unnecessary to follow the river further, and decided on taking a south-easterly route to Peak Downs and the Mackenzie River.

Latitude by a Pegasi 21 degrees 57 minutes 45 seconds.

6th November.

At 6.30 a.m. crossed the Belyando, and steered south through brigalow scrubs till 9.0; then entered a box and Moreton-Bay ash flat, in which was a small gully with rainwater, near which a camp of blacks was observed; but they ran into the scrub on our approach. At 9.30 changed the course to south-east towards some rocky hills, which were reached at 11.0. From this we saw several distant ranges to the westward; but the intervening twenty to forty miles was very flat. The route was now over scrubby sandstone hills for three hours, and then descended into an open flat, with box, bloodwood, and Moreton-Bay ash, triodia, and grass growing on a sandy loam. At 3.30 p.m. camped at a pool of rainwater in a small creek. In crossing the sandstone range we had a view of some high peaks twenty to thirty miles distant to the south-south-east; but to the east the country was quite level.

Latitude by a Pegasi 22 degrees 13 minutes 10 seconds.

7th November.

Started at 6.5 a.m., steering south-east; the whole country appeared perfectly level with brigalow scrub and patches of open sandy country, producing triodia and a little grass; the timber Moreton-Bay ash and box. Towards noon the country was more open. At 1.30 p.m. passed a shallow pool of rainwater at the edge of a scrub. About a mile further on Melville's horse fell, and so bruised his rider that we had to return to the water and camp.

Latitude by a Pegasi 22 degrees 23 minutes 36 seconds.

HORSE-SKIN SOUP.

8th November.

The water being exhausted, the party had to move on in search of a further supply where we could halt until Melville had recovered from his injuries. Steering south-east for one hour, came to a fine creek with grassy flats and a stream of muddy water, indicating that there had been heavy rain in the ranges to the south. Having camped, we shot the filly, which was now eleven months old, cut the flesh into slices and hung it up to dry in the sun during the day and over a charcoal fire at night. The skin was cleared of hair, and was thus made into a species of gelatine, from which excellent soup was subsequently prepared. The saddlery had become much worn by passing through the scrubs, and the party was fully employed in repairs and shoeing the horses, many of which were very lame from injury among the fallen timber.

9th November (Sunday).

Melville somewhat better, but scarcely able to walk. The meat drying well.

Latitude by a Pegasi 22 degrees 26 minutes 16 seconds.

10th November.

At 7.40 a.m. left the camp and followed the creek up for an hour south-south-east; then steered south-east through brigalow scrub, which gradually changed to open ironbark and box flats well grassed. At 2.0 p.m. came to broken country covered with a dense scrub of acacia and ironbark, deep gullies intersecting the country in every direction; at 3.30 ascended a ridge of mica schist, from which a high range was seen twenty miles to the south-east, but the scrub was so dense that the view was imperfect. Followed a gully, which changed from south round to north-west till 5.15, when we camped at a small pool of rainwater. There were good grassy flats along the watercourse, but the hills were covered with scrub. It is evident that we are now approaching the watershed of the Fitzroy River, and hope soon to emerge from the vast tract of scrub which occupies the valley of the Suttor River. On the plain we observed that more than half the box-trees had died within the last three years, and that they had not been killed by bush fires, as the old timber which lay on the ground was not scorched.

Latitude by a Andromedae 22 degrees 42 minutes 13 seconds.

PEAK RANGE.

11th November.

Leaving the camp at 6.30 a.m., steered south-east over ironbark ridges of very scrubby character with open grassy valleys; the ridges increased in height, and at 11.0, having reached the most elevated summit, got a view of Peak Range about thirty miles to the north-east; to the north-west the view was obscured by wooded ranges, but from north to east-south-east the country consisted of low-wooded ridges for ten miles, beyond which fine open grassy plains extended from east-north-east to east, along the foot of Peak Range. Descending from the range, followed a small watercourse east-south-east for two hours, and then north-east, and at 2.30 p.m. encamped in a fine grassy flat with a small pool of rainwater in a gully, the larger creek being dry. The country generally consists of low ridges of schist, which, by decomposition, forms a gravelly loam, the gravel being derived from the quartz veins which intersect the schist in all directions. The forest consists of ironbark and acacia; grass everywhere abundant. Many of the horses are very lame from the splinters of dead wood in the scrub, and some have to be relieved entirely of their loads.

Latitude by a Pegasi 22 degrees 48 minutes 17 seconds; longitude by lunar distances 147 degrees 30 minutes 30 seconds.

12th November.

At 7.25 a.m. steered north 110 degrees east, over grassy ironbark ridges, with small watercourses trending north; at 11.0 entered a dense brigalow scrub with a few Moreton-Bay ash-trees, the soil very poor and derived from the decomposition of a coarse conglomerate; small watercourses trending to the south. At 12.45 p.m. emerged from the scrub into open box forest, with limestone and quartz gravel, and a soft black soil producing rather dry scanty grass. At 1.45 entered a well-grassed plain with limestone ridges covered with bottle-tree scrub; the grass was good at this season, green but much mixed with salsola; the summits of Peak Range showed well above the ridges, and from the cliff around the tops seem to be capped with sandstone or more probably porphyry. There being little prospect of finding water in an easterly direction, at 4.0 altered the course to south-east; a heavy squall and thunderstorm brought some rain, but it was all immediately absorbed by the hot dry soil, at 5.0 came to a watercourse trending south, followed it till 6.30, and camped without water; about a mile north from the camp saw a small box-tree marked AB, and near it a large sheet of bark which had been cut about two years before.

Latitude by Saturn 23 degrees 18 seconds.

13th November.

Resumed the journey at 6.20 a.m., steering south down the watercourse; at 7.0 saw some blacks, who, when asked by signs where water could be found, pointed down the creek and into the scrub; at 9.20 came to a pool of rainwater and camped. This part of the country is very poor and scrubby, with large Moreton-Bay ash trees, the soil formed by the decomposition of sandstone and conglomerate, with intervals of schist and trap-rock.

CROSS THE PEAK DOWNS.

14th November.

At 6.50 a.m. steered south-east; we soon entered a grassy plain with ironbark ridges and belts of acacia scrub, trap, and limestone on the plains, and sandstone on the ridges; at noon passed a belt of cypress and entered extensive open downs covered with beautiful green grass. Following a shallow watercourse, passed some blacks at a distance, and at 4.20 p.m. came to a small pool of rainwater, and camped. The country to the north-east appeared level, and the grassy downs apparently extend to the foot of Peak Range. To the south-west it appeared to be a fine open country for three to eight miles, and then rose into wooded hills of moderate elevation, at the base of which a creek appeared to run to the south-east. If this part of the country were well supplied with water it would form splendid stations for the squatter; but from its level character and geological structure, permanent surface-water is very scarce, and where it does exist it is surrounded by scrubby country, which renders it almost unavailable.

THE MACKENZIE RIVER.

15th November.

At 6.40 steered east-south-east and soon entered an open acacia scrub with some grassy patches; the soil a fine black loam; limestone, trap, and quartz-pebbles occurring on the surface in the open plain; at 9.0 entered a fine box flat, and passed some pools of water; the flat extending east three miles; then entered a scrubby tract of country, the soil a black mould with much salsola growing even in the thick scrub; at 11.0 came on a fine creek from the north with pools of permanent water (Crinum Creek), but the banks covered with scrub. Changing the course to south-east, at 12.20 p.m. came to a fine river with high grassy banks and several deep channels which were now full of water and running in consequence of the late rains. It had been slightly flooded this season, and the previous year had risen twenty-five feet above the present level. This river is the Mackenzie of Leichhardt. The course of the river is to the east-south-east, and we crossed to the right bank without much difficulty, the bottom being firm and the bank sandy; followed the river till 2.40, and camped. The country on the banks of the Mackenzie is scrubby, with occasional open flats; the timber box, with good grass. The little lemon-tree was in full bearing, and though the fruit is only half an inch in diameter, was excellent eating when boiled with sugar. The day was cool and cloudy, and it rained lightly for some hours during the night.

Latitude by Procyon 23 degrees 28 minutes 19 seconds.

16th November (Sunday).

Remained at the camp. The morning was cool and cloudy, but cleared towards noon, and at night got sights for latitude.

LEICHHARDT'S CAMP.

17th November.

Resumed our journey at 6.40 a.m. Followed the Mackenzie south-east through level country with much scrub till 9.25 a.m., when we crossed a large creek from the south, which proved to be the Comet River of Dr. Leichhardt. The whole bed of the Comet did not exceed seventy yards, and the smaller channel only five to six yards wide, and even below its junction the Mackenzie only had a channel ten to thirty yards wide in the bottom of a bed 150 yards wide from bank to bank. Just below the junction of the Comet we found the remains of a camp of Dr. Leichhardt's party on its second journey. The ashes of the fire were still visible, and a quantity of bones of goats were scattered around. A large tree was marked thus:

DIG arrow pointing down L

but a hollow in the ground at the foot of the tree showed that whatever had been deposited had long since been removed. We, however, cleared out the loose earth, but found nothing. The river now turned east-north-east, and our course being east, we receded from it, and at noon we ascended a rocky hill of sandstone covered with scrub; we therefore steered north for an hour and came to the Mackenzie, and encamped in a fine grassy flat, but beyond the immediate flats of the river the country was covered with scrub. Near the camp a large flooded-gum tree had been marked:

Solid square [symbol ??]

some years before. The day was cloudy with easterly breeze. Marked a tree:

120 solid Delta

this being the 120th camp since starting from the Victoria River.

18th November.

Rain commenced at 7.0 a.m. and continued till noon; at 6.25 steered east and soon entered a dense scrub of acacia, box, sterculia, and Moreton-Bay ash. Ascending to the level tableland by a steep sandstone slope, at 11.25 passed a gully with deep waterholes which appeared permanent, and at 1.40 p.m. encamped at a deep creek with a small pool of water. To the south-east of the camp about five miles distant a range of hills rose abruptly from the level country to a height of 800 to 1000 feet. The summits were flat and surrounded by high cliffs of red sandstone (Expedition Range).

Latitude by Procyon 23 degrees 33 minutes 40 seconds; variation of compass 7 degrees 50 minutes east.

19th November.

Resumed our route at 6.30 a.m.; steered east through dense scrubs with open patches of grassy forest, the soil a light loam, very sandy in the open forest. Small watercourses trended north; at 10.0 turned to south-east to avoid a large scrubby hill which lay detached from the principal range; at 11.0 again steered east, ascending a steep sandstone hill from which the country to the north and east appeared extremely level, we then crossed a series of ironbark ridges with scrub at intervals, and fine flooded-gum and box flats in the valleys; casuarina and cypress grew on some of the ridges, but the country generally was well grassed; at 3.30 p.m. encamped at a small pool of water in a shallow watercourse trending north-east.

Latitude by Saturn 23 degrees 37 minutes 23 seconds.

20th November.

At 7.40 a.m. steered east over open country, thinly timbered with box and ironbark; at 10.0 crossed a dry creek, on the banks of which were recent tracks of horses and cattle; at noon there was a heavy thunderstorm, and at the same time entered a dense scrub of brigalow and casuarina; at 2.0 p.m.

the country was more open, and at 4.10 camped near a small gully with pools of rainwater; heavy rain during the night.

21st November.

Continued an east course; at 6.50 a.m. crossed some wooded ridges, from which ranges of hills were imperfectly seen about twelve miles to the east; descending the ridges, entered a brigalow scrub, and at 11.40 came to the Dawson River, about eighty yards wide, with long shallow pools of water, the scrub coming close to the bank on both sides, leaving a narrow grassy flat; followed the river upwards to the southward till 2.50 p.m., and camped on the left bank of the river. The flats on the bank of the river are here much wider and well grassed, and we observed the tracks of horses.

REACH THE FIRST STATION ON THE DAWSON RIVER.

22nd November.

At 6.15 a.m. resumed our route up the river south-east, and at 8.0 came to a dray-track, which was followed east-north-east two miles to Messrs. Connor and Fitz' station, where we met with a most hospitable reception.

Latitude by Procyon 23 degrees 51 minutes 15 seconds.

The party having thus reached the occupied country travelled by the dray-tracks past Mr. Hay's station Rannes, on the 25th November, and thence by Rawbelle, Boondooma, Tabinga, Nanango, Collinton, Kilkoy, Durandur, and Cabulture stations, reached Brisbane on the 16th December, 1856.

1857. NEW SOUTH WALES LEGISLATIVE ASSEMBLY

DR. LEICHHARDT, PROPOSED EXPEDITION IN SEARCH OF

Ordered by the Legislative Assembly to be Printed, 28th October, 1857.

PROCEEDINGS OF THE EXECUTIVE COUNCIL ON THE 14TH SEPTEMBER, 1857, WITH RESPECT TO AN EXPEDITION IN SEARCH OF DR. LEICHHARDT

MINUTE NUMBER 57-44.

His Excellency the Governor-General, at the instance of the Honourable the Colonial Secretary, brings under the consideration of the Council a proposal which has been made to organise another Expedition to ascertain, if possible, beyond doubt, the fate of Dr. Leichhardt, who left Sydney some nine years ago with the intention of exploring the north-western interior of Australia. This proposal has its origin in a public meeting, held in Sydney on the 11th instant, at which resolutions were passed invoking the assistance of the Government, and it is recommended to favourable consideration at the present moment by the circumstance that Mr. Gregory, who recently returned from a successful exploration in the same direction, has intimated his willingness to undertake the conduct of the proposed Expedition.

2. The Council express themselves desirous of seizing so favourable an opportunity of pursuing this inquiry, and they therefore advise that Mr. Gregory should be at once invited to submit, for approval, a definite proposal having for its object: 1st, to ascertain the fate of the late Dr. Leichhardt; and, 2nd, to connect the exploring surveys of Mitchell and Kennedy with his own; such proposal to be accompanied by an estimate of the probable expense which it will be necessary to incur.

EDWARD C. MEREWETHER,

Clerk of the Council.

Executive Council Office,

Sydney, 22 September, 1857.

A.C. GREGORY, ESQUIRE, TO THE COLONIAL SECRETARY.

Sydney, 15 September, 1857.

SIR,

Adverting to your verbal communication of yesterday, with reference to the proposed Expedition in search of traces of Dr. Leichhardt, I have the honour to furnish a memorandum of the arrangements I would suggest for the organisation and conduct of a party calculated to effect the objects in view, together with an estimate of the probable cost.

These documents I have submitted to such of the gentlemen composing the Committee of the Leichhardt Association as I have had the opportunity of consulting, and I have availed myself of their experience of the District in which the Expedition would be organised.

Although I have allowed extreme rates for many of the items of expenditure, yet, as in all undertakings of this description unavoidable and unforeseen contingencies are certain to arise, I should scarcely feel justified in naming the gross amount which should be available, though not necessarily expended, at a less sum than 4,500 pounds.

I have, etc.,

A.C. GREGORY.

The Honourable the Colonial Secretary.

MEMORANDUM FOR THE ORGANISATION OF AN EXPLORING EXPEDITION FOR THE PURPOSE OF SEARCHING FOR TRACES OF DR. LEICHHARDT'S PARTY

The objects of the proposed Expedition would be primarily to search for traces of Dr. Leichhardt and his party, who started from the settled districts of New South Wales in April, 1848, with the intention of proceeding to Western Australia, and, if possible, to ascertain the fate of that unfortunate explorer. Secondly, the examination of the country both in the intervening spaces between the tracks of previous explorers, and also beyond the limits of that hitherto explored, with a view of developing its resources, especially with reference to its capabilities for settlement.

The party despatched by the Colonial Government, under Mr. Hely, in 1851-2, traced Dr. Leichhardt to a spot near the head of the Warrego River.

Beyond this spot Dr. Leichhardt had expressed his intention of proceeding down the Victoria River to its northern bend, and then shape his course along the interior slope of the ranges which he supposed existed at the sources of the streams flowing to the northern coast.

The proposed route of the searching Expedition would therefore be to reach Leichhardt's last known camp, and then to examine the banks of the Victoria River to the junction of the Alice River, at the northern bend, where especial search would be made, as Dr. Leichhardt intended to leave letters there, and would probably encamp for several days to recruit before finally entering the unknown country; and the non-existence of marks at this point would be almost conclusive evidence that the party had perished nearer to the settlements.

In the search for traces of the missing party beyond this point (as it could only be at the camping places that any traces would remain after so long an interval), it would be necessary to follow such natural features as would probably have influenced the party in the selection of its route, assuming that the general course would be north-west.

The investigation having been carried to the fullest extent that time and circumstances would admit, the searching party would adopt such a route on its return as would intersect the greatest extent of unexamined country. To effect these objects it is proposed to organise a party at one of the outer stations, say at Surat, on the Lower Condamine River, from which Leichhardt's last known camp is 230 miles, and the junction of the Alice with the Victoria River, 370 miles, not allowing for deviations.

The party to consist of two sections, which may be termed the Exploring and the Auxiliary parties.

The first would comprise eight persons, equipped and provisioned for 5 months, and for the conveyance of which 32 horses would be required, as follows:

Commander.

Assistant.

Overseer, etc.

4 Stockmen.

1 Aboriginal Stockman.

The second section would be composed of six persons, provisioned etc., for 2 months, and for the conveyance of which 13 horses would be required, as follows:

1 Leader.

4 Stockmen.

1 Aboriginal Black.

These two sections would proceed together to the junction of the Alice and Victoria Rivers, and would be sufficiently strong to detach parties to examine points out of the more direct line of route which the main body would follow.

On reaching the spot above referred to, the Exploring Party would be fitted out in the most efficient manner for continuing its operations, by selecting the strongest and most serviceable portion of the horses, equipment, etc., while the Auxiliary Party would return with the remainder to the settlements; thus affording nearly all the advantages of a depot, without incurring the greater expense or inconvenience attending the otherwise necessary return of the Exploring Party by the same route.

It is scarcely necessary to advert to the many advantages which would be derived from this arrangement, for enabling the Exploring Party to reach the extreme known point of country, with its strength impaired in the least possible degree, while it would afford an opportunity of testing the capabilities of the party to be finally selected.

ESTIMATE OF THE COST (IN POUNDS/SHILLINGS/PENCE) OF THE EQUIPMENT, ETC., OF THE EXPLORING PARTY

PROVISIONS.

1400 pounds Flour : 17/10/0.

500 pounds Bacon : 25/0/0.

400 pounds Sugar : 10/0/0.

70 pounds Tea : 7/0/0.

750 pounds Meat Biscuit : 37/0/0.

70 pounds Tobacco : 8/15/0.

20 pounds Sago : 0/13/4.

6 pounds Pepper : 0/6/0.

50 pounds Salt : 0/5/0.

50 pounds Soap : 0/18/8.

6 pounds Sperm Candles : 0/9/0.

150 pounds Dried Beef--800 pounds fresh meat : 10/0/0.

1000 pounds Fresh Meat : 12/0/0.

subtotal : 130/7/0.

TRANSPORT.

45 Horses, at 40 pounds : 1800/0/0.

14 Riding Saddles, at 60 shillings : 42/0/0.

31 Pack Saddles, at 77 shillings 6 pence : 120/2/6.

45 Bridles and Headstalls, at 9 shillings : 20/5/0.

45 Horse Blankets, at 8 shillings : 18/0/0.

100 Hobbles, at 4 shillings : 20/0/0.

20 Pairs Girths, at 4 shillings : 4/0/0.

31 Canvas Saddle-bags, at 25 shillings : 38/17/0.

100 Provision Bags, at 60 shillings : 15/0/0.

40 Yards Canvas, at 1 shilling 6 pence : 3/0/0.

10 Horse-bells, at 6 shillings 6 pence : 3/5/0.

Materials for repairs, etc. : 20/0/0.

90 Horse-straps and Nails : 10/0/0.

100 Saddle-straps, at 1 shilling : 5/0/0.

subtotal : 2119/9/6.

ARMS AND AMMUNITION.

13 Double guns, at 5 pounds : 65/0/0.

13 Revolvers, at 5 pounds : 65/0/0.

30 pounds Gunpowder : 6/0/0.

150 pounds Shot and Lead : 3/0/0.

5000 Percussion Caps : 1/10/0.

14 Belts and Pouches : 3/10/0.

14 Gun-buckets : 4/18/0.

Sundries : 10/0/0.

subtotal : 158/18/0.

CAMP EQUIPAGE.

14 Calico Sheets for Tents, at 1 shillings : 8/8/0.

50 yards Calico, at 6 pence : 1/5/0.

6 Camp Kettles, at 5 shillings : 1/10/0.

40 Pannikins, at 8 pence : 1/6/8.

3 Leather Buckets, at 17 shillings 6 pence : 2/12/6.

20 Tin Dishes, at 9 pence : 0/15/0.

2 Frying-Pans, at 4 shillings 6 pence : 0/9/0.

2 Water Bags, at 30 shillings : 3/0/0.

14 Water Holders, India-Rubber, at 10 shillings 6 pence : 7/7/0.

2 Socket Shovels, at 2 shillings 6 pence : 0/5/0.

2 spring Balances, at 7 shillings : 0/14/0.

Materials for repairs, etc. : 20/0/0.

subtotal : 27/12/2.

INSTRUMENTS, ETC.

1 Sextant : 10/0/0.

1 Prismatic Compass : 3/0/0.
1 Artificial Horizon : 4/0/0.
2 Aneroid Barometers : 7/0/0.
3 Thermometers : 1/1/0.
1 Lever Watch : 9/0/0.
Stationery : 5/0/0.
subtotal : 40/1/0.

CLOTHING.

20 Trousers, at 7 shillings : 7/0/0.
20 Serge Shirts, at 6 shillings : 6/0/0.
20 Cotton Shirts, at 3 shillings : 3/0/0.
20 Pairs of Boots, at 15 shillings : 15/0/0.
14 Blankets, at 10 shillings : 7/0/0.
14 Oiled Capes, at 10 shillings : 7/0/0.
subtotal : 45/0/0.

total equipment : 2521/7/8.

CONTINGENCIES.

Medical Stores and Drugs : 20/0/0.
Petty Contingencies : 50/0/0.
Collection and Forage for Horses prior to starting : 100/0/0.
Freights and Passages from Sydney to moreton Bay : 50/0/0.
Conveyance of Stores from Brisbane to Surat : 200/0/0.
Contingent Expenses in the Collection of the Party at Surat : 100/0/0.
Total Contingencies : 520/0/0.

SALARIES.

Commander, 9 months, 600 pounds per annum : 450/0/0.

Assistant, 7 months, 300 pounds per annum : 175/0/0.

Overseer, 6 months, at 150 pounds per annum : 75/0/0.

4 Stock men, 6 months, at 2 pounds per week : 208/0/0.

1 Aboriginal Stock man, 6 months : 20/0/0.

Leader of the Auxiliary Party, 3 months : 104/0/0.

4 Stock men, 3 months : 208/0/0.

1 Aboriginal Stock man, 3 months : 10/0/0.

Total salaries : 1117/0/0.

RECAPITULATION.

equipment : 2521/7/8.

Contingent Expenses : 520/0/0.

salaries : 1117/0/0.

total : 4158/7/8.

A.C. Gregory.

Sydney, 16th September, 1857.

1858. LEGISLATIVE ASSEMBLY, NEW SOUTH WALES

EXPEDITION IN SEARCH OF DR. LEICHHARDT.- -REPORT ON PROCEEDINGS

Ordered by the Legislative Assembly to be Printed, 1 September, 1858.

REPORT OF THE PROCEEDINGS OF THE EXPEDITION IN SEARCH OF DR. LEICHHARDT AND PARTY

8TH DECEMBER, 1857, TO 11TH JANUARY, 1858.

Having received instructions from the Honourable the Secretary for Lands and Public Works to organise an expedition for the purpose of searching for traces of Dr. Leichhardt and party, who left New South Wales in 1848 with the intention of proceeding overland to Western Australia, I proceeded to Moreton Bay with such portions of the equipment as had been prepared in Sydney. On reaching Ipswich forty horses were purchased, and having despatched the stores to Mr. Royd's station, on the Dawson River, by drays, the party were collected at that place; but, owing to unforeseen delays in the transport of the stores, the equipment and organisation of the expedition was not complete till the latter part of March.

The following list of the party, horses, stores, etc., will show the principal arrangements.

The party consisted of nine persons, namely: Commander A.C. Gregory; assistant commander, C.F. Gregory; assistant, S. Burgoyne; overseer, G. Phibbs; stockmen, etc., R. Bowman, W. Selby, T. Dunn, W. von Wedel, and D. Worrell. The stock consisted of horses alone, comprising thirty-one pack and nine saddle horses, completely equipped. Provisions comprised the dried meat of two bullocks and four sheep, weighing, as butcher's meat, 16 hundredweight; but when dried and the bones removed, reduced to 300 pounds. In addition to this 500 pounds bacon, 1600 pounds flour, 100 pounds rice, 350 pounds sugar, 60 pounds tea, 40 pounds tobacco, and some minor articles. The arms and ammunition were: one minie rifle, eight double-barrel guns, nine revolver pistols, 25 pounds gunpowder, 150 pounds shot and balls, percussion caps, etc. For the conveyance of water two leather water-bags were provided, each holding five gallons, besides which each of the party was furnished with a water-bag of India-rubber holding three pints. The tents were made of calico, each suited for the accommodation of two persons, and the several articles of camp equipage were of the lightest construction consistent with the service required. The instruments employed were an eight-inch sextant, box-sextant, prismatic compasses, pocket compasses, double axis compass, aneroid barometers, thermometers, and artificial horizon, etc. Including forty sets of horse-shoes, farrier's and carpenter's tools, together with sundry material for repairs, etc., the total weight of the equipment was about 4,600 pounds, exclusive of the saddles and harness, which gave an average load of 150 pounds as the net load carried by each pack-horse.

THE PARTY START FROM JUANDA STATION.

24th March to 27th March.

These arrangements being complete, the expedition left Juanda, and proceeded by the road to Mr. Cardew's station at Euroomba, from which, under the guidance of Mr. Bolton--whose local knowledge was of material service--we made our way through the dense scrubs and broken country to the west for about thirty miles, to the head of Scott's Creek, a small tributary of the Dawson River.

29th March.

The general course was now west-north-west through a country with rich grassy valleys and dense scrubs of brigalow acacia on the higher ground. Green grass was abundant at this time; but I fear that in seasons of drought few of the waterholes are permanent; the timber consists of ironbark, box, and a few other species of eucalyptus--the brigalow acacia attaining the height of thirty feet; soft brown sandstones of the coal measures are the prevailing rock, forming hills with table summits.

2nd April.

With some difficulty, owing to the dense scrubs, we crossed the basaltic ridge which divides the eastern waters flowing to the Dawson River from those trending to the west into the basin of the Maranoa River, a tributary of which--probably the Merivale River--was followed westward. The country became more sandy, timbered with ironbark, cypress, etc. The whole was, however, well grassed, and suited for grazing, if not too heavily stocked.

5th April.

Reaching the Maranoa River in about latitude 25 degrees 45 minutes, water was scarcely procurable in the sandy bed, and we had to dig wells to obtain a supply.

7th April to 12th April.

Warned by the fact that Messrs. H. Gregory and Haly had been unable to penetrate the country to the west from scarcity of water, even three months earlier in the season, we followed up the Maranoa to Mount Owen, and having found a sufficient supply of water and grass for a few days' halt, I proceeded to reconnoitre the country to the west, and at length found a practicable route to the tributaries of the Warrego River, to which the party was advanced. A heavy shower of rain had filled the gullies in this locality, and green grass clothed the country, forming a striking contrast to the dry and waterless valley of the Maranoa.

15th to 16th April.

Fine openly timbered valleys, well suited for pasture, alternated with ridges of scrub of brigalow acacia till we reached Mount Playfair, a basaltic hill on the sandstone ridge which separates the Warrego Valley from that of the Nive, a small branch of which was followed down to its junction with the main channel in latitude 25 degrees 6 minutes. The soil in the valley of the Nive is sandy, thinly grassed, and openly timbered with ironbark spotted gum, etc.; the back country rising into low sandstone ridges, covered with dense scrub of brigalow acacia. Some pools of permanent water containing small fish were passed, on the bank of which the remains of numerous native camps were seen.

17th April.

From the Nive River a north-north-west course was pursued through a nearly level sandy country, covered with a scrub of acacia, eucalypti, bottle-tree, etc., which offered great impediments to our progress, till within six miles of the Victoria River, when we suddenly emerged from the scrub on to open downs of rich clay soil; but the drought had been of such a long continuance that the whole of the vegetation had been destroyed and swept away by the wind, leaving the country to all appearance an absolute desert. The bed of the Victoria was scarcely ten yards wide, and perfectly dry, so that it was only after a prolonged search along its course that a small puddle of water was found in a hollow of the clay flat, and near it, fortunately for our horses, a little grass growing in widely scattered tufts.

THE BARCOO RIVER.

19th April.

Being now on the line of route which Dr. Leichhardt had stated his intention of following, the party was divided, so that both sides of the river were examined in all probable positions in which his camps might have been situated; but as the high floods appeared to have inundated the country for nearly a mile on each bank last year, all tracks of previous explorers were necessarily obliterated, and it was only by marked trees, or the bones of cattle, that we could hope to discover any trace. During the first two days' journey down the river only a few small pools of water were seen, and these not of a permanent character, while the rich vegetation on the open downs, which had excited the admiration of Sir T. Mitchell on his discovery of the country in a favourable season, had wholly passed away, leaving little but a bare surface of clay, the deep fissures in its surface giving evidence of long-continued drought.

20th April.

In latitude 24 degrees 37 minutes, longitude 146 degrees 13 minutes, a small sandy creek, of equal size with the Victoria, joined from the east, and just below the first permanent pool of water was found. There was a slight improvement in the grass, but dense scrubs prevailed in the back country, and even approached the river at intervals.

LEICHHARDT'S MARKED TREE.

21st April.

While collecting the horses near this pool of water I detected a party of armed natives watching one of the stockmen, evidently, from their position in the scrub and general movements, inclined to hostilities, and I imagine that it was a knowledge that we were aware of their intentions which prevented my being able to establish any communication with them. I may here remark that this party, which numbered about eight, were the first natives seen during the journey. Continuing our route along the river (latitude 24 degrees 35 minutes; longitude 36 degrees 6 minutes), we discovered a Moreton-Bay ash (Eucalyptus sp.), about two feet in diameter, marked with the letter L on the east side, cut through the bark, about four feet from the ground, and near it the stumps of some small trees which had been cut with a sharp axe, also a deep notch cut in the side of a sloping tree, apparently to support the ridge pole of a tent, or some similar purposes; all indicating that a camp had been established here by Leichhardt's party. The tree was near the bank of a small reach of water, which is noted on Sir T. Mitchell's map. This, together with its actual and relative position as regards other features of the country, prove it not to have been either one of Sir T. Mitchell's or Mr. Kennedy's camps, as neither encamped within several miles of the spot, besides which, the letter could not have been marked by either of them to designate the number of the camp, as the former had long passed his fiftieth camp, and the latter had not reached that number on the outward route, and numbered his camp from the farthest point attained on his return journey. Notwithstanding a careful search, no traces of stock could be found. This is, however, easily accounted for, as the country had been inundated last season, though the current had not been sufficiently strong to remove some emu bones and mussel shells which lay round a native camping place within a few yards of the spot. No other indications having been found, we continued the search down the river, examining every likely spot for marked trees, but without success. The general aspect of the country was extremely level, and even the few distant ridges which were visible had but small elevation above the plain, the highest apparently not exceeding 200 or 300 feet. Timber was wholly confined to the bank of the river, and though open plains existed, acacia scrubs were the principal feature. Water became very scarce in the channels of the river, and we were principally dependent on small puddles of rainwater from a recent thunder-shower; but as we approached the northern bend some fine reaches of water were passed.

THE ALICE RIVER.

6th April to 28th April.

In latitude 26 degrees 2 minutes we observed a small dry creek joining from the north-east. This I traced upwards for a few miles; but as its relative position with regard to the adjacent country, as well as the latitude, did not correspond with that of the Alice River on the chart, we continued our route. Finding, however, that the general course of the river changed to south-west, I left the party at a small lagoon and rode up the river again, making a second search, more especially at the junction of the small dry creek, which proved to be identical with the Alice River, though more than five miles to the south, as the Victoria River never reaches the parallel of 24 degrees. Our position was now becoming very critical, as a long continuance of drought had not only dried up all the water, except in the deepest hollows in the channel of the main river, but the smaller vegetation, and even the trees on the back country were annihilated, rendering the country almost impracticable from the quantity of fallen dead branches, and even in the bed of the river, where the inundation derived from heavy rain near the sources of the river last year had somewhat refreshed the grass, it was scarcely possible to find subsistence for the horses. Under existing circumstances, it would have been certain destruction to attempt a north-west route from this point; and the only course that appeared opened to us was to follow down the main river to the junction of the Thompson River, and ascend that watercourse so as to intersect Leichhardt's probable line of route, had he penetrated in that direction, favoured by a better season. At the same time, it was probable that, like ourselves, he had been repulsed, and would then follow down the river, and search for a more favourable point from which to commence his north-west course, in order to round the desert interior on its northern side; and we therefore continued our search down towards the Thompson River.

29th April to 2nd May.

The country was perfectly flat on both sides of the river, and showed traces of tremendous floods. The soil near the river was often deeply-cracked mud, water very scarce, and grass seldom seen. The back country was covered with scrubs of dead acacia, the soil a red sand or gravel; and such was the unpromising appearance that I began to fear that our horses would soon fail for want of food and water; but having camped at a waterhole during Sunday to rest the party, heavy rain commenced, and though the greater portion of the water was absorbed by the dry soil, some of the channels of the river filled and commenced to flow. This relieved us from much difficulty as regarded the want of water, and enabled us to seek for grass in positions which were otherwise inaccessible.

3rd May.

Just as we were leaving our camp a party of seven natives made their appearance; but though they came up to us, and talked much, I could get no useful information from them. As the party moved on they followed us, and thinking they were not observed, made an attempt to throw a spear at one of the men; but Mr. C. Gregory, wheeling his horse quickly and presenting a revolver at the intending aggressors, they ran away, and left us to pursue our journey in peace.

THE THOMPSON RIVER.

4th May to 6th May.

The abundance of water was not without its inconveniences, and had the rain continued the party would have been annihilated, as our camp was between the deep channels which intersected the plain; and in attempting to extricate ourselves from the plains subject to inundation, found ourselves so completely entangled among the numerous deep channels and boggy gullies, in some of which the horses narrowly escaped suffocation in the soft mud, that after having forded one branch of the river, carrying the whole equipment across on our own backs, constructing a bridge over a second for the transport of the stores, and dragging the horses through as we best could with ropes, after three days of severe toil we had scarcely accomplished a direct distance of five miles. The dry weather which followed rapidly hardened the surface of the clay plains, and I attempted to steer due west to the Thompson, but found the country so destitute of feed, and covered with dense acacia scrub, that we were compelled to return to the plains on the bank of the river.

8th May.

The valley of the river trending west was somewhat contracted, and did not exceed five or six miles in breadth; the plains were firmer, salt-bush and grass more abundant, and the horses recovered slightly from the effects of the barren country. Keeping back from the right bank of the main channel, we passed some ridges of drift sand, and came on a fine lagoon nearly a mile in length. Here we surprised a party of natives, who decamped on our approach, leaving a net, fish, etc., which we of course left untouched, and camped at a spot lower down the lagoon.

9th May.

The next day being Sunday, we remained at our camp, and the party of natives, consisting of seven or eight men, three or four women, and some children, approached us, and remained the greater part of the day near the tents. They were very anxious to enter the camp, but this was not permitted. By signs they expressed that they had observed we had not taken away any of their property the evening before, when they ran away and left their nets, and were therefore satisfied our intentions were friendly; but we could not procure any information relative to the objects of our journey or the character of the country before us. At 4 p.m. they informed us they were going to sleep at the most distant part of the lagoon, and would return next morning at sunrise, and then departed. After dark, however, the natives were detected attempting to crawl into the camp through the bushes, and though we called to them in an unmistakable tone to retire, they would not withdraw. As the position they had taken up was such as to command our camp, and render it unsafe in the event of an attack, it was necessary to dislodge them. I therefore fired a pistol over them, but was answered by a shout of derision, which no doubt would have been soon followed by a shower of spears had we not compelled them to retreat by a discharge of small shot directed into the scrub, after which we were not further molested.

10th May.

We were now approaching the junction of the Thompson River, but the country became worse as we advanced, and the last five miles of the plain were absolutely devoid of vegetation. Our hopes were, however, raised on finding that the late rain had caused the Thompson to flow, though the current was not strong; we had, however, to travel upwards of twelve miles up its course before any grass could be found for the horses.

11th May.

Continuing our route up the Thompson, nothing could be more desolate than the aspect of the country; except the few trees which grew on the immediate bank of the river there was scarcely a tree left alive, while the plains were quite bare of vegetation, except a few salsolaceous bushes. At the distance of five miles low ridges of red drift sand showed the desert character of all around; even the lower surfaces of the clouds assumed a lurid tinge from the reflection of the bare surface of red sand.

12th to 15th May.

In latitude 24 degrees 40 minutes low sandstone hills, or rather tableland, approached both banks of the river, and the gullies which intersected them had supplied the water lower down, as the channel was dry above. We, however, succeeded in reaching latitude 23 degrees 47 minutes, when the absence of water and grass--the rain not having extended so far north, and the channels of the river separating into small gullies and spreading on the wide plains--precluded our progressing further to the north or west; and the only prospect of saving our horses was to return south as quickly as possible. This was a most severe disappointment, as we had just reached the part of the country through which Leichhardt most probably travelled, if the season was sufficiently wet to render it practicable. Thus compelled to abandon the principal object of the expedition, only two courses remained open--either to return to the head of the Victoria River and attempt a northern course by the valley of the Belyando, or to follow down the river and ascertain whether it flowed into Cooper's Creek or the Darling. The latter course appeared most desirable, as it was just possible that Leichhardt, under similar circumstances, had been driven to the south-west. In order to ascertain whether any large watercourses came from the west, the return route was along the right bank of the Thompson, but only one small creek and some inconsiderable gullies joined on that side; nor was the country of a better character than on the left bank--consisting of barren plains, subject to inundation, low rocky ridges covered with dense scrub, and sandy ridges producing triodia.

22nd to 23rd May.

We had nearly reached the Victoria River, when, in crossing a gully, Worrell's horse fell and hurt him so severely that we had to halt for some time before he could be placed on his horse again, and it was therefore fortunate that a small patch of dry grass was found on the bank of the river, which enabled us to halt the next day, which was Sunday. Travelling down the right bank of the river, the principal channels were full of water, but the clay plains between were quite dry, the rain which had caused the river to flow not having extended so far south; nothing could well be more desolate than the unbounded level of these vast plains, which, destitute of vegetation, extended to the horizon. Our horses were reduced to feeding on the decayed weeds, and even these were so scarce that they eagerly devoured the thatch of some old native huts.

27th May.

We had nearly reached the furthest point attained by Mr. Kennedy when the horses showed signs of failing strength, and the channels on the east side of the plain being dry, I conceived it prudent to cross to the western side again. The dry mud was so deeply cracked that the horses were continually falling, and one horse was so completely exhausted that we had to abandon him.

KENNEDY'S MARKED TREE.

28th May.

Steering a westerly, and then a north course, we reached the small waterhole at Mr. Kennedy's second camp on the return route; there was just sufficient water to supply the party for one night, and a few scattered tufts of grass near it, but quite insufficient for the supply of so large a number of horses. Close to the waterhole we found Mr. Kennedy's marked tree; it was a large box-tree, marked on the north side thus:

K II.

The cuts of the axe and chisel were still quite clear, though twelve years had elapsed; but the slow growth and decay of trees in the interior may be attributed to the dryness of the climate.

29th May.

Steering north-west, after toiling nearly thirty miles across this fearful waste of dry mud, we at length reached a small patch of grass on a sandy hummock, but only just in time to save the horses, as many could scarcely keep on their legs, and we had to remove their loads to those which were less exhausted.

30th May.

Long before the next morning our hungry animals had consumed every blade of grass, and the small patch round the camp was reduced to the same barren appearance as the surrounding plain. We therefore started in search of food for them, and were fortunate in finding a second patch of grass, about three miles to the south, and halted for the remainder of the day, which was Sunday, thankful that Providence had enabled us to make it a day of rest.

PLAINS OF DRY MUD.

31st May.

The running channel of the river being still to the west of our position, we steered south-west, over barren clay plains, to some low ridges of drift sand, beyond which we found the channel full of water, with a slight current; but it terminated in a large reach of water which had not yet filled, and the channel lower down was dry. Low ridges of red drift sand were now frequent on the plain, and appeared to be the higher points of the former sandy desert, the clay plains resulting from the deposition of mud in the hollows between which had in course of time filled it to one uniform level.

Latitude 26 degrees 2 minutes.

1st June.

The channels on the western side of the plain were very irregular, sometimes completely lost on the level surface, and again collecting into large hollows, with box-trees on the banks, in which fine sheets of water still remained, some 100 yards wide and more than a mile in length. We therefore did not experience so much inconvenience with regard to the supply of this necessary element as from the absence of sufficient grass, and the all but impracticable nature of the mud plains.

4th June.

In latitude 27 degrees, low sandstone tableland approached the west side of the river, and we attempted to travel along the slope between it and the mud plains, but found it so stony that the horses' hoofs were soon worn to the quick, as we had been compelled to remove their shoes to enable them to traverse the mud plains. Had it not been for green bushes of salsolae, and some similar plants which had sprung up since the rain, this tract of country exactly resembled the stony desert described by Captain Sturt as existing 200 miles to the westward. These remarkable features forming the declivities of the sandstone tableland through which Cooper's Creek forces its way, and by confining the waters to a narrower space during floods, causes the fine deep reaches of water which characterize it.

8th June.

By following the western limits of the plains we reached latitude 27 degrees 30 minutes, when the sandstone tableland receded, and a boundless expanse of mud plain was before us; the lines of box-trees which had hitherto marked the channels nearly ceased, polygonum and atriplex constituting the main feature of the vegetation.

COOPER'S CREEK.

9th June.

After toiling south-west a day and a half over this level surface to latitude 27 degrees 50 minutes, we approached some low ridges, at the foot of which there was a lagoon 100 yards wide, exhibiting signs of a current during flood to the north-west; and as there was an evident westerly trend in all the smaller channels previously crossed, it was evident they would soon merge in Cooper's Creek. Steering west-north-west, the several channels collected together, and soon formed a deep watercourse, with fine reaches of water. The sandstone tableland closed in on both sides; the soil of the intervening plain was much firmer, but showed by the vegetation that saline nature which so often attends the development of the upper sandstones in Australia. Grass was abundant, and it was surprising with what rapidity the horses recovered their strength.

BOUNDARY OF SOUTH AUSTRALIA.

12th June.

Approaching the 141st meridian, which is the boundary of the province of South Australia, stony ridges closed in on both banks of Cooper's Creek, forming almost a natural division, across which we followed a well-beaten native path; and here I observed the only instance which has come under my observation where the aborigines have taken the trouble to remove natural obstacles from their paths. The loose stones had been cleared from the track, and in some places piled in large heaps.

14th June.

After passing the stony ridge the valley became wider, the hills receding suddenly, in longitude 140 degrees 30 minutes, both to the north and south; and the whole of the country to the west seemed to consist of a succession of low ridges of red sand and level plains of dry mud, subject to inundation. Shortly before reaching the branch of Cooper's Creek named by Captain Sturt Streletzki Creek, we observed the tracks of two horses, one apparently a cart-horse, and the other a well-bred animal, but as none of their tracks were within the last month, the rain had obliterated them to such an extent that they could not be traced up, as they had left the bank of the creek on the first fall of rain, as is the usual habit of horses whose wanderings are uncontrolled. There can be little doubt that these horses belonged to Captain Sturt, who left one in an exhausted state near this locality, and also lost a second horse, whose tracks were followed many miles in the direction of this part of Cooper's Creek.

16th June.

Streletzki Creek, which separates nearly at a right angle from the main channel, appears to convey about one-third of the waters of Cooper's Creek nearly south, and, as we afterwards ascertained, connects it with Lake Torrens. We, however, continued to follow the channels which trended west for thirty miles, but large branches continually broke off to the south and west, and at length the whole was lost on the wide plains of dry mud between the sand ridges; and, as there was no prospect of either water or grass to the west, I steered south and south-east for fifty miles over a succession of ridges of red drift sand, ten to fifty feet high, running parallel to each other, and in a nearly north and south direction. Between these ridges we occasionally found shallow puddles of rainwater, or rather mud, as it was so thick with clay as to be scarcely fluid. Fortunately a great quantity of green weeds had grown up since the rain, and the horses improved in condition, and did not require much water.

21st June to 25th June.

In latitude 28 degrees 24 minutes we again came on Streletzki Creek, and then followed it nearly south-south-west between sandy ridges to latitude 29 degrees 25 minutes, when it turned to the west and entered Lake Torrens. No permanent water was seen in the bed of the creek, though there were many deep hollows which, when once filled, retain water for several months, and this, combined with the existence of a fine reach of water in Cooper's Creek immediately above the point where Streletzki Creek branches off, renders it far the best line of route into the interior which has yet been discovered. Passing between the eastern point of Lake Torrens and what has hitherto been considered the eastern arm, but now ascertained to be an independent lake, the space between (about half a mile) was level sandy ground, covered with salicornia, without any apparent connecting channel. The course was continued south-south-west towards Mount Hopeless, at the northern extreme of the high ranges of South Australia, which had been visible across the level country at a distance of sixty miles.

26th June.

As we approached the range of hills tracks of cattle and horses were observed, and eight miles beyond Mount Hopeless came to a cattle station which had been lately established by Mr. Baker. As the nature of the country we had traversed was such as not to admit of any useful deviations from it if we returned to New South Wales by land, I deemed it advisable to proceed forthwith to Adelaide, and, disposing of the horses and equipment, return with the party by sea to Sydney.

ARRIVE IN ADELAIDE, SOUTH AUSTRALIA. GENERAL OBSERVATIONS.

31st July.

We therefore proceeded by easy stages towards Adelaide, experiencing the greatest hospitality at the stations on our route, while our reception in the city was of the most flattering nature. His Excellency Sir Richard Macdonald kindly gave me the use of an extensive paddock for the horses, and provided quarters for the men during the period which necessarily elapsed before the sale of the equipment of the expedition was effected. I have also to express my acknowledgments of the kind assistance rendered by the Honourable the Commissioner of Crown Lands, to the Surveyor-General, and the Superintendent of Telegraphs, for valuable data connected with the construction of the map of the route, as well as to many other gentlemen whose cordial co-operation greatly facilitated my arrangements. It is extremely gratifying to record my appreciation of the untiring zeal and energy which distinguished every individual composing the expedition; and it is to the unvarying and cheerful alacrity with which each and all performed their respective duties, that, under Providence, the rapidity and success of the journey is to be mainly attributed. With reference to the probable fate of Dr. Leichhardt, it is evident, from the existence of the marked camp, nearly eighty miles beyond those seen by Mr. Hely, that the account given to that gentleman by the natives of the murder of the party was untrue; and I am inclined to think only a revival of the report current during Leichhardt's first journey to Port Essington. Nor is it probable that they were destroyed until they had left the Victoria, as, if killed by the natives, the scattered bones of the horses and cattle would have been observed during our search. I am therefore of opinion that they left the river at the junction of the Alice, and, favoured by thunder-showers, penetrated the level desert country to the north-west; in which case, on the cessation of the rain, the party would not only be deprived of a supply of water for the onward journey, but unable to retreat, as the shallow deposits of rainwater would evaporate in a few days, and it is not likely that they would commence a retrograde movement until the strength of the party had been severely taxed in the attempt to advance. The character of the country traversed, from the out-stations on the Dawson River to the head of the Warrego River, was generally that of a grassy forest, with ridges of dense brigalow scrub. A great portion is available for pastoral purposes, but not well watered; and the soil being sandy, the grass would soon be destroyed if too heavily stocked. As we advanced into the interior it became more barren, and, except along the banks of the larger watercourses, destitute of timber, and the character of the vegetation indicated excessive droughts. North of latitude 26 degrees dense scrubs of acacia prevailed on the level country beyond the influence of the inundations, but to the southward sandy and stony deserts, with low shrubby vegetation, were the characteristic feature. West of longitude 147 degrees, nearly to the boundary of South Australia, in 141 degrees, the country is unfit for occupation, for, though in favourable seasons there might in some few localities be abundance of feed for stock, the uncertainty of rain and frequent recurrence of drought renders it untenable, the grasses and herbage being principally annuals, which not only die but are swept away by the hot summer winds, leaving the surface of the soil completely bare. On Cooper's Creek, near the boundary, there is a small tract of second-rate country, which, being abundantly supplied with water, may eventually be occupied. The best part is, however, within the province of South Australia. Between Cooper's Creek and Lake Torrens about 120 miles of sandy country intervenes. This tract is destitute of surface water, but as it is probable that it could be obtained by sinking wells of moderate depth, I think it might be occupied to advantage during the cool season, and thus relieve the stations which are now established within Lake Torrens, though I fear that the summer heat would be too great to admit of permanent occupation. The geological character of the country is remarkably uniform. Carboniferous sandstones and shales, containing occasional beds of coal, with superincumbent hills and ridges of basalt, extend from Darling Downs to the 146th meridian, where these rocks are covered by horizontal sandstones with beds of chert and water-worn quartz pebbles. This latter formation extends as far as Mount Hopeless, where the slate ranges of South Australia rise abruptly from the plain. The sandy deserts and mud plains are only superficial deposits, as the sandstones are often exposed where the upper formation is intersected by gullies. The direction of the parallel ridges of drift sand appear to be the result of the prevailing winds, and not the action of water, it being sufficient to visit them on a windy day to be convinced that it is unnecessary to seek for a more remote and obscure cause than that which is in present operation. It is, perhaps, with reference to the physical geography of Australia that the results of the Expedition are most important; as by connecting successively the explorations of Sir T. Mitchell, Mr. Kennedy, Captain Sturt, and Mr. Eyre, the waters of the tropical interior of the eastern portion of the Continent are proved to flow towards Spencer's Gulf, if not actually into it, the barometrical observations showing that Lake Torrens, the lowest part of the interior, is decidedly above the sea-level. Although only about one-third of the waters of Cooper's Creek flow into Lake Torrens by the channel of Streletzki Creek, there is strong evidence that the remaining channels, after spreading their waters on the vast plains which occupy the country between them and Sturt's Stony Desert, finally drain to the south, augmented probably by the waters of Eyre's Creek, the Stony Desert, and perhaps some other watercourses of a similar character coming from the westward. This peculiar structure of the interior renders it improbable that any considerable inland lakes should exist in connection with the known system of waters; for, as Lake Torrens is decidedly only an expanded continuation of Cooper's Creek, and therefore the culminating point of this vast system of drainage, if there was sufficient average fall of rain in the interior to balance the effects of evaporation from the surface of an extensive sheet of water, the Torrens Basin, instead of being occupied by salt marshes, in which the existence of anything beyond shallow lagoons of salt-water is yet problematical, would be maintained as a permanent lake. Therefore, if the waters flowing from so large a tract of country are insufficient to meet the evaporation from the surface of Lake Torrens, there is even less probability of the waters of the western interior forming an inland lake of any magnitude, even should there be so anomalous a feature as a depression of the surface in which it could be collected, especially as our knowledge of its limits indicate a much drier climate and less favourable conformation of surface than in the eastern division of the continent. The undulations of the surface of the country are nearly parallel to the meridian, gradually decreasing in height from the dividing range between the eastern and western waters till, instead of the waters of the rivers being confined to valleys, they occupy plains formed by a slight flattening of the curvature of the sphere. Thus the sides of the plain through which the river ran before it turned west to Cooper's Creek were 150 feet below the tangential level of the centre channels, and even the summit of the sandstone tableland which rose beyond was below the visible horizon. It is this peculiar conformation which causes the stream-beds to spread so widely when following the course of the valleys from north to south, and it is only where they break through the intervening ridges that the water is confined sufficiently to form well-defined channels. The existence of these extensive valleys trending north and south over so large a tract of country render it by no means unlikely that they continue far beyond the limits of present explorations, and it is not unreasonable to infer that the great depression which has been traced nearly five hundred miles north from Spencer's Gulf through Lake Torrens to the stony desert of Sturt (or rather the mud plains contiguous to its western limit) may be continuous for an equal distance beyond to the low land at the head of the Gulf of Carpentaria; a theory also supported by the fact that the rivers flowing into the Gulf either come from the east or west, apparently from higher land in those directions, while there is not a single watercourse from the south, or any indication of elevated country in that direction. Captain Wickham having named an important river discovered by him in H.M.S. Beagle, on the north-west coast, the Victoria, several years prior to Sir T. Mitchell having attached that name to the upper portion of Cooper's Creek, which had also been previously discovered and named by Captain Sturt, I would suggest that the term River Cooper be adopted for the whole of the main channel from its sources, discovered by Sir T. Mitchell, to its termination in Lake Torrens; as, while it does not interfere with the rule that the name given by the first discoverer should be retained, will prevent the recurrence of the misapprehension and inconvenience of having two important rivers with the same designation on the maps of Australia. With regard to the numbers and habits of the aborigines, I could collect little information, as only a collective number of about 100 men, a few women and children, were seen, in small scattered parties; but, judging from the number of encampments seen, at least a thousand must visit the banks of the river; and it is probable that the whole of the inhabitants for at least 100 miles on each side are dependent on it for water during the dry season. Neither sex wear any clothing. Their weapons and utensils are similar to those used on the eastern coast; nor was there any characteristic by which they could be observed to differ from the aborigines of other portions of Australia. Fish, rats, grass seeds, and a few roots, constitute their chief food. On the upper part of the river they bury their dead, piling wood on the grave; near the junction of the Thompson they suspend the bodies in nets, and afterwards remove the bones; while on Cooper's Creek the graves are mounds of earth three to four feet high, apparently without any excavation, and surmounted by a pile of dead wood. In the last-named locality the number of burial mounds which had been constructed about two years ago greatly exceed the proportion of deaths which could have possibly occurred in any ordinary season of mortality, even assuming the densest population known in any other part of Australia; and it is not improbable that the seasons of drought which proved so destructive to the tree vegetation higher up the river may have been equally disastrous in its effects on the aboriginal inhabitants of this portion of the interior.

A.C. GREGORY.

Sydney, 27 August, 1858.